ROME IN CANADA
*The Vatican and Canadian Affairs
in the Late Victorian Age*

In the three decades after Confederation, an aggressive Anglo-Saxon nationalism struggled to imprint its cultural model on the emerging Canadian state. It was countered by a defensive French-Canadian nationalism chiefly articulated by a majority within the Roman Catholic clergy. Roberto Perin explores the role of the Vatican in the struggle and in the political, religious, and cultural life of Canada during the period.

Perin begins by charting the historical development of the Catholic church in Canada in its all-important regional dimension. He suggests that Rome acted as another Canadian metropolis, where decisions concerning the young country's future were taken by clerical bureaucrats, mostly Italians, who had never set foot in North America.

Rome and its apostolic delegates to the Canadian church took positions on a wide range of Canadian matters. They included the political controversies of the day, Catholic education (particularly after Manitoba abolished denominational schools), immigration, and the relations between the upper and lower clergy. Placing the discussion in international and diplomatic contexts, Perin finds that such questions as Catholic education and immigration were influenced by events in the United States as well as by interest groups in Great Britain and continental Europe.

Ultimately, the Vatican failed to support the French Canadians' brand of nationalism, despite the fact that they represented three-quarters of the Catholic population in Canada. That failure of support contributed to the victory of an Anglo-Saxon Protestant nationalist version of Canada.

ROBERTO PERIN is Associate Professor in the department of History at Atkinson College, York University. He is co-editor, with Franc Sturino, of *Arrangiarsi: The Italian Immigration Experience in Canada.*

ROBERTO PERIN

Rome in Canada

*The Vatican and Canadian
Affairs in the Late
Victorian Age*

UNIVERSITY OF TORONTO PRESS
Toronto   Buffalo   London

© University of Toronto Press 1990
Toronto Buffalo London
Printed in Canada

ISBN 0-8020-5854-X (cloth)
ISBN 0-8020-6762-X (paper)

∞

Printed on acid-free paper

Canadian Cataloguing in Publication Data

Perin, Roberto
Rome in Canada

Includes bibliographical references.
ISBN 0-8020-5854-X (bound) ISBN 0-8020-6762-X (pbk.)
1. Catholic Church – Relations (diplomatic) –
Canada. 2. Canada – Foreign relations – Catholic
Church. 3. Canada – Politics and government –
1867–1896.* 4. Canada – Politics and government –
1896–1911.* 5. Catholic Church – Canada. I. Title.

BX1421.P4 1990   327.45′634′071   C89-095479-8 64449

PICTURE CREDITS: **Archives du Séminaire de Québec** Cardinal Ledochowski,
Cardinal Rampolla, Benjamin Pâquet, Callixte Marquis, Bishop Conroy,
Archbishop Bégin; **National Archives of Canada** Apostolic delegation
Ottawa PA 10545, Henri Smeulders c52222, Merry del Val c51965; **National
Gallery of Art, Washington** Diomede Falconio; **Map** Janet Allin

This book has been published with the help of a grant from the Canadian
Federation for the Humanities, using funds provided by the Social
Sciences and Humanities Research Council of Canada.

Contents

Acknowledgments

I would like to express my thanks to a number of people who made this study possible. First among them is Pierre Hurtubise o.m.i., rector of St Paul University, Ottawa, who first suggested the topic to me. My deep appreciation also goes to the staff at the archives of the Vatican: Josef Metzler o.m.i., prefect of the Archivio Segreto Vaticano, archivists Monsignor Charles Burns and especially the late Monsignor Ottavio Cavalleri, who led me to the papers of the apostolic delegation to Canada, as well as Claudio De Dominicis who has done tremendous work organizing these papers and those of the apostolic delegation to the United States; Monsignor Marcello Camisassa, the prelate in charge of the archives of the Congregation for Extraordinary Ecclesiastical Affairs, as well as a former assistant in these archives, Suor Dominguez; finally, the anonymous but ever efficient staff at the archives of the Propaganda Fide.

I would also like to express my gratitude to the Canadian Academic Centre in Italy for facilitating my research and especially to Antonella D'Agostino, its executive assistant, for her incomparable adeptness at opening doors in Roman officialdom. The Canadian embassy to the Holy See, through the very able Jacqueline Petrassi, was also most helpful. Yvon Beaulne, then ambassador, received me with the exquisite courtesy that distinguishes him and impressed me with his breadth of interests, including those concerning the problems studied below. I would like to thank Leonard Boyle o.p., prefect of the Vatican Library, and Robert Robidoux p.s.s., rector of the Pontifical Canadian College, for their encouragement during my stay in Rome. I am also indebted to Monique Benoit, Matteo Sanfilippo, Luigi Bruti-Liberati, and Nicoletta Serio whose inventories of Canadian documents in the Vatican archives proved invaluable in checking sources.

I would like to acknowledge the precious assistance of Atkinson College, York University, for providing a leave fellowship which allowed me to write my manuscript unencumbered by teaching and administrative responsibilities. Special thanks go to Daniel Drache, colleague and friend, whose long tirades against free trade kept me in touch with the real world during my writing. Intellectual encouragement came from Pierre Savard, Paul Crunican, Cornelius Jaenen, Matteo Sanfilippo (bis), Gabriele Scardellato, and finally Luca Codignola, who never tires of speaking about the riches of the Vatican archives to Canadian academics. I am indebted to Gerry Hallowell of the University of Toronto Press for his kind encouragement and concern in shepherding the book through the various stages of production, and to Diane Mew whose professional editorial hand and critical mind made the manuscript ready for publication. Last but not least, a fond thanks to my wife Yvonne (who did not type this manuscript) and to my children, Pier-Paolo, Dominique, and Alexis, for their patience with what they so reverently called my enthusiasm for 'dead priests.' To them this book is dedicated.

The building of the Collegio della Propaganda Fide in Rome: front façade by
Gian Lorenzo Bernini

Mieczyslaw Ledochowski, Cardinal Prefect of Propaganda Fide, 1892–1902

Mariano Rampolla del Tindaro, Cardinal Secretary of State, 1887–1903

Benjamin Pâquet, archdiocesan agent of Quebec in Rome, superior of the Séminaire de Québec, and rector of Laval University, 1887–93

Callixte Marquis, Roman agent for Archbishop Taschereau, seen here with a page and relics of St Anne brought back from Rome

Mansion of the apostolic delegation, Ottawa, 1913

Bishop George Conroy, apostolic delegate, 1877–8

Dom Henri Smeulders, apostolic commissioner, 1883–4

Rafael Merry del Val, apostolic delegate, 1897

Archbishop Diomede Falconio, apostolic delegate, 1899–1902, painted by
Thomas Eakins

Adélard Langevin, archbishop of St Boniface, 1895–1915

Louis-Nazaire Bégin, archbishop of Quebec, 1898–1925

ROME IN CANADA

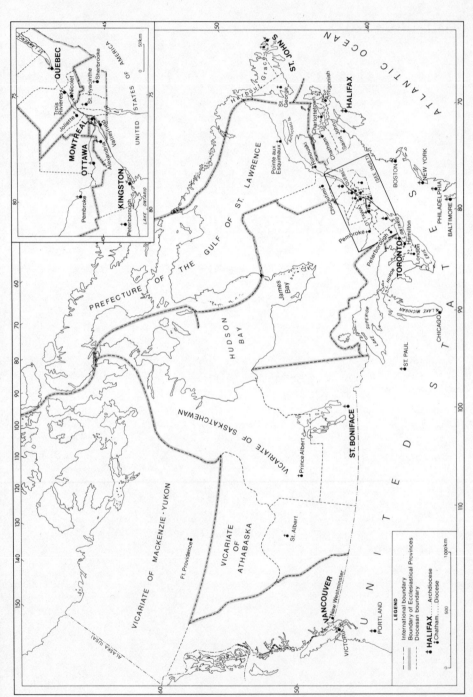

Dioceses of Canada, 1904

Introduction

The original *Rome in Canada* was written shortly after Confederation by a grandson of William Lyon Mackenzie. The author, Charles
Lindsey, sought to show how the Vatican was extending its dark
dominion to the free-born Britons of Canada by pursuing in this
country the aggressive policies which marked its relations with the
Protestant and liberal states of Europe. The instrument of this
sinister infiltration, Lindsey contended, was the Quebec church; not,
he hastened to add, the institution which in the past had 'acted in
perfect accord with the national instincts, and aided the Government
in periods of national crisis.'[1] That institution, the Gallican church
which proved its loyalty to Britain in 1775, 1812, and 1837, had given
way in the Union era to a new body led by obscurantists such as
Bishop Ignace Bourget of Montreal and his phalanx of Jesuits who
had drunk deeply of the heady Roman doctrines of ultramontanism
as exemplified by Pope Pius IX in *Syllabus of Errors*. These were the
enemies within that threatened the very freedoms upon which Canada stood.

But this brief synopsis of *Rome in Canada* should not lead us
astray. The book was well documented, its author obviously well
informed. Although its message was alarming, the tone of the treatise
was free from the hysterics characterizing the gothic productions of
the period. Its assumptions and conclusions, though rarely articulated by active politicians who feared the effect on party unity,
probably were shared by a good many English-speaking Protestants.
After all, the liberal nationalist Charles Lindsey echoed fears about
Rome rule expressed almost contemporaneously in two controversial
pamphlets by the Conservative Alexander Tilloch Galt.

Lindsey may have been well informed; but he was clearly an unsympathetic outsider. His views of 'the inside' were influenced by values current in his own culture, notably an ascendant English-Canadian nationalism. Although in its infancy, this ideology was beginning to express a national vision and aspirations to national grandeur, which made little allowance for French Canada. It never occurred even to those few English-Canadian intellectuals who genuinely tried to find a space in the new nation for their French-speaking fellow citizens that French Canada might be an equal partner or that it could play a significant role in the development of national institutions on its own terms. In any event, *Rome in Canada* saw contemporary French Canada, the land where ultramontanes were hatching their schemes of dominion, as a threat to its own dream of Dominion. The book shared in the psychology of aggressive majorities who mask their ambitions of domination by projecting them onto the minority. They thus create an imaginary scapegoat which facilitates the realization of their own objectives.

That the grandson of the leader of the rebellion of 1837 should have articulated such ambitions is indicative of a change of perspective. Before the Union of 1840, hopes for political and social change were expressed in the language of mutual respect for the autonomous development of the Canadas. Forty years later, Mackenzie's physical heir no longer entertained dreams of partnership. Nor was he comfortable with the reality of cultural difference. His approach invited ethnic discord, in which the majority showed its intolerance of the minority. Of course political, not to mention demographic, realities had changed in the intervening years. So, too, had cultural ones. Religion came to play an important role in Canadian life as a whole, while in Quebec, the church increased its power.

Yet if Lindsey had known where Rome stood on Canadian questions, he might at least have spared himself some anxiety. He might even have altered his interpretation of events (although this is unlikely in light of his overall outlook). The author presented his readers with a monolithic Catholic church intent on robbing Canadians of their fundamental political freedoms. With the possible exception of Bourget's rival, Archbishop E.A. Taschereau of Quebec City, who was cast in the role of a Gallican hero, Lindsey's work is peopled only by villains. It is true that the church at Rome and in Quebec were at one in championing ultramontane doctrines. But the political corollaries of such doctrines and the opportuneness of their application

– questions in short which were at the heart of Lindsey's concerns – found Rome and the bulk of the Quebec church on opposite sides, as we shall soon see.

Contrary to what Lindsey may have thought, the Holy See did not support Bourget and his chorus of hard-liners. These men were seen as intemperate clerics who were pushed to commit excesses by their lack of education. Rome believed instead that conciliation, moderation, informed argument, and rationality were the most effective means not only of avoiding a disastrous confrontation with the Protestant majority in Canada, but of bringing the English-speaking peoples of America and Britain back to the Roman fold. These characteristics were regarded as being the almost exclusive preserve of English-speaking bishops. Minimizing the fact that the Catholic church in Canada was overwhelmingly French-speaking and deluded by false hopes of conversion, Rome placed itself squarely on the side of the majority, of the strongest, of the big battalions. Still, Lindsey's view of a monolithic church strongly influenced the popular mind in English Canada, as well as historical writing.

A parallel historiographical current originated around the same period in French Canada and had a more immediately political focus. It denounced the Quebec church's lengthy persecution of the Liberal party. The struggle between these antagonists, described in truly epic tones, pitted the Liberal David against the clerical Goliath. In their polemical writings, L.O. David and Charles Langelier[2] attributed the clergy's actions to rabid partisanship. Their clerical allies in Rome, on the other hand, suggested that Quebec priests were simply misguided, that they were confusing doctrinal and political liberalism. Either version of this interpretation was repeated by Laurier's biographers shortly after his death and has been accepted by political historians ever since.

Recently, however, this view was challenged. In a masterful study, Paul Crunican showed that the actions of the clergy in the controversy over Catholic education in Manitoba, and particularly in the crucial election of 1896, were generally neither misguided nor partisan.[3] While limited to one political crisis, Crunican's work dispels an all-too-facile depiction of the Liberals as innocent victims of a malevolent (partisan) clergy. At the same time, it invites broad reflection prompted by a critical examination of *Rome in Canada*: were those who cried wolf the loudest not themselves wolves in sheep's clothing?

If nothing else, the Liberals' lengthy exile in opposition had given them the opportunity to reflect on which combination of political forces would bring them to power. Their opponents' success had been predicated on the unlikely alliance between the country's Protestant majority and the Catholic church. The Conservatives had managed up to a point to hold these antagonistic elements in balance. But the fundamental problem was that the church regarded a number of public issues as essentially religious in nature, while the Protestants, as we have seen, had their own agenda for nation building. Still, for a variety of reasons, the Liberals found enough support within the two constituencies to win the 1874 election. However, bringing this coalition together and making it function were two quite separate things. Unable to resolve these contradictions effectively in their first years of office, they sought to be free from the unrelenting pressures of the more turbulent elements of the Quebec clergy in order to deal with controversial questions according to the exigencies of the moment.

Liberal spokesmen turned to Rome for help. They presented themselves as innocent victims of clerical aggression. Yet they were neither innocent nor victims since as a government they knowingly pursued policies that provoked the church's ire. The Liberals, however, knocked at the doors of the Vatican at an opportune moment. The Holy See's recent policies of confrontation with the liberal states of Europe and America had produced meagre results and to influential inside officials seemed counter-productive. Vatican diplomacy was anxious to establish normal relations with governments, especially if these proclaimed their devotion to Rome as earnestly as did Canada's representatives. In the wake of the 1877–8 mission of Bishop George Conroy, whom Rome sent to Canada to resolve major politico-religious questions, the Liberals were assured that the Holy See would not hinder their management of the affairs of state. They therefore sought to have a permanent apostolic delegation established in Canada as early as 1878.

The Liberals' objective here was to contain potential clerical opposition to their initiatives. For, in the process of determining state policy on controversial religious questions, the Liberals would be dealing with only one ecclesiastical intermediary, an outsider with an English point of view. At the same time, this official would be expected to keep a tight rein on the more unruly elements within the church. Like the French and British governors of the past, the

Liberals saw this as the most effective means of minimizing the church's intervention in political affairs. Whether they realized it or not, they were harking back to Gallican traditions. They did this not from doctrinaire ideals, as some of their clerical opponents maintained, but from political opportunism. In any event, they emerged clearly victorious from their struggle with the Quebec church. In this second instance, Rome chose not to support the position taken by the institutional mainstay of Canadian Catholicism. The Quebec church, however, was not weakened by this defeat; it had weathered similar, if not worse, crises in its two and a half centuries of history. Rather it was a particular concept of Canada and of French Canada's place in it that was undermined. Rome's actions also unwittingly strengthened the control of political parties in Canadian social and intellectual life.

The current study looks at the Holy See as a third Canadian metropolis. After Paris and London, Rome was a decision-making centre for this country. From their offices in the elegant Palazzo di Propaganda on the Piazza di Spagna or at the Vatican Palace, Italian churchmen decided on some vital Canadian issues. They did this not in a vacuum, but in consultation with local clergy and public figures, and in the broader context of British and American relations. The process was one that Lindsey could only surmise, the results of which would have been beyond his wildest dreams.

If categories are helpful, this work is partly institutional and partly intellectual history within an international relations context. Although some of the issues examined here have been dealt with elsewhere in political histories or in broader works such as that by Robert Rumilly,[4] my approach differs from these in two important respects. Political histories have tended to concentrate on particular crises, measuring their impact on political parties and, by extension or identification, the country as a whole. The emphasis has been on the episode and epiphenomenon, rather than process and continuum. This is particularly the case in their treatment of the politico-religious question of the last quarter of the nineteenth century. It seemed as though inevitably one chapter ended with the Conroy mission, while another began with the Merry Del Val visit in 1897. Little attempt was made to link the two events together, to see the issues and personalities in the context of what went before. And yet were not the actors themselves conscious of a continuity and measured their actions accordingly?

Rumilly, for his part, was a chronicler, interested above all in getting his reader to follow him from the beginning of his story to the end. His characters are vividly portrayed, perhaps too vividly, with all their peculiarities and eccentricities. In the end they appear as personalities out of an *opéra bouffe*. If they fight, it is only for form's sake, since they are all members of one happy family which no issue can seriously divide. Laflèche's political actions appear as quirks, about as interesting as Joly de Lotbinière's ample sideburns. By the same token, the Liberals' dispatch of envoys to Rome make entertaining divertissements in an otherwise turgid account of the political machinations in Quebec City and Ottawa. Some historians maintain that, in his detailed coverage of this period, Rumilly has said all there is to say. Anything more would be hackneyed. But surely what is missing, and what the current study proposes, is an interpretation.

This is the first study of late nineteenth-century Canada based almost exclusively on untapped material contained in the various archives of the Vatican, notably the Propaganda Fide, Extraordinary Ecclesiastical Affairs, and Vatican Secret Archives (especially the rich collection of the apostolic delegate to Canada). It is true that part of this material may be found in Canadian diocesan archives. But Rome has the advantage of bringing together documentation scattered throughout the length and breadth of Canada, some of which is still restricted or inaccessible due to the oftentimes arbitrary decision of the local bishop or archivist. In any event, the archives of one or two dioceses cannot assess the broad policies followed by the Holy See, nor can they indicate how such policies were reached. As well, the all-important international dimension is missing. Even in formulating decisions for a particular country, the Holy See, as a world-wide organization, was rarely influenced solely by conditions specific to that country. My treatment of questions relating to immigration, the establishment of an apostolic delegation in Canada, and the Manitoba schools question bears this out. It is clear, too, that the archives of religious bodies necessarily provide a different perspective from the papers of public figures or organizations and are likely to give rise to different interpretations. By its sources, perspective, and interpretation, this work seeks to establish its distinctiveness.

In the course of my research I was asked by specialists and non-specialists alike about the relevance of my study of an ecclesiastical theme to this secular age. The question was not intended to be flattering! The primary interest of this work, however, is not with the church as such, but with minority-majority relations which in the nineteenth century assumed a religious idiom. This point has been blurred by the overly linguistic emphasis given to Canadian ethnic relations in our secularistic age. Although Catholic-Protestant tensions constitute a central theme of this study, my intention is certainly not to stir up denominational hostilities (nor for that matter to beat the drum for a political party) which a misreading of the text might suggest.

My focus is instead on the dynamic which in this crucial period in Canada's development led to an accommodation between Protestants and Catholics, happier for the former than for the latter. This was a long-term process, the fruit of bitter confrontation and of a succession of crises, in which the Catholic church played an essential brokerage role. The dynamic was complicated by the fact that the minority, especially its religious leadership, was culturally divided. Historical memory and rapid population increase made French Canadians express the superiority of their culture by accentuating their separateness from the North American environment. For the Irish, however, sense of place, and therefore historical memory, had been jolted by immigration from the British Isles. At the same time, they could not find strength in numbers since the Irish Catholic proportion of the population, especially, but not only, in Ontario, kept on declining in this period. In the face of these realities, they asserted their cultural superiority by imitating prevailing North American cultural norms. While French Canadians fiercely defended their religious-linguistic patrimony, Irish Catholics expressed all the ambivalent attitudes of a Dickensian Uriah Heep: publicly thankful for the place assigned to them in Upper Canadian society, while privately resenting the petty harassments that daily reminded them of their station. Instead of directing their frustration to their tormentors, however, the Irish clergy and laity, particularly in Ontario and the West, turned the French Canadians into scapegoats, and thus lent the majority a helping hand in its struggle with the minority.

But the personalities, as much as the issues, are what made the topic fascinating to me. This intense confrontation of the era brought into sharp relief the qualities and weaknesses of the actors involved. In some of the historical figures with whom I spent my time sporadically over the past five years, I admired the keen insight and culture, in spite of past and present stereotypes, of the nineteenth-century Quebec clergy. They were certainly not stars in the intellectual or cultural firmament of their day. But who in the colonial Canada of the period could make such claims? Some public figures did play up their European connections, took pride in introducing into this country fashions from abroad, and saw themselves as heirs of a noble old-world intellectual or political tradition. Yet they were followers, not innovators, and their legacy ultimately was shallow and derivative. The men of the Institut canadien, for example, who professed unbounded admiration for Galileo, Voltaire, and the encyclopaedists, when given a choice between their intellectual convictions and their religious affiliation, all chose bourgeois conformity and respectability. Not one cherished freedom of thought and expression enough to say: 'Here I stand!' As for the intellectuals of the Liberal party, they placed their beloved ideals of tolerance and liberty in the strait-jacket of federal-provincial relations and capital accumulation.

The men of the cloth had no such ideals and made no claim to them. Neither broad-minded nor urbane, these men of authority rejected the social and intellectual currents of their time, longing instead for a mythical past characterized by simple faith and blind submission. Nor were they generally known for their sense of humour. In short, they did not possess the qualities that constitute the finer specimens of humankind. Their shortcomings were numerous and very real. Yet the best among them were earnest in a period of public cynicism; they were men of conviction amidst sordid compromises, of drive among public figures driven by ambition, of broad faith in an age without a transcendent vision. These are not in themselves qualities. In fact, under certain conditions such traits may be dangerous. But they were informed by a generous sense of practical tolerance and accommodation. These are characteristics not often used to describe nineteenth-century clergymen. Even so, the church's apparent rejection of the modern world never prevented these men from coming to terms with industrial society. Their aversion to doctrinal error was no impediment to their living in peace with mainstream Protestant churches. This tolerance, allied with their strong sense of identity, is perhaps their more lasting legacy.

Chapter One

Towards a National Church?

Diomede Falconio looked out on the Rideau Canal from the window of his ample greystone mansion. It was a warm bright day, one of the last in that Indian summer of 1902. Ottawa was ablaze with the fiery colours of autumn. As he gazed, Falconio felt a sense of relief and satisfaction. He would be spared another unbearable Canadian winter.[1] The prospect of his new post as the Vatican's representative in Washington filled him with excitement. At the same time, though, he thought back with pride on his tenure as the first apostolic delegate in Canada. The delegation and the Canadian church had come a long way in that short three-year period. He remembered how, on his arrival in Ottawa, he had had to accept cramped lodgings at the university, accommodations scarcely befitting his elevated status. Now he could entertain in a dignified manner the prime minister and other leaders of government and the opposition in his comfortable, although not overly spacious, residence which he shared with two secretaries and the three sisters who kept house for him. As for the Catholic church in Canada, at first he was shocked by its lack of cohesion and conformity to canon law. But thanks to the key role played by the delegation, it was becoming a national institution. This goal, the archbishop believed, was not yet a reality, but it was certainly within the grasp of his successor.

Falconio was at least correct in his assessment regarding the heterogeneity of the Canadian church. Thirty years earlier at Confederation, the institution very much mirrored the diversity of the regions entering into the new agreement. The situation had not improved by the turn of the twentieth century. Part of the problem was that the church lacked a national structure. Back in 1844 the Holy See had given Canadian Catholicism an organizational form by creating the ecclesiastical province of Quebec, whose boundaries spanned all of British North America except for the Atlantic colonies. The driving force behind this move was Ignace Bourget, bishop of Montreal, who expressly called for greater uniformity within the church in British North America. The prelate was evidently disappointed at Rome's exclusion of the Atlantic dioceses from the new ecclesiastical province. And although the Holy See expected the Atlantic bishops to attend the councils of Quebec as observers, only Charlottetown and St John's were represented at the first such meeting held in 1851. In fact, it was the last time any Atlantic prelate would be in attendance.

THE STRUCTURE OF CANADIAN CATHOLICISM

The national character of Canadian Catholicism was further eroded as church structures evolved at the local and regional levels.[2] The ecclesiastical province of Halifax was erected in 1852. In 1870 Rome divided the enormous ecclesiastical province of Quebec into three parts, raising its western components at Toronto and St Boniface to metropolitan status. Except of course for the Atlantic bishops, Canadian prelates met together in a provincial council for the last time in 1868. Further fragmentation of Canadian ecclesiastical structures occurred in 1886 and 1889 when three more provinces were created, at Montreal, Ottawa, and Kingston.

The existence of an organizational framework at the regional level did not necessarily entail greater co-ordination and consolidation within each ecclesiastical province. Halifax, Toronto, and St Boniface only ever held one provincial council or synod – in 1857, 1875, and 1889 respectively. Quebec was the only archdiocese in Canada to have surpassed this phlegmatic performance with a record seven synods between 1851 and 1886. The reason for this was largely due to the dynamic Bishop Bourget who provided the impetus for the first five councils. The last two synods were convened to deal with pressing issues affecting the strife-torn Quebec church, notably the division of the ecclesiatical province. It is interesting to note that once this division was effected, only one other provincial council was held in French Canada, in the archdiocese of Montreal in 1895. Still, as a result of these various meetings, the French-Canadian church, despite its internicine quarrels, was probably the most cohesive institution in Canadian Catholicism by the end of the century. Quebec councils passed decrees reaffirming church dogma, defining ecclesiastical discipline (the responsibilities of the hierarchy, lower clergy, and laity), safeguarding and expanding Catholic education, and standardizing the liturgy, cathechism, and calendar of feast days. This process fostered a degree of uniformity and consultation among French-Canadian dioceses.[3]

The fact remains, however, that the Canadian church as a whole, including its Quebec wing, was not as structurally developed as its American counterpart; nor was it keeping pace with Roman trends towards centralization and standardized church government. In the United States the episcopate had held provincial councils since 1829 and, when the metropolitan see of Baltimore was divided twenty years later, the whole American hierarchy gathered together in plenary councils, the third and last of which occurred in 1884.

Many Canadian bishops even failed to call diocesan synods. The Council of Trent required that they be convened regularly, and although such synods had been fashionable in the 1850s in the wake of the excitement generated by Rome's centralizing policies, they soon fell into disuse in most areas. Bishops tended instead to communicate with their clergy at diocesan retreats held annually or biennially; however, this communication tended to be a monologue. Relations between the lower clergy and the episcopate therefore depended largely on the individual bishop's personality and on local circumstances. While recorded instances of flagrant abuse of episcopal authority were not that frequent, the dearth of structures at all levels of the Canadian church was proving increasingly inadequate to meet the needs of a complex industrializing society.

This situation harked back to a time when the church functioned under missionary conditions. Consequently there existed a wide variation in ecclesiastical practices, not only in discipline, as we have seen, but also in matters relating to liturgy, clerical education and dress, and the observance of religious feast days. In the latter half of the nineteenth century, standardization evoked a mixed response from the Canadian episcopate. Some bishops advocated wholesale adoption of Roman forms and usages; others were quite content with things as they were; still others were proponents of gradual change so as not to offend sensibilities and vested interests.

While standardization was a desirable objective, clearly there were limits to what could be standardized. Ecclesiastical structures, though useful, can only provide partial insight into the institutional life of local churches, which were born and developed under particular circumstances. But by looking briefly at each church through such issues as legislative provisions affecting its development, internal ethnic relations, and its own position with regard to the Protestant communities, we can come to appreciate the diversity within Canadian Catholicism.

At this point, a comment is in order. The history of the Catholic church outside Quebec is still largely undeveloped. Making generalizations about local churches when the most basic studies are quite often lacking is at best dangerous, at worst risky. Still, some good theses have recently appeared. These, together with the mass of information – often turgid and undigested – ferreted out by pious local historians, invite attempts to outline the features of Canadian Catholicism. It would appear that the church had four distinct components at the turn of the last century and these may best be described as Maritime, French Canadian, Ontario Irish, and Oblate missionary. The boundaries of these local churches were more reflective of ecclesiastical than political realities.

MARITIME CATHOLICISM

The Maritime church was a distinct entity by the end of the eighteenth century.[4] The bishops of Quebec, under whose authority the region fell, made repeated and genuine efforts to provide clergy for the ethnically diverse population. But the difficult situation created by the Conquest stymied these efforts. Irish and Scottish immigrants to the area required English- and Gaelic-speaking priests. This fact was given partial recognition in 1817 when the Holy See made mainland Nova Scotia into a vicariate under the authority of Bishop Edmund Burke.[5] Two years later Prince Edward Island, the Magdalen Islands, Cape Breton, and New Brunswick were given a bishop of their own in the person of Angus MacEachern; he was, however, made subject to the diocese of Quebec.[6]

Throughout this period Catholics in the Maritimes suffered from the same disabilities as their co-religionists in Britain, even though colonial administrators tended to be more complaisant than their superiors in London. Catholic emancipation in England brought an end to these restrictions in 1829. As a result, the governing structures of the local church could be organized more freely. Rome named MacEachern titular bishop of Charlottetown in 1830. As such, he was no longer dependent on Quebec. A number of dioceses were then erected: Halifax (1842), New Brunswick–St John (1842), Arichat-Antigonish (1844), Chatham (1860). Subsequently, colonial governments gave these dioceses civil recognition by passing acts of incorporation.

Maritime Catholics belonged to three ethnic groups: Irish, Scots, and Acadian. These formed fairly compact communities throughout the region. Tensions nevertheless developed very early on between the Scots and Irish members of the hierarchy, and between these two and their Acadian flock.[7] Generally mindful of these difficulties, Rome gave the diocese of Arichat and Charlottetown to Scots, and those of Halifax, St John, and Chatham to Irishmen. Within this territorial arrangement, strong local institutions deeply rooted in ethnic communities flourished. Such was the case of St Francis Xavier University at Antigonish and St Dunstan's at Charlottetown.[8]

The Acadians, however, were shut out of this ethnic division of power until they obtained their first bishop in 1912. Acadian national pride had been both stirred and offended ten years earlier when Rome had named the English-speaking Thomas Barry bishop of the overwhelmingly Acadian diocese of Chatham. This pride had been built up over the years since Confederation as the Acadians, largely through their own efforts, established educational and other social service institutions staffed by members of various Quebec religious communities. In this process of institutionalizing the Acadian culture, the English-speaking bishops were either sympathetic bystanders or simply hostile. Their attitude is difficult to understand, given the fact that in the latter part of the nineteenth century the number of Maritime Catholics was growing both in absolute terms and relative to the Protestant population largely because of the phenomenal birthrate of the Acadians (see Table 1).

In thirty years, the Acadian population rose by 78 per cent in New Brunswick, 73 per cent in Prince Edward Island, and 30 per cent in Nova Scotia. As Table 2 shows, the Catholics of New Brunswick and Prince Edward Island would have suffered a net decline in numbers had it not been for Acadian fecundity. As for Nova Scotian Catholics, those of French origin were increasing faster than their British counterparts. Rome's failure to recognize the Acadians' impressive cultural and demographic achievements by the end of the century im-

TABLE 1
Percentage of French in the Overall Catholic Population of the Maritime Provinces

Year	Nova Scotia	New Brunswick	Prince Edward Island
1871	32	47	20
1901	35	64	30

TABLE 2
The Population of the Maritime Provinces

Province	French origin	Total Catholics	Total population
Nova Scotia			
1871	32,833	102,001	387,800
1901	45,161	129,578	459,574
New Brunswick			
1871	44,967	96,016	285,594
1901	79,979	125,698	331,120
Prince Edward Island			
1871	8,000 approx.	40,442	94,021
1901	13,862	45,796	103,259

pelled the latter to do some intense lobbying which culminated in the appointment of Edouard Le Blanc as bishop of St John in 1912. This event signalled their entry into the complex mosaic of Maritime Catholicism.

When dealing with the question of the place of Catholicism within the life of the wider community, we get the distinct impression that the church was integrated into Maritime culture and society. Of course there were instances of anti-Catholic fanaticism, in Nova Scotia and Prince Edward Island in the late 1850s and early 1860s and in New Brunswick in the 1890s.[9] On the whole, however, there existed a tradition of religious tolerance which had well-established

TABLE 3
Percentage of Catholics in the Total Population
in the Maritime Provinces.

Year	Nova Scotia	New Brunswick	Prince Edward Island
1871	26	34	43
1901	28	38	44

historical roots[10] and was maintained by the relative numerical importance of Catholics to the overall population (see Table 3).

Access to political power is a barometer of the integration of a minority group or institution into the broader community. The most striking example of Catholic political influence was Archbishop Thomas Connolly of Halifax, whose control of patronage appointments at the provincial and federal levels is legendary.[11] By all accounts, the archbishop was a formidable figure and he is credited by some with having dispelled the denominational tensions of the late 1850s in Nova Scotia.[12] Both he and his suffragan, Colin Mackinnon of Arichat, who at various times had a brother on the Executive Council of the colony, enjoyed warm relations with Charles Tupper. A Catholic was appointed puisne judge of the Nova Scotia Supreme Court in 1873, probably through the good offices of the once antipapist Joseph Howe.[13] John Thompson became the first Catholic premier of the province some twenty years later. In Prince Edward Island, Bishop Peter MacIntyre was quite cynically courted by politicians of both political parties in their scramble for power. The island had a Catholic premier in 1879 when William Wilfred Sullivan formed a Conservative administration. These facts are not cited in a hagiographic spirit to flatter Catholic pretensions to prominence; they are given to show that the church and its followers were not marginal but quite at home in the Maritimes.

It may be argued that it was the close relationship between politicians and prelates that prevented the latter from successfully defending Catholic educational rights, which were restricted in all three provinces. Connolly in particular maintained unswerving support for Charles Tupper despite the premier's steadfast refusal to guarantee Catholic educational rights. On the whole, Maritime bishops followed a strategy of quiet diplomacy when confronted with legislation establishing non-denominational schools. Nevertheless, governments sooner or later realized that these acts could not be implemented without the co-operation of the Catholic community. Tupper reassured Connolly that since the administration of the new legislation lay with a Council of Public Instruction composed of the entire Cabinet, Catholics would never be excluded from the policy-making process. A similar structure was established in Prince Edward Island under the Public School Act of 1877. In New Brunswick, after a period of political and judicial confrontation and instances of violence such as the Caraquet Riots, the government finally came to terms with reality.[14]

As a result, there evolved in both Nova Scotia and New Brunswick a publicly funded system of Catholic schools in which religious instruction, garb, and symbols were permitted and textbooks containing passages offensive to Catholics edited out or annotated. In addition, teachers belonging to religious communities were either exempted from provincial licensing exams or allowed to take them before a separate board. The Acadians were the only group left out of this gentleman's agreement. In their struggle to protect linguistic and religious rights, they had to confront hostile English-speaking trustees or inspectors, while the Irish or Scots episcopate did little or nothing to support their cause.

Still, in assessing the position of Catholicism in the Maritimes, the important point to remember is that Catholic schools developed out of common school legislation. They had no status in law and were very much dependent on the tolerance of the wider community. Since this system was never seriously challenged, the observation that Catholicism was at home in the Maritimes appears to be sustained. Bishop John Cameron of Antigonish summed up the situation very neatly when he told the apostolic delegate that 'proselytism in Nova Scotia has become so intensely unpopular that no self-respecting Protestant would take any part in it.'[15]

THE IRISH ONTARIO CHURCH

The contrast with Irish Ontario Catholicism could not have been starker. The Irish character of this church developed in the wake of the famine migration of the 1840s which had vastly increased the number of Catholics in the region. The prelates who emerged to become its leaders reaped the benefits of the work done by an earlier generation of Scots and French-speaking clergy.

The church in Ontario had in fact evolved under the protective wing of its mother church in Quebec. In 1818 Upper Canadian Catholics were entrusted to the care of Bishop Alexander Macdonell, suffragan to the bishop of Quebec.[16] Six years later, the colony became a diocese, the episcopal see being at Kingston, which was made ecclesiastically dependent on Quebec. New dioceses then were erected at Toronto (1841), London (1856), and Hamilton (1856). Despite the Quebec hierarchy's efforts to recruit incumbents whose mother tongue was English, the first bishops in Canada West were either French Canadians or Irishmen trained in Quebec seminaries.[17] The Quebec church also provided parish priests for many Ontario missions, as well as members of male and female religious congregations to staff schools and hospitals.

Ontario Catholicism became distinctly Irish with the appointment in 1860 of John Joseph Lynch to the see of Toronto. Unlike other Ontario prelates at the time, Lynch was born and trained in the old world and then served in the United States for fourteen years. He was administrator of a seminary at Lewiston, New York, before his episcopal nomination. The bishop's Canadian experience was rather limited. However, he did share with the Irish clergy and the American episcopate, most of whom were Irishmen, the idea of the providential mission of the Irish people. He once stated:

Ireland was subdued ... in order the more effectively to amalgamate the inhabitants with the English nation ... They resisted but were compelled by force to learn the language. God has his designs in this. Little did Irish children suspect when they were whipped in school for not knowing the English lesson that God destined the English language in their mouths to spread the true faith of his Divine Son throughout the greater part of the world.[18]

Superficially it would seem that this messianism was not much different from its French-Canadian equivalent. In fact, both focused on the historical experience of subjugation which was somehow redeemed by a divinely ordained mission of national grandeur. But the two differed in one fundamental respect. Lynch's vision was predicated on assimilation – the historic assimilation of the Irish to the English language, and the inevitable assimilation of non-English-speaking Catholics to prevailing North American cultural norms.[19] French-Canadian messianism was based on the innate superiority of

French Catholic culture which by virtue of its *rayonnement* ultimately would be recognized by the Anglo-Saxon majority. It did not seek to thrust this culture upon others. Irish messianism, on the other hand, implicitly required that other ethnic groups follow the Irish example and blend into the dominant culture.

It must be stressed, however, that in the eyes of Lynch and his Irish colleagues, assimilation was merely an instrument to achieve the pre-eminent aim of converting the English-speaking peoples. This often meant adopting forms that were culturally acceptable to the Protestant majority in order better to diffuse Catholic dogma. For example, priests in the ecclesiastical province of Toronto were not required to wear the Roman collar and soutane, garb which Pius IX prescribed after the Roman Revolution of 1848 to highlight the separation between the clergy and the world. Instead, they wore the soutanella, a knee-length coat which went over their trousers. In this way, it was hard to distinguish the Catholic from the Protestant clergy. Similarly, Lynch appropriated the Sunday evening lecture, which he regarded fondly as an intellectual forum for the rational exposition of articles of faith to cultured Protestants. These lectures were delivered regularly in St Michael's Cathedral and sometimes were published in the local press. The archbishop was also proud of his letters that appeared from time to time in influential newspapers such as the *Globe*.

Lynch believed that he was very much a part of Toronto's social élite and that, as the head of the local church, he should be highly visible. Consequently, he poured scorn on his Quebec colleagues, who expressed surprise when he attended the funeral of the rabidly anti-Catholic George Brown. It was imperative, the prelate argued, that the man who occupied the most important position in society after the lieutenant-governor be seen at such functions! Clearly, Lynch considered that he and his church were well integrated into Ontario society and that they exerted considerable influence within it.

Illusion was one thing, reality quite another. The fact is that Lynch was – and was perceived by the socio-political élite of his day to be – an ethnic leader, a familiar figure in our age of multiculturalism. Despite all his attempts at blending in, the archbishop remained much more attuned to Irish than Canadian questions. He spearheaded petitions to Queen Victoria in favour of Home Rule and the establishment of a Catholic university in Ireland. In protest against the British government's Irish policies, he refused some years later to allow the ringing of church bells to mark the sovereign's golden jubilee.[20] The Irishness of his Catholicism also got the better of his attempts to present the rational face of his faith to the Protestant élite. Lynch's devotion to Our Lady of Knock, especially to the restorative qualities of the plaster used in the construction of the shrine, and his support of Francis McSpirit, priest and healer,[21] scarcely enhanced his claims that the Irish were chosen instruments for the propagation of the faith among the English-speaking peoples of the world.

While he threw himself wholeheartedly behind Catholic causes in Ireland, questions involving Catholic rights in Canada, particularly when championed by French-speaking protagonists, did not seem to excite his enthusiasm. In the aftermath of the Red River uprising, for example, he declined to sign a petition to the governor general in favour of an amnesty for Louis Riel, who among other things had defended the right to denominational education in the area. In addition, the archbishop's public support for Catholic educational rights in New Brunswick was little more than tepid. Clearly his attempts to blend in with the majority culture of Ontario while remaining faithful to his Irish Catholic roots involved him in contradictions. He failed on some crucial occasions to show solidarity with the French-Canadian episcopate, never imagining that in the eyes of Ontario's élite he was as much an ethnic leader as were the Quebec bishops.

Lynch had a distorted view of his place not only in Ontario society, but also within the church. It is clear that he considered himself to be the senior prelate of the Catholic church in Canada.[22] It is not clear on what this claim rested, since the archbishop of Halifax, whose ecclesiastical province was established earlier and contained roughly double the population as that of Toronto during this period, was better placed to assert this privilege among English-speaking prelates. The archbishop of Toronto summarily dismissed any pretensions to pre-eminence by members of the French-Canadian hierarchy. The province of Quebec, he asserted, was 'yet in the thirteenth century,'[23] and its clergy were narrow-minded, imprudent, ignorant, backward, and motivated only by petty ethnic interests.[24] He accused them of antagonizing politicians and thereby endangering the rights and privileges of the Catholic church in Canada. It never seemed to occur to him that his own involvement in Irish politics and his tempestuous relations with Canadian politicians might produce the same results. Lynch once likened the French in Canada to the Cajuns of Louisiana and concluded that they 'will not leave a single permanent mark on this country.'[25]

The prelate certainly did occupy a central place within Irish Ontario Catholicism. Toronto was raised to archiepiscopal status in 1870 and was given Kingston, Hamilton, and London as suffragan sees. Lynch would have preferred his ecclesiastical province to be coterminous with the boundaries of Ontario, but he encountered stiff resistance from the French-Canadian hierarchy who wanted to keep the diocese of Ottawa within their territory. This dispute gave rise to acrimonious confrontations between the bishops of Quebec and Ontario.[26] Nevertheless, within his province Lynch was undisputed leader and placed like-minded men in vacant episcopal sees. He even recruited incumbents directly in Ireland, such as James Vincent Cleary and James Joseph Carbery, bishops of Kingston and Hamilton respectively, who were preferred to local candidates. Prospective bishops need not always have been Irish, although this was almost invariably the case, as long as they were loyal. When, for example, the Holy See created the vicariate of Northern Canada (the future diocese of Peterborough), Lynch was content to see it administered by a trusted collaborator, the Frenchman Jean François Jamot.

The ecclesiastical province of Toronto was divided in 1889 when Kingston became a metropolitan see. This administrative decision gave Irish Ontario Catholicism a second vigorous spokesman in the person of Archbishop Cleary, whose territory included Peterborough, now headed by Bishop Richard O'Connor, and Alexandria, a diocese with a French-Canadian majority ruled by a bishop of Scottish origin, Alexander Macdonell.

This distribution of ecclesiastical power raises a fundamental question about the ethnic composition of Ontario Catholicism. Table 4 indicates the crucial role played by French Canadians in maintaining the proportion of Catholics to the overall population. In thirty years the French-Canadian presence in Ontario increased by 113 per cent. If we consider that the Catholic population excluding those of French origin rose by 15.2 per cent and that the total Ontario population went up by 34 per cent, we come to appreciate just how vital the French-Canadian presence was to Ontario Catholicism. It was this presence which allowed the proportion of Catholics to the overall population to remain constant at just under 20 per cent in this period.

These statistics, of course, refer to the whole of the province, in-

TABLE 4
The Population of Ontario

Year	Total	Catholics	French origin
1871	1,620,851	274,162	75,383
1901	2,182,947	390,304	161,181

cluding that Ontario portion of the diocese of Ottawa. But if we were to exclude Ottawa from our consideration and focus instead on the territory occupied in 1871 by Irish bishops – that is, the ecclesiastical province of Toronto – some rather startling figures on the ethnic distribution of the Catholic population is revealed. In 1871 the French numbered 49,267 and comprised 22 per cent of the Catholics of the ecclesiastical province of Toronto.[27] If we assume that Catholics of Scottish, German, and origins other than Irish accounted for another 24,000 people,[28] we are left with 148,468 Irish Catholics, or 67 per cent of the Catholic population of the ecclesiastical province.[29]

Thirty years later, through immigration from Quebec and natural increase, French Canadians comprised 40 per cent (46,536) of the Catholic population of the archdiocese of Kingston and 26.5 per cent (43,202) of that of Toronto, including 47.6 per cent (28,281) of Catholics in the diocese of London.[30] By adding those Catholics whose ethnic origins were Scottish, German, Italian, and Indian to these numbers, it would appear that by 1901 the Irish only constituted a slight majority within the boundaries of Irish Ontario.[31] In fact, their numbers had remained constant in thirty years, while the French had almost doubled. Not only were the expectations that Irish providentialism nurtured an illusion; the population base on which Irish Ontario Catholicism rested seemed very fragile indeed.

What of the position occupied by Catholicism in Ontario life? Was it roughly the same as in the Maritimes? Superficially at least there were similarities. Lynch, whose sense of self-worth was certainly equal to that of Connolly, developed close ties with the Mowat administration. This alliance made it easier for Catholics to have access to patronage and Lynch often acted as broker in these nominations. The provincial cabinet under Mowat always included Catholic members and the minister of education periodically consulted the hierarchy before submitting legislation to the Assembly.

A symbol of this new spirit of *bonne entente* was the *Globe*, the once rabidly anti-Catholic Reform organ. By the 1870s and 1880s the newspaper blessed all aspects of what some derisively called the Lynch-Mowat Concordat and accused the opposition press of disturbing religious harmony in the province.[32] It also staunchly upheld the civil rights of Catholics during the Jubilee Riots of 1875. From this it would seem that by the third quarter of the century, Ontario reached the same level of religious tolerance and harmony as the Maritimes, after a period in which both regions had experienced intense denominational factionalism. But we must be wary of suggestions that a newspaper which had a political stake in harmonious relations between Catholics and Protestants necessarily reflected opinion in the broader community. So, too, must we question the view of a number of Canadian historians who hold that what went on in the political sphere somehow encompassed the totality of life within a given community. Anti-Catholicism was deeply rooted in Ontario culture. The Jubilee Riots, for instance, indicate that despite injunctions from the party political press in favour of denominational concord and against street hooliganism, a substantial number of Torontonians (anti-Catholic rioters were estimated at between six to eight thousand) agreed with their mayor and with the Protestant press in denying Catholics the right to hold religious processions.[33]

Recently historian Greg Kealey has tried to explain the cause of the violence (which he described as 'undoubtedly the bloodiest sectarian struggle in Toronto's history')[34] by arguing that Catholics had transgressed the informal limits set for public religious events. But this surely begs the question of who set these limits. Was this a mutually acceptable, though informal, accord? Is it likely that Toronto Catholics would have agreed to give up an integral part of their religious ritual? In a society where Christian denominations were recognized as being equal before the law, what was excessive about Catholics participating in a normal religious function which happened to be held outdoors? It should be remembered in this regard that Catholics rejected the Protestant notion which relegated religion to the private sphere. If, then, processions had not been previously held in the streets of Toronto, it was not because of some tacit understanding, but for fear of a Protestant backlash. Those who defined Kealey's limits of acceptable religious public display clearly were Protestants who regarded this notion as totally foreign to their own religious experience. And they were numerous enough that priests did not wear ecclesiastical garb or insignia in the streets of southern Ontario cities for fear of being molested and the bishops of Toronto, Lynch included, were insulted, sometimes assaulted, in public. Catholics thus perceived themselves to be, and indeed were, a besieged minority.

It might be argued that Ontario Catholics were the only minority, excepting Quebec Protestants, to enjoy constitutional guarantees regarding denominational education. But it bears repeating that legislation creating and extending Catholic education in Canada West was opposed by a majority of politicians from that region; and that such legislation was enacted only because of the overwhelming support of members from Canada East, a fact frequently and resentfully invoked by the opposition Conservative party and press in the 1870s and 1880s.

Guarantees to Catholic education in Ontario were in fact rather limited when compared with the generous conditions which obtained for Protestant schooling in Quebec. For example, Ontario refused to provide public funds for Catholic secondary schools as well as for separate teacher training throughout the latter part of the last century. And minority schools in Ontario were not, as in Quebec, administered by a separate structure at the provincial level. Instead, the Catholic educational system was forced into a voluntarist straitjacket: the state provided constitutional guarantees for basic education but precluded access to equitable funding, and at the same time required Catholic schools to follow departmental norms set by Protestant administrators. The minority, therefore, had to assume the financial burden of improving an under-financed system, of creating its own secondary schools, and of training its own teachers.

Of course, the hierarchy lobbied to extend Quebec's provisions for minority education to Ontario, but in the era of 'no popery' elections they were forced to fight a rearguard action.[35] In fact, several bishops believed that, despite constitutional guarantees, Catholic schools in Ontario were in imminent danger of being suppressed. In this context, it might be well to reflect on historian Franklin Walker's contention that the Catholic vote represented a force strong enough to dissuade Ontario politicians from attacking either Catholics as a body or their schools as a system.[36] Such a view is misleading, since it suggests that Catholics felt assured about their position in society. Yet had they not heard political and religious spokesmen decry the existence of separate schools and the sordid political manoeuvrings from which they had sprung? Such arguments were hardly likely to inspire confidence in the minority's future prospects. Between the Conservatives' open hostility and the Liberals' imperturbable voluntarism, Ontario Catholics read between the lines of the official discourse of religious concord and understood that they occupied a narrow and insecure space in the life of their province.

In any event, the hierarchies of Ontario and the Maritimes certainly expressed divergent views about their respective positions in the wider community. We get an intimation of this difference when comparing the letters written to the apostolic delegate by members of the Ontario episcopate with the one cited above by Bishop Cameron. Ontario bishops complained that they lived in a fundamentally Protestant society. Social life, wrote Bishop Fergus McEvay of London, was anti-Catholic. Wealth was securely in the hands of Protestants and as a result everything Catholic was considered inferior. In this context, both he and Archbishop Dennis O'Connor of Toronto bemoaned the lack of strong Catholic leaders. 'Leading Catholics are rare,' stated O'Connor, 'and do not distinguish themselves by zeal for Religion.'[37] This vacuum led to a double tendency: the more prosperous Catholics sought out Protestant company 'because it commonly constitutes what is called *good society*,'[38] while poorer young men, faced with lack of opportunities in Ontario, emigrated to the United States. In either case, the outcome was mixed marriage, which the Ontario hierarchy universally deplored. O'Connor observed that half the children of these unions were lost to the church in the first generation and fully three-quarters in the second.

In general, these prelates felt that Ontario politicians had little regard for Catholics. McEvay affirmed: 'In the past both parties have abused and persecuted us, and either party would do so again to gain political advantage.'[39] There was a feeling as well that Catholics did not have a fair share of patronage. The provincial of the Basilian Fathers in Toronto maintained: 'A chances égales de succès, le protestant est toujours préféré et le catholique n'occupera guères que de postes inférieurs, où son salaire ne sera jamais bien élevé et son influence à peu près nulle.'[40] Protestantism therefore expanded its influence through the social standing and political power of its members, but equally through the public schools and welfare institutions. The Basilian provincial summed up the position of Ontario Catholics with a quote from John Walsh, former archbishop of Toronto: they (the Protestants) tolerate us while seeking to take away all our freedoms.

TABLE 5

Number and Percentage of Catholics to the Overall Population of Some
Canadian Cities

City	Population	Catholics	%
Toronto	209,892	28,994	14.0
Hamilton	52,634	8,872	17.0
London	37,976	(less than) 5,000	13.0
Peterborough	11,239	2,690	24.0
Kingston	17,961	4,782	26.5
Halifax	40,832	(approx.) 17,000	42.0
St John	40,711	(approx.) 12,000	30.0
Charlottetown	12,080	4,995	41.0
Chatham	9,068	3,302	36.5
Sydney	9,747	3,877	40.0

One further factor must be borne in mind when comparing the
relative status of Catholics in the Maritimes and Ontario. Catholics
were a far more important element of the urban population in the
Maritimes than in English-speaking Ontario. Figures taken from
the 1901 census are revealing (see Table 5).

THE OBLATE MISSIONARY CHURCH

The Catholic church in the lands governed by the Hudson's Bay Company was very much an offspring of Quebec. Established in 1818
primarily for the spiritual care of French Canadians and Métis, it
placed a great deal of importance as well on missionary service to the
Amerindians. In light of the sheer size of the North-West and its
distance from the Canadas, the Holy See soon realized that pastoral
and missionary activities would have to be organized locally. As a
result, permission was granted for Joseph-Norbert Provencher, one
of two Quebec priests who were the first to work in the area, to be
raised to the episcopate. Provencher was consecrated bishop in 1822
and, as with MacEachern and Jean-Jacques Lartigue, was designated auxiliary and suffragan to the bishop of Quebec.[41] Rome
officially gave Provencher a vicariate to administer in 1844. Three
years later, he was made titutlar bishop of the North-West, an area
initially stretching west to the Rocky Mountains and north to the

Arctic Ocean. Well into the twentieth century, Provencher's successors in what was soon known as the see of St Boniface, the mother church of the Canadian West, were French Canadians. During most of Provencher's episcopate, human resources were at a premium. Until the Oblates arrived in 1845, the bishop never had more than four or five priests at his disposal, all of whom were French Canadians.[42]

The arrival of the Oblates heralded an ecclesiastical revolution. Backed by the human and financial resources of the order, with solid Canadian bases in the diocese of Ottawa and also in Montreal, the Oblates made a commitment to perform the pastoral and missionary work of the western church. They were at once guarantors of stability and expansion for the fledgling institution. In return, they exercised a control of ecclesiastical life which paralleled the Hudson's Bay Company's virtual monopoly of civil life. The Oblates held all the episcopal positions in the West until the first decade of the twentieth century, monopolizing Catholic missionary work among the Amerindians and Inuit and most of the pastoral activity among white and mixed-blood communities. The Oblates in Canada reflected the recent European origins of the order: most were French and Belgian, a few French Canadian. This gave the western church a pronounced French character.

Effective missionary work soon required a better organization of the vast territory covered by the diocese of St Boniface. Rome created the vicariate of Athabaska-Mackenzie in 1862, headed by Bishop Henri Faraud, a missionary who had resided in the area for over ten years and worked among the Athapaskan Indians. The vicariate was very isolated from the outside world. It took Faraud's coadjutor seventy-five days to travel by cart from St Boniface to Lac La Biche,[43] while Faraud himself only heard of the death of Pius ix four and a half months after the event.[44] Apart from the North, the Oblates also became active beyond the Rockies in mainland British Columbia, founding a mission in the Okanagan valley in 1859. Five years later the vicariate of British Columbia was established under the care of Bishop Louis d'Herbomez, whose see was at New Westminster.

Although members of the order had been present on Vancouver Island even before coming to the mainland, the Oblates never managed to dominate ecclesiastical life there. Modeste Demers, a Quebec priest recruited by Provencher to do missionary work on the Pacific coast, was made bishop of Vancouver Island in 1847 and his

TABLE 6
The Population of Manitoba

Year	Total	Catholics	French
1871	12,228	5,452	approx. 3,000
1881	65,954	12,246	9,949
1901	255,211	35,672	21,357

diocese was incorporated into the ecclesiastical province of Oregon. It was only in 1903 that Victoria was detached from the American church and raised to archiepiscopal status, with New Westminster and the new vicariate of Mackenzie-Yukon as suffragan sees.

The western church was given a tighter organizational structure in 1871. St Boniface was raised to metropolitan status and covered the whole of the Territories, as well as mainland British Columbia. The Holy See created the diocese of St Albert under Bishop Vital Grandin. St Albert ran like a swathe south-west to north-east, from the foot of the Rockies to the northern half of Hudson Bay. Twenty years later this diocese was divided to create the vicariate of Saskatchewan, administered by Bishop Albert Pascal.

The Catholic population of the western church underwent dramatic changes in the period under study. As Table 6 shows, Catholics rapidly became a small minority in Manitoba in the decade after its entry into Confederation. Because of heavy immigration from Protestant Ontario in those ten years Catholics, who constituted 45 per cent of the population in 1871, fell to 18.5 per cent by the next census. At the turn of the century they had fallen further back to 14 per cent. But in these thirty years the French continued to comprise over half of the Catholic population: in 1871 they were 55 per cent of the total, rising to 81 per cent in the following decade, and dropping to 60 per cent by the beginning of the century. This last figure, however, is open to question, since the census failed to take into account many recently arrived Catholic immigrants from Central and Eastern Europe. There were, for example, over ten thousand Catholic Ukrainians, as well as an indeterminate number of Germans and Poles. From this it is obvious that English-speaking Catholics were but a tiny part of the total Catholic population.

The situation in the Territories, organized and unorganized, presented a different picture. There the number of Catholics, while always a minority, increased faster than the overall population (see Table 7). This was undoubtedly due to steady immigration from Catholic Europe. By the turn of the century, while the French formed nearly half (44 per cent) of the Catholic population, it is clear that they were not, as in other parts of Canada, the motor which fuelled the significant rate of increase of Catholics to the overall population. Even more than in Manitoba, the members of the western church were ethnically varied, with sizeable numbers of French, Ukrainians, Amerindians, Germans, and Poles.

In British Columbia, Catholics remained steady at about 20 per cent of the total population during the period of study (see Table 8). This was the only Canadian region where the French did not comprise a significant element of the Catholic population.

These early years in the history of the western church were marked by generally good ethnic relations. The Oblates made an honest effort to cater to the varied cultural communities living under their care, whether these comprised Irish sailors in the port of Esquimault, Italian railway workers in the interior of British Columbia, Polish, German, or Ukrainian settlers in the prairies, or nomadic Amerindians pursuing their traditional way of life.[45] Many Oblates were or became polyglot. Catechisms and missals written in Cree and Athapaskan bear eloquent testimony to the efforts made by missionaries to reach people in their own idiom. And yet this statement must be qualified. As we shall see later, the western church had difficulty coming to grips with the special needs of Ukrainian Catholics who belonged to the Eastern rite and this gave rise to many years of ethnic and religious tensions. In addition, one gets the impression from contemporary and present-day accounts of missionary activities that, despite efforts to adapt European religious precepts and practices to aboriginal cultures,[46] the clergy tended to treat the Amerindians like children.[47] This was surely one of the factors which made conversion to Catholicism so arduous among these peoples.

The church's relations with the civil authorities were also generally positive, particularly in the early years. The Hudson's Bay Company undoubtedly recognized the important function of social control which the church could exercise among both Catholic employees and Amerindian suppliers. As a result, missionaries were transported at the company's expense to the various posts which dotted the North-West. While at the official level relations were warm and cordial, cases of tension between individual clerics and

TABLE 7
The Population of the Territories

Year	Total	Catholic	French
1881	56,446	4,443	2,896
1901	211,641	39,653	17,493

TABLE 8
The Population of British Columbia

Year	Total	Catholics	French
1881	49,459	10,043	916
1901	178,657	33,639	5,103

factors were not uncommon, particularly when the latter favoured Protestant preachers. Rivalry between Catholic and Protestant missionaries sometimes was intense and company officials could play a decisive role in favouring one denomination over another.

Some churchmen managed to rise above these petty difficulties and to be prominent members in western society. Men such as Archbishop Taché and Father Albert Lacombe were universally recognized as leaders of their communities, spokesmen for various socio-cultural groups, and government mediators. Taché undoubtedly controlled a lot of patronage in the decade after Manitoba's entry into Confederation. However, the influence wielded by such clerics waned quickly before the steady advance of Protestant immigration. As Catholics resigned themselves at the end of the century to forming small minorities, their ecclesiastical leaders became increasingly pessimistic about the position and rights of the church in the West. Taché and others were demoted to the status of ethnic spokesmen.

QUEBEC CATHOLICISM

The Quebec church was the heart of Canadian Catholicism. It was the oldest, most numerous, best organized, and richest of the local churches. And yet this cliché is deceptive because up to 1840 it was still experiencing the harmful effects of the Conquest. Imperial policy sought to make the Quebec church a malleable and dependent institution. Over the years the British relaxed their grip as the clergy showed continued fidelity to established authority. But the fact remains that the church's institutional development was thwarted. The ecclesiastical province of Quebec, for example, was created only eight years before that of Halifax. Montreal became a diocese after Kingston, Charlottetown, and the vicariate of Halifax were erected. As well, the Quebec church suffered from a chronic shortage of priests, a situation which may not have been created by the Conquest but was certainly exacerbated by it. Finally, the church lived in the shadow of fear, a constant fear that the crown might use certain constitutional provisions or the articles of the Gallican church against it.[48]

The institution's potential was very real, however, and its release depended only on a favourable climate. In the midst of the troubles leading up to the rebellions of 1837–8, the British lifted their veto to the Holy See's creation of a second diocese in Quebec, implicitly admitting that the church no longer required the tight control exercised upon it in the past. As a result, Montreal finally became a diocesan see in 1836.[49] Subsequently the crown's recognition of Sulpician property rights, which had been contested since 1763, signalled an end to the period of tutelage. After the erection of the ecclesiastical province of Quebec, other dioceses were established in quick succession: Trois-Rivières and St-Hyacinthe (1852), Rimouski (1867), Sherbrooke (1874), Chicoutimi (1878), Nicolet (1885), Valleyfield (1892).

It was in the conservative context of the Union period that the Bourget revolution took place. The second bishop of Montreal (1840–76) had a keener awareness than any of his ecclesiastical peers of the needs of the church and more energy to respond to them. Under his firm direction, Quebec Catholicism evolved into a mature institution; it acquired the personnel, both secular priests and religious communities, to care for the spiritual and physical requirements of an expanding and increasingly industrialized population; it diffused expressions of Roman culture, from liturgy to architecture to ideology, which enhanced the French Canadians' sense of distinct identity.[50] In collaboration with conservative politicians of both Canada East and Canada West, the church obtained a series of legislative concessions that made it an omnipresent institution in Quebec until the Quiet Revolution.

But the impressive spectacle of power and discipline which the church presented to the outside world masked the deep divisions that plagued it, particularly during the second half of the last century. These divisions were not ideological, as some commentators have held, dramatically depicting a struggle between ultramontanists on the one hand and Gallicans and Liberal Catholics on the other; nor were they based, as others imagined, on conflicting political loyalties.[51]

Dissension sprang instead from competing interest groups within the church. On one side there was the archdiocese of Quebec and the seminaries of Quebec and Saint-Sulpice, who all clung tenaciously to their long-standing privileges and to the old order on which these were based. 'Le mieux est ennemi du bien' asserted a Sulpician superior.[52] On the other side there were prelates such as Bourget and Laflèche and religious communities such as the Jesuits, who tended to challenge these entrenched privileges as being out of step with the exigencies of the times. Who, for instance, could have doubted the wisdom of dividing the enormous Sulpician parish of Notre Dame which served nearly one hundred thousand Catholics in Montreal by the mid 1860s? Who would have challenged Montreal's right to its own French-speaking university when McGill and Bishop's already catered to the city's English-speaking community? Who would have stopped the Jesuits from settling their claim over land confiscated from them by the crown after the Conquest, land which could serve the ever expanding needs of education? And yet these initiatives encountered the unrelenting opposition of vested ecclesiastical interests, which provoked sterile confrontations and undermined the church's effectiveness.

These quarrels were also fed by personality conflicts. Archbishops Baillargeon and Taschereau were distant, cerebral, cautious, and suspicious of change. Bishops Bourget and Laflèche on the other hand were warm, impulsive, impatient, and, in the latter's case, almost compulsively driven to action. The context of the period was one of change. Rome's centralizing policies and Quebec's era of industrialization, with its attendant phenomenon of population increase and mobility, required more sophisticated ecclesiastical institutions. The requirements of the times exacerbated both the conflicts of personalities and vested interests.

In Canada the context was not only one of social change but cultural conflict. The latter third of the last century saw a bitter ethnic struggle regarding the future cultural character of the country: was Canada officially to be Anglo- Saxon and Protestant or would it accommodate the Catholic and French-speaking elements in its political culture? At this time in Canada's history, religion was an essential component of nationality. As a result those who advanced the interests of one generally promoted the other. Over the years Bourget fought hard to have legislation reflect Quebec's condition as a Catholic society (without this affecting the status of the Protestant population), and also to defend the educational rights of Catholic minorities in the other provinces of the new Dominion. For example, he led the lobby to amend Quebec's newly formulated Civil Code so that it might better reflect the principles of canon law. At the same time he was a staunch advocate of an amnesty for Louis Riel in the aftermath of the Red River uprising and of Catholic educational rights in the New Brunswick schools controversy. The bishop was not a nationalist. In fact, political theorists would be perplexed and a little bemused by his identification of 'true nationality' with the 'spirit of charity,'[53] surely not the stuff with which modern ideologies are made. And yet his vision of a Catholic Quebec whose special mission it was to defend Catholic minorities in Canada coincided with and was an integral part of the affirmation of a French-Canadian presence within the new polity. His actions unwittingly contributed to the expression of a form of French-Canadian nationalism.

Bourget's public stands and his tactics on these questions alienated the more cautious members of the hierarchy. Prelates such as Taschereau were not anti-nationalist – in fact, they essentially shared Bourget's vision – but they were annoyed by his methods. Disagreements over political strategies combined with conflicts of personality and vested interests to deepen the rift. A theoretical debate regarding the rights of the church in Canada broke into the open shortly after Confederation: one school asserted that the church had a constitutional right to organize itself as it saw fit; the other maintained that in a country with a Protestant majority these rights could be secured, not through ringing declarations, but through negotiation and quiet diplomacy. The latter school worried out loud about the dangers of a Protestant backlash should Bourget and his followers persist in their tactics.

The Liberal party was worried also. In the early 1870s the Quebec wing of the party repudiated its Rouge origins and through the parti national tried to woo moderate nationalists, including the clergy. When Alexander Mackenzie formed a Liberal administration in Ottawa in 1873, however, back-benchers from Quebec abandoned their nationalist stand on the Riel amnesty and the New Brunswick schools controversy and closed ranks behind their leaders. Worse still, after a few months in office the government introduced legislation on undue electoral influence, which was clearly aimed in Quebec at intimidating unfriendly clergymen. Feeling betrayed, Bourget and his followers persuaded other members of the hierarchy to write a joint pastoral letter against Catholic liberalism. The clergy had clearly met the Liberals' challenge. Faced with the prospect of massive clerical opposition in future election campaigns, the party determined to act in order to neutralize the church. At this point the interests of the Liberals converged with those of Bourget's ecclesiastical opponents. The latter provided Joseph Cauchon, president of the Privy Council and a member of Parliament for Quebec City, with an entrée to the Holy See. Cauchon fanned the fears of the Roman bureaucracy by proclaiming that Canada was teetering on the edge of sectarian warfare because of the imprudent actions of some Quebec clergymen. The combined pressure of Archbishop Taschereau's advisers and of the Liberal party convinced the Holy See to dispatch to Canada the first apostolic delegate, Bishop George Conroy. The long-term consequences of these actions was, as we shall see, to make the Quebec church an ineffectual institution in defending Catholic minority rights, a strong French-Canadian presence within Confederation, and a pluralistic model of cultural development.

The Quebec church was characterized by a high degree of ethnic homogeneity, as Table 9 shows. French Canadians accounted for over 90 per cent of the Catholics in Quebec in this period. Although non-French-Canadian Catholics increased in number, their percentage of the overall Catholic population dropped during these thirty years. Still, in some dioceses, particularly in the Montreal area, their numbers were not inconsiderable. In 1901, for instance, the archdiocese of Quebec had roughly sixteen thousand non-French Catholics, that of Montreal almost fifty thousand while Rimouski and Valleyfield each had around seven thousand. For purposes of comparison, the archdiocese of Montreal had more non-French Catholics than the dioceses of Kingston or Hamilton had faithful.

TABLE 9
The Population of Quebec

Year	Total	Catholics	French origin
1871	1,191,516	1,019,850	929,817
1901	1,648,898	1,429,212	1,322,513

The proportion of Catholics to the total Quebec population rose slightly at this time, because of the rapid natural increase of French Canadians. The pattern that we have seen in the Maritimes and in Ontario was repeated in the homeland of Canadian Catholicism: French Canadians were responsible for the proportional increase of Catholics to the total population.

Despite this strong ethnic character, the Quebec church did accommodate English-speaking Catholics. The Irish had their own parishes in Quebec City, Montreal, and Ottawa, as well as a number of schools and social service institutions. Bishops even appointed priests to serve English-speaking communities in their own language in rural and outlying areas of the province. Generally, ethnic relations within the church were good, with the possible exception of Ottawa where Irish spokesmen became increasingly restive at the end of the century, arguing that their countrymen were not being given their due in the upper echelons of the diocesan administration and the university.[54]

As for the English-speaking Protestants of Quebec, the wealth and political power of the dominant élite ensured that they would enjoy virtual autonomy in running their community institutions. Large-scale sectarian violence was unusual in Quebec. When it did occur, it was often sparked by the over-zealousness of anti-Catholic or anti-papal preachers, such as Alessandro Gavazzi in the 1850s. But French Canadians were certainly not immune from religious intolerance, as when a riot broke out to prevent the Salvation Army from parading through the streets of Quebec City in 1887.[55]

CONCLUSION

As Falconio observed in the autumn of 1902, it was time for the Catholic church in Canada to come out of the desert. The church was no longer a missionary institution, nor was it labouring under the difficult conditions imposed by the British Conquest. Consequently it had to abandon the state of nonconformity in which it found itself and adhere to the standards and practices prevailing among the more established churches. By the turn of the century it was high time to standardize diocesan administration, regularize relations between the episcopate and the lower clergy, improve clerical education, and institute a uniform liturgy. Yet these were not new themes in the history of the Catholic church in Canada. Bishop Bourget had advocated the creation of an ecclesiastical structure embracing all of British North America when he proposed that the Atlantic bishops be included in the ecclesiastical province of Quebec. Rome did not accept this suggestion, nor did it follow up on its own expressed wish to see Atlantic prelates attend Quebec provincial councils as observers. At the diocesan level as well, it was Bourget's administration that led the way. The bishop had created a cathedral chapter and an ecclesiastical tribunal in his diocese; he had reformed the liturgy and seminary studies. Perhaps these initiatives did not go far enough, but they were a step in the right direction. Yet few of his colleagues followed in his footsteps. He received little recognition for these achievements and was in fact heavily criticized by traditionalists in the hierarchy. Of course, it may be argued that in this troubled period Rome had better things to do than to encourage a turbulent bishop or watch over a small and remote church barely emerged from its colonial past. It is significant, however, that Falconio made no acknowledgment that a tradition of change was already present within the Canadian church, thereby implying that the motor of reform must come from the Holy See.

A closer adherence to external norms and forms was one thing; a fusion of the various traditions from which the local churches sprang was quite another. And yet in urging the creation of a national ecclesiastical structure, was not Falconio also trying to achieve the second objective? What model did he have in mind for the national church? Was it the Quebec church, which enjoyed a special status among its sister institutions, with well-entrenched rights concerning the tithe, Catholic education, marriage, the recording of births and deaths, the management of ecclesiastical property? Was it the Maritime church, whose prerogatives existed more in fact than in law thanks to the large number of Catholics living in the region? Was it the Ontario church, whose education rights were certainly better established in law than in the Maritimes, but which suffered from demographic and social weaknesses? In this respect it is worth bearing in mind that in 1871 the Catholic population of Ontario exceeded that of the Maritimes by only 15 per cent. Although this figure rose to 30 per cent by the beginning of this century, the fact remains that Ontario did not have significantly more Catholics than the Maritimes throughout this period. What model of leadership would be preferred in relations between prelates and politicians? Whose style would prevail: would it be that of Lynch, Taschereau, Connolly, or Bourget?

To answer these question, we must see how Rome viewed the local churches and what events impelled the Holy See to send apostolic delegates to Canada.

Chapter Two

Rome: Another Canadian Metropolis

Henri Smeulders, the second of three papal legates who smoothed the way for the establishment of a permanent delegation in Canada, was given plain advice on preparing reports for the Propaganda: 'You must go to the heart of the matter,' he was told, 'I must insist even more on this way of proceeding because their Eminences the Cardinals having to deal with varied and complicated questions in General Congregation do not have time to read long reports.'[1]

Quebec sociologist Fernand Dumont once referred to Rome as yet another distant centre of decision-making on which the lives of French Canadians depended.[2] The image of Rome as metropolis, while particularly apt for French Canadians whose attachment to the Holy See was much more intense and immediate than for English-speaking Catholics, is none the less applicable to Canada as a whole, especially for the period under study. At that time the Roman bureaucracy still was overwhelmingly Italian. The process of its internationalization had only just begun, and very timidly at that. For all practical purposes, Italians controlled the major decisions affecting the Catholic church in various countries around the world. Brief and concise reports, in which complex issues were reduced to their simplest and barest expression, were the watchword of this and every other metropolitan bureaucracy. And like every other bureaucracy, decisions in Rome tended to be influenced by effective lobby groups.

But in contrast to the classical relationship of colony to metropolis, the cement that bound Canada to Rome was essentially spiritual in character. This is not to say that there was no economic dimension to this tie. In fact, through Peter's Pence, Catholics contributed to the Holy See's maintenance. Canadians had even made a modest contribution to the Vatican's vast art treasures. When he heard that Smeulders would be visiting an Indian reservation during his stay in Quebec, Cardinal Simeoni wrote: 'I am sending you a copy of the circular from this Sacred Congregation regarding the Museum. If the opportunity arises for you to find some interesting objects for the said Museum, I would urge you to arrange to have them collected.'[3] Evidently Simeoni was counting on the generosity of Canada's native peoples since he did not specify how Smeulders was to pay for these objects. In the final analysis, however, Rome's power rested on the spiritual sanctions that could be applied against local churches or their members, and this determined the relationship of dependency which tied Canada to the Holy See.

DECISION-MAKING AT THE PROPAGANDA

Formally at least, these relations dated back to 1622 when Pope Gregory xv established the Sacred Congregation 'de Propaganda Fide.' Broadly speaking, this Congregation existed, as the name suggests, to propagate the faith in Christian countries where Catholics constituted a minority and in non-Christian parts of the world. Practically, however, the Propaganda's day-to-day activities revolved around the interests of Catholics living in those areas. Its jurisdiction extended to places as disparate as England, Holland, Greece, the Americas, India, and the Near and Far East. The faithful living in these regions did not deal with the Holy See through regular channels – that is, through its various congregations according to the matter to be discussed. Instead all issues were funnelled through the Propaganda. At times this Congregation might wish to refer an important question to another department or to consult with it; but it was the Propaganda that communicated the results of these consultations to Catholics under its authority.

The structure of the Congregation was quite simple. Day-to-day administration was handled by the head of the Propaganda, the cardinal prefect, assisted by a Secretary. Correspondence most often came to them from diocesan bishops, but also from priests, religious, and the laity. The prefect and the Secretary met weekly in private session to decide on routine matters such as dispensations, complaints, requests for information, and reports from the field. Larger questions such as the appointment of bishops, the division of dioceses, the approval of the constitutions of religious communities, and major conflicts of various kinds, were usually referred to monthly meetings of the Propaganda's general congregation, composed of cardinals of the Curia (at that time a dozen or so were active members).[4] A number of consultants, usually canon lawyers, provided the general congregation with their expertise in assessing complex cases. A printed brief describing the question to be discussed was prepared by the Secretary assisted by *minutanti* or secretaries, who were usually *monsignori*. The *minutanti* were very influential since they often determined how a case would be presented for discussion. The results of the cardinals' deliberations, the *Acta*, formed part of the church's legislation. It is important to note that many of the questions discussed by the Propaganda were not merely spiritual or religious. They might relate to education, church-state relations, politics, civil liberties, aboriginal cultures.

Canada and the problems of its church were certainly not uppermost in the minds of these officials, quite the opposite. This may explain why in earlier times documents relating to America might be found under the rubric 'Armenia' or those on Canada under 'Candia,' as the island of Crete was then known to the Holy See. Distance and the difficulties of communication meant that some authorities had only the vaguest notions of the lands with which they were dealing.

By the nineteenth century these technical difficulties largely had been overcome, and the Holy See had amassed a large body of documentation relating to Canada. Even so, Rome had only the most approximate notion of the socio-cultural or even geographical conditions of the country. Well into this century, one important Vatican congregation classified Canadian material under 'England,' along with documents relating to Malta and Ireland. Roman policies were determined not so much by the fact that Canada achieved a large degree of internal autonomy with Confederation, but that it was a distant appendage of the British Empire. The fact too that Canada was part of a largely English-speaking continent began to influence the perspective of Vatican officials, particularly toward the end of the nineteenth century as the American church, with its twelve million faithful, emerged as an important element in Catholicism.

In any event, the Vatican bureaucrat continued to have a Euro-centred, and especially southern European, clerical view of the world. It must have been difficult for even the most well-informed among them to understand the diverse cultures under Rome's authority. 'What the Holy See needs,' wrote Cardinal Manning, 'is a body of men in Rome who have travelled and have made themselves masters not only of their languages but of the actual state of foreign countries. I fear that there is much to be learned and to be done in this respect.'[5] For this reason, foreign cardinals, ambassadors to the Holy See, apostolic nuncios, and the heads of the various national colleges in Rome acted as go-betweens. Canadian ecclesiastics availed themselves of the services of the directors of the English, French, or Irish colleges who for a fee made themselves interpreters of Canadian concerns. Yet this formula was soon found wanting, since these men had themselves only a remote knowledge of Canada.

The practice developed after the mid nineteenth century of using as agents priests who were sent to Rome to pursue their theological studies. Needless to say, this did little to promote learning. Nevertheless, these students obtained a different type of education. As the careers of Benjamin Pâquet and Joseph Desautels show, Canadian priests resident in Rome acquired the more or less subtle skills of lobbying and diplomacy. The more astute among them realized the importance of courting influential members of the Curia; to this end they sought out allies among canon lawyers, diplomats, and omnipresent bureaucrats.

In the antechambers of power they discovered the importance of patience, perseverance, concise argument, quick rebuttal, and gratuities. Pâquet, for instance, was reputed to do his lobbying at the Propaganda armed with mass intentions, which were payments made by the faithful so that masses could be said for specific purposes.[6] This money, his critics claimed, was used to influence decisions. Although Pâquet hotly denied these charges, the American hierarchy's agent in Rome commonly resorted to such practices during the same period.[7] These agents also learned not to rely on the good words of Vatican officialdom who, it was well known, liked to please. They had to persist, even at the risk of importuning people, knocking often at the same door, constantly repeating the same arguments, and seizing upon chance encounters to make their point. After all, in Rome, brashness was hardly a vice! This informal system of agencies began to wane when the Canadian church established its own college in Rome in 1886.

QUELLING POLITICAL QUESTIONS

By the 1870s, however, the Propaganda's normal administrative machinery was proving inadequate to deal with dissension in the Quebec church. Rome particularly disliked the fact that the bishops were washing their dirty linen in public. For the Holy See, the issue was politics, into which older conflicts relating to rival interest groups and personalities were subsumed. But, as noted earlier, underlying this tangle of controversies was French-Canadian nationalism. Insensitive to this dimension and faced with unseemly journalistic quarrels over the merits of the *programme catholique*, the Roman Congregation charged with maintaining the purity of the faith, the Inquisition, ordered the Quebec bishops to stop their public polemics and reduced them to silence on the notorious *programme*. But the problem would not go away; it returned in different guises and always assumed seemingly more alarming proportions.

In order to break the vicious cycle of competing claims and bring concord to a strife-torn Quebec church, the cardinal prefect of Propaganda, Alessandro Franchi, decided to send a trusted friend and collaborator who was alien to the factionalism of the local church to do *in situ* what the Congregation had been unable to achieve from a distance. Named Papal Ablegate, officially Monsignor Cesare Roncetti was to bring the cardinal's hat to John McCloskey, archbishop of New York. Unofficially, however, he was to stop over in Quebec to investigate the Jesuit Estates question, one of a number of issues involved in the university controversy. The prefect's hope was that Roncetti might, if not bring about agreement on the vexed question of Jesuit lands, at least collect basic facts on which the Propaganda could formulate a decision.

The Congregation's decree of 1876 on the university was in fact based on Roncetti's report, which reduced the conflict in the Quebec church to a question of vested interests. The problem was serious enough, in the Ablegate's mind, to warrant vigorous action in defence of institutions whose very existence was being undermined by these tensions.[8] The Propaganda therefore ordered Bourget to establish in Montreal a branch of Laval University at his own expense. The bishop, however, resigned rather than implement a sentence which was unworkable given the hostility between Laval and Montreal.

Confronted by an ever more complicated crisis, Cardinal Franchi quickly became convinced of the need to dispatch an apostolic delegate to Canada. He confided his thoughts to Ignazio Persico, former bishop of Savannah, Georgia, who for reasons of health was residing in the suburbs of Quebec City. Franchi asked Persico for an on-the-spot account of the crisis in the Quebec church and may also have been testing the latter's availability for the mission. The cardinal prefect told the bishop that he was thinking of someone 'who would reside in Quebec and direct the Bishops both on current problems and on those that could subsequently arise,' and he solicited Persico's opinion, among other things, 'on the manner in which Your Lordship considers it expedient to put it [the mission] into practice and the difficulties that might arise.'[9] The fact that Persico soon requested permission to return to Italy, apparently unwilling to spend another winter in Canada, put an end to his candidacy.[10] In any case, he was already deemed to be *persona non grata* by the Laflèche faction of the Quebec clergy, since the Italian prelate was too closely identified with Archbishop Taschereau's Liberal entourage.[11]

Franchi, however, was deeply preoccupied by the political aspects of the crisis. It appeared as though the local church were on a collision course, not only with the governing party in Canada, but with British traditions of justice. Already in this period, key Vatican officials were rethinking the policies that during the heyday of Pius ix (1846–78) had led to head-on confrontations with civil governments in a number of areas deemed by the church to be of joint jurisdiction, such as marriage, education, and the legal status of the Catholic church. The idea was not so much to abandon the principles proclaimed with such flourish in an earlier period, as to try to reach some short-term understanding with the civil authorities, which was seen as a first step to implementing these principles in the more distant future.[12] Although the new policy was devised to respond largely to European events, it was so central to the thinking of top officials at the Holy See that it influenced their perspective on problems arising in other parts of the world. Rome certainly would not have viewed with equanimity the prospect of a major conflict with the Canadian and possibly British governments over the actions of some members of the Quebec episcopate.

Shortly after seeking Persico's advice on the institution of an apostolic delegation, the cardinal prefect replied to Joseph Cauchon's letter of complaint regarding the Quebec clergy's interference in politics. Franchi expressed grave concern about the situation and about its implications on the country's constitutional and religious stability. He assured Cauchon that he was actively seeking solutions to this problem and thanked him for his interest in writing to Rome and 'even more for your prompt attention in defending the interests of the Church.'[13] The tone and content of this letter showed that Franchi took Cauchon's accusations very seriously. By the same token, the cardinal prefect refused to deal with specific complaints of clerical interference.[14] This indicated that Franchi considered the question best resolved at the governmental level – that is, between the Holy See and Canada – rather than on a case-by-case adjudication of the facts.

It may be thought that distance and detachment gave Rome special insight into the problems of the Quebec church and that its policies, being consistent over time, were arrived at unanimously. This was far from the case. Cardinal Franchi was very much influenced on this and other issues by Benjamin Pâquet who happened to be in Rome during this crucial period. Pâquet was no stranger to the Propaganda. A decade earlier as a student of theology at the Collegio Romano, he had often acted as archdiocesan agent in Quebec's quarrel with Bourget. As a result, he knew a host of minor and major officials in the Roman bureaucracy and had an easy entrée to the antechambers of power.[15] Pâquet was close to Persico and Roncetti,[16] and was also well connected with prominent politicians in the Liberal party. These contacts doubtless gave him an exaggerated sense of his own importance. He once boasted, for example, that it was he who had determined the Holy See's choice of apostolic delegate, as well as the terms of the mission.[17] There was no one in Rome of Pâquet's stature to provide the Curia with an alternative view of things. But the agent never took chances and this perhaps accounted for his success. On hearing that Bishop Laflèche intended to come to Rome to reverse the Holy See's decision on Bourget's resignation and possibly to influence its choice of an apostolic delegate, Pâquet quickly tried to marshal influential support. He urged his friend Cauchon to involve both the archbishop of Toronto, who was a close and devoted ally of Alexander Mackenzie, and possibly Lynch's suffragans in his campaign to protect the Liberal party.[18]

But neither was Laflèche without influence in the Roman bureaucracy. At the very least he could count on the support of the Secretary of Propaganda, Monsignor G.B. Agnozzi, as well as that of Luigi

Cardinal Oreglia di San Stefano, prefect of the Congregation on Indulgences. It comes then as no surprise that the general congregation which decided to send an apostolic delegate to Canada was a tumultuous affair in which an unnamed high-ranking official apparently indicted the Propaganda's past policies.[19]

Despite these differences of opinion among Roman officialdom, a consensus was clearly evident on the need for an apostolic delegate.[20] The Propaganda considered that, for the time being at least, the appointment should be made to appear temporary. For this reason preference was given to a candidate who either was a diocesan bishop or had some fixed responsibilities at the Holy See. But the cardinals obviously thought that in the long term a permanent delegation was desirable. The delegate, they agreed, 'should sound out the possibilities or find the means of ensuring that the visits to the Canadian Union by a Representative of the Supreme Pontiff become more regular or better still less infrequent.'[21] Evidently Propaganda officials wanted to give themselves time to assess the success of this mission before considering the option of a permanent delegation.

In the minds of some cardinals at least, the delegation would have a predominantly diplomatic coloration. For this reason the nationality of the prospective candidate was of importance since it was specified that he should be 'possibly Italian or at least British.'[22] Similarly, the general congregation instructed the cardinal prefect to announce the Holy See's decision to Cauchon, making it appear as if its action were in direct response to the Canadian cabinet minister's letters of complaint. The Propaganda proposed George Conroy, the forty-five-year-old bishop of Ardagh and Clonmacnois, as apostolic delegate, a choice that was ratified by the pope.

As for the mission, Franchi gave Conroy detailed instructions that do not appear to have been drawn up collectively in general congregation, but by the cardinal prefect alone. The delegate was asked to inculcate a sense of unity in the episcopate and, through them, discipline in the lower clergy, using if necessary canonical sanctions to achieve these objectives. Not surprisingly, issues related to the political question took up the lion's share of these instructions, but Conroy was also given guidelines for resolving the controversies dividing various interest groups within the Quebec church, notably on the university question, always on terms favourable to the archdiocese of Quebec.[23]

Before leaving for Canada, Conroy already had an accurate idea of the difficulties that awaited him, especially in trying to reconcile such bitterly divided factions. Considering how deeply their passions and animosities ran, he was undoubtedly concerned about maintaining his own authority. From Ireland he wrote to an Italian cleric about the forthcoming visit to Rome of two Quebec prelates who belonged to the Laflèche faction: 'I hope that the Canadian pilgrims will be made to understand that Propaganda has full confidence in the Delegate. Otherwise they will go back ready to resist.'[24]

And resist they did. This faction had powerful patrons in Rome, prelates such as Oreglia and Agnozzi, who felt that the objectives of the mission were being betrayed. They soon turned against the apostolic delegate and actively encouraged a movement of clerical opposition.[25] Conroy was shaken by rumours of Roman interference in his mission and urged Cardinal Franchi in confidential dispatches to take effective action to remedy the situation.[26] The delegate subsequently reported that news of the dissidents' alleged close contact with a high-ranking official at the Propaganda had become public knowledge.[27] Conroy stated that he did not wish to give credence to the possibility of betrayal by Roman prelates. But he still took the precaution of warning Franchi that the cardinal prefect was himself under attack. In fact, the clergy were preparing a memorandum and petition which they intended to present directly to the pope, without going through a by now suspect Propaganda.[28]

By the time these documents reached Rome, changes were occurring in the upper echelons of the Holy See's administration, resulting from the death of Pius IX. Giovanni Cardinal Simeoni, former Secretary of State, took over from Franchi as the new Prefect of Propaganda. Within a few months it was clear that Simeoni shared his predecessor's views on the Quebec church. He wrote letters to the Laflèche faction, urging them to maintain the unity of action established by the delegate and discouraging any initiatives that might be seen as a challenge to already established policies.[29]

But that unity of action was as fragile as the delegate's health. By the end of August 1878 the Holy See learned of Conroy's death in Newfoundland. The Liberal party responded swiftly to the news. The Quebec members of the federal and provincial cabinets, together with the lieutenant-governor of the province, offered the cardinal prefect their condolences and expressed the hope that Rome would name a new delegate to complete the mission begun by Conroy.[30] The Secretary of State for the Holy See wasted no time in replying that the appointment of a new apostolic delegate was being given very serious consideration. Luc Letellier de Saint-Just then urged the pope to name someone having 'l'expérience des institutions britanniques, la connaissance approfondie de la Constitution, de la [sic] langue, des moeurs, des traditions et des usages du pays.'[31]

As Conroy's achievements rapidly came undone, the cardinals of the Propaganda met away from the stifling summer heat in the coolness of the Palazzo di Propaganda, designed two centuries earlier by the two rival geniuses of baroque architecture, Bernini and Borromini. On the agenda was the future of the delegation. Their eminences recognized the remarkable services rendered by the Irish prelate to the Canadian church and fully endorsed his recommendations. But while convinced of the need to continue his work, they were forced to defer a final decision on the matter of a successor for lack of suitable candidates.[32]

Several months later Ignazio Persico proposed his own candidacy, confiding to the Propaganda that he was bored with the work of bishop of a diocese just south of Rome. He stressed the opportuneness of this appointment since, in the wake of the aborted attempt to establish an apostolic delegation in the United States, the delegate in Canada could also unofficially represent the Holy See's interests in the neighbouring republic. He pleaded with Rome to act quickly, adding that, at fifty-nine, he should not be made to waste in his diocese the little energy he had left, when he could spend it more fruitfully elsewhere.[33] Bishop Laflèche got wind of Persico's manoeuvres and bluntly told the cardinal prefect that the Italian bishop would simply be 'une seconde édition de la délégation de Mgr Conroy. Je conjure V[otre] E[minence] d'épargner ce malheur à notre chère Église du Canada.'[34]

SHORING UP THE TASCHEREAU FACTION

In the mean time, tensions within the Quebec church intensified as clergymen descended to ever lower levels of pettiness in their quarrels with each other. New alliances were formed around current problems which were nothing more than old controversies under a different guise. The apple of discord this time was the tutelage which Laval University exercised over its Montreal branch, an arrangement encouraged and sanctioned by the apostolic delegate. Laflèche led the faction, supported by one or two bishops, some activist clerics from Montreal, the École de Médecine which was excluded from Conroy's settlement of the university question, and the nuns of Hôtel Dieu Hospital.[35] The Taschereau faction was backed by a majority of bishops, including Fabre. The latter, of course, would have liked to settle the controversy on terms favourable to his diocese, but felt bound to follow the direction set by Taschereau and Rome.

The Holy See received deputation upon deputation from Quebec, each fully resolved to set the record straight once and for all.[36] Roman documents of the period make it fairly clear that Cardinal Simeoni and the new Secretary of Propaganda, Domenico Jacobini, were wary of the Laflèche faction. But some of Simeoni's colleagues, while prepared to uphold decisions collectively adopted in general congregation, were none the less quite sympathetic to the bishop of Trois-Rivières on specific issues, while others were simply unwilling to reassess policies already adopted for the Quebec church.[37]

The fact remains that during these years Taschereau's faction continued to have the upper hand in Rome. They had many friends at the Propaganda. These included the head *minutante*, who was also the official responsible for Canada, Monsignor Zefferino Zitelli;[38] a consultant at the Congregation, Henri Brichet, who was also a long-time bursar at the Collège français, where Taschereau and his entourage stayed when in Rome;[39] the omnipresent Bishop Persico, who apparently was working quietly but effectively behind the scenes on behalf of his archdiocesan friends;[40] and Edward Henry Cardinal Howard, a member of the Propaganda and agent of the English church in Rome.[41] Taschereau also had a very wily agent in the person of Callixte Marquis, who busily defended the archbishop's interests.

But Marquis, a priest from the diocese of Trois-Rivières and an inveterate enemy of Laflèche, was more likely to exacerbate tensions than to ease them. In fact Conroy had described him as 'a man who does not deserve the confidence of the Holy See ... Always preoccupied with secular matters, a conspirator who is little concerned with the welfare of his own parishioners ... he has left disorder everywhere he goes.' He added that the priest was forever absent from his parish on missions of various sorts, often running off with the keys of the tabernacle, much to his parishioners' dismay.[42]

Marquis's correspondence reflects the rage generated by this crisis which found expression in quite an astonishing level of verbal violence. It is well worth citing some examples of this truculent language to capture the mood of a much tormented institution. In Taschereau's entourage, Laflèche was seen as the source of all evil. The learned Louis Nazaire Bégin, future archbishop of Quebec, who would live to regret his words, stated: 'Quelle pitié que d'avoir des évêques aux idées si croches et si étroites! ... Ces chicanes [sont] suscitées par l'ignorance et aussi par la mauvaise foi.'[43] Writing about his own bishop, whom he described as 'un fou malfaisant,' Marquis advocated that Rome threaten Laflèche with suspension. Only then would the prelate comply 'avec la rapidité de l'éclair; on ne s'apercevrait même pas qu'il boite!'[44] Such vicious sentiments were echoed by Bégin: 'Ce serait le temps de *l'écrapouter* ... Il veut agir à sa tête et être indépendant de l'autorité; est-ce que l'autorité ne pourrait agir, elle aussi à sa tête et l'envoyer *in partibus infidelium*?'[45]

The bishop of Montreal, who was seen by both factions as weak and indecisive, also came under heavy fire. On Fabre's treatment of the nuns of the Hôtel Dieu, one priest in Taschereau's circle observed: 'Et l'Évêque de Montréal se propose d'*agir avec énergie*, comme s'il en était capable! Le voilà arrêté par une poignée de religieuses ... Ne pouvait-il pas ... les forcer à donner *par écrit, hic et nunc*, leur adhésion au décret ... sinon interdire la communauté, enlever le chapelain et le St-Sacrement; et les laisser là comme les vieilles folles Jansénistes de Port-Royal? Il me semble qu'un homme doit être capable d'avoir raison de cette poignée d'imbéciles.'[46] The young bishop of Sherbrooke agreed. In Montreal, 'on veut ménager celui-ci et celui-là, comme on fait dans un salon où les femmes dominent. Mais ce sont des évêques qui doivent gouverner et obéir [le Saint-Siège] et non des femmes.'[47] Racine concluded: 'Et dire que ce Mgr Fabre veut être archevêque!! Il n'est pas capable de conduire sa maison, et il voudrait conduire une province. Il tient dans ses mains la quenouille, et non le bâton pastoral.'[48]

Once again Catholics were engaged in bitter public wrangling which, although deadly serious in its implications, presented all the characteristics of an *opéra bouffe*. By 1883, in fact, Rome feared an open schism. Taschereau and Fabre publicly declared the École de Médecine and the nuns of Hôtel Dieu Hospital rebellious to the Holy See, and as such excluded from the sacraments. Only an eleventh-hour intervention by Simeoni overturned this condemnation. And once again the call went up for an apostolic delegate. A member of Taschereau's party saw it quite simply: 'Il n'est pas nécessaire qu'il [the delegate] sache toutes les langues; une âme droite, une volonté ferme, voilà tout.'[49]

But the Propaganda came to realize that its hard-line policies in support of the archdiocesan position had to be tempered.[50] In August 1883 Leo XIII decided to send a delegate to Quebec to try to restore harmony to a much troubled church. This solution was welcomed by both parties, although Laflèche warned Simeoni that certain prospective delegates were not acceptable.[51] The Holy See's choice fell on Henri Smeulders, a fifty-seven-year-old Belgian Cistercian resident in Rome.

Although Smeulders was not a bishop, as a representative of the Holy See he was given precedence over the archbishop and bishops of Quebec. The pope conferred upon him the title of apostolic commissioner, which indicated that his mandate was not as extensive as that of Conroy's. His instructions dealt in detail with the university question. Smeulders was asked to produce an accord on terms largely favourable to Laval's interests, although he was encouraged to apply pressure on the university should it prove to be intransigent. The commissioner would have to submit the broad outlines of an eventual agreement to Rome for ratification. On other matters the Belgian was directed to enforce rigorously the Holy See's order to the Quebec clergy to remain silent on political questions. He was asked for an opinion on the proposed division of the diocese of Trois-Rivières and on whether the Jesuits should receive compensation for the settlement of the Estates question.[52] These directives were a clear indication of Rome's perspective on the controversies dividing the Quebec church.

Although initially Smeulders shared this perspective, by the spring of 1884 it was quite obvious that he sympathized with the Laflèche party. Hearing of this change of heart from his Roman friends who had access to the commissioner's reports and letters, Taschereau abruptly left for Rome, where he spent the next eight months. A few years earlier the archbishop had indignantly condemned his episcopal opponents for just such behaviour. But now that his interests were at stake, Taschereau sought to circumvent the apostolic commissioner and make a direct appeal to the Propaganda.

His efforts, together with those of the ever-active Marquis, were not entirely fruitless. Except for some minor details, the Propaganda largely preserved Laval University's status.[53] At best Smeulders only managed a holding action in the university dispute in favour of those institutions opposed to Laval. On other questions he did not even achieve that much. After initially indicating unwillingness to divide the diocese of Trois-Rivières, the Propaganda reversed itself under pressure from Taschereau and Marquis. The bishop of Trois-Rivières clearly emerged as the loser in this latest round.

Even so, the Taschereau party was far from happy. A strange letter allegedly written by a Montreal printer to Cardinal Simeoni was proof of their discontent. The document reflected as well their knowledge of the minutest details of internal Vatican politics. Using a pseudonym, the author threatened to publish amazingly accurate information on secret aspects of the Smeulders mission obtained, he claimed, from a consultant at the Propaganda. The letter accused Simeoni of being influenced by the pro-Jesuit Cardinal Franzelin to the detriment of Laval's interests.[54]

But if the Taschereau faction was unhappy, the mood in the Laflèche camp was one of despair and alienation. The division of the diocese was carefully carried out by Bishop John Cameron of Antigonish, named apostolic commissioner by the Holy See especially for this circumstance. Meanwhile Laflèche's allies bitterly complained of being excluded and ignored by the Holy See.[55] In this climate of doom, Rome thought it prudent to adopt a policy of largesse, which did not however extend to Laflèche's party. Taschereau was given a cardinal's hat. Montreal was raised to metropolitan status which gave Fabre, now an archbishop, a freer hand in running the Montreal branch of Laval University. This trend was confirmed when in 1889 Rome published the papal bull *Jamdudum*, which made a genuine attempt to satisfy all parties in the university dispute. Callixte Marquis, for his part, was given the honorary title of prothonotary apostolic. The old tensions which had plagued the Quebec church, for the moment at least, seemed to be abating.

CATHOLIC EDUCATION IN A NEW-WORLD PERSPECTIVE

In fact, a new-found harmony was taking root, partly favoured by a growing sentiment that the enemy was not to be found within the church but outside of it.[56] Antoine Labelle, famous curé of St-Jérome and deputy minister of colonization in Honoré Mercier's government, rang the alarm early in the new decade. The problem, he maintained, was an aggressive Anglo-Protestant expansionism which threatened to crush the Catholics of Eastern Canada by taking complete possession of the North-West. Labelle lamented the fact that in this confrontation Irish Catholics chose to ally themselves not with their French-Canadian co-religionists, but with their English-speaking brethren.[57] Claiming that French Canadians were responsible for 'le progrès du catholicisme dans les provinces anglaises elles-mêmes,' Labelle called on Rome to intervene 'en protégeant l'église catholique française qui le mérite à tous les égards en Amérique, comme le Souverain Pontife l'a déjà fait pour l'Église catholique italienne aux États-Unis.'[58] The question of *la survivance* had taken on a North American dimension and, in the brief heyday of Cahenslyism in the United States, French-Canadian clerical leaders saw their struggle as part of a wider continental campaign for the preservation of cultural diversity against the forces of Anglo-Protestant homogenization. But the issue quickly assumed concrete dimensions at home with the drawn-out controversy over the Manitoba schools.

The Manitoba government's institution of a common school system in 1890 raised the question of what means should be taken by Ottawa to meet the legitimate aspirations of the province's Catholic minority. As with the New Brunswick schools question, it was the Quebec church which, in co-ordination with Archbishop Taché, took the initiative in defending Catholic rights in the West. But whereas twenty years earlier the Quebec episcopate was divided on strategy, this new issue created a remarkable unity and will to act in the ranks of the French-Canadian clergy.

This change occurred partly because the creation of two new ecclesiastical provinces in French Canada had allowed for the smoother resolution of conflicts among interest groups. But more important still was the transformation of the Quebec hierarchy during this decade, as a new generation of bishops replaced the old guard. Louis Nazaire Bégin was named administrator of the archdiocese of Quebec, replacing Cardinal Taschereau who by the beginning of the 1890s had become totally mentally incapacitated. Taschereau's inglorious departure from the scene occasioned the gradual eclipse of his old advisers, men such as Benjamin Pâquet, whose deafness increasingly insulated him from the larger world. And although Bégin had been an unconditional and at times quite intemperate follower of Taschereau, the new climate of the nineties altered his political perspective dramatically. The dioceses of Rimouski, Chicoutimi, and

Sherbrooke all had new incumbents, and they would be followed in the early years of the new century by every other diocese in Quebec.

The Propaganda too had a new administration in this period. Cardinal Simeoni and Ignazio Persico, who had risen to become Secretary of the Congregation and a cardinal to boot, both died. The new prefect, Mieczyslaw Cardinal Ledochowski, a Polish archbishop formerly of Gniezno and Poznan in the German Empire, was a victim of the Bismarckian *Kulturkampf*. He had spent two years in a Prussian jail, among other things for advocating religious instruction in the Polish language.

But there was now another Vatican player on the Canadian scene. In 1893 the Holy See appointed Archbishop Francesco Satolli as the first apostolic delegate to the United States. On taking up his new appointment, the prelate found himself in the midst of the ethnic turmoil which disrupted the American Catholic church and divided it roughly into two camps – the Irish and the others. Since the French-Canadian immigrant élite took a leading role in agitating against Irish hegemony over the church, the apostolic delegate kept a wary eye on Canada as well. He even visited the country in the autumn of 1894. As professor of dogma at the Urban College in Rome, Satolli had taught a number of American clerics. Consequently, he came to the United States with a marked sympathy for the Americanist faction within the church and for the Irish clergy as a whole. Cardinal Ledochowski, on the other hand, worried about the fate of German and Polish immmigrants who were being forced into the Irish-American mould, much to the detriment, he thought, of their faith.

The Manitoba schools question mobilized the French-Canadian hierarchy, who kept Rome well informed about the political and judicial convolutions of the crisis – a crisis that jolted them and gave them a deeper sense of political realism. Archbishop Taché, who persistently placed his faith in the Conservative party, came face to face with some bitter truths in the last days of his life. He condemned the party's ineptitude, its inertia, and even doubted its good faith in handling the issue.[59] Using words that Conservative politicians had not heard from prelates in twenty-five years, the anguished archbishop accused the minister of public works, Joseph Aldéric Ouimet, of playing to the gallery, making statements more for his partisan supporters' gratification than to clarify issues.

Si on ne veut pas nous venir en aide, qu'on dise que la volonté fait défaut. Si on ne veut pas nous protéger, qu'on avoue son impuissance, mais au moins qu'on nous épargne l'humiliation d'être traités comme si nous étions tout à fait déraisonnables et incapables de comprendre la situation dans laquelle on nous place. Ce n'est pas un ennemi qui vous adresse ces paroles, c'est un compatriote; un enfant de cette commune patrie; un de ceux, auxquels les événements semblent dire aujourd'hui qu'il n'y a plus de place pour eux sous le soleil du Canada.[60]

Like Taché, Archbishop Bégin was critical of Conservative inaction: 'Le gouvernement fédéral ... n'a pas jugé prudent, n'a pas osé désavouer cette loi scolaire ... il a craint une guerre des races et de religion. Ces craintes sont-elles fondées?'[61] Twenty years earlier the archdiocese of Quebec itself fanned fears of an impending sectarian war in Canada in its campaign against an overly political clergy. These rumours, we may recall, led to decisive action on the part of the Propaganda. If in 1894, when the entire Canadian episcopate publicly became involved in the Manitoba issue and when anti-Catholic organizations such as the Protestant Protective and the Equal Rights Associations were at their apogee, Bégin could question the probability of inter-denominational violence, we may well wonder how real had been the danger in 1876. That the archbishop was not alone in holding this view is clear, since a few years later the Quebec episcopate as a body repeated these arguments in an attempt to refute alleged Liberal fears of sectarian warfare.[62] Clearly, over the past twenty years the universe of the Quebec church had been transformed.

While bishops were critical of the Conservatives, the Liberals with their penchant for common schools provided no alternative. What Canadian Catholics needed, according to Laflèche, was political unity of action. 'Les Catholiques sont les 2 cinquièmes de la population fédérale, 2 millions contre trois. Si nous avions pour nous l'union des Catholiques almands [sic], il nous serait possible et même facile de faire respecter nos droits.'[63] But, he lamented, the spirit of Catholic liberalism prompted many Catholic politicians to sacrifice principle to personal or party interest. In 1895, at least, the Quebec hierarchy did not believe that a solution to the crisis was in the offing.[64]

Not only was Rome informed of events, its help was also sought in redressing the grievances of Manitoba Catholics. At the request of Elphège Gravel, bishop of Nicolet,[65] Ledochowski asked the archbishop of Westminster, Herbert Cardinal Vaughan, to intervene in the manner he considered most appropriate on behalf of Manitoba Catholics. The prefect allowed himself to suggest that Vaughan remind the British government, and especially the colonial secretary, of the promises regarding Catholic education made in the name of the sovereign by Lord Carnarvon at the time of Manitoba's entry into Confederation. Vaughan should also imply that failure to act on these solemn promises 'would produce a sense of disgust and alienation that could be exploited by political agitators who were not lacking in Canada.'[66] Ledochowski also followed Gravel's advice by writing a letter to the Canadian episcopate, strongly condemning the concept of non-sectarian education and encouraging them to fight against it.[67] The Quebec bishops drew comfort from this support. Soon, however, even their assessment of the dismal state of Canadian politics changed when the Conservatives reluctantly committed themselves to remedial legislation. As a new Conservative administration prepared to fight an election over the issue, Archbishop Bégin gave his candid assessment of its French-Canadian members. 'S'ils n'ont pas l'éloquence et le génie de Démosthène,' he admitted, 'ils ont au moins le mérite d'être d'excellents Catholiques, des hommes fermes, convaincus, et non disposés à transiger avec l'ennemi.'[68]

Rome's support of episcopal action continued unabated in the crucial year of 1896. Ledochowski agreed with the principle underlying the Quebec episcopate's insistence that Catholic politicians and their electors were morally bound to uphold legislation re-establishing Catholic schools in Manitoba. He had reservations, however, about the way in which the bishops proposed to enforce this moral imperative. The prefect feared that they might unwittingly provide the church's enemies with an excuse for persecution. He also worried about punishing those who in good faith went against the hierarchy's advice.[69]

The Conservatives may have exulted at the prospect of the church's endorsement during the upcoming electoral contest, but the Liberal party was less pleased. For as long as the church, and especially its militant Quebec wing, kept insisting upon the full restoration of Catholic rights in Manitoba, a political solution that would appeal to both English- and French-speaking Canadians would be improbable and the Liberals' agonizingly long quest for power frustrated. Consequently, in an attempt to break the hierarchy's unity of action, Laurier sought to woo the archbishop of Toronto. Referring to an earlier conversation in which John Walsh appeared to show some flexibility on the vexed question of Manitoba schools, Laurier asked the prelate to comment on his proposal for a commission of inquiry. The archbishop confessed that a few months earlier 'I had but cursorily examined that question and the principles that underlie it'; but now he rejected the Liberal leader's idea out of hand. Instead, he wanted Catholic schools to be established in Manitoba on the same basis as they existed in Ontario.[70]

KEEPING THE CLERGY IN LINE

But this brief and unsuccessful flirtation with a prominent member of the hierarchy did not exhaust Laurier's stock of tactics. Somehow the Quebec clergy would have to be kept in line. So it was that Senator L.G. Power of Halifax, following up on an earlier meeting with Satolli in Boston, formally wrote to the apostolic delegation in the United States. He complained of clerical interference in politics and, as Cauchon had done years earlier, raised the twin spectres of sectarian strife and secularism if things were not remedied.[71] Power begged Satolli to press the Holy See for the creation of a delegation in Canada or for the extension of his jurisdiction north of the forty-ninth parallel. That the very Liberal Lady Aberdeen tried to achieve the same results suggests that Laurier saw an invaluable ally[72] in Satolli, who had certainly had his own fill of meddling French-Canadian priests in the American church.[73]

This time Laurier would not be disappointed. Before the Quebec bishops published their collective pastoral that sought to prepare the electorate for the 1896 federal elections, Satolli took it upon himself to sound out Canadian archbishops and their suffragans on the establishment of an apostolic delegation in Canada.[74] Replies came mainly from Quebec and Ontario: the prelates of Quebec were generally reticent but willing to go along with the idea, while those of Ontario were staunchly opposed. According to John Walsh, a delegation was 'not necessary, certainly inopportune and even dangerous' in view of Canada's Protestant majority.[75] His colleague, Archbishop Cleary of Kingston, agreed. Ontario's population, he emphasized, was over 80 per cent Protestant, most of whom belonged to anti-Catholic secret societies. The creation of a delegation would arouse their anger and imperil the Catholic school system in Ontario. Better to leave well enough alone, he thought, since nothing warranted this papal presence in Canada: there were no public scandals, no problems of internal church discipline, no burning question dividing Canadian Catholics.[76]

As for the French-Canadian hierarchy, they were primarily worried about having to pay for its establishment. Archbishops Fabre and Duhamel questioned the timeliness of the proposal. The country was young, they maintained, and many dioceses were poor. There was no pressing need for a delegation at that moment. Still, if the Holy See insisted, Fabre assured Satolli that his suffragans would submit to the decision.[77] Archbishop Bégin was the only one who wholeheartedly supported the initiative, at least in principle. He stressed the need for greater co-ordination among the bishops of Canada since there was no Dominion-wide mechanism to bring them together on a regular basis, as was the case in Quebec through the Council of Public Instruction. Bégin admitted that he preferred the convening of a plenary council of the Canadian hierarchy as a first step to the eventual creation of a delegation, but Satolli's idea was none the less sound.[78]

These replies reached the delegation in Washington together with fresh complaints from Senator Power about clerical interference, this time during the federal election campaign. Satolli subsequently wrote to the Secretary of State, Mariano Cardinal Rampolla del Tindaro, informing his superior of the Liberal victory in Canada in the following terms: 'Since the bishops generally worked in favour of the other party [the Tories] even obliging their priests to do so, should we not fear for the Church's interests in that vast region? The Liberal Party has many excellent Catholics and if the clergy had kept themselves above partisanship, they would see today the results of such a dignified course.'

The delegate also transmitted the results of his survey of Canadian archbishops, freely interpreting their reactions for the Secretary of State. Satolli claimed that 'All replied that if the Holy Father sends him [a delegate], they would receive him meekly and willingly, except for their having to support him (They feared where there was no fear), but they do not see the need for it.'[79]

As in 1874, the victorious Liberals now set about putting the clergy, particularly those from Quebec, in their place. They dispatched deputations and documents to Rome. A former zouave, Gustave Drolet, arrived with armfuls of signed affidavits alleging clerical meddling in federal and provincial elections, together with petitions from Ottawa and Quebec City Liberals calling for action against partisan priests. The names of Taschereau, Conroy, and Simeoni were invoked in these appeals.[80] Drolet was seconded by Jean-Baptiste Proulx, pastor of Laurier's parish of Saint-Lin and former vice-rector of the Montreal branch of Laval University – the man who single-handedly and very astutely wrested financial autonomy from the mother-institution. Proulx came armed with a document written in his hand but signed by Fabre, accusing five bishops of electoral manipulation and calling for an apostolic delegate.[81]

International pressure was also brought to bear on the Vatican in favour of Laurier. The papal nuncio in Brussels wrote to Rome at the suggestion of a Belgian minister, a friend of Drolet, warmly supporting the Canadian prime minister's views.[82] The leading Catholic layman in England, the Duke of Norfolk, backed Laurier's call for an apostolic delegate, specifying that the candidate should be 'well acquainted with the English language and with the constitution and political history of Canada.'[83] As well, Cardinal Vaughan obligingly provided letters of introduction to two new representatives of the Canadian government in Rome, Solicitor General Charles Fitzpatrick and Charles Russell, Canadian legal agent in London. In these letters, the archbishop of Westminster, stressing Laurier's sincere desire to reach a settlement of the crisis, reiterated the British foreign secretary's opinion that such a settlement would benefit not only Canada but the Empire as a whole.[84]

A few days later, the *Tablet*, the Catholic weekly from London, published Edward Blake's legal opinion on an important aspect of the Manitoba schools question, as well as an editorial urging the appointment of an apostolic delegate. It is not surprising that this issue found its way to Rampolla's office.[85] The Laurier lobby at the Holy See stressed the legal dimensions of the question because they sought to counter the Canadian archbishops' key contention that the Catholic rights in Manitoba were founded on the law of the land.[86] Significantly, this lobby was aimed at the Secretary of State, rather than the Prefect of Propaganda.

In addition to legal arguments, Laurier's agents emphasized two major points. One was the political weakness of Catholics in the Canadian parliament, most of whom, they made sure to note, were

Liberals. This was intended to show that nothing could be accomplished in Ottawa without the goodwill of either the Protestant majority or the Liberal party. The second point was that the actions of the Quebec bishops who had thrown themselves 'body and soul' in the election campaign were not supported by the majority of the hierarchy who did not associate themselves with their pastoral letter. Since Winnipeg was as far from Quebec as Rome was from St Petersburg, it was clear that Ontario bishops had a more immediate appreciation of events in Manitoba than their Quebec colleagues. In any event, relations between the Quebec hierarchy and the government were so strained, they argued, that an apostolic delegate was needed to restore harmony. The dispatch of a papal representative could in no way be seen as an act of censure against the Quebec bishops since everyone recognized that they had acted in good faith.[87]

Even if the Secretary of State's office became a centre of lobbying at this point, the Propaganda did not remain idle. Ledochowski approved of Bégin's suggestion that the pope write an encyclical on the Manitoba schools question.[88] The archbishop of Quebec then prepared a draft of the papal letter which, among other things, warned Canadians against the spirit of partisanship; refused to identify the church with a particular political party; and maintained that the Judicial Committee of the Privy Council gave the federal government leave to restore Catholic educational rights in Manitoba.[89] Meanwhile Ledochowski himself urged the new archbishop of St Boniface, Adélard Langevin, to make a public statement during the negotiations on Catholic education which were going on between the federal and Manitoba governments to the effect that he would reject any settlement not consonant with the constitution and the Privy Council's judgment.[90]

THE PROPAGANDA CIRCUMVENTED

But in the new year a dramatic change occurred at the Curia. The Secretary of the Congregation for Extraordinary Ecclesiastical Affairs, Monsignor Felice Cavagnis, informed the Propaganda that the pope had ordered his congregation to carry out an investigation on 'the interference of the clergy in the Manitoba School Question (Canada) and consequently in the elections.'[91] With this letter the Propaganda was formally relieved of the entire matter. Until now, historians had assumed that the Drolet and Proulx missions had been unsuccessful and that it was Fitzpatrick and Russell who determined the change in Vatican policy. The fact, however, that Cavagnis's letter was written before the arrival of these two envoys disproves this assumption. Proulx and Drolet may have found Vatican diplomacy somewhat trying, but their message certainly reached the proper channels.[92]

Extraordinary Ecclesiastical Affairs was one of the more recent congregations of the Holy See. It was created by Pius VI in the wake of the French Revolution to deal with the thorny questions of church-state relations in France. His successor, Pius VII, broadened its mandate to include relations with civil governments. Extraordinary Ecclesiastical Affairs was under the immediate authority of the pope and, unlike the other departments of the Holy See, had no prefect. The Secretary of State was only an ex-officio member, even though matters dealt with by the congregation properly fell within his jurisdiction. He was expected, however, to implement its decisions once these were approved by the pope and to sign all official correspondence. A Secretary administered the day-to-day affairs of the congregation. In 1897 fourteen cardinals, including Ledochowski, were active members of Extraordinary Ecclesiastical Affairs, eight of whom were also members of the Propaganda.[93]

Despite this change of administrative responsibility, Ledochowski maintained an ongoing interest in the Manitoba schools question. He made sure that Extraordinary Ecclesiastical Affairs received Bégin's reaction to the Laurier-Greenway agreement, variously described by the archbishop as a 'lâche abandon,' 'criminel sacrifice,' 'traité honteux,' 'ignominie,' and 'acte absolumment immoral.' Nor was Bégin any kinder to the politicians who were its architects: 'L'audace et l'impudence de ces politiciens sont incommensurables comme leur insigne lâcheté.'[94] The Prefect of Propaganda also made himself the spokesman of the Quebec hierarchy in urging a quick publication of the encyclical on Manitoba schools, adding that 'the Liberal Party is anxious that such a response [the encyclical] not arrive before the upcoming elections in the Province of Quebec, so as to emerge victorious in this contest as well.'[95]

But it was in his resumé of the Manitoba schools question submitted to Extraordinary Ecclesiastical Affairs that Ledochowski played his hand most explicitly. While reiterating his reservation about the public commitment required of candidates during the June election, the cardinal nevertheless praised the Quebec episcopate's joint pastoral letter. Ledochowski believed that in light of Laurier's ambiguous position in the crisis, the bishops were justified in their fears and suspicions regarding the future of Catholic education in Manitoba and elsewhere. At the same time, judging by the reaction of the partisan press, the prelate considered that the letter had not offended the Liberal party. Indeed, he felt that the joint pastoral produced good results as a majority of Quebec Liberals committed themselves to remedial legislation during the electoral campaign. Since the Conservatives had already championed this course while in office, the new Liberal administration had at its disposal a potentially broad parliamentary consensus in favour of remedial legislation. But caught in the contradictions between current political realities and his former position, Laurier preferred to conclude an accord with the Manitoba government which sanctioned the principle of non-sectarian education. This 'compromise' was rejected by the episcopate. 'But the work of the bishops,' noted Ledochowski, 'is interpreted by some as undue interference and is opposed.'[96] Speaking once again on their behalf, the cardinal urged the pope to give them the support and guidance they so badly needed.

But the pope did not follow his prefect's counsel. It does not even seem that Ledochowki was involved in elaborating the Holy See's policy which was arrived at in private session, probably between the Secretary of State and the Secretary of the Congregation.[97] The background paper on which the final decision rested was an interesting amalgam of Ledochowski's initial resumé, the various petitions addressed to the pope from Liberal politicians, together with the opinions of Blake and Fitzpatrick on the constitutional dimensions of the question.[98]

The decision was a complete triumph for Laurier's point of view. Rome praised the episcopate for their zeal in defending Catholic educational rights, but pointed out that they had interpreted too freely the judgment of the Judicial Committee of the Privy Council. Since this opinion did not explicitly order the re-establishment of Catholic schools in Manitoba, any coercive action taken by Ottawa would be bound to fail and this failure might have disastrous repercussions on Catholic minorities throughout Canada. The Holy See then announced the dispatch of an apostolic delegate to Canada. This mission was necessary, Rome maintained, because on the one hand the Laurier-Greenway agreement was considered to be inadequate, and on the other because the active interference of the Canadian clergy in politics made their relations with the government difficult. The delegate's role would be to bring about a rapprochement between the church and the government, as well as to gain new concessions for the Manitoba Catholics.[99] In the mean time, the hierarchy was asked to refrain from taking any action on this question.[100]

The Holy See's perspective on the matter may well have been influenced by an earlier agreement reached between John Ireland, archbishop of St Paul, Minnesota, and local public school authorities regarding the funding of parochial schools in the towns of Faribault and Stillwater. The archbishop secured state support for these establishments, in return for a promise that religious instruction would be given only after hours. The understanding unleashed a storm of protest from elements in the American hierarchy who considered it contrary to church practices and to policies approved at the plenary council of Baltimore in 1884. To counter this opposition, Ireland got Rome to send Francesco Satolli on a fact-finding mission to the United States, a move strongly opposed by Ledochowski. It was in these troubled circumstances that the apostolic delegation was established in the United States. Soon after arriving on American soil, Satolli announced to an astonished population that he would remain in the country as a permanent apostolic delegate. He proceeded to give Ireland's position broad support and was instrumental in shaping the Holy See's policy on public funding of Catholic schools in the United States. Leo XIII's encyclical on this question, dated May 1893, encouraged the traditional concept of Catholic education, but left local bishops free to allow children to attend public schools.[101] By 1897 Satolli was back in Rome, a full-fledged cardinal and a member of the Propaganda. It is not clear whether he personally intervened in the Manitoba schools question, but Secretary of State Rampolla, in preparing the new apostolic delegate's instructions, asked for and obtained a copy of the Faribault and Stillwater arrangement.[102]

Rome named thirty-two-year-old Monsignor Rafael Merry del Val, a Spanish prelate who was brought up and educated in England, as apostolic delegate.[103] This announcement threw the Quebec bishops into consternation. Paul LaRocque of Sherbrooke considered the nomination to be an indirect declaration of non-confidence in the episcopate. 'Ce serait le *triomphe* de nos *libéraux-catholiques* qui voudraient reléguer l'évêque dans son palais, le curé dans sa sacristie.' He earnestly pleaded that Rome spare the Canadian church this humiliation.[104] The bishops of Nicolet, Chicoutimi, Trois-Rivières, and St-Hyacinthe trembled at the thought of a mission 'si grosse de mauvaises conséquences.'[105] Archbishop Duhamel of Ottawa noted that, by arriving after Parliament's ratification of the Laurier-Greenway agreement, the delegate simply would be faced with a *fait accompli*. Duhamel predicted that this would presage an end to the church's influence not only in areas of mixed jurisdiction, but in religious ones as well.[106]

The Quebec episcopate took quick action. They designated Bégin to defend them in Rome. Once again the tactic of circumventing the delegate was tried. The archbishop of Quebec carried with him a statement signed by all his colleagues designed to counter the allegations made against them at the Curia. But Bégin returned from Rome empty-handed. To ensure that the voice of the bishops was heard in the Curia, however, he appointed a Dominican, Dominique Gonthier, as episcopal agent.[107]

The Merry del Val mission did nothing to soothe the Quebec episcopate's concerns; it only exacerbated them. Rome received letters which complained that the delegate was muzzling the more active bishops and sowing discord in clerical ranks to the greater glory of a cynical Liberal party. Oddly enough, at the end of Merry del Val's mission, a printer again threatened to publish extensive documents dealing with the delegation. The author ended his letter to Rome with the following assessment of the delegate's accomplishments, faithfully echoing episcopal sentiments: 'Il a parlé comme un homme pour le moins naïf, irréfléchi, sans aucune expérience du monde et des affaires, susceptible comme une femme, qualifiant de déplacé et de *cosa brutta* tout ce qui le contrariait un peu.'[108]

PRESSURES FOR A PERMANENT DELEGATION

Merry del Val may have caused the Quebec bishops anguish, but Laurier and his Liberals were certainly jubilant. Replying after some months to Rampolla's letter announcing the delegation, the prime minister referred to the 'happy results' produced and called for the establishment of a permanent delegation. At the same time, while recognizing that the Laurier-Greenway agreement did not satisfy the legitimate aspirations of the Catholic minority, he intimated on the basis of contacts with Manitoba Liberals that the province would adopt a number of measures which would go some way to meeting them.[109]

With Laurier's position on the Manitoba schools articulated, Merry del Val considered his mission at an end. The government had now made its position clear and any hopes the Holy See may have had of encouraging more cordial relations between Laurier and the episcopate were stillborn. The bishops were ordered not to make any public statements on the schools question and to await the pope's directives.[110] At the same time Rome sought to mollify a troubled Quebec hierarchy by appointing Paul Bruchési as Fabre's successor to the see of Montreal.

Intense lobbying went on in the uncompromising heat of a Roman August as Merry del Val busily wrote his report for the Vatican. Gonthier kept up the pressure on behalf of the Quebec hierarchy, while Laurier took advantage of his famous trip to London for the Queen's Jubilee to make a slight detour to Rome where he begged the Secretary of State to allow Merry del Val to remain longer in Canada. In the autumn he was followed to Rome by Archbishop Bruchési and Charles Russell.

Those who hoped that Bruchési's elevation would signal a modification of Vatican policy were quite mistaken. Extraordinary Ecclesiastical Affairs closely followed the recommendations of Merry del Val's report. In October the broad outlines of the papal encyclical were formulated. As well, reminders were given to the clergy not to meddle in politics, nor to confuse moral and political questions. Reprimands were administered to the bishops of Antigonish and Chicoutimi for their harsh actions during the 1896 elections. Recommendations were formulated for the archbishop of St Boniface to remain firm on Catholic rights in Manitoba, but at the same time not to reject practical improvements to the Laurier-Greenway accord.[111]

In the wake of the Merry del Val mission, Leo XIII published his much-awaited encyclical *Affari Vos* on the Manitoba schools question. This document inspired mixed feelings in the episcopate: joy because the Laurier-Greenway agreement was declared to be unsatisfactory; bitterness because the bishops were asked to work for the improvement of legislation that they knew could never give satisfaction to the Catholic minority. Very soon their fears were realized when negotiations between the archbishop of St Boniface and the federal government over improvements to the Laurier-Greenway agreement reached an impasse.

Rumours began to circulate concerning the establishment of a permanent apostolic delegation. These were greeted with scepticism in ecclesiastical circles. Bégin frankly observed: 'Ceux qui la sollicitent n'ont en vue que des intérêts politiques, leur but est encore de gagner du temps, d'amuser le Saint Siège avec d'artificieuses négociations, de jeter du discrédit sur l'épiscopat et de faire croire aux fidèles qu'un Délégué est devenu nécessaire pour le tenir en tutelle.'[112] Still, his colleagues in the Quebec episcopate hoped that the new delegate would secure substantial changes in the status of Catholic schools in Manitoba.[113]

Meanwhile the Canadian prime minister kept up his pressure in favour of a permanent apostolic delegation in Canada and had Quebec Premier Félix-Gabriel Marchand and Charles Russell do the same.[114] In December, Extraordinary Ecclesiastical Affairs expressed approval in principle of the delegation and recommended that the incumbent be a 'prudent and learned' bishop, knowing both English and French. But the cardinals rejected Merry del Val's candidacy on the grounds that he was too disliked by many bishops. They proposed that the delegation be delayed until public reaction to the papal encyclical *Affari vos* could be determined.[115]

Impatient with Rome's procrastination, Laurier turned to Cardinal Vaughan for help.[116] The archbishop of Westminster again interceded on the prime minister's behalf and probably convinced Rampolla to grasp the nettle. The Secretary of State soon wrote to Diomede Falconio, archbishop of Matera and Acerenza in the rugged and destitute Basilicata region of southern Italy, informing him that he was the Holy See's choice. Falconio had been picked 'because of your knowledge of the English language and your experience with American affairs.'[117] The official announcement of the nomination was quite fittingly made on 1 July 1899.

With Falconio's designation as permanent apostolic delegate, the close involvement of Roman congregations in the life of the Canadian church largely came to an end. The delegate took over the role played in the past by the prefect of Propaganda and the Secretary of State. These men continued to be important players in shaping the overall direction of the Canadian church, but their influence was likely to be indirect and more remote. This new arrangement may be seen as a decentralization of the Holy See's administrative apparatus and to a certain extent as a response to the real difficulties experienced by a metropolitan bureaucracy in keeping abreast of developments within national churches through 'brief and concise reports.' Cardinal Simeoni's formula was proving inadequate to cope with the complex problems of local institutions. The creation of apostolic delegations – Canada's was one of three established in 1899 – broadened the Holy See's Roman horizons by producing a larger pool of experienced diplomats who came in direct contact with local realities. Cardinal Manning's dream of a more cosmopolitan bureaucracy was very slowly becoming a reality.

CONCLUSION

It is important to see the bureaucracy of the Holy See as it was seen by clerics in Quebec and elsewhere, as a human institution whose perspective could be influenced, modified, or reversed by effective lobbying. The dictum 'Roma locuta est, causa finita est' was never as definitive as it was meant to sound. Judgments often contained loopholes or technical errors which could be exploited by astute clerics. This is not to impugn the Quebec church's attachment to the Holy See. It would be hard in this period to find a more Roman institution in terms of loyalty to dogma, practices, and symbols. When Rome spoke at this level it could expect absolute conformity and submission. But the affairs of God were one thing, those of man another.

Under Taschereau the Quebec archdiocesan lobby was effective partly because the archbishop and his closest collaborators studied in Rome around the same period and established solid and useful contacts with their professors, their fellow students, and officials in the Curia. At the same time, their Roman education set them apart from the bulk of the French-Canadian clergy and gave them a definite sense of superiority. In the context of a church bitterly divided by factionalism, they saw themselves as a minority under siege defending superior values.

This self-image gave them a fierce determination to uphold their cause. The archbishop and his collaborators were prepared to spend months and perhaps years in Rome in pursuit of their objectives. The only other clergyman to show such determination was Bishop Bourget, but he was removed from effective action when forced to resign in 1876. Laflèche, on the other hand, worked mostly alone. He lobbied personally and seemed generally reluctant to involve trusted collaborators in the defence of his interests at the Curia. Perhaps this in part explains his repeated failures during this period.

Apart from contacts and tenacity, the success of the archdiocesan lobby may be due to the use of arguments which had a definite resonance in Rome. At a time when the Holy See was involved in a bitter struggle with Risorgimento Italy over the state's powers in areas traditionally administered by the church, archdiocesan agents stressed that the Canadian Liberal party had no quarrel with the church. Why then needlessly antagonize an institution that was favourably disposed to Catholicism, they asked? At a time when Catholics in large parts of Europe were complaining of persecution at the hands of Protestant and secularist majorities, Canadian Protestants, they emphasized, had shown a remarkable degree of tolerance of the Catholic minority. Harmonious interdenominational relations were based on mutual understanding and a generous spirit of give and take. But if Catholics should now abandon this spirit in favour of an aggressively militant posture, could Protestants be expected to stand idly by? For those unfamiliar with local conditions, these arguments were certainly very compelling.

Context was also important in effectively presenting the archdiocesan position in Rome. As a beleaguered minority within the Quebec church, Taschereau and his entourage tended to set the defence of their interests in a wider Canadian, rather than Quebec, perspective. It comes as no surprise then that they favoured papal investigators who were British because these were most likely to see things as they did. While situating their own concerns in a broad context, archdiocesan lobbyists reduced their opponents' arguments to questions of narrow interest and partisanship. If Laflèche and his followers attacked the Liberal party, it was because they were rabid Conservatives. If they lashed out at Laval University, it was because they were jealous of its prestige and wanted a university of their own. And these petty interests, it was argued, portended ruin for the church and for Catholics in Canada.

When the Liberal party first made representations to Rome, the ground had already been prepared. Archdiocesan agents in effect legitimated the arguments subsequently restated by Canadian politicians. As a result, it was unnecessary for the Holy See to investigate the latter's assertions and accusations. Like their archdiocesan precursors, the Liberals also presented their interests within a broader Canadian context, even if for electoral purposes they had appealed in the early 1870s to Quebec nationalism through the formation of the *parti national*. They too wanted apostolic delegates who spoke the language of the country and who had a British perspective.

With the Manitoba schools question, however, the convergence of interests between the archdiocese and the Liberal party ended. But just as the Liberal party's credit began to wane in some ecclesiastical circles, Laurier proved himself to be a superb tactician, calling upon

Catholics of impeccable standing in England, the United States, and continental Europe to reiterate arguments that seemed to have tarnished with time. By a sublime twist of fate Archbishop Bégin, who had at long last created a relative consensus in the Quebec church, was defeated in Rome by the very arguments articulated by his predecessor only twenty years earlier.

As we have seen, however, behind the supposedly uniform edifice of Roman policy towards Canada there was disagreement. If Cardinals Franchi, Simeoni, Persico, and Rampolla had one view, Cardinals Oreglia and Ledochowski and Monsignor Agnozzi had another. Laflèche may not have been an effective lobbyist; he may not have chosen the best collaborators, nor presented his arguments in the most convincing fashion, but his case certainly had plausibility, if not credibility. The actions of Laflèche and his followers in Quebec society might not be judged opportune, but they were not outside the pale of what was tolerated and, in some cases, encouraged within the universal church. Indeed, they elicited sympathy from the likes of Cardinal Ledochowski and, as we shall see, Henri Smeulders. Is it mere coincidence that both men came from minority cultures struggling for survival?

The policy which prevailed, however, looked at Quebec not as a distinct entity, as did the majority of the Quebec clergy and their Roman sympathizers, but as part of a wider Canadian, North American, and certainly British context. It is understandable why Rome adopted this perspective: political realism, diplomatic necessity, and even the fashionable view that North America constituted a separate entity within the universal church encouraged such thinking. But Canada was not the United States, nor was Quebec Ireland. It is not clear that the Holy See's perspective, when applied to a country where French speakers constituted over 70 per cent of the Catholic population in 1870 and 75 per cent in 1901, was well advised. Nor is it clear that this perspective illuminated such questions as the clergy's involvement in politics – or the Manitoba schools question, for that matter. On the other hand it did profoundly wound the Quebec clergy's sense of space and history, contributing to their deep sense of alienation which first manifested itself during the Conroy mission. Of course, the apostolic delegates played an important role in shaping and reinforcing this perspective and it is to their work which we now turn.

Chapter Three

The Delegation: An Outsider's Inside View of the Church

Falconio was very proud of his delegation. He worked hard at getting it firmly established. Immediately on arriving in Canada in October 1899, he had been faced with a choice regarding its location. Would he reside in Montreal, the centre of Canadian Catholicism, or in Ottawa, the national capital? The episcopate were divided on the issue. However, the delegate claimed that a majority favoured Ottawa, as indeed did the civil authorities. Although he asked Rome to decide, Falconio left little doubt as to what were his own preferences. 'Ottawa, aside from being the Capital and seat of government, is more centrally located, having on one side the provinces dominated by the French element, and on the other, the English.'[1]

At the same time Falconio was somewhat anxious about his own place of residence. 'I would like to know,' he asked his superiors, 'if I should call upon the generosity of the bishops and faithful for the funds necessary to buy a residence. For the time being I am living at the University.'[2] Cardinal Rampolla advised him to stay in temporary lodgings for the short term and to consider the advisability of buying a residence later on, but only after having consulted again with Rome.[3] Cardinal Ledochowski was even more categorical: under no circumstances should the Catholic population be called upon to support such a project.[4] But before this letter reached him, Falconio had already sounded out the archbishops of Quebec and Montreal on the matter.[5] A few days later he was forced to beat a hasty retreat. The delegate informed the archbishops that, on second thought, he considered it imprudent to appeal to the laity. 'Si le Délégué ne peut pas faire construire de maison, il se contentera d'en louer une. Pour le moment je me trouve bien à l'Université.'[6]

The matter, however, did not end there. Falconio soon told Ledochowski that, although he was prepared to submit to the Propaganda's directive, a 'spontaneous movement' in favour of a residence had arisen among the episcopate and prominent Catholics who were 'unhappy with the fact that His Holiness' representative did not have his own residence as in the nearby United States.'[7] Falconio added that he did not feel the delegate would be compromising his dignity by accepting such a gift. The truth was, however, that the archbishops initially had been very cool to the idea of a direct appeal to the faithful but, faced with the delegate's pressing solicitation, offered to dip into general diocesan funds to support the scheme.[8] Ledochowski, in answer to Falconio's news, thought it prudent to restate his position: the delegate could only accept a residence if it were offered to him spontaneously.[9]

One year later Falconio's urgent wish became a reality. At an Ottawa meeting the archbishops of Canada made him the much anticipated offer. 'The residence has been bought and in a few days will be furnished thanks to the absolutely spontaneous offerings of the Bishops and to a donation provided by the good Sulpician Fathers of Montreal, without the slightest solicitation on my part.'[10] The house cost $7,015. An additional $8,500 was spent on renovations, and by the time the residence was furnished the total cost to the Canadian church reached a hefty $22,000. Initially the episcopate also paid municipal taxes, as well as the costs of upkeep and insurance.

By 1903 these financial obligations had become such that the archbishop of Ottawa unburdened himself to Rome. He recalled how the Canadian episcopate had become involved in this affair.

Mgr Falconio nous fit part de son désir d'avoir une résidence à Ottawa, et nous crûmes comprendre d'après ses paroles que tel était aussi le désir du Saint-Siège.

Malgré les oeuvres nombreuses dont ils sont tous chargés dans leur diocèse, les évêques regardèrent comme un devoir d'accéder au voeu qui leur était exprimé.[11]

He explained that after having done all that was possible for the delegation, the bishops no longer had the resources to continue assuming the costs involved.

For Falconio, however, the important thing was that he had achieved his goal. The apostolic delegation in Canada, which to his mind was in no way inferior to its American counterpart either in prestige or power, was now firmly entrenched on Canadian soil. The residence was a fitting symbol of permanence, a culmination and at the same time a departure from the efforts of temporary Vatican envoys, from George Conroy to Rafael Merry del Val, who had laboured over the previous twenty-five years to bring the Canadian church in line with the Holy See's directives.

PERSICO: THE PRECURSOR

The history of the apostolic delegation in Canada begins with Ignazio Persico, the first candidate to be solicited by Cardinal Franchi for the position of temporary delegate. From the Holy See's perspective, Persico had all the attributes of an ideal papal envoy. Of good birth, he was related on his mother's side to the Italian branch of the Acton family. He was a man of the world, a linguist, a scholar, and a diplomat. He served as a missionary in India and rose to become vicar apostolic of Agra at the time of the mutiny. As Rome's special envoy to London he carried out a delicate and successful mission in defence of the church's interests in the Indian subcontinent. Reasons of health, however, compelled him to return to Italy, where his English-language skills were put to good use at the Propaganda. In 1870, after a three-year stay in the United States, he was made bishop of Savannah.

It was in the American South that he met Louis-Honoré Pâquet, Benjamin's brother, who also taught at the Séminaire de Québec. Because of recurring problems with his health, Persico resigned his charge in 1873 and, through Pâquet's good offices, took up residence in Quebec as pastor of Sillery.[12] There he lived a quasi-monastic existence, devoting himself totally to the care of his parishioners and travelling very little.[13] The Sillery presbytery was, however, a lively meeting place for a number of priests from the Séminaire de Québec and their friends. It was in these circumstances that Persico's rather negative opinions of the Quebec church, and particularly of its episcopate, were formed.

In general, the former bishop of Savannah felt that his Quebec colleagues neither measured up to the standards of their office nor the requirements of their times. He was especially critical of the archbishop of Quebec. In this particular case, Persico's views clearly were influenced by priests, like those at the Séminaire de Québec, who had the opportunity to observe the archbishop at close range. A Quebec City pastor in the course of his regular duties simply would not have had access to the first-hand information which Persico provided Rome. What is astonishing is that the Italian bishop's criticisms of Taschereau were very similar to those of the archbishop's opponents. Persico maintained that, although Taschereau gave the impression of being a cool, self-confident, and thoughtful person, he really acted haphazardly, precipitately, and without counsel. His circulars to the clergy were a tissue of contradictions and revealed his lack of judgment.

To emphasize the archbishop's instability, Persico cited his behaviour over resolutions passed by provincial councils of the Quebec church prohibiting university professors from engaging in political activity.[14] At first the archbishop vigorously opposed this proposal, which was adopted in any case. Then, to everyone's surprise, he subscribed to it. But when the rector of Laval came to him for guidance concerning its implementation, Taschereau told him simply to ignore it. University administrators were only too happy to follow this advice, but discovered some time later that the episcopate, including the archbishop, censured them for failing to respect the bishops' wishes. The rector then went before the hierarchy to justify his actions and, on that occasion, received Taschereau's support. Persico concluded that in the face of such weak and ineffectual leadership,[15] only an apostolic delegate could bring harmony to a much divided church.[16]

THE CONROY MISSION

This advice was heeded and Conroy became the man of the hour. Like Persico, the Irish bishop had credentials that would have impressed Roman bureaucrats. He pursued higher theological studies at the Urban College in Rome where over the years he had acquired a thoroughly Roman perspective, as well as fluency in spoken and written Italian. Shortly after his return to Ireland, Conroy's scholarly merits and ideological orientation were recognized when he was appointed joint editor of the *Irish Ecclesiastical Record*, a publication designed to promote Roman ideas and devotions. He soon became secretary to Paul Cardinal Cullen, archbishop of Dublin and the most powerful prelate in the Irish church. Consecrated bishop of Ardagh and Clonmacnois in 1871, Conroy was clearly Cullen's right-hand man; the new bishop was soon involved in delicate diplomatic manoeuvrings with the British government over educational reform. Since the cardinal had himself spent thirty years in Rome, Cullen could not have been alien to the Holy See's choice of apostolic delegate.

Conroy arrived at Halifax in May 1877 in time to consecrate Connolly's successor, Michael Hannan, as the new archbishop of that city. This gave him the opportunity to meet most of the Canadian bishops and to get their views on the problems of the Quebec church.

One week later he was in Quebec City where an enthusiastic crowd twenty thousand strong turned out at the port to greet him. A procession of archbishops, bishops, two hundred priests, the professoriate of Laval University in academic garb, the officers of various societies in formal dress, and the students of the university and seminaries accompanied the delegate through the streets of the old capital. 'Tout cela formait un spectacle grandiose, saisissant et je me suis cru transporté aux grandes fêtes du Moyen Age lorsqu'on recevait les légats *a latere* du Pape,' wrote an enraptured Archbishop Lynch, who evidently had ambivalent feelings about the Middle Ages. That evening a wonderful literary event was organized at the university. 'Un superbe portrait de Pie ix de grandeur héroique placé au fond de l'immense salle et entouré de guirlandes et de couronnes, dominait majestueusement tout l'auditoire qui ressemblait à une grande famille réunie autour d'un Père bien aimé.'[17]

No one, however, was deceived by this spectacle of unity, least of all the apostolic delegate. He confided to Franchi: 'All that Your Eminence has heard regarding the condition of things in Canada are understated, as much for the good as for the bad. The good is greater than one might believe and the bad is also greater. It would be difficult to imagine a people more worthy and yet more cruelly tormented by internicine quarrels.'[18]

The apostolic delegate expected to be in Canada for some six months. He would then proceed to the United States, where the Holy See had asked him to carry out a fact-finding mission also. Evidently the idea of spending the winter in Canada horrified him and he sought to avoid such a prospect at all costs. But at various times clerical unrest punctuated Conroy's stay in Canada and made havoc of his schedule. In October the delegate told Cardinal Franchi that he was ready to leave for United States, confident that Rome 'will not want to condemn me to suffer the horrors of the Canadian winter.'[19] The Propaganda, however, was more concerned with the storm that was brewing in the lower clergy than with the climatic disturbances of the approaching season. Conroy therefore agreed to stay on until, as he put it, the cold became too intense. The new year of 1878 still found him in Montreal where he reported, 'I have suffered greatly for some weeks from the atrocious cold of this climate. Yesterday the thermometer showed thirty degrees below zero!'[20] Although the delegate soon escaped the cold, the clergy's discontent followed him to the farthest and warmest reaches of the adjacent republic.

Clerical dissent simply confirmed Conroy's image of French Canadians as a people who were by nature litigious. His report stated that for the previous twenty years a succession of political and religious controversies had rocked the Quebec church. Bishops, priests, and the laity descended into the public arena with a 'furia più che francese.' 'Quebeckers love to write and scheme; they are not happy unless they are obstructing or counter-obstructing on paper ... One single trouble-maker would succeed in having ten different memoranda signed all by the same people.'[21] These clerics, like the monks of Nitre and Tabenna at the time of St Cyril, were no less orthodox and no more educated. (Conroy was referring here to the primitive monastic communities of fifth-century Egypt composed of plebeian illiterates on the fringes of respectable society who went about disrupting and intimidating non-Christian and rival Christian factions.)[22]

The Quebec clergy were factious, Conroy believed, because they had an appalling lack of education. Only a small minority actually completed their theological studies, and many never saw the inside of a seminary. Since young ecclesiastics were used to staff the province's numerous classical colleges, they were expected to pick up theology in their spare time. A hard day's teaching and supervision, however, hardly inclined these young men to scholarly activity after hours. They were thus given holy orders without possessing a firm foundation in many branches of the ecclesiastical sciences. Their bishops were no more inclined to remedy the situation and showed more interest in staffing these second-rate institutions than providing the clergy with a solid educational foundation. Given this situation, the only remedy, according to Conroy, was to make the completion of theological studies mandatory for accession to the priesthood.

It was also necessary to make educational achievement a prime condition for promotion to the episcopate. Since the bulk of the Quebec clergy thus would be rendered ineligible, ideal candidates, the Delegate believed, could be drawn from among the directors and professors of the university and major seminaries or the members of religious communities. One thing was certain; the current composition of the Quebec episcopate left much to be desired. Apart from Taschereau, who had always led a studious life, Conroy thought that the local church could not boast one prelate distinguished for his erudition. The institution was thus complacent and lacked dynamism. Whereas in English Canada and the United States, 'Catholic truth' exerted a strong attraction on Protestants and produced many conversions, in Quebec the opposite was the case. Protestant meeting places in Montreal, for example, were teeming with apostates, people whom the church had alienated.

Thus this lack of a Catholic intellectual movement is largely due to the Quebec prelates' mediocre intelligence. The English dominant race which justly appreciates the abilities of the mind wherever these exist will bend down with difficulty before mediocrity even when it is seated on an episcopal throne. Thus the Catholic Church does not advance as one would so justly expect in a country where it finds itself in such a singularly favourable position as in Canada.[23]

But there seemed to be an ambiguity in Conroy's thinking. For if more advanced clerical studies were the remedy to the ills of the Quebec church, then the crisis would persist for a long time to come. Elsewhere, however, the delegate intimated that the problem was also a lack of ecclesiastical authority for which he thought his mission had provided a quick remedy. Conroy claimed that the ambitious men who had taken advantage of the power vacuum created by a divided hierarchy and who somehow believed that the governance of the church was on their shoulders were being put in their place. 'It seems to me that the time has already come to make these priests understand that such questions are not of their authority, but that it is their strictest duty to obey their ecclesiastical superiors.'[24] Of course, the lower clergy had a completely different view of the crisis. Claiming to be victims of episcopal autocracy, a large number of priests called for the institution of diocesan synods where the voice of the lower clergy finally could be heard.[25]

Conroy's report, which dealt mostly with the political question, also formulated some recommendations regarding the Quebec church. But, contrary to Persico, the delegate did not make personality an issue. Even his private correspondence revealed little in this regard. The learned bishop took the high ground. Whatever judgments he may have had on individual bishops were kept largely to himself. This attitude, together with his firmness, probably explain the success he achieved while he was in Canada. Still, the few references gleaned from his letters confirm the thrust of his actions, the meaning of which escaped no one, least of all his enemies.

While he never met Ignace Bourget, it is clear that he considered the aged prelate to be the leader of the extremist faction, a man who readily mixed politics and the sacraments, a potentially explosive combination.[26] He regarded the bishop of Rimouski as singularly lacking in judgment. Who else would have pushed things so far in the question of undue clerical influence as to place Catholic doctrine in open opposition to the laws of the British Empire? Indeed, for the first time in imperial history, the fact of being a Catholic was made incompatible with holding judicial office.[27] In Bishop Laflèche, on the other hand, Conroy found a man thoroughly devoted to Rome, a sure support to his mission, and a zealous promoter of sound ecclesiastical studies.[28]

The delegate's admonitions to the clergy could not conceal the fact, however, that the edifice which he so laboriously constructed during his stay in Canada rested on unstable ground. It was based on episcopal consensus, which in turn depended on Conroy's powerful presence. But in the summer of 1878 the Irish bishop headed back to Rome, confident that the main objectives of his mission had been achieved. In Newfoundland the strain of months of intense work in the four corners of the continent took its toll. First the Irish prelate was afflicted with a liver ailment. Then he developed congestion in the lungs. Leeches were applied by the two attending physicians, but not all was left to the devices of modern medicine: 'Pictures and relics of His Holiness Pius the Great were not forgotten.'[29] All this was to no avail. Conroy died on 4 August 1878.

THE SMEULDERS MISSION

During the next few years Laflèche, on whom Conroy had especially relied to quell the movement of dissent, led those who opposed the Irish bishop's legacy. Conflict was rife. A new papal investigator was dispatched on the scene to defuse a potentially explosive situation. Henri Smeulders was born and educated in Mol, a town in Antwerp province, Belgium. Like Conroy, he had spent seven years in Rome, first as a student at the Jesuit Collegio Romano, where he obtained a doctorate in theology, and then as professor at the Cistercian monastery of San Bernardo alle Terme. He was obviously a very promising young man since he soon became a consultant to the Congregation of the Index and, shortly after his return to Belgium, was made secretary to the general of his order. In this capacity he visited Cisterician monasteries in France, Belgium, and Austria-Hungary. Smeulders returned to Rome as procurator general of his order and was responsible for defending its interests at the Holy See. Following the death of the Cistercian general, he was invited to become head of the order, but declined. In 1880 he became a consultant at the Propaganda.[30] The new papal envoy had wide-ranging administrative experience, keen intellectual abilities, was well travelled, and above all enjoyed the confidence of his superiors in the Roman Curia.

Smeulders left Belgium for New York after being warned by Simeoni not to travel on the same boat as Laflèche, who was himself returning to Canada from Rome. The apostolic commissioner, accompanied by two secretaries, chose first-class accommodations on a ship especially recommended to him. Smeulders confessed: 'I am not one of those saints who could make a boat out of their cloak or who walked on the waves of the sea.'[31] The envoy arrived in Quebec City from New York in October 1883 and gave the Propaganda his initial impression of the local church. 'Combien vive est la foi dans le coeur du Canadien; combien grand est son attachement au Saint-Siège.'[32] While he carefully avoided any public acts which might be interpreted as favouring a particular faction, his sympathies at first were with Taschereau's group.[33] After spending six weeks in Quebec City, Smeulders left for Montreal, where he remained for a year as a guest of the Oblates. There his perspective changed under the influence of Archbishop Taché, who had expressly left St Boniface for three months in order to advise the papal visitor.

Smeulders was meticulous and thorough in carrying out his mandate. He spoke at length with all members of the Quebec hierarchy, carefully examined Laval University's accounts, and spent long hours negotiating separately with the two sides in the university dispute. Taschereau's hurried departure for Rome in the midst of these negotiations certainly did not make Smeulders's task any easier. The archbishop in fact remained in Rome for eight long months. In any event, by immersing himself completely in the intricacies and complexities of these controversies, Smeulders developed an overview of the problems afflicting the Quebec church and society.

The apostolic commissioner had no other task but to resolve the internal problems of the Quebec church. Unlike Conroy, he did not travel to the United States, nor to English Canada. This may in fact explain why the Holy See chose a French-speaking cleric as its delegate. These different parameters undoubtedly shaped the apostolic commissioner's perspective.

The image that emerges from Smeulders's letters and reports is that of the church as a rudderless ship. The hierarchy was plagued by a lack of authority, moral integrity, and vision. Happily, Laflèche stood out among his peers for his learning, his exceptional piety, his virtue, and his single-minded defence of the rights of the church. Catholics of all ranks revered him. Smeulders also praised Jean Langevin of Rimouski and Thomas Duhamel of Ottawa. The latter was singled out for his prudence, intelligence, independence of mind, and sound principles. Unlike many of his colleagues, Duhamel ruled his diocese with a firm hand and a kind heart.[34]

But these men were not at the helm and if the ship was adrift, prime responsibility had to be assumed by Archbishop Taschereau. Smeulders depicted the archbishop's actions as often contradictory, incomprehensible, and quite astonishing. While on a personal level he was certainly well meaning, in his position of authority he seemed to be a prisoner of his entourage. This clique, or *camarilla* as Smeulders termed them, controlled the seminary and the university. In the power vacuum created by the archbishop's chronic indecisiveness, they ruled the Quebec church according to their whims and interests. These clerics were narrow, petty, and inordinately ambitious. Their pretensions for Laval University were an offence to common sense and rocked the very foundations of faith in the province.[35] The commissioner felt quite sincerely that 'the Archbishop and his foxes were destroying the vineyard of the Lord.'[36]

The Belgian prelate's opinion of the other bishops was scarcely more flattering. They were men of no enduring principles and so were easily influenced. Acting either from a false sense of obedience or from overweening ambition, they blindly followed the prevailing current. Smeulders cited Persico's opinion that some should never have been raised to the episcopacy.[37]

The situation produced by the dominance of the Taschereau faction was serious. What evidence did Smeulders have of this? He cited the treatment of the Catholic École de Médecine and the Hôtel Dieu sisters by Taschereau and Fabre. The archbishop had gone so far as to declare null and void a contract between the hospital and the legally incorporated medical school, without first seeking their consent and without compensation. Were the school or the nuns flirting with heresy, Smeulders asked? No, they simply and justly believed that decrees of the Holy See were not to be treated as dogma, but that they allowed for negotiation. And yet the means taken to deal with the school and the sisters were out of all proportion to the issues involved and went well beyond the bounds of reason. Smeulders added that the best elements in Quebec Catholicism, Bishop Laflèche and the Jesuits for instance, were slandered and threatened.[38] Meanwhile the Séminaire de Québec cast covetous glances at Jesuit properties to finance its grandiose university projects. As well, it held the whole province to ransom, demanding enormous sums for Laval, without which it threatened to close the university's doors.[39]

What is significant about Smeulders's perspective is not its faithfulness to the clichés of the ultramontane discourse, but its similarity to the views of Persico and Conroy. All three prelates were extremely critical of the Quebec hierarchy. Persico was the first to alert the Propaganda to the archbishop's irresoluteness and his observations were now seconded by Smeulders. And although the Belgian monk disagreed with Conroy about Jean Langevin, their common perspective on Laflèche is striking.

Smeulders's recommendations to Rome were straightforward. He believed that it was crucial to remove Taschereau from the scene. A new energetic archbishop would provide order and direction to his diocese and to the whole ecclesiastical province. Taschereau for his part could be given a cardinal's hat and summoned to Rome. There, the prelate 'would be freed from harmful influences and, being in constant contact with the wisest of Roman prelates and cardinals, soon would change his ideas and be of service to the Holy See.'[40] Smeulders considered that this action would help to restore unity to the archdiocesan clergy, nine-tenths of whom were opposed to Taschereau's administration, and to the episcopate as a whole.

As for the university question, considering the impossibility of bringing about an understanding between Laval and the medical school ('they have always been two roosters amidst a collection of hens'), he proposed that Montreal be granted its own university.[41] Like Conroy before him, he strongly advised against dividing the diocese of Trois-Rivières, which could only be interpreted as a public humiliation of Laflèche. Such a move would profoundly discourage the church's friends, give comfort to her enemies, and in practical terms reduce the good bishop to penury.[42] But Smeulders was not an unconditional apologist for all of Laflèche's causes and allies. He was a critical investigator, able to distinguish the trivial from the substantial.[43]

The commissioner felt that he had to end his mission with an apologia since he was no longer sure of his superiors' support in Rome. 'I certainly know,' he admitted to Simeoni, 'that I am a monk, not an astute diplomat.'[44] He took comfort in the fact that his actions met with the approval of men of the highest social standing, but offered to correct any mistakes he might have made.

Not surprisingly, the commissioner's departure sparked angry comments from the Taschereau faction. Using terms remarkably reminiscent of his opponents' reaction to the Conroy visit, the archbishop portrayed the commissioner as a dupe of the forces of evil: Smeulders had been content to repeat without the slightest investigation slanders and accusations levelled against those who happened to disagree with Laflèche.[45] In terms one might have expected to hear more from the bishop of Trois-Rivières than from his metropolitan, Taschereau alleged that the Belgian prelate protected rebels against the Holy See's authority who '[font] ainsi l'oeuvre du libéralisme et de la franc-maçonnerie.'[46] In apocalyptic tones the bishop of Chicoutimi considered that Smeulders had pushed Quebec a little closer to the abyss and repeated St Peter's anguished cry: 'Domine salva nos, perimus.'[47] The future bishop of Nicolet, the diocese soon to be carved out of Trois-Rivières, called for another delegate and suggested rather curiously: 'Il doit être possible de trouver dans le clergé romain, ou ... de l'empire britannique, un Prélat, qui puisse quitter son travail ordinaire, pour quelque temps, sans qu'il soit nécessaire de recourir à des étrangers. Nous ne voulons plus d'étrangers: celui qui vient de nous quitter nous a fait trop de mal.'[48]

RAFAEL MERRY DEL VAL

Gravel's wish came true, but in a way that would have made him bitterly regret his words, had he remembered them. Thirteen years later, an English-speaking prelate, resident in Rome, did indeed come to Canada to put some order in the Canadian church. Merry del Val was steeped in diplomacy. He was born in London, the son of the secretary of the Spanish embassy and the maternal grandson of a Spanish count. He studied in the best schools of England and Belgium. As a young man he pursued his theological studies in Rome and graduated from the Pontifical Academy of Noble Ecclesiastics. Even before his ordination, Merry del Val's diplomatic skills were recognized when Leo XIII entrusted him with special missions to London, Berlin, and Vienna. He was held in such high esteem that at the young age of twenty-seven he entered the pope's household as secret papal chamberlain. Five years later he was made special apostolic delegate to Canada. (At the time of this designation, Merry del Val's father was Spanish ambassador to the Holy See.) This was the beginning of a meteoric rise which would see him named a cardinal and Secretary of State to the new pope, Pius X, by 1903.[49]

The apostolic delegate, accompanied by his secretary, spent a few days in England before boarding the *Umbria* at Liverpool for the journey to New York. In London he met with 'authoritative personalities,' both Catholic and Protestant, who gave him their impressions of events in Canada. The prevailing opinion in the English capital was that if the Quebec bishops continued their passionate campaigns of excommunications and denunciations, they were sure to unleash a disastrous persecution against the Catholic church. At the same time, though Merry del Val was very upset to learn that the Manitoba government had formally approved the Laurier-Greenway agreement even before he had a chance to set foot on Canadian soil.[50] It took all of Charles Russell's diplomatic skills to convince him the night before his departure for the new world that the accord could in any case be modified.[51] In New York Merry del Val met with Archbishop Michael Corrigan and other 'prudent' people who 'all deplored the painful state in which many Catholics in Canada are reduced as a result of political conflicts, and of the imprudent behaviour of many members of the clergy.'[52] He left New York for Montreal in the company of Thomas Shaughnessy, the president of Canadian Pacific Railway, who put a special railway car at his disposal for the journey.[53]

Merry del Val spent three and a half months in Canada, residing mostly in Ottawa, although he did visit Quebec City, Trois-Rivières, Montreal, Toronto, and Winnipeg. His mission began on 30 March 1897 in Quebec City, where he received a warm welcome which he described as a spontaneous and imposing demonstration. But official acts contrasted sharply with private sentiments. And if the delegate harboured any predispositions against the French-Canadian clergy, these could only have been strengthened by the events surrounding the inception of his mission.

For one thing, the metropolitan of the oldest ecclesiastical province in Canada, Archbishop Bégin, was not there to greet him. Instead he was in Rome appealing against the delegate's mission. Merry del Val even suspected that a couple of weeks earlier Bégin deliberately avoided him in England on his way to the Eternal City.[54] For another thing, the Quebec episcopate immediately presented the papal envoy with a self-justificatory statement on the Manitoba schools question. Merry del Val considered the document offensive to the Holy See because it suggested that Rome had been misled. The delegate also noted that although claiming to represent the sentiments of the Canadian episcopate, the statement was signed only by Quebec bishops, some apparently under duress.[55] Finally, he was outraged by Vicar General C.A. Marois's letter to the Quebec episcopate which expressed fears that the delegate's tacit acceptance of the Laurier-Greenway agreement would cause deep divisions in the church. Bégin's administrator considered remedial legislation the only recourse. 'I protested vehemently,' Merry del Val wrote, 'against his disloyal behaviour and audacity by which he privately intervened in the relations between the Bishops and the Representative of the Holy See.'[56] If Merry del Val's reception in French Canada was less than cordial, he felt quite welcome in the English part of the country. He pointedly noted that the bishops of Ontario 'far from considering themselves humiliated, saw the arrival of the Delegate as a great consolation.'[57]

This only served to confirm impressions which the delegate had already formed in Rome, London, and New York. The Catholic church in Canada, he believed, found itself in an extremely serious, indeed perilous, condition. 'The unfortunate position in which religion finds itself in Canada today and more especially in the French speaking provinces'[58] were the sombre tones Merry del Val used to begin his report to the Vatican. Once completed, the delegate's depiction of the situation in Canada was truly catastrophic. The recent crisis 'placed the faith of thousands of people in imminent danger, made people hate the sacraments of the Church and disdain the authority of the Bishops and Clergy; it destroyed all ecclesiastical discipline, alienated non-Catholics ever more, ruined family harmony, and occasioned the loss of many many souls.'[59] Elsewhere in his report Merry del Val positively asserted that the faith of the people had declined, as indeed had the prestige and authority of the clergy.

But at this point the papal envoy was careful to make an important distinction. The crisis had not compromised the Canadian episcopate as a body, but only its French-Canadian component. 'The assertion that the Canadian Episcopate was inspired in this [crisis] by political motives is absolutely false, as is the suggestion that the Episcopate of

Canada as such identified itself with one or other political party occupying the scene.'[60] The problem lay instead with the French-Canadian bishops who made themselves blind instruments of the Conservative party.

Like Smeulders, Merry del Val depicted the Quebec episcopate as a ship cast adrift. At one time Cardinal Taschereau had with the support of the Holy See succeeded in separating religion from politics, especially in the New Brunswick schools question. But 'there is indeed no one who could today guide the Episcopate in the wake of the illness which has stuck the eminent Cardinal Taschereau.'[61] His legacy now lay in tatters. And while the delegate praised Bégin for his knowledge and virtue, he had to confess that the archbishop was surrounded by men who took advantage of his good nature[62] – compromised men like Vicar General Marois and the bishops of Chicoutimi, Rimouski, and Trois-Rivières whose violent and imprudent actions aggravated the crisis.[63]

However, Merry del Val could not be entirely negative about Laflèche. He felt compelled to acknowledge the bishop's virtue and his zeal.[64] He did the same for Adélard Langevin. At the beginning the archbishop of St Boniface had made an unfavourable impression of the delegate. Merry del Val observed on first meeting him that 'the prudence of the distinguished Prelate's hurried gait is certainly questionable.'[65] Later on he deplored the excesses committed by the archbishop, who had thrown many a conscience into the greatest turmoil. But during his visit to Winnipeg the delegate recognized Langevin's strong points – his zeal, his kind heart, his devotion to the Holy See.[66] The papal envoy saw very few worthy men among the Quebec clergy. He singled out N.Z. Lorrain of Pontiac, and Médard Emard of Valleyfield whose Roman education had given him a greater knowledge of theology and canon law than most bishops.[67] Merry del Val was also impressed by the rector of Laval University, J.C.K. Laflamme, a man uncompromised by political events and 'one of the few people that I have so far met among the clergy of Canada with a truly elevated perspective.'[68] In fact, the delegate's analysis of the causes of the crisis relied very heavily on Laflamme's views.

Both men, repeating Conroy, believed that the Quebec clergy's lack of theological education and culture was at the root of the crisis. This led priests and bishops to commit the worst excesses in the name of a just cause. Another factor was the Quebec church's failure to abide by the prescriptions of canon law. In many dioceses the will of the bishop was the only rule, which left the lower clergy and the laity without due recourse. The church unhappily was also prey to the traditional opposition between the English and French in Canada, as well as to divisions internal to French Canada itself. Quebeckers were split into two hostile camps, 'some of whom seek to unite themselves more with the English element, while the others want to hold on to the reserved and almost exclusive attitudes of the past.'[69] These problems were all the more tragic since the Canadian church had tremendous potential in Merry del Val's eyes. 'Canada should and could be the bulwark and main support of the Church in the whole North American continent; but if things continue as they are going today, it will definitely lose its traditional position and will do nothing in the future.'[70]

The only bright spot in this otherwise sombre assessment of Canadian Catholicism was the Irish Ontario church which the delegate portrayed in glowing terms. He reminded Rome that although a minority in the province, Catholics always had let themselves be guided by prudence so that not only were their rights universally recognized, but their leaders found themselves at the apex of society. The episcopate of Ontario stood out among their peers for their knowledge, their experience, and their diplomatic skills.

They have earned the esteem of politicians and even of Protestants so that their influence is enormous in the country. After a long and persevering struggle, they obtained their own separate schools, large subsidies for their main Catholic institutes, and the easiest of terms for their Catholic works. But these things they did not obtain with violence, by denouncing people, by forbidding newspapers and the sacraments, and by offending political parties on the one hand and Protestant fanaticism on the other. They neither diminished nor hid their Catholic principles, but in applying them, appealed instead to common sense and to their fellow citizens' sentiments of justice so as gradually to improve their position.[71]

The papal envoy was very much impressed by the fact that he had heard both Liberals and Conservatives praise the Irish archbishops of Ontario. Because he could count on the latters' discretion, foresight, and unanimity of views, Merry del Val worked closely with them in achieving an understanding with the federal government over the Manitoba schools question. Not so, of course, with the French-Canadian bishops, except for Lorrain and Emard. For this reason, the main recommendation of Merry del Val's report was that on issues involving either serious disagreements with the federal government or the interests of the Canadian church as a whole, bishops not issue collective documents unless these were signed by the entire Canadian episcopate.

At the end of his mission, and like Smeulders before him, Merry del Val defended himself against his detractors. 'I cannot hope to escape the denunciations of those who from the beginning opposed the dispatch of a Delegate, and who later would have liked to direct his actions.'[72] Nevertheless, he expressed a willingness to explain his behaviour and to accept any criticisms which might be deserved.

'Une des plus pénibles épreuves et l'une des plus grandes calamités que Dieu ait infligées à l'Eglise du Canada.'[73] So Bégin described the Merry del Val mission. Five years after the delegate's trip to Canada, the archbishop presented Rome with a passionate thirty-five-page typewritten refutation of Merry del Val's report, denouncing its numerous inaccuracies and its lack of seriousness.

Bégin's criticism of Merry del Val was partly one of process. He and his colleagues in the Quebec episcopate obviously felt the sting of the delegate's cool and distant manner, as well as his refusal to involve them in any meaningful way in his mission. 'Il est vrai qu'il a su leur faire sentir à ses manières et au ton de son langage qu'ils étaient assez peu de chose à ses yeux.'[74] These sentiments were echoed elsewhere by Bishop Moreau, who complained that the delegate constantly and disfavourably compared the Quebec episcopate to their English counterparts, whereas Merry del Val hailed Laurier as another Duke of Norfolk.[75]

Bégin admitted that, not having fifteen hundred years of tradition behind it, the Quebec church might lack a certain sophistication. Still, he was convinced that some of the products of that church, if they were to show a little less modesty and were given wider scope for action, could become truly superior churchmen. 'Les aigles parmi nous sont comme partout l'exception. Nous admettons facilement qu'il y en a davantage dans certains pays; mais bien des aigles d'Europe deviennent des oiseaux fort ordinaires quand nous les voyons de plus près, soit ici, soit dans leur propre pays.'[76]

There was more, however, to the bishops' reaction than personal pique. Moreau maintained that Merry del Val's comparison of the Quebec and English churches was spurious because it failed to take into account the differences in context: English Catholics did not enjoy the same status as their Canadian counterparts and, as a result, their bishops adopted different strategies. Implicit in Bégin's refutation was the conviction that the Quebec bishops were the bearers of an historical consciousness and tradition. But Merry del Val had only granted them two or three hours of his time. Instead he preferred the company of unscrupulous and ambitious men more interested in political power than historical truth, and of a coterie of ecclesiastical confidants 'qui [n'ont] sûrement le monopole ni de l'intelligence ni de l'amour désinteressé de l'Église.'[77] How could the delegate then pretend to understand the historical background of the Manitoba schools question? How could he substantiate his judgment that the crisis was but a symptom of twenty years of political abuse by the Quebec clergy? 'Cette page n'est pas la moins malheureuse de ce malheureux rapport.'[78] The archbishop wondered how the delegate could in four short months acquire an in-depth understanding of the religious situation in Canada: his lack of experience in the affairs of men, his ignorance of Canadian history, the length of time spent at official functions – all these factors contributed to a very superficial appreciation of the facts.

From process, Bégin turned to the report itself. He ridiculed its Cassandra-like tones depicting a catastrophic situation, which only existed in the mind of the delegate 'et de certaines têtes plus chaudes que solides qu'il a eu l'extrême bienveillance de prendre au sérieux. Un étranger seul pourrait se méprendre à ce point.'[79] The archbishop was amazed that the delegate gave credit to rumours flying in Anglican circles about the impending apostasy of numerous Catholics because of the episcopate's electoral excesses. 'Mais sans doute les protestants pourvu qu'ils parlent l'anglais, sont mieux en état de renseigner le St-Siège sur le véritable état de l'Eglise ... que ses malheureux "évêques de langue française."'[80] Bégin wondered how the Holy See could have displayed such little insight in making episcopal nominations in Quebec over the previous twenty years, if even half the things the delegate said about the Quebec hierarchy were true.

The archbishop rejected Merry del Val's contention that, apart from partisan motives, the politico-religious polemics of previous years were inspired by the natural antagonism between the French and the English in Canada. The clergy were not by nature nationalistic. Before the Manitoba schools question, Bégin maintained, nationalism had been totally foreign to religious controversies. And if it suddenly surfaced in the current crisis, this ideology was a defensive reaction against a campaign on the part of a certain number of Protestants to oppress all that was French in order better to overcome the Catholic church in Canada. The Protestant cause was indirectly assisted by the apathy of a large number of English-speaking Catholics who failed to uphold Catholic rights when these primarily involved French-speakers. If nationalism was a sin, clearly the sinners were in the other camp. With this confrontational situation in mind, Bégin dismissed as pure fantasy the delegate's contention that part of the French-speaking population showed a tendency to anglicization.[81]

DIOMEDE FALCONIO

The French-Canadian bishops were still feeling very aggrieved when the appointment of a permanent apostolic delegate was made two years after Merry del Val's mission. The news revived hopes for a new climate of understanding and conciliation. Archbishop Diomede Falconio was no stranger to North America, having spent twenty of his fifty-seven years on this continent. Born in the Abruzzi region of central Italy, Falconio entered the Franciscan noviciate at the age of eighteen. Five years later he was sent to the United States as a missionary. It was there, in fact, that he was ordained a priest by the bishop of Buffalo and soon became rector of the Franciscan parish in New York as well as a teacher at a Franciscan college in New York State. In 1868 he was entrusted with a special mission in Newfoundland by a compatriot and fellow Franciscan, Enrico Carfagnini, then bishop of Harbour Grace. He remained in this diocese for fifteen years, rising to the post of chancellor. After a brief return to the United States, Falconio went back to Italy where he was soon appointed procurator general of his order. He was consecrated bishop in 1892 and archbishop of Matera and Acerenza in 1895.[82]

Falconio left Europe from Liverpool on the steamer *Vancouver* accompanied by his two secretaries[83] and arrived to an enthusiastic reception in Quebec City on 10 October 1899. During his three-year term as apostolic delegate, he travelled the length of the country and dealt with several important questions, including Manitoba schools, European immigration, and especially the spiritual care of Ukrainian immigrants, the Acadian revival, French-Irish rivalry in the Ottawa area, and relations between the lower clergy and the episcopate.[84]

The delegate's initial impression of Canadian Catholicism was very positive. He told Ledochowski that he was edified by the bishops' zeal, the clergy's self-denial, and the faithful's genuine faith. 'In general, Catholics really practise their religion. Should someone miss Mass on holy days or not observe his Easter duty, that failure is noted by the community.'[85] Canadian churches were magnificent, and educational and social service institutions, colossal.

That first impression would not undergo dramatic change. In general, Falconio later observed, the episcopate was venerated and respected. Their administration was truly paternal.[86] Their conduct was exemplary. Through pastoral letters, canonical visitations, spiritual exercises, and instructions, they educated the faithful to their Christian duties.[87] As for the lower clergy, their life was characterized by fraternal goodwill, evangelical simplicity, cordial hospitality, pastoral zeal, and administrative acumen. The Catholic laity, composed essentially of Irish and French Canadians, were less ambitious and enterprising than English-speaking Protestants and still seemed burdened by a servile past to which Protestant fanaticism condemned them both. Although the Irish were less demonstrative in their religious practice than the French Canadians, their faith was more solid and constant, especially in the face of Protestant proselytizers. Still, the church lived its life most freely in Quebec where the legal system recognized its existence. As for the other nationalities, their faithfulness to the church was much less constant. Overall, Falconio warmly described the Canadian church as being among the most flourishing portions of Christ's kingdom on earth.

But the kingdom had not yet come in Canada. There were areas in which major improvements could be made. For one thing, relations between the upper and lower clergy, and between clerics and the laity, were too often marked by arbitrariness. There was no code of law defining these relationships, which not infrequently resulted in abuses of authority and provoked disenchantment, even apostasy. Falconio noted that French Canadians were particularly sensitive to such abuses and some were known to leave the church for a mere trifle. There were hardly any restraints on episcopal authority and this engendered a servile spirit in the lower clergy. Another dark spot was the rivalry between Irish and French-Canadian clerics and the generally low level of clerical education, although on this last point the Delegate noted some improvements.[88]

Falconio proposed one major solution to these difficulties – the convening of a plenary synod of the Canadian church. Such a body would give uniformity to ecclesiastical discipline, raise the standards of clerical education, and get French-Canadian and Irish clergy used to working together. Ledochowski, however, urged caution and considered that above all the delegate should instil 'concord among the Prelates of rival nationalities.'[89] The cardinal prefect considered the convening of a national synod to be a longer-term objective, achieved through episcopal consensus.

Not one to tarry, Falconio soon consulted with the archbishops in much the same way as he had done on the issue of the residence. His letter to them began: 'Je sais déjà que presque tous les Archevêques et les Evêques du Canada sont favorables à la réunion d'un Concile plénier.'[90] He added that the national synod, an institution approved by the pope, had produced excellent results in the United States. The Canadian hierarchy, he suggested, could not afford to be left behind.

But the results of this survey were not as enthusiastic as expected. The bishops of the provinces of St Boniface, Kingston, Ottawa and Quebec (except for Bishop Blais of Rimouski) all endorsed the idea without reservation. Those from Halifax (except for Bishop Rogers of Chatham) all opposed it. Toronto and Montreal were divided. Although Archbishop Dennis O'Connor approved of the idea, his suffragans, Fergus McEvay of London and Thomas Joseph Dowling of Hamilton, merely stated their willingness to comply with Rome's wishes. In the province of Montreal the bishops of St-Hyacinthe and Sherbrooke were opposed on the grounds that the special status enjoyed by the church in the province would be compromised by the standardization of discipline. Archbishop Bruchési found their arguments compelling, but in the interests of the whole church he offered to accept the will of the majority.[91] Only Médard Emard of Valleyfield gave an unqualified yes. The final tally was fifteen bishops supporting the idea unreservedly, three lukewarmly, and eight opposed.[92] Nevertheless, Falconio reported to Girolamo Cardinal Gotti, Ledochowski's successor as prefect of Propaganda, that the bishops 'almost unanimously' accepted the proposal. Those who did not were troubled by such questions as the ethnic diversity of the Catholic population and the disparity of disciplines among the local churches. But the delegate thought it inconceivable that an otherwise zealous episcopate could not manage to rise above ethnic prejudices in a country governed so harmoniously by leaders belonging to different national backgrounds.[93]

Throughout the last year of the delegate's tenure, rumours flew regarding his impending promotion to Washington. Archbishop Ireland for one considered that Falconio was not the man for such an important position. 'Il ne possède ni le talent intellectuel ni les

manières courtoises qui commanderaient le respect et l'estime ... Puis
enfin – ceci est certain, il s'exprime en conversation de manière à
marquer clairement qu'il a peu de sympathies avec les États-Unis et
le gouvernement à Washington, et en même temps avec un certain
nombre d'évêques.'[94] Opinions such as these may explain why the
anouncement of his nomination was only made in mid September of
1902. For some unknown reason, the appointment of his successor in
Ottawa, Donato Sbarretti, was also delayed for two months before
finally being confirmed.[95]

Bishop Sbarretti also had experience in the new world, although
not as extensive as that of his predecessor. He was born in 1856 in the
Umbria region of central Italy. His insertion into the bureaucracy of
the Holy See was facilitated by his being the nephew of Enea Cardinal
Sbarretti. After being ordained he was appointed professor of ethics
at the Urban College, where he doubtless met a number of American
clerics who were pursuing higher degrees. Soon he was named
secretary of the Propaganda for American Affairs and later for
Oriental Affairs. When the apostolic delegation in the United States
was established, he became a consultant to Francesco Satolli. Shortly
after the Spanish-American war he was consecrated bishop of Ha-
vanna and as such became an intermediary between the population
of Cuba and their American conquerors. In 1902 he was appointed
extraordinary apostolic delegate to the Philippines.[96]

Sbarretti arrived in Ottawa shortly after the new year in 1903 and
took over the residence Falconio had worked so hard to acquire. The
building was indeed a fitting symbol of Rome's permanence in
Canada. But did it embody continuity in the succession of Apostolic
Delegates since Conroy who had occasion to observe the troubles of
the Canadian church at close range?

CONCLUSION

The papal envoys who came to Canada during this twenty-five-year
period had a number of things in common. For one thing, they were
well-travelled men who had lived in a number of countries in the
Atlantic world and, as a result, they were polyglots. For another, by
the clerical standards of their time they had received an excellent
education, part of which was pursued in Roman institutions. Finally,
they all possessed first-hand experience of the bureaucracy of the
Holy See.

Considering these common traits, it is quite astonishing how subjective their perceptions of Canadian events and personalities could be. It is true that they were sent to Canada for different purposes: Conroy to resolve a number of issues, including undue clerical influence, the university question, the conflict between the bishop of Montreal and the Sulpicians; Smeulders to diffuse the explosive situation engendered by the crisis in the university dispute; Merry del Val to deal with the Manitoba schools question; Falconio and Sbarretti to bring about unity of purpose within the Canadian hierarchy and harmony between clerics and politicians. The nature of their assignments had a certain influence on the length of their stay: Conroy and Smeulders spent about one year in Canada, Merry del Val three months, and Falconio three years. These factors may have affected their perceptions. In addition, things did change in this quarter-century. At the beginning of the period the Quebec church was torn by internal fighting, whereas at the turn of the century it had achieved a harmony about which Taschereau and Bourget could only dream some two decades earlier. And yet the crisis persisted, a crisis which everyone, including Rome, were aware of, a crisis which underpinned the numerous disputes of the period.

The most striking contrast in the envoys' perceptions of the Canadian church occurred within a short span of three years. It was almost as if Merry del Val and Falconio were describing two completely different institutions. Merry del Val had quite simply a cataclysmic view of the church marked by loss of faith on the part of the laity and loss of authority on the part of ecclesiastical rulers. Falconio described Canada as one of the most fertile parts of the Lord's vineyard.

The envoys' analysis of the roots of the crisis in the Canadian church was equally confusing. One school of thought, which was articulated by Roncetti but found some support with Conroy and Merry del Val, believed that the church was prey to serious internal conflicts based on personalities and vested interests. The expectation was that peace would be achieved by removing some protagonists from the scene. Consequently, the Holy See accepted Bourget's resignation; Conroy isolated the Jesuits, the École de médecine, and 'ultramontane' laymen; Fabre, too, pursued this policy, ridding himself of Bourget's cathedral chapter, a painful daily reminder of his predecessor's legacy. By the end of the century the ranks of the episcopate were completely renewed. Personalities came and went, disputes erupted and subsided, but the crisis remained.

Another school of thought, especially dear to Conroy and Merry del Val, although Falconio also gave it some weight, attributed the clergy's excessive behaviour to a lack of theological education and culture. The problem with this view, however, is that the clergy in the Catholic world of the nineteenth century were not generally distinguished by their knowledge and erudition. Could the situation in the archdiocese of Quebec have been much worse than in Falconio's own archdiocese of Matera, for instance? Were Quebec clerics considerably more ignorant than their Irish, Spanish, or English-Canadian counterparts for that matter?[97]

The only evidence we have on this score are some delegates' judgments framed in absolute terms. However, it is helpful to point out that the same Conroy during the American segment of his mission to the new world observed that only ten out of the sixty-eight American bishops displayed any kind of talent. The rest 'hardly reach a decent mediocrity, and in theological knowledge they do not even reach mediocrity.'[98] He added that parish priests were chosen not for their intellectual or pastoral qualities, but for their financial abilities. Complaints about the American clergy's ignorance were commonplace at the time.[99]

Theological education improved in Quebec in the last quarter of the century, as Falconio himself observed. And yet the malaise continued. Some delegates seemed to argue that the problem was not so much the poor level of clerical education as the excessive behaviour that it engendered. Smeulders's report, however, clearly emphasized that educated men such as Archbishop Taschereau could be just as intemperate. That the prelate could have envisaged in all serenity the excommunication of nuns and Catholic doctors as a solution to a problem which, in Smeulders's mind at least, allowed for differing interpretations, starkly showed that the crisis was not as one-sided as some delegates thought. Moral rigorism was clearly not the preserve of the uneducated. The correspondence of Taschereau's agent in Rome in the early 1880s further underlines the fact that educated men could be as petty and narrow-minded as the most ignorant country priest.

A third school of thought argued that the Canadian church was plagued by indiscipline. But while most papal envoys accepted this theory to varying degrees, they disagreed on the causes of the phenomenon. Conroy in particular blamed an unruly lower clergy who, in the face of a divided hierarchy, took it upon themselves to run the affairs of the church. Persico and Smeulders bemoaned the lack of authority within the Quebec episcopate and held Taschereau especially responsible for this situation. Smeulders, however, disagreed with Conroy as to who was usurping episcopal prerogatives. While the former looked to Quebec City, the latter turned instead to Montreal. In any case, twenty-five years later, the perception of the problem was totally different; Merry del Val and Falconio both considered the disorder in the church to be the result of the bishops' abuse of power. The absence of canon law and of 'national' ecclesiastical structures meant that every bishop was a law unto himself in his diocese. Yet could the situation have evolved so rapidly in a quarter of a century that bishops went from being weak and ineffectual rulers to despots?

It may be useful to mention a common trait characterizing the perceptions of those delegates with experience in English-speaking countries. They all placed a heavy, if not unfair, burden on the Quebec church in the North American context. They believed that this church had a potentially vital role to play in the conversion of North America to Catholicism. They therefore implicitly rejected the thesis dear to many a Quebec cleric that language and faith were indissolubly linked. The appeal to North American Protestants could not be made on the basis of a particularistic culture, but by publicly displaying values which the majority held dear. Protestants would have to be won over on their own terrain. This is why these delegates placed such a heavy premium on intellect. Conroy and Merry del Val, who had both grown up in Britain, understood that superior intelligence was the key to acceptance in Protestant society. In their minds, the vitality of North American Catholicism depended on conversion and the eyes of the continent were therefore on Quebec.

This view of things was quite simply unrelated to reality for, as we have seen, the growth of Canadian Catholicism depended on French-Canadian fertility. In addition, in English Canada (and probably in the United States) there were more Catholics lost to the church through mixed marriages than gained by conversion. Of course there were 'apostasies' in French Canada, as Conroy and Falconio observed, but these were simply not significant enough from a demographic point of view to affect the growth of the Catholic population in Canada. But somehow most delegates tied this growth to the education and political behaviour of the French Catholic clergy who were thus blamed, whereas they should have been praised for the spiritual care they provided to the population that fed this growth.

Chapter Four

Tutto è politica:
A Question of Undue Influence

Rodolphe Laflamme, in his youth an *enfant terrible* of the Rouge party, but in political maturity an eminently respectable Liberal minister, gave Bishop Conroy detailed information, including signed affidavits, concerning clerical interference in his 1876 re-election in the Montreal riding of Jacques Cartier. Asked to comment on Laflamme's allegations, Edouard Fabre, the newly appointed bishop of Montreal, dismissed the evidence out of hand. The first priest incriminated in the documents had been dead for eleven years – a truly redoubtable opponent! Another had pronounced Liberal sympathies and was therefore unlikely to fight his own friends. The last four had visited the constituency where their families happened to be living during the campaign, and while they may have talked privately about politics, they did not actively participate in partisan activities.[1] As for the sworn statements, Bishop Fabre stated that they came from a family in the county, one of whose members was such an ardent follower of Laflamme 'qu'il est prêt à faire toutes les sottises possibles pour le soutenir.'[2] The priests whom they impugned were, he assured Conroy, men above reproach.

This incident indicates that the phenomenon of undue clerical influence is not as straightforward as generally assumed by political historians, who have tended to represent it as widespread in the province of Quebec and working to the detriment of the Liberal party. As Fabre's comments suggest, sworn affidavits could be inspired by political motives, and the evidence which they contained organized, or even manufactured, to suit partisan purposes. In Quebec only two elections were invalidated because of undue clerical influence, one in the provincial riding of Bonaventure in 1875 and the other, on appeal to the Supreme Court of Canada, in the federal constituency of Charlevoix in 1876. The decisions were based on *ex parte* evidence such as sworn affidavits. No priest was ever charged; nor has there ever been a detailed inquiry either by civil or Roman authorities into alleged political abuses by the clergy.[3]

It would be foolish to deny that priests intervened in politics. Even bishops admitted that some of their clerics got carried away in the heat of political battle; but they insisted that such excesses were not widespread. The episcopate's view raises a fundamental question: what was meant by undue clerical influence? It was generally admitted that the clergy should remain above the affairs of men. But were there times when their intervention in the secular sphere was justified? And among the various possible forms of intervention, including private opinion, pastoral letters, exhortations from the pulpit, the use of the sacraments, were some more appropriate than others? Should some never be used? But apart from these theoretical or theological questions, how did the clergy actually perceive their involvement in politics? And finally, how did Rome and its delegates view the political situation in Canada and the clergy's activities in this field?

CLERICAL POLEMICS ABOUT POLITICS

Eighteen seventy-six was a year heavy with political consequences for the Quebec church. On the eve of the new year a Liberal minister, Lucius Seth Huntington, reacting against the episcopate's joint pastoral on Catholic liberalism of September 1875, denounced the clerical offensive against electoral freedoms. A short time later one of his long-time Conservative opponents, Alexander Galt, publicly warned Quebeckers that there would be a repetition of the disastrous events of 1837 if the Catholic hierarchy persisted in their attempts to control the minds of British subjects, even if these happenned to be French-speaking.[4] The short-lived formation of a Protestant Defence Alliance was another signal of Protestant concern over the Catholic church's apparently gross interference in the affairs of the state. That year, also, two cases alleging undue spiritual influence were heard before the courts. If politicians were upset with the hierarchy, the bishops in turn were unsettled by these events. The partisan press fed the climate of tension and hostility. Never one to temporize in the face of adversity, Bourget published his famous 'J'écoute mon curé' letter against Catholic liberalism.

Politicians were not the only ones to find fault with the episcopate's actions. In an open letter to Prime Minister Mackenzie, Archbishop Lynch of Toronto dissociated himself from his Quebec colleagues' stance. In the characteristically magisterial tones he reserved for his French-speaking counterparts, Lynch explained his point of view to Bourget. There was, he proclaimed, a fundamental difference between a liberal Catholic and a Catholic Liberal. The Liberal party as such had no quarrel with the Catholic church. Indeed, its highest officials had given him positive assurances that the church's status in Quebec was firmly entrenched in the constitution.[5] Still, the archbishop admitted, 'there is a party in the Catholic Church [in Quebec] with which thank God we are not afflicted here.' This was the Rouge or infidel faction of the Liberal party, as he termed it. But just as the church in Ontario had to contend with the Orange Order which was allied to the Conservatives, so the church in Quebec had to deal with the Rouges. This did not give either church licence to declare war on an entire party.

Lynch conceded that Orangemen were easier to combat because they were outside the church, whereas the wives and children of the Rouges were Catholics. But he insisted that it was unwise for priests to turn the pulpit into political hustings and so give offence to respectable families by descending to the level of personalities. Indeed, this imprudent strategy would succeed only in strengthening the Rouges. It would be more gentlemanly instead for priests, after consulting their bishop, to express their opinions privately and discreetly. 'It appears to me that the remedy ought to be to make them good Catholics by the means Christ employed.'[6]

But the 'means Christ employed' were easier to prescribe than practise. It is ironic that a short month after writing these letters, Lynch became embroiled in a public controversy with the trustees of the Toronto Separate School Board, who were trying to assert their prerogatives and wrest control of school administration from the archbishop. Suddenly Lynch found liberal Catholics where previously none had existed. From the pulpit of St Michael's Cathedral, scene of many edifying sermons for the Protestant élite's gratification, Lynch accused the trustees of being equal to the Conservatives in falseness. On another public occasion he likened them to Italian anti-clericals. The prelate even refused absolution to their chairman who, he alleged, had given public scandal by threatening to take their disagreement to court. In a subsequent school board by-election, the archbishop stated that it was a sin to vote for a non-practising Catholic. At the same time he assured his listeners that he was not meddling in politics and that he would never take it upon himself to tell people how to vote in secular matters.[7]

Lynch's open letter to Mackenzie had prompted a private response from Taschereau. The archbishop disapproved of Lynch's action, interpreting it as a public censure of the Quebec episcopate. 'C'est pour cela que vous avez reçu un très grand nombre (very many) des [sic] lettres de reconnaissance. Je ne sais si V[otre] G[randeur] a droit de s'en réjouir ... Ceux qui ... veulent faire la guerre à l'*Ultramontanisme* et *à quelques prélats*, c'est à dire à l'Église Catholique, remercient celui qui leur fournit un grand argument pour cacher leur sinistre dessein.' The contradiction in Lynch's behaviour was patent to Taschereau: he accused the Quebec hierarchy of partisanship while he himself flaunted his political preferences in a public letter to the prime minister.

Taschereau also took exception to Lynch's pretension that the Ontario hierarchy had a more genteel way of dealing with political issues, through private admonitions. 'Nous croyons nous, que l'avis peut se donner quelquefois publiquement; la convenance de l'une ou de l'autre méthode dépend de bien des circonstances que chaque Evêque peut et doit apprécier. Ce qui peut offrir des inconvénients dans Ontario, peut ne pas en avoir dans Québec [sic]...' The archbishop concluded his letter with the observation that Huntington's sortie against the Quebec hierarchy was a truly portentous event in recent history which fully justified their collective action.[8]

Yet this is the same prelate who in the days before and after this letter was consulting his suffragans about the advisability of publishing a new joint pastoral to elucidate the 1875 one and specifically deal with the question of whether the episcopate meant to condemn the Liberal party. Here was a man who had himself written the September 1875 pastoral; who considered Huntington's speech a scarcely veiled attempt to intimidate the church; and who, mindful of this context, chastised Lynch for giving comfort to the enemies of Catholicism, now effectively undermining the objective of that pastoral.

As Bourget and Laflèche reminded the archbishop, a new episcopal statement would have the same effect as Lynch's letter – it would only serve to minimize the meaning of the initial pastoral. It would allow political parties and candidates to claim that it was business as usual and that the hierarchy's stance had nothing to do with them. This is why Taschereau's suffragans urged silence. The bishop of Montreal stated unequivocally: 'Nous n'avons pas à condamner le Ministère fédéral, ni à l'approuver autrement qu'en établissant solidement les vrais principes qui doivent diriger les Catholiques ... Cela fait, notre mission est remplie.'[9]

During these months of crisis, Taschereau's actions did indeed appear to be ambiguous. The Charlevoix by-election which sparked the first court case on undue spiritual influence occurred in his own archdiocese. Taschereau apparently made no attempt to stop the patent abuse of religion in the campaign. At the same time he refused to allow accusations of clerical intimidation to be tried in diocesan court. In fact he called a couple of priests to order only when one of the candidates formally complained of their behaviour.

The other case of clerical interference involved priests in the neighbouring diocese of Rimouski. Bishop Langevin had been a staunch ally of Taschereau in previous years; yet instead of exercising the prerogatives of a metropolitan and a friend by calling Langevin's attention to clerical abuses, Taschereau remained silent. On the one hand, when his suffragans pressured him to take a stand against Catholic liberalism, he wrote the joint pastoral. On the other hand, when priests in his entourage who were Liberal supporters emphasized the inopportuneness of the document, he effectively retracted it by issuing his own pastoral letter of May 1876. In moments of crisis Taschereau showed an exasperating inability to make up his mind, a trait severely criticized by Persico. Perhaps this mental instability was a forerunner to the illness that would incapacitate him at the end of his life.

CONROY AND THE OMNIPRESENCE OF POLITICS

While priests and politicians argued about clerical interference in politics, Ignazio Persico was giving Rome his own interpretation of these events. If the Italian prelate was hard on Taschereau, he was merciless with his suffragans. Most bishops, he maintained – those, that is, who were not weak and timorous – acted out of blind political passion, 'not to defend religious principles, but simply for political or personal ends.'[10] And their aim was quite simply to destroy those who were politically opposed to them. This was especially evident in the September 1875 joint pastoral which was intended to crush the Liberal party.

But, emphasized Persico, their excessive partisanship went against a fundamental fact of Canadian life for, in this country, 'tutto è politica.' 'The social life of Canada,' he explained, 'is eminently political. Even commerce together with the arts and industry is intimately dependent on politics.'[11] Everyone became politically active, he noted, in order to benefit from the government's favours and encouragement, especially the professional classes whose prospects often depended on public patronage. The bishops were therefore in fundamental contradiction with themselves, since on the one hand they proclaimed their right to intervene in politics and on the other they denied this right to laymen who happened to choose the opposing party.

Persico's opinions were decisive in Rome's appointment of Bishop Conroy as apostolic delegate and in the formulation of his instructions regarding the political question.[12] If Rome was anxious to mend fences with an aggrieved Liberal government, it is equally clear that Ottawa found it opportune to be in Rome's good graces. The instrument of this rapprochement was the governor general, Lord Dufferin, who, like Conroy, was an Irishman. The queen's representative wasted no time in wooing the pope's envoy. He invited Conroy to spend a few days with him as a guest at Rideau Hall. 'I accepted his invitation, and I hope to receive from him information which will be of no little use in expediting the affairs of this Delegation.'[13] Dufferin offered a dinner in Conroy's honour attended by several cabinet ministers. This gave the delegate the opportunity to speak to Alexander Mackenzie, who put his best foot forward in justifying the Liberal party's stand against the Quebec church's interference in politics.[14]

After convincing the Quebec hierarchy to publish the joint pastoral letter of October 1877 exonerating the Liberal party, Conroy was once again Dufferin's guest. 'He receives me with the most exquisite courtesy and treated me with all the regard due to an ambassador of some great power ... He placed his stately carriage at my disposal and did everything to overwhelm the unworthy Representative of the Holy Father with honours.'[15] The governor general hosted another gala dinner at which 'the most prominent people in Ottawa' were invited. Conroy reported that, together with his government colleagues, the prime minister, although a Protestant, did him the honour of attending a lecture which he delivered in the cathedral in Ottawa. Finally, when he left the capital the delegate was accompanied to the train station by the minister of the interior. The government clearly did not miss an opportunity to impress the papal legate.

On this and other occasions, Dufferin allowed himself to speak his mind. He often thanked Conroy for the immense good that his mission was producing in Canadian public life and told him how much the government appreciated his work. The governor general did not hide his outrage at certain clerical pretensions to ecclesiastical supremacy in the judicial sphere, particularly in cases involving undue influence. The province of Quebec, he added, would not be allowed to become an *imperium in imperio*.[16] There was no country in Europe, he believed, where the Catholic church was better treated than in Canada. Why then should this church identify itself with a particular political grouping? Dufferin stressed that whatever the Liberal party had been in the past, it did not now distinguish itself as hostile to Catholicism. But if antagonized, the Liberals would retaliate and the church could expect the worst.[17] Conroy faithfully transmitted these views to his superiors.

But while relations between the Holy See and the Canadian government blossomed, Conroy's dealings with the lower clergy in Quebec became increasingly strained. An opposition movement sprang up in Montreal and eventually encompassed all areas of the province, gaining momentum after the publication of the joint pastoral on Catholic liberalism in October 1877 and especially after the delegate's public exegesis of the document. Conroy's resolution of the complex university question only confirmed the clerical dissidents' worst fears.

They were convinced that the delegate's actions amounted to a disavowal of the joint pastoral of 1875 and a public exoneration of the Liberal party which, they pointed out, had done nothing to repudiate dangerous doctrines and malevolent men. Conroy had rehabilitated the leaders of Quebec liberalism, the Laflammes, Doutres, Dessaulles, Huntingtons, Lauriers, and Langeliers. He whitewashed their attempts to deceive the people with crafty arguments designed to subvert the spirit of religion and nationality. He put the friends and enemies of the nation on the same footing. But who could deny that from its very inception the party of liberalism had fought against the survival of French Canada by espousing the principle of representation by population? And was not the conservative party the party of order, of respect and submission to the church, of religion and nationality? Yet, when the clergy fought against pernicious political doctrines that trespassed upon the moral sphere, 'Mgr Conroy semble ... nous faire croire que nous avons combattu un fantôme.' They accused the Irish prelate of muzzling the Catholic press. No longer able to deal with political issues from a religious perspective, these newspapers became 'une institution où l'on traite uniquement de finances et de nouvelles à sensations.'

These sentiments were undoubtedly shared by a great many clergymen. One memorandum was signed by forty-three priests from the diocese of Montreal and the Collège de St-Hyacinthe. Another had no less than 106 signatures. Underlying the clergy's overtly political concerns was a deep-seated French-Canadian nationalist reaction. They felt that the delegate was insensitive to the special status of Quebec as a French and overwhelmingly Catholic province within Confederation, fundamentally different from Ontario or, for that matter, Ireland. 'Mgr Conroy semble n'avoir sous les yeux que les instructions données à nos Gouverneurs à une certaine époque, dans le but de nous protestantiser ...' He failed to realize that the Catholic church was totally free in Quebec, which was described as 'le boulevard du catholicisme dans la confédération de l'Amérique Britannique du Nord,' and that its rights were universally recognized. Not even the fanatical designs of some British ministers had prevailed against these truths.

The document further maintained that, in order to preserve Quebec's special character, it was necessary to demand rights guaranteed by the constitution, not to beg favours. If the delegate did not understand these realities, it was because he had not grown up with them. 'Peut-il dans l'espace de quelques mois mieux connaître notre pays que des Evêques qui y ont vécu et qui y ont suivi depuis leur jeunesse, la marche des idées.' From San Francisco, Conroy had had the temerity to dictate the episcopate's actions during the provincial election of 1878, 'comme si à plus de quatre cent mille milles [sic] de distance, il pouvait mieux juger des circonstances, que ceux qui se trouvent sur les lieux!'[18] That slip of the pen spoke reams about the state of alienation of the Quebec clergy. They firmly maintained that Conroy's mission was a failure.

It is clear that the apostolic delegate considered the political question to be his highest priority and he devoted to it his best energies. His final report to the Propaganda is a reflection of this concern. It is essentially an incisive analysis of the Canadian political situation.

According to Conroy, the thirst for wealth was the moving force behind Canadian politics: 'He who succeeds in getting himself seated, as a Minister, at the banquet of the nation, becomes rich. He who does not belong to the winning party stays poor. Thus in Canada, perhaps more than anywhere else, it is common for a politician to go from one party to another for reasons of personal interest.'[19] In such a process, political ideas were not so much an end in themselves as a means to achieve election. Once elected, however, politicians who wanted power were compelled to form alliances with the most disparate political groups. This is what made Canadian politics so utterly bewildering. Parties were in effect strange combinations of antagonistic elements.[20] Thus, depending on which particular faction an observer had in mind, it was possible to express the most varied and even contradictory opinions on political parties, each opinion being correct in its own right.

But a proper assessment of the situation could only come from looking at the political party as a whole, not at one of its parts. Unfortunately, the reverse was all too common a tendency in Canada.[21] Conroy warned that partial descriptions, like inadequate definitions, inevitably led to error. He then turned to Canadian political history to try to evaluate the tendencies of the two parties as moral entities.

Conroy found some very bad elements in the Liberal party, particularly in its early years of existence.[22] The Grits (partito Grito!) had been fanatical opponents of the Catholic church. Their Quebec counterparts, Papineau's Liberal Democrats, were unbelievers and anti-clericals who looked for inspiration to the blood-stained Europe of 1848. This political current was still very much alive within the party and even had a spokesman in the cabinet in the person of Rodolphe Laflamme. This politician's private life could scarcely be described as Christian and in the public sphere he was a shameless champion of anti-clericalism and Gallicanism. He and his associates made the Guibord affair a *cause célèbre*. 'His companions on that and other occasions vomited the most lurid blasphemies against the Church, the Papacy, and the Clergy.'[23] Conroy admitted, however, that these elements had become more moderate in recent years. But the Liberal party also contained another bad strain, the Liberal Catholics of the Montalembert school.[24] And it was against these last two currents that the Quebec clergy unleashed their well-deserved hostility.

Within the party, however, there were also orthodox Catholics, men such as former Conservative Joseph Cauchon, who exemplified the inconstancy of partisan attachments by following Fortune's star into the Liberal fold. Another was the Commons Speaker, Timothy Anglin. In the face of a House generally hostile to Catholicism, this exemplary Catholic always began daily prayers with the sign of the cross recited in Latin. Well-intentioned Protestants formed a significant element within the party, and in Ontario they were responsible for sheltering the church from the attacks of Conservative Orangemen. This explained why Ontario Catholics largely supported the Liberals. The heterogeneity of political parties was reflected as well in public opinion which, despite regional, religious, or ethnic boundaries, was fairly evenly divided between the two political groups. 'Thus,' maintained Conroy, 'the party, as an organization, does not assume responsibility for the erroneous doctrines of some of its members, when these errors have been removed from the party's platform.'[25]

The delegate's conclusion was that neither party 'had a monopoly of virtue or political orthodoxy.'[26] There was good and bad in each, and the learned bishop cited Horace to prove his point: 'Et intra Iliacos muros peccatur, et extra' (And there was sin both inside and outside the walls of Troy).[27] Conroy repeated Dufferin's opinion that neither party was interested in fighting the church; but by the same token either would not hesitate to sacrifice Catholic interests if political advantage so dictated. But the irony of Canadian politics, according to the Irish prelate, was that the church's security lay in this competition for political power, which guaranteed that extremist elements could never achieve their objectives. 'This is so true, that before 1841 when there was no Parliament French Catholics were treated as slaves by their English masters. But from the time that the parliamentary system began to operate ... Canadian history is a story of the continuous progress of Religion.'[28] Given this situation, Catholics still had an obligation to denounce political error and resist any attacks against the church. By the same token, however, they were perfectly free to vote for whatever party they felt would advance Canada's prosperity.

Unfortunately, the Quebec church was not guided by such a prudent view of things. Clerical opposition to the Liberal party sprang from a number of sources, including personal interest, nationalist ideology, but especially from a concern over its anti-clerical faction. Thus a holy war had been unleashed. 'From the pulpit, in the confessional, in religious newspapers, in Pastoral Letters, the Catholic Clergy for many years ceaselessly has denounced the Liberal Party as impious, without distinguishing the good from the bad, and without attention to the heterogeneity of the elements which make up the party.'[29] Quebec was the only place in Canada where politics had become a religious question and this holy war fed the extremist wings of both political parties.

The clergy had clearly gone beyond the bounds of reason in their political activities. Conroy cited two examples of this behaviour. In the diocese of Rimouski, where a law professor from Laval University was seeking election as a Liberal, Langevin had told the faithful that they could not vote Liberal without offending God. Similar opinions, the delegate noted, were found in the Montreal newspaper *Franc Parleur*. In both dioceses it was common practice for priests actually to deny absolution to penitents, unless they first promised never again to vote Liberal. Was it not unwise, Conroy asked, to make it a sin to support a political party backed by half the electorate? And was it not incongruous that what in one province was considered a sin was not in another?

Conroy's report dealt in some detail with the incidents surrounding the 1876 Jacques Cartier by-election. On that occasion the parish priests of the district, after consulting their bishop, adopted a common policy regarding penitents who voted for Rodolphe Laflamme. They agreed to question in detail penitents who supported 'dangerous candidates.' Confessors would assume that penitents could not invoke good faith in their defence because of the clergy's repeated warnings against Catholic liberalism. 'Puis ... on leur fera comprendre leur tort en toute douceur et fermeté, et on exigera qu'ils s'engagent à faire mieux à l'avenir avant de recevoir l'absolution.'[30] As a result of this common policy, twelve men were refused absolution. These appealed to Fabre, who in the end absolved them. Conroy considered the parish priests' behaviour bad enough, but he noted that they then had the temerity to ask their bishop to explain himself and even accused him in scarcely veiled, but certainly outrageously disrespectful, terms of being a liberal. The delegate vowed to put an end to such excesses.

The six parish priests did try to justify themselves to Conroy. They informed the delegate that they were not novices to political campaigns and although they always had reservations about the Liberal party – less trustworthy in their eyes than the Conservatives – they had never opposed a Liberal's election. They only did so when Laflamme first ran for office in 1872. At that time the candidate presented two contradictory images of himself. Before Catholic audiences he spoke as a man of good faith, whose principles were harmless to the interests of religion. He even promised to withdraw from the Institut canadien, a promise which subsequently he showed no hurry to fulfil. Before his Rouge supporters, however, he boasted of being the man of *Le Pays*, *l'Avenir*, and of the Guibord affair. During the campaign parish priests were very careful to mention no one by name in their admonitions to the faithful. When Laflamme was elected, Bourget advised confessors to withhold absolution from his supporters, unless they showed signs of repentence. Despite these punitive measures, the parish priests assured Conroy that the number of communicants had not decreased.

But they stressed that, after being elected, Laflamme continued to show bad faith. He only withdrew from the Institut a few short weeks before the elections of 1874. During that campaign he pandered to Catholic interests, yet a year later he was the prime instigator behind attempts to have the provincial election annulled in Jacques Cartier because of undue clerical influence. He whipped up Protestant feeling against the Catholic clergy and played up his Rouge connections by showing himself in the company of Joseph Doutre. Still, in the 1876 by-election the clergy again refrained from mentioning anyone by name in the pulpit. 'Plus nous comparons notre règle avec la Théologie de St-Liguori moins nous pensons avoir eu tort en l'adoptant,' they concluded.[31]

Conroy had in hand other documents surrounding this question, which make it clear that the clergy applied the same rule to Laflamme's supporters as to other public or habitual sinners; such as moneylenders, tavern-keepers who operated their establishments on Sundays or without a licence, or those who frequented 'dangerous' dances condemned by the bishop. In all of these cases, penitents were required to show true repentence before receiving absolution.[32] Sinners were not being refused the sacraments because of the way they had voted, insisted the clerics, but because of their refusal to show true repentence.[33] Exclusion from the sacraments was even being used by some laymen to political advantage. The parish priests cited the example of some parishioners who, having received absolution from Fabre, rudely and ostentatiously paraded themselves before the public either as headstrong opponents of the local clergy or as friends of a bishop who would not support his own clergy on this question.[34]

These documents also suggest that Fabre's conduct in the whole affair was far from clear. To the parish priests who asked for direction, the bishop, repeating Liguori, replied that confessors should look to the conscience of the penitent, not to the wrongs of the political candidate. With care and in the spirit of charity, they had to distinguish the leper from leprosy, sin from the sinner. Excommunications and the use of the pulpit for personal denunciations were neither wise nor prudent.[35] But writing to some laymen three weeks later, Fabre stated that it was difficult to forgive those who knowingly voted for a party that advocated bad principles. He added, rather enigmatically, 'Le libéral catholique et le parti libéral canadien sont deux choses distinctes mais il peut arriver que le programme, les projets, les argumens [sic] etc d'un parti politique soient tellement remplis des erreurs du Libéralisme que l'on soit naturellement porté à considérer ce parti comme une personnification de cette erreur.' [36] The bishop took the opportunity to remind these men that reading anti-clerical newspapers was strictly forbidden. Conroy did not comment on Fabre's conduct except to say that he had shown remarkable restraint and kindness. Still, the delegate expressed grave concerns for the future of religion in Canada if clerical abuse of religion was not firmly suppressed.

SMEULDERS AND THE 'STATE OF QUEBEC'

In the five years that separated the Conroy and Smeulders missions, the political question was simply not the point of contention it had been earlier. For one thing, the cardinal prefect of Propaganda kept the Quebec clergy tightly in line, firmly discouraging initiatives that might in any way revive the ire of the Liberal party. For another, the Liberals were no longer in office either provincially or federally. As for the Conservatives, they were spared the agony of divisive 'national or religious' issues for well over another decade. (The Riel Rebellion of 1885 would not rally some members of the upper clergy as had the Red River uprising in 1869.)[37] These factors would be decisive in shaping the Smeulders mission. It is important to bear in mind that the apostolic commissioner was not sent to Canada at the request of politicians, as was the case with Conroy. His had none of the diplomatic trappings of the Irish bishop's visit. Smeulders was not wined and dined by vice-regal officials in Ottawa and Quebec City, nor was he courted by interested politicians.

Consequently his perspective was different from that of his Irish predecessor. According to the Belgian prelate, the danger threatening Canadian political parties came from politico-religious liberalism which, while not as bad as its doctrinaire counterpart, certainly was just as dangerous. He cited the recent history of Belgium to show that in time and through various artifices this milder form of liberalism became the vehicle for the triumph of the doctrinaire variety.[38] Although extremist liberals were not numerous in Quebec, Smeulders believed that they did exist. France was the social model they were trying to replicate on the banks of the St Lawrence. These admirers of modern French culture revered the name of Prime Minister Léon Gambetta and his slogan; 'Le cléricalisme, voilà l'ennemi.' By their skilful manipulation of Catholic liberals who were more numerous and influential in Quebec, they had succeeded in muzzling Catholic authors and newspapers and in spreading doubt and indifference among the supporters of the Catholic cause.[39]

But who were these Catholic liberals? They were men like Joseph Cauchon. The apostolic commissioner was shocked by this politician's cynical use of religion for partisan purposes. After being appointed lieutenant-governor of Manitoba in 1877, Cauchon apparently boasted in public of the enormous influence he wielded over the Roman Curia thanks to his clerical friends in Quebec City. The ex-politician had the temerity to suggest that Conroy's report simply repeated arguments he himself had made to Rome. He admitted that it had been difficult getting the delegate to 'swallow' Laflamme; but all went smoothly once he persuaded the *enfant terrible* to make a public profession of his Catholic faith. For his stunning victory over the Quebec episcopate, it was rumoured that anti-clericals had dubbed Cauchon the theologian of the Liberal party, while Mackenzie himself thanked him for resolving 'Quebec's ecclesiastical problems.'[40] Although a practising Catholic, Cauchon allowed himself to be a tool of blindly partisan and even anti-clerical men who sought to keep the church under control and who at the same time failed to uphold Catholic rights in Canada. This was the stuff with which Catholic liberals were made. By undermining the church's influence, Smeulders believed, such men were paving the way for the advent of a secular society.

Smeulders's perspective was predicated on the belief that Quebec enjoyed a special position in Confederation: the province had the power to act fully independently from the federal government in matters involving religion and education. As a result, he came to share the view that the 'State of Quebec' could make its laws conform in all respects to the prescriptions of the Catholic church without danger and without difficulty.[41] He believed as well that Quebec politicians stood ready to introduce such reforms.

But the Taschereau faction, for whatever reason, was blocking the objective of an officially Catholic state in Quebec. In the university question, for example, Laval sheltered academics who justified the anti-national and anti-Catholic stances of prominent politicians, particularly in such questions as New Brunswick schools, the Red River rebellion, and undue electoral influence. Smeulders could only conclude that Taschereau and his advisers 'directly and indirectly, and perhaps unconscious of the danger, either were promoting Liberalism and Freemasonry which covertly were infiltrating society, or at the very least they were not sufficiently resisting their spread.'[42] In other words, the archdiocese of Quebec had become an instrument of liberalism.

And in their obstinacy, they cut themselves off from the over-whelming majority of the Catholic population. The apostolic commissioner was struck during his brief stay in the provincial capital by the isolation of archdiocesan institutions. Smeulders explained why this was so. 'The Archbishop and the Gentlemen from Laval attribute this antipathy to [their opponents'] lack of education and to their not keeping up with the daily progress of civilization; be that as it may, it seems to me that not all of them are asses, especially considering the quality of the people concerned. These include top men on the bench and in the legal profession, lawyers of the highest reputation who completed with distinction their courses in Rome etc. etc. I would rather be inclined to say: "Vox populi, vox dei".' [43]

THE RETURN OF POLITICS

The issue of clerical intervention in politics subsided briefly, but returned with a vengeance when legislation to reinstate Catholic educational rights in Manitoba became a focus of the federal election of 1896. As we have seen, the Propaganda fully supported the restoration of minority rights, but Cardinal Ledochowski expressed concerns over the sanctions which the Quebec bishops wished to impose on those who would not follow their electoral directives. Anxious to allay the cardinal's fears, the archbishop of Quebec justified the stance taken by the hierarchy in their pastoral letter of 1896. The fact was, he stressed, that the Manitoba government was implacably hostile to its Catholic minority. In this context, a negotiated settlement with Manitoba, the course favoured by the Liberals, would only leave the minority prey to further administrative harassment and arbitrariness by the province. The only sure way of restoring Catholic education in the province was remedial legislation. The difficulty, he recognized, was that since only one political party, the Conservatives, supported such a measure, the hierarchy appeared to be taking a partisan position in the elections. But, Bégin continued, it was the Liberals, not the hierarchy, who made Manitoba schools a political issue. The party had sought by every device to embarrass a government honestly intent on passing remedial legislation.[44]

The English-speaking bishops, however, dissociated themselves from this movement. The Ontario hierarchy feared that by adhering to the collective pastoral, they would arouse the sleeping giant of anti-Catholicism in their midst. They were also concerned that such action might alienate a not unfriendly provincial Liberal government. Their Maritime colleagues, for their part, were equally quiescent.[45] Even some members of the Quebec hierarchy had been reticent and it took some hard lobbying to convince Fabre and his suffragan, Médard Emard of Valleyfield, about the opportunity of collective action. When the letter was finally drafted, however, Fabre expressed full satisfaction that the clergy's action was not motivated by partisan interests. 'Nous voulions non seulement dégager l'idée religieuse de l'idée politique, mais encore donner aux chefs des deux partis l'occasion de remplir leurs promesses respectives et d'exécuter leur programme.'[46] Emard, on the other hand, still harboured deep doubts about the effects of the letter to which he subscribed under pressure. In his isolation, he sought solace and possibly a justification of his position from Rome.[47]

Clerical involvement in the 1896 campaign has been exhaustively and competently analysed elsewhere.[48] But in order to place this question in the broader context of the history of undue spiritual influence, it might be useful to dwell briefly on some aspects. The archdiocese of Quebec asked local Liberal candidates to sign a declaration formally committing them to remedial legislation according to the terms of the Privy Council decision. The declaration stipulated that when such legislation was again introduced, it would have to meet with the episcopate's prior approval. The pledge ended with these words: 'Si Mr Laurier arrive au pouvoir et ne règle pas cette question dès la première session conformément au mandement, je m'engage soit à lui retirer mon appui ou à résigner.'[49]

Asked whether Catholics could vote for candidates who refused to sign this declaration, Vicar General Marois, speaking in Bégin's name, replied: 'Si quelqu'un vous dit: en dépit de vos raisonnements, j'ai plus de confiance en Mr Laurier et je vote pour son candidat ... cet électeur à moins d'avoir perdu le sens commun sera coupable de faute grave et par conséquent mortelle.'[50] Unfortunately, one of the recipients of this letter read it from the pulpit to his parishioners. He was promptly chastised by a mortified Marois, who reminded him that the hierarchy strictly forbade any public comments on the joint pastoral. The vicar general added, however, that the priest could use the letter to give his parishioners *private* advice, since candidates were not mentioned in it by name.[51] In any case, he strongly emphasized the fact that priests could not say that it was a serious sin to vote for a candidate, no matter how dubious his past, who committed himself to Bégin's declaration.[52] The archbishop made his own perspective on the clergy's role in the election quite plain:

Je ne veux ni approuver ni répudier les candidats qui briguent les suffrages des électeurs: ce n'est pas mon rôle ... En adhérant *formellement et solennellement* à ce document vous ne pouvez être ostracisé par les électeurs catholiques ni être réputé indigne de leurs suffrages.[53]

The clergy's behaviour in the archdiocese of Quebec was typical of what went on in other parts of the province, except in Trois-Rivières where Laflèche denounced the 'rationalist' Laurier from the pulpit.

A few weeks later Bégin reported that the elections had gone smoothly and only a few priests compromised themselves by overtly partisan behaviour.[54] It is clear, however, that clerical intervention in politics was a two-way street. Bishop Moreau, for example, was indignant at Emard's attempts to undermine the joint pastoral letter. He accused his colleague of letting his personal political preferences determine his moral assessment of the issues.[55] Certainly Emard's predilection for Laurier was transparent when he commented on the results of the elections: 'Au fond, la préoccupation la plus générale des Canadiens français (la question du Manitoba étant mise de côté, par l'adhésion au mandement) a été de donner le pouvoir à l'un des leurs, ce qui arrive pour la première fois depuis la Confédération. Et peut-on faire de cela un crime?'[56]

Despite Emard's strong intellectual qualities and his concise, rigorous, and logical exposition against collective episcopal action,[57] his unabashed excitement at 'this unique event' in Canadian history may have made him insensitive to the soundness of his colleagues' actions. But Emard was not alone. Laflèche confided that more than half of the young clergy in the Quebec City area were 'grands admirateurs du rationaliste et libéral Wilfrid Laurier.'[58]

But it was the Laurier-Greenway agreement that marked a definite break between the Quebec hierarchy and the newly elected government. Laflèche did not mince words. He described the accord as the Liberals' 'applatissement devant le fanatisme protestant et libre penseur ... [qui a] rendu leur trahison religieuse et nationale si évidente qu'il[s] ... pourrai[en]t fort bien ... passer du Capitole à la roche tarpéienne.'[59] Bégin believed that the accord sanctioned the federal government's alliance with the mighty against the weak and oppressed. 'Il n'était pas nécessaire d'aller faire semblant de négocier si longtemps à Winnipeg pour arriver à ce minuscule compromis.' Whatever tiny concessions had been wrested from Manitoba could be revoked at any time, he thought, by this government known for its hostility to Catholic rights.[60]

Archbishop Fabre's funeral in January 1897 gave the Canadian hierarchy an opportunity to discuss their reactions to the agreement. Once again, it was the Quebec episcopate that arrived at a common position. Among other things, the bishops were concerned about the constitutional position of Catholics in the wake of the Laurier-Greenway agreement. They pointed out that the educational provisions of the 1870 Manitoba Act had been formulated to protect Protestants who then constituted a minority. Now that Protestants were a majority, had these provisions suddenly become invalid? 'Y aurait-il donc, deux poids et deux mesures?' The Quebec bishops endorsed a declaration repudiating the accord as a desertion of the Catholic minority and a legal justification for the violation of established rights. They deplored the fact that Catholics no longer had the control and administration of their schools and that religion had lost its central place in the curriculum. The bishops, however, agreed to defer publication of the document until after the pope issued his long-

awaited encyclical. Bégin reassured Rome that the episcopal statement was moderate in tone: it threatened no one and made no
political allusions.[61] Laflèche saw it as a much-needed support for
Archbishop Langevin who 'comme un autre Jean Baptiste ... a dit à
ces deux Chefs du Gouvernement de Manitoba et d'Ottawa: *Non
licet*. Il ne vous est pas permis de vous emparer ainsi des enfants
Catholiques!'[62]

MERRY DEL VAL AND THE REALITIES OF CANADIAN
POLITICAL LIFE

Merry del Val stepped into this confrontational situation, with directives from Rome to end once and for all the clergy's political excesses.
As with Conroy, his mission was essentially diplomatic. Consequently the government spared no effort in orchestrating a lavish
reception for the pope's representative. It seemed like a replay of the
Conroy mission twenty years earlier. Merry del Val was met at the
Ottawa train station by the secretary of state, Richard Scott, who as
architect of the separate school system in Ontario was a very astute
choice for the occasion. The following day he received a visit from
Laurier and they talked at length. The delegate obviously was
flattered by the amount of time the prime minister granted him. In
the next few days he had the opportunity of dining with all the
ministers of the crown.

But the papal envoy was particularly impressed by the solicitude
of the governor general, Lord Aberdeen. 'Upon hearing of my arrival
in Ottawa, he dispatched his aide-de-camp to invite me immediately
to dinner ... In his courtesy he went so far as to offer with great
insistence that I should reside in his palace; and yesterday he came
to get me in his carriage to give me the opportunity to speak freely of
my mission. For the public, particularly for English Protestants, this
demonstration on the part of the governor is of no small consequence
since it holds up high the prestige of the Holy See.'[63]

The delegate attached a great deal of importance to his visit to
Toronto and provincial Liberals did not disappoint him. Merry del
Val told the Secretary of State, Cardinal Rampolla, that the official
welcome organized by the government of Ontario surprised everyone. It was, he considered, a great triumph for Archbishop Walsh,
who only a few years earlier had been greeted 'with stones' when
taking possession of his archdiocese. Not only had the premier of this

most Protestant province held a banquet in the Parliament buildings in the delegate's honour, at which the most prominent citizens were invited, but the assembled guests applauded when Merry del Val mentioned the pope's name.[64] Even the lieutenant-governor of the province had invited him to dinner.

The *bons mots*, the good fare and heady wines, however, were merely a prelude to serious business. Merry del Val set about to defuse the potentially explosive relationship between the Quebec church and the Laurier government, by taking the Laurier-Greenway accord as the basis for an eventual understanding. His position in this was much closer to that of the government which declared in the speech from the throne of 1897 that the arrangement was the best possible under the circumstances, than to that of the Quebec bishops, who rejected it outright. Subsequent negotiations on improvements to the agreement coloured the delegate's perspective on Canadian politics. As a result, Merry del Val's report to Rome does not contain that historical perspective, that breadth of vision, found in Conroy's.

Both delegates nevertheless shared a number of common assumptions about Canadian politics. They emphasized the extreme heterogeneity of political parties. According to Merry del Val, it was because the Liberals had been out of power for so long that they were an even more diversified group than the Conservatives. Like Conroy, he admitted that there were dubious elements within the Liberal fold, doctrinaire men of the European variety. He accepted the commonly held opinion that Laurier himself was not a practising Catholic. But the delegate argued that on questions of principle, the prime minister sinned more from a lack of religious instruction and blind partisanship than from malice: 'They say that thus far he has always shown himself to be both upright and a gentleman.'[65] The delegate shared Conroy's view that, while there was a larger number of respectable men within Conservative ranks, good Catholics could be found in both political groupings.[66] But the fundamental fact of Canadian life remained Protestant domination of both political parties, which meant that Catholic interests were not secure in either. Consequently he repeated Conroy's admonition that the church not identify itself publicly with any one political party.

Unfortunately, however, this is precisely what the Quebec episcopate wanted to do. Merry del Val saw a continuity between the current crisis and those that had shaken the Quebec church in previous years. The Manitoba schools question was simply an extension of earlier controversies. In the past 'Cardinal Taschereau with his prudence and energy and with the support of the Holy See succeeded in subduing emotions and imposing a distinction between religion and political interests, despite the violent opposition of the Bishop of Trois-Rivières and others. Now that he has disappeared from the scene, efforts are being made to destroy his achievements.'[67]

The Quebec episcopate, lamented the delegate, now were blind instruments of the Conservative party and were generally perceived to be acting solely in its interests. Indeed, the bishops' relationship with the party was so totally symbiotic that he confessed being unable to rely on their discretion or collaboration. Party people very often articulated positions taken by Quebec bishops, which were then presented as official church documents. Merry del Val had been shocked in this regard to find in the Montreal archdiocesan archives drafts of the 1896 joint pastoral which had actually been written by some politician. Even the Roman correspondence of the learned archbishop of Quebec was in some instances nothing more than the writings of rabidly partisan men such as Senators Philippe Landry and Thomas Bernier.[68] By the same token, any private discussion of controversial matters by the clergy uncannily found its way into the party press or some politician's speech.

The bishops, Merry del Val went on to say, lived in an imaginary world totally cut off from the reality which surrounded them.

They do not understand that in a constitutional and parliamentary system ... in which many opposing religious, political, and commercial interests are ceaselessly being debated and where because of contacts with the United States and continuous relations with Europe modern ideas and aspirations, good and bad, are ever more being disseminated, it is not possible for a Bishop or Parish Priest to succeed in imposing on politicians from the pulpit or the confessional the programme which they must follow.[69]

In any event, the delegate stated that he had no intention of instituting a formal inquiry into the clergy's electoral wrongdoings for fear of stirring up a hornet's nest. But he took the trouble to document the more spectacular cases of what he termed 'untheological behaviour' which threw many consciences into profound turmoil.

Bishop Labrècque of Chicoutimi, for example, required that absolution be withheld from those reading certain Liberal newspapers, which were not formally condemned either in his or any other diocese. He even ordered his priests to carry out investigations at the post office as to their subscribers' identity in order to question them more effectively in the confessional. The diocesan clergy were also forbidden, under pain of suspension, from saying anything that could be construed as a justification of the Laurier-Greenway agreement. Apart from the extreme severity and imprudence of these measures, Merry del Val stressed the incongruousness of an act being a sin in one diocese and not in another.

For his part, Archbishop Langevin intimidated penitents who voted Liberal in the 1896 election by imposing upon them a formula which contravened theological precepts. This formula which was leaked to the press read as follows: 'M. X regrette le passé et est bien disposé à demander conseil à son archevêque, désormais, dans les circonstances où la conscience catholique est concernée. Tout prêtre peut l'entendre en confession.' The last sentence in particular was untenable because it restricted the right of each penitent to lay bare the state of his conscience.[70]

Bishop Cameron of Antigonish had his parish priests warn the faithful from the pulpit that they were obliged in conscience to vote for the Conservative candidate in the 1896 election. In Heatherton forty parishioners walked out of the church when this statement was read. Cameron required that before the protesters could be readmitted to the sacraments, they sign a retraction in which they admitted having given public scandal. Yet the delegate had positive assurances that these men were all honest and practising Catholics.

Merry del Val cited Laflèche's tempestuous denunciations of Laurier during the federal campaign, as well as Vicar-General Marois's electoral admonitions, as other examples of the clergy's total lack of restraint. He insisted, however, that in the face of the Canadian episcopate's internal divisions over Manitoba schools, such stringent measures were simply uncalled for. They were dictated not by theology, but by personal or local interests, by political or nationalist passions.[71] The remedy to these excesses was greater episcopal unity under the wise guidance of the Holy See and of the more prudent members of the Canadian hierarchy.

The archbishop of Quebec replied to these allegations on behalf of his colleagues in the French-Canadian church in a long memorandum addressed to the Propaganda. Bégin claimed that Merry del Val accused the Quebec clergy without instituting a proper inquiry and rested his case solely on signed affidavits. Yet what weight could be attached to these declarations which were made by men 'auxquels le parjure est aussi naturel que le mensonge, quand ils sont aveuglés par la passion et l'esprit de parti'?[72] Bégin gave the example of two such affidavits forwarded to him by the delegate during the 1897 provincial election with a request that they formally be investigated. When the archbishop summoned the plaintiffs to his diocesan court, they confessed that their accusations against two priests were false. The archbishop admitted that there had been some clerical interference in the electoral process in the past; but such incidents were isolated and the episcopate always attended to them. Bégin added that these cases usually involved priests who favoured the Liberal party, which certainly did not prevent the latter from making political capital by holding the clergy constantly responsible for their electoral failures.

Bégin characterized as totally gratuitous Merry del Val's contention that the bishops were manipulated by the Conservatives: 'c'est le fait de ces hommes trop aveuglés eux-mêmes par l'esprit de parti pour ne pas comprendre que des évêques puissent n'être pas pris du même aveuglement.'[73] Apart from the Manitoba schools question, the Quebec episcopate had never had anything to do with political parties. And he stressed that their intervention in the 1896 election was not inspired by partisan motives. What they sought instead was 'de jeter dans la balance parlementaire un vote catholique compact' to redress the wrongs done to Manitoba Catholics. The episcopate's impartiality during the campaign was recognized by the partisan press. Only after their victory did the Liberals take off their masks. 'Mais avant les élections, il fallait simuler le respect aux évêques et l'obéissance pour capter le vote catholique; le vote obtenu, on calomniait sciemment les intentions des évêques pour les amoindrir et les discréditer et se donner un prétexte de ne tenir nul compte de leurs réclamations.'[74] The archbishop even defended Laflèche's intervention in the campaign, the sole purpose of which was to get Laurier to repudiate his claim that Catholic politicians could not be bound by Catholic morality in assessing public questions. But it was the venerable bishop's fate to be showered with the grossest insults by the Liberal press.

In a separate document, Archbishop Langevin rejected the delegate's accusations that he had denied the sacraments to those who had voted Liberal in the St Boniface by-election of 1897. He explained that he had simply requested these penitents to see him in order that he might give them his point of view. Langevin stressed that the sacraments were only withheld from those who tried to have elections annulled on the grounds of undue spiritual influence.[75]

Since Merry del Val had not taken the trouble to investigate allegations of clerical misconduct, Bégin concluded that the delegate, not the Quebec hierarchy, was the blind instrument of political manipulation on the part of Russell, Fitzpatrick, and Laurier. The supposedly impartial men consulted by the papal envoy 'étaient appointés par des chefs libéraux et payés fort cher pour servir leurs intérêts.'[76] Bégin also turned around Merry del Val's comments about the Quebec episcopate's lack of discretion. 'Tous cependant ne signeraient pas des deux mains le certificat d'absolue discrétion qu'il s'octroie.'[77] The archbishop noted that the contents of supposedly secret documents were known by laymen in minute detail, as were the broad outlines of the delegate's report even before it was submitted to Rome.

Bégin noted that Catholics were the victims of a Protestant campaign to homogenize the country. And where were the Liberals in this campaign? There was a current within the French-Canadian wing of the party 'qui n'a jamais eu de sympathies actives que pour les idées protestantes et les intérêts protestants.'[78] What seemed to escape the attention of the apostolic delegate was that within the Liberal party hostility to the church, its institutions, and to Christian ideas generally came from among Catholic members. It was no use saying then that there were bad elements within both political groupings: the Conservatives had their Orangemen and the Liberals their doctrinaire elements. 'Si l'on veut avoir une notion vraie des deux partis, il faut comparer protestants à protestants, catholiques à catholiques, et parti à parti – et non point les protestants d'un parti aux catholiques qui sont dans l'autre. C'est ce que S. Ex. a eu l'habilité de ne pas faire. Il n'est pas toujours plus difficile d'être habile que d'être sérieux et sincère.'[79]

Of course, Bégin agreed that there were excellent Catholics within Liberal ranks and that the party could not be held responsible for the errors of individual members. But when such errors were committed by the 'partie active et dirigeante' of the organization which itself consistently declined to disavow them, was not the party as such at fault? Bégin questioned the good faith of the Liberals' change of heart toward the church since 1876. For while they publicly proclaimed their fidelity to the institution, and covered themselves with Taschereau's good words, they also openly displayed their old anti-religious spirit on a number of occasions. But Bégin assured the Propaganda that his predecessor never said what the Liberals so casually attributed to him. In stating that the Liberal party as such was not condemned by the church, Taschereau never meant to imply that the party was free of dangereous tendencies. 'Il n'a jamais nié ni méconnu que ce parti est le rendez-vous ordinaire des utopistes, des déséquilibrés, des doctrinaires et des impies de tout le pays ... et que tous les dangers pour l'avenir religieux du pays viendront de ce côté-là.'[80]

If, then, Bégin kept his distance from the Liberal party, it was not out of blind partisanship. '[Il ne s'est] jamais laissé conduire ni aveuglement ni les yeux ouverts par aucun chef politique.' It was rather out of a long experience which proved to him that its leaders were capable 'de toutes les fourberies et de toutes les trahisons.'[81] In the past the episcopate failed to act against certain Liberal leaders and their press for fear that their actions would be widely interpreted as a condemnation of the whole party. But episcopal indulgence only encouraged the spread of bad principles and movements.

The archbishop assured Rome that he subscribed to such constitutional truths as the need for a bipartisan system and to such practical realities as the expediency and even necessity for Catholics to participate in both political parties. He did not believe in the formation of a Catholic party, which would only provoke the hostility of the Protestant majority. At the same time, Catholics who became involved in one political grouping should not abandon their Catholic ideas, otherwise they could not expect the electorate to support them.

Merry del Val's report essentially indicted the episcopates of Quebec and Manitoba who constituted, Bégin reminded Rome, fully two-thirds of the bishops of Canada. These prelates 'pour être français, ne manquent absolument ni de vertu, ni d'expérience, ni de sens pratique et ont été choisis par le Saint-Siège pour faire autre chose que des sottises.'[82] The Holy See should then encourage and work closely with these active elements in the defence of Catholic rights in Canada, instead of with the forces that traditionally were hostile to the church and advanced Protestant interests.

In the end, Bégin wondered, what were the concrete results of Merry del Val's mission to Canada? 'Toutes les négociations du

Délégué ... n'ont abouti qu'à des paroles doucereuses, à des dîners, à des réceptions brillantes, à des protestations intéressées de religion ... se heurtant à l'impossibilité de faire davantage.'[83]

FALCONIO: THE END OF CLERICAL POWER?

When the first permanent apostolic delegate arrived in Canada, the archbishop of Quebec repeated his advice that Falconio work with, and not against, the episcopate.[84] Only then would the delegate's mission be successful. In this the archbishop was simply reflecting the general wariness with which his Quebec colleagues viewed the establishment of a permanent delegation. Falconio for his part was just as chary in taking up his new posting, forewarned as he had been about the clergy's political eccentricities. Undue spiritual influence was certainly an important item in his first major report to the Propaganda, but it took the form of a suggestion that in view of the upcoming elections of 1900, the Holy See might wish to repeat long-standing directives against clerical interference.[85]

The climate of crisis which had marked Merry del Val's mission was largely dissipated by the time of Falconio's arrival, and this facilitated the delegate's relations with the Quebec clergy. Falconio may not have agreed with the French-Canadian episcopate about the moral worth of Canada's major political parties,[86] nor about the dangers which threatened the Catholic church in this country.[87] There is also no doubt that he viewed the Laurier government as favourably as had his predecessor. The delegate did not hide his delight at the Liberals' re-election in 1900: 'The victory of the Liberal Party headed by a Catholic and a large majority of Catholic MPs makes us hope for better treatment of our holy religion.'[88] Falconio was also convinced of the government's goodwill in attempting to vindicate Catholic rights in Manitoba.[89]

But he did not share Merry del Val's predispositions against the Quebec hierarchy. In the wake of the 1900 elections, he reported that the clergy had generally respected the Holy See's directives, adding that the crushing defeat of episcopal candidates in the preceding election made everyone understand that 'the political power of the clergy had come to an end.'[90] References in his reports to clerical intervention in politics certainly persisted, but they tended to be perfunctory, almost *pro forma*, and limited to pious wishes about its elimination. The climate of extreme tension which had charged

Merry del Val's relations with the Quebec hierarchy over the Manitoba schools was displaced and contained in Falconio's time to the delegation's dealings with the archbishop of St Boniface. The delegate held Langevin in low regard, not least because the archbishop's alleged partisan passions were impeding a settlement of the schools question.[91]

So the issue that erupted with such suddenness on the Canadian political scene in 1876 petered out just as suddenly at the beginning of the new century. Yet it is clear that clerical intervention in politics did not begin in 1876, nor did it end in 1900. A thorough understanding of this phenomenon awaits a larger study which would make more intensive use of local sources, the correspondence of parish clergy, for example, and documents showing the relations between the diocesan bishop and his priests over this issue. What was attempted here was to place the question in some kind of context and, even more important, to try to assess in this quarter-century marked by change the elements of continuity within the Quebec church. Such an assessment in turn facilitates an evaluation of the policies pursued by the Holy See and its Delegates with respect to the Canadian church.

CONCLUSION

The years 1876 and 1896 were high points in the history of undue spiritual influence in Quebec. The first date may be seen as the apogee of the Bourget era, the second as that of the Taschereau era. The literature of the past twenty years on Quebec ultramontanism has tended to represent Bourget and his ally Laflèche as extremist, fringe, and even deranged elements who caused much mischief in the church and society, particularly from the time of the publication of the *programme catholique* in 1871 to the Riel crisis of 1885.[92] By implication, Taschereau appears as a wise and moderating influence who guided the ecclesiastical barque through the stormy politico-religious controversies of the period and whose legacy continued unaltered through his successors, eventually prevailing over the old forces of reaction. Crunican's findings about the clergy's generally moderate behaviour during the general election of 1896 lends weight to this interpretation.[93] In this view historical continuity within Quebec Catholicism passes through Taschereau. Thus 1876 and 1896 are seen as very different, indeed opposite, epochs.

But if we look at the period as a whole rather than focusing on the specific crises that punctuated it, what do we find? We find Taschereau's successor, Nazaire Bégin, sounding in his long memorandum to Rome remarkably like the archdiocese of Quebec's perennial arch-enemy, the 'unbalanced' bishop of Trois-Rivières. In this document, which reads like a *cri de coeur*, it is as if the archbishop recognized that Laflèche had been right all along. Bégin, like Laflèche, defended the integrity of the clergy on the question of undue influence. Both demanded an impartial inquiry to establish the facts; both accused the Liberal party of exploiting religion for political purposes, even to the point of raising the false spectre of sectarian warfare; and both upheld the rights of French Canadians and Catholics when these were under attack. Would it not be more appropriate to say that historical continuity in Quebec Catholicism passes through Bourget and Laflèche? This hypothesis becomes more plausible when we consider the testimony of Persico, Smeulders, and even some arch-diocesan counsellors, who represented Taschereau not as a great helmsman but as one whose course was steered by the prevailing currents, whatever their origin.

Undue spiritual influence at times has been treated as comic opera, as in the case of the writer Robert Rumilly, at times as a terrible blight on the history of the church and society. Still, as Crunican so accurately observed, this issue lends itself easily to alchemy, anecdotes being readily transmuted into fact. But what are the facts? From the documents cited above, it would seem that priests generally did not name candidates from the pulpit, their admonitions to parishioners being couched rather in terms of principle than personality. They did not use the sacraments indiscriminately against the Liberals, only against those candidates deemed dangerous from a doctrinal point of view and their supporters. These men were treated in the same way as public or habitual sinners. Finally, the clergy applied rigorous sanctions against those who read anti-clerical or irreligious newspapers. Of course there were some clerics who diverged from this general rule of conduct. Bégin, like Bourget before him, had to chastise certain zealous priests. Sometimes, too, priests and bishops, such as Jean Langevin, were not called to order when they ought to have been. But clerical involvement in politics was far from an unruly affair, dictated by personal political caprice.

Discussion of this issue as applied to English Canada is at best sporadic. English-speaking bishops, like their French counterparts, claimed to have a right as citizens to express their political opinions.

Some prelates, such as archbishops Connolly and Lynch, did so quite openly at election time. But opinion was one thing and coercion quite another.

Spiritual coercion certainly existed in English Canada. How widespread a phenomenon it was is difficult to establish at this point. Archbishop Lynch's quarrel with the Toronto separate school board has already been cited as evidence. In the late 1880s Archbishop Cleary of Kingston ordered his priests to withhold the sacraments from the supporters of the provincial Conservatives who were accused of trying to do away with Catholic education.[94] Catholics who failed to uphold the separate school system apparently were routinely denied the sacraments by the Ontario hierarchy.[95] As for the Maritimes, Merry del Val himself dealt with Bishop Cameron's intemperate behaviour in the 1896 election, which certainly was not an isolated incident.

Yet the English-speaking bishops who so blatantly practised spiritual coercion were precisely those regarded by Rome and its delegates as exemplary prelates. Bishop Cameron, for instance, had been educated in Rome, was a polyglot, and was esteemed for his theological learning. The Holy See even appointed him apostolic commissioner in the division of the diocese of Trois-Rivières. Archbishop Cleary, for his part, was identified by Merry del Val as one of the few prudent and learned men in the Canadian church. It would then seem that the connection made by Conroy and Merry del Val between clerical interference in politics and lack of theological education was tenuous indeed. In any case, the scattered references to spiritual coercion in English Canada tend to indicate that Quebec was not wildly out of line with what was practised in the rest of the Canadian church.

Why then such a fuss? Clerical intervention in politics stretched back to the beginning of the nineteenth century. Yet it suddenly became an issue in 1876 because of legislation passed two years earlier by the Mackenzie government on undue electoral influence. The Liberals' earlier attempts to woo the clergy by appealing to their nationalism, while partly successful in the beginning, foundered after Mackenzie took office. The government's handling of *la question Manitoba-Brunswick* left some members of the clergy, particularly in the Montreal area, bitter and disillusioned. Legislation on undue influence turned this bitterness into rage and hostility.

A new strategy was called for, one that would accuse the clergy of political interference not in the courts of Canada, but in Rome.

Cauchon was the man for the job. An ex-Conservative with many friends in Archbishop Taschereau's entourage, he gained easy access to the highest officials of the Curia. His testimony was corroborated by the archbishop's counsellors who already enjoyed a solid reputation in Rome. Ignazio Persico clinched these arguments for the Propaganda. Pastor of the Quebec City suburb of Sillery for the three years he remained in Canada, Persico was close to Taschereau's advisers and frequented a number of parish priests who had good friends in the Liberal party. His view was therefore their view. But while the Italian prelate certainly had first-hand experience of Taschereau's foibles since he worked in the archdiocese, his knowledge of the rest of the ecclesiastical province was limited. Persico took his pastoral duties so seriously that he rarely travelled outside his parish. Nevertheless, his testimony on the state of the church in Quebec became the standard version of the facts in Rome.

This version determined the Propaganda's instructions to Bishop Conroy and the direction of his mission. In turn, this version was corroborated by what the delegate saw and heard during his Canadian stay. In the diocese of Montreal Conroy was witness to a chaotic situation brought on by the sudden departure of Bourget and the advent of a weak successor. The ensuing vacuum gave the lower clergy licence to play politics. Conroy held Bourget responsible for these abuses. Yet the Holy See and the delegate could not have it both ways: by forcing Bourget's resignation, they could not blame him for the excesses committed under his successor, who lacked the will or the ability to repress them.

Conroy's perspective, which was largely that of the government was also confirmed by ecclesiastics whose own views were partial or biased. One of the priests consulted by the delegate admitted that he was unable to read French newspapers, but this did not stop him from assuming that priests in Quebec were meddling in politics. Archbishop Lynch, who already had crossed swords with the Quebec episcopate over his plan to annex the diocese of Ottawa to his own ecclesiastical province, was only too happy to provide the delegate with yet another example of the French-Canadian clergy's inferiority by dwelling on their electoral abuses. The good archbishop saw the mote in his neighbour's eye and not the beam in his own.

In this way an image of the Quebec clergy was created, which in the years following the Conroy mission was often reaffirmed by the archdiocese of Quebec. By the end of the century it was not hard for

Laurier to revive it, with the help of Satolli, Russell, Fitzpatrick, and Proulx. Now we may well ask; what was the harm in this? Did the Liberal party not have a right to defend itself? Was the clergy not charging at windmills when they attacked it as impious and dangerous? What did the clergy mean when they condemned Catholic liberalism?

Bégin correctly asserted that the hierarchy was not interested in political parties as such. The bishops as a whole only intervened in politics when they believed Catholic rights to be at stake. To this end Bourget openly fought with both Conservatives and Liberals over their failure to take up the cause of New Brunswick Catholics. His clergy combated Rodolphe Laflamme because of his Rouge connections, his betrayal of Catholic rights in *la question Manitoba-Brunswick*, and his quite cynical use of religion for electoral purposes. In the minds of Conroy and those he consulted, however, electors were free to support nominal Catholic candidates as long as the party they represented was not hostile to the church.

But it was on this last point that Conroy met resistance in Quebec. For, while it was generally agreed that as an institution the Liberal party was not suspect from a doctrinal point of view, it was still thought to represent some dangerous tendencies. The first was its failure to defend Catholic rights, the second its manipulation of religion for electoral purposes. But were not the Conservatives also guilty on both these counts? The hierarchy replied that the Conservatives did not try openly, by legislation and court cases, to silence the clergy who opposed them at election time. By doing so, the Liberals undermined ecclesiastical authority, a charge which they took very seriously indeed. Contrary to Conroy, the Quebec clergy believed that nominal Catholics could be supported, but only if the party they represented did not itself present a threat to the rights of the church.

It was precisely because the moral standing of the Liberal party was different in Quebec than it was in English Canada, and because the moral worth of candidates from the same party differed from constituency to constituency, that the episcopate spoke in terms of principle, not political party. The more conscientious bishops such as Bourget and Bégin ensured that the application of principle to political reality did not involve personalities. It is difficult, then, to understand why Merry del Val was so offended by the fact that what was a sin in one riding or diocese was not in another, since these bishops were concerned with principle, not party. Cleary made it a sin to vote Conservative in the archdiocese of Kingston in 1889; but Catholics elsewhere in the province and in Canada were free to support the party. Surely the bishops had a right to respond to local conditions without putting into question the whole edifice of Catholic morality. And if Cleary could withhold the sacraments from those who failed to support Catholic education in the Ontario elections, why could his Quebec counterparts not do so in 1896 when the same principle was at stake in Manitoba? Of course, Laurier claimed that he, too, was in favour of Catholic education and that the debate was thus about strategy, not principle. The Liberal leader was deluding either himself or others in thinking that Catholic education was synonymous with common schools providing religious instruction after hours. The Quebec hierarchy on the whole had the wisdom to see his error and was prepared to do something about it, the leaders of the Irish Ontario church were not.

If the Quebec episcopate was discredited in 1896–7, it was because the image of the local church as a rabidly partisan institution was a widely accepted fact. The archdiocese of Quebec under Taschereau was responsible for giving credence to this fact. Elsewhere we have shown that Bourget kept the partisan activities of his clergy well in check while he was bishop.[96] If partisanship existed elsewhere – and it probably did to some degree – it was due to the failure of local bishops to suppress it. We have seen that Taschereau was one of these. The archbishop's weaknesses, in neglecting to deal effectively both with political abuses in the clergy and the religious manipulation of some Liberal politicians, weighed heavily on the Quebec church's future ability to exercise moral leadership. If Taschereau had been with Bourget rather than against him in the 1870s, the Quebec church conceivably might have been more effective in the defence of French and Catholic rights during the Laurier years. The church's failures in this period not only reflected upon itself but upon the political position of French Canada in Confederation.

Chapter Five

A House of Cards:
The Laurier-Greenway Agreement
and Its Aftermath

'Eminence, obedient to the wishes of the Supreme Pontiff, I left my diocese to go to these regions where for approximately six months we are covered in ice and snow and where bitter disputes have for years and years disturbed public peace. To all this, I resigned myself.'[1] These words might have been written by a Roman emissary sent to scarcely Christianized and dimly perceived northern stretches of Europe in the eleventh century. Instead they were modern sentiments expressed in 1901 about Canada by its first permanent apostolic delegate, Diomede Falconio, sentiments of exasperation at the lack of progress made in the question of minority Catholic education in Manitoba, sentiments shared by other apostolic delegates who grappled with this same issue. These prelates found themselves in a no-man's-land between the ideal to which they aspired but governments refused to countenance, and the real which they abhorred but politicians accepted as they held out the elusive prospect of further concessions.

The Laurier-Greenway agreement in effect created a political vacuum which neither the federal nor the provincial government felt inclined to fill, on the grounds that the people of Manitoba were overwhelmingly opposed to the restoration of Catholic educational rights. Since Rome effectively prevented the Quebec hierarchy from exerting their weight on behalf of Manitoba Catholics after January 1897, it fell to Archbishop Langevin to fight the minority's battle alone. Except for a hard core of contemporary hagiographers, Langevin has had a bad press from Laurier's time onward. In his own day he was accused of being fanatically partisan and unrealistic. Current historians have seen him as intractable, intransigent, little inclined to subtlety, and betraying a siege mentality common to minority groups. On the one hand he has been portrayed as so narrow that he lost the confidence and support of English-speaking Catholics, and on the other as so demanding that he sacrificed the interests of French speakers to those of other Catholic linguistic groups.[2] Langevin was certainly the *bête noire* of more than one apostolic delegate. Yet contemporary observers and latter-day historians have shown little sensitivity to the difficult situation which he inherited from his predecessor and from the political authorities.

In any case, because of him apostolic delegates from Merry del Val to Sbarretti spent a great deal of time trying to come to terms with the problem. This chapter of the Manitoba schools question largely has been ignored by historians,[3] perhaps because they assumed, together with the politicians of the day, that the Laurier-Greenway agreement put an end to the crisis. Certainly the delegates and Langevin did not see it that way. This period may then be taken as a case study to assess the delegates' perspective, diplomatic role, and achievements, and better understand the position in which Langevin found himself.

RESTORING CATHOLIC RIGHTS IN MANITOBA?

The elections of 1896 placed Archbishop Langevin of St Boniface in the odd postion of having to negotiate Catholic education with a government whose fundamental policy for Manitoba was common schools. He wrote of his dilemma to Rome. Citing the unhappy example of North-West Territories Catholics who were suffering under the restrictive terms of the 1892 school legislation,[4] the prelate stressed the importance of Catholics controlling their own schools. But, he insisted, if he were to reject any solution which fell short of this objective, 'on va m'accuser d'intransigeance et de parti pris; on va s'en prendre à ma jeunesse, à mon inexpérience et pour tout couronner on va chercher à mettre en doute ma bonne entente avec le Saint-Siège ... [Cependant] les racontars des journaux ... et les injures des politiciens n'ont pas le don de m'émouvoir. *Levavi oculos meos in montes unde veniet auxilium.*'[5]

But Langevin's colleagues endorsed his position. Bégin continued to stress the importance of remedial legislation which constitutionally would entrench minority rights, 'sanctionnant le droit de celles-ci [minorities] d'en appeler au Parlement en cas de préjudice, et le droit du Parlement d'intervenir pour le protéger efficacement.'[6] Archbishop Cornelius O'Brien of Halifax warned Langevin against compromises that would undermine the ultimate objective of Catholic schools. 'You are not playing a game of politics, you want your rights and you do not care which party grants them. If the present Government will obtain them, all right! If not, they run the risk of defeat. You need not have any hesitation in looking for justice no matter what party may be hurt thereby.'[7] Not all prelates were as categorical, however. Archbishop Walsh did not believe that Catholic control of schools was essential and considered the Ontario model of separate schools satisfactory. In contrast to O'Brien, his support of Langevin's position was much less strong: 'Hold out for your full rights, for all you can get,' he advised, 'and whilst you may perhaps accept certain substantial concessions, do so under protest, and without prejudice to your full rights.'[8]

In real terms, the Laurier-Greenway accord of November 1896 changed nothing in the situation created for Manitoba Catholics by the government's abolition of denominational schools. It simply gave legal sanction to an arrangement which emerged in some rural areas of the province after 1890. Because French-speaking Catholics formed compact settlements in these localities, they controlled municipal taxes, which partly financed the running of their schools. So in many cases they retained their Catholic teachers, textbooks, and religious exercises, while their establishments were officially designated as public schools.[9] This local control remained fully effective even after the Greenway government tightened its grip on education by requiring municipalities to withhold subsidies from schools not complying with the law – a provision that was simply ignored in many Catholic rural areas.

The government's restrictive legislation hit Catholics directly, however, in urban centres where they formed a minority. In Winnipeg and Brandon five schools with a total enrolment of twelve hundred children, one-quarter of the Catholic student population, felt the full impact of the government's intolerance. There, parents could be liable to pay twice for their childrens' education, once in compulsory public school taxes and again in tuition to privately supported Catholic schools. As the front-line victims of the Greenway government's restrictive measures, they found little relief and nothing to cheer about in the Laurier-Greenway accord.

In these circumstances it is understandable that the Canadian hierarchy should have rejected the agreement outright, since it did not advance the position of Catholic education beyond what already existed in fact. But had not the Judicial Committee of the Privy Council affirmed in the Brophy judgment of 1895 that the minority had a legitimate grievance? The Liberals, however, played on the apparent ambiguity of the judgment. While their Lordships acknowledged that Ottawa had the power to redress the wrongs done to Manitoba Catholics, at the same time they affirmed that 'it is certainly not essential that the statutes repealed by the Act of 1890 should be re-enacted.' Since the new system of common schools answered the needs of the vast majority of population, 'all legitimate ground of complaint would be removed if that system were supplemented by provisions which would remove the grievance upon which the appeal is founded, and were modified so far as might be necessary to give effect to these provisions.'[10] Since the nature of the Manitoba Catholics' complaint had to do with the elimination of their schools, any accommodation which did not restore such schools in fact as well as in law would go against the intent of the Privy Council's judgment. The Laurier-Greenway agreement, however, simply gave limited privileges *to any denomination* within the public school system. These privileges related to religious instruction after hours and the possible provision of teachers of the same denomination as students where numbers so warranted. Catholics were still liable to the legislative and administrative harassment inherent in the provincial school law. It is difficult to see, therefore, how the Laurier-Greenway accord satisfied the intent of the Privy Council's judgment. Despite their pronouncement's sybilline wording, their Lordships had more in mind than simply appending after-hours religious instruction to the common school system. If we consider that in 1890 Manitoba had simply copied Ontario's school legislation without the separate school clauses,[11] then very likely it was this 'supplement' and this 'modification' of the Manitoba legislation of which their Lordships were thinking. They undoubtedly sought to grant the minority Catholic public schools, but not the dual administrative system of education, copied from Quebec, which had existed in Manitoba until 1890.

In any case, the federal Conservatives went beyond the terms of this decision with their remedial legislation which would have fully restored the system abolished in 1890. During the 1896 election Laurier promised to achieve the substance of the remedial bill

without the attendant acrimony and divisiveness. Langevin therefore felt betrayed by the accord formulated shortly after the Liberal
victory which, far from reviving the old order, denied the very
concept of Catholic education. The agreement in effect did not allow
Catholics to form school districts under their own jurisdiction.
Langevin would have nothing less than this.

In taking this stand, was the archbishop of St Boniface being
intransigent or simply expecting politicians to fulfil electoral commitments? Was he jeopardizing the *modus vivendi* painfully established
by French-speaking Catholics in rural districts or simply trying to
entrench these achievements in law, thus sheltering them from the
vexatious measures of future governments hostile to the minority?
Indeed, by insisting that Catholic rights enjoy clear legal protection,
the archbishop proved to be more far-sighted and realistic than most
French-speaking Manitobans, who seemed content to live within the
terms of the agreement, oblivious to what the morrow might bring. At
this particular juncture Langevin had the backing of the entire
Canadian hierarchy and of the Propaganda. When the accord was
concluded the archbishop submitted three questions to Cardinal
Ledochowski and would have been much heartened by the prelate's
replies, made as marginal notations, had they been sent to him.
Could the archbishop of St Boniface, he asked, sanction the establishment of school districts subject to the provisions of the accord? No.
Could he order priests and laymen to remain outside of the agreement? Yes. Could he say that the refusal to accept it was a matter of
conscience. Yes. At the same time Langevin proposed to the cardinal
that the Canadian episcopate be allowed to appeal to the Queen for
redress,[12] knowing that on the whole the Quebec hierarchy fully
backed his interpretation of the constitution. His colleagues in fact
believed that the Privy Council's decision gave the minority three
rights: to build and manage their own schools; to obtain public
subsidies for them; to be exempt from what was termed 'double
taxation.'[13]

But Rome heard discordant voices on the Brophy judgment. Using
a legal opinion which Edward Blake provided for the occasion,
Fitzpatrick and Russell argued that the Laurier-Greenway agreement fully satisfied the terms of the Privy Council's decision. Cardinal Rampolla and the Congregration for Extraordinary Ecclesiastical Affairs must have been impressed with the Canadian envoys' sincerity and their authoritativeness. After all, Blake was one of Can-

ada's most distinguished jurists who represented the Catholic minority before the Judicial Committee of the Privy Council in the Brophy case. Russell was the son of the Lord Chief Justice of England, Charles Baron Russell of Killowen, considered the greatest advocate of his time, an Irish Catholic and attorney general in two Gladstone governments.[14] Fitzpatrick was Canada's solicitor general. It is not surprising that the cardinals found their opinions more convincing than those of the Quebec bishops. And it was this view that formed the premise of Merry del Val's Canadian mission.

MERRY DEL VAL: THE ART OF THE POSSIBLE

The apostolic delegate quickly immersed himself in the complexities of the Manitoba schools question. His analysis of the historical background convinced him that this was not a partisan issue. Catholics had been the victims of both political parties in equal measure. The 1890 legislation had been supported, after all, by Protestants on both sides of the assembly.[15] And if, six years later, the remedial bill failed to carry the day in Ottawa, the fault belonged equally to the two parties.

Since the Quebec hierarchy held the federal Conservatives in such high esteem, Merry del Val felt it necessary to catalogue the party's sins of omission and commission in this affair: its six years of inactivity; its failure to remedy the crisis quickly and effectively through disallowance; its repeated and deliberate evasion of responsibility by foisting the issue onto the courts. On this last point, the delegate was perhaps being slightly ironic when he observed: 'I want to believe that not a few members of the party sincerely expected a favourable sentence from the courts.'[16]

The Conservatives acted only when forced to by the highest tribunal in the British Empire and again only in the last days of the seventh Parliament. Their remedial bill was so complex that it would have taken months of debate to secure its approval. Merry del Val doubted the government's death-bed conversion and was certainly not prepared to absolve them of their past sins. Indeed, he stressed their insincerity. Presenting legislation which in their hearts the Conservatives knew would not pass allowed them to maintain Protestant support in Ontario, while at the same time posing as champions of the Catholic cause in Quebec. The parliamentary debate and its aftermath only served to highlight even further the party's bad faith.[17] And in this sordidly ambiguous situation, Archbishop Langevin was imprudent enough publicly to support the government measure.

Nor were the Liberals without sin. They had shown more concern for their own future than for that of Manitoba Catholics. The party 'felt itself close to power which it coveted for so many years ... On the eve of what it considered such important elections, it did not want to alienate a large section of the Electorate by lending its support to an odious measure, nor give the advantage to the Conservatives.'[18] But quite apart from such partisan considerations, sincere Liberals had reservations about the remedial bill. They saw its flaws, they were anxious about the little time allotted for its discussion, they wondered about its efficacy. Merry del Val assured Rome that, except for some radicals and extremist Protestants, the party did not question the minority's right to Catholic schools. Instead, there was genuine concern about how to interpret the Judicial Committee's judgment and how best to reach an accommodation with the Manitoba government. Merry del Val believed that the principle of religious education was acknowledged by party leaders. Once this principle was implemented, the rest should be left to the individual's judgment.[19]

The delegate then turned to the current situation and stressed the seriousness of the moment. Laurier 'finds himself in circumstances that are most difficult, and he does not wish to hide from me the fact that at this time the Holy See holds his political position in its hands.' Merry del Val questioned the wisdom of precipitate action 'in the current acute phase of the question. A move that is less well balanced might lead to political and religious upheavals of the utmost gravity.'[20] As a result, it was not a question of what was 'desiderabile,' but 'praticabile, prudente, e possibile.'[21]

In the opinion of observers whom the Delegate valued for their learning and impartiality, remedial legislation was both impossible and inopportune. For one thing, the governor general did not even mention it as a viable option in his most recent speech from the throne. For another, the measure certainly would be opposed by the Protestant majority in Parliament and rejected outright by the government and people of Manitoba. Of course, the Conservatives, now in opposition, feigned support for the bill as a tactic to embarrass Prime Minister Laurier who unquestionably would endanger his career by following such a course.[22] In fact the delegate believed that if Charles Tupper, the leader of the opposition, were really sincere about remedial action, he would seize the initiative by moving an amendment to the speech from the throne. But he was prevented from doing so by the same political realities that dictated Laurier's actions.

Remedial legislation inevitably would provoke a government crisis and lead to new elections, with disastrous results for religion, the episcopate, and the Holy See. The same party likely would be re-elected, 'only this time with an enormous majority of Protestants more than ever determined to deny Catholics the smallest concession.'[23] Catholic interests then would be in imminent peril.

Now I ask: ... would it not be little less than criminal to sacrifice 50,000 Catholic children in Ontario and as many in the Maritime provinces, and provoke Protestant hostility against Catholics in all walks of life, in employment and in public offices, even in families, simply because we wanted to defend abstractly, without in practice even succeeding, that which could in an absolute sense be considered the rights of 4,000 Manitoba children who for the time being could be looked after by administrative and other arrangements?[24]

Merry del Val insisted that the benefits enjoyed by Catholics in many parts of the country depended on the goodwill of the Protestant majority. He dismissed the fears of some bishops that failure to entrench minority rights in Manitoba would make Catholics elsewhere in Canada vulnerable to Protestant aggression. Rather, the opposite was true, the imposition on a Protestant majority of federal legislation framed specifically for Catholics would provoke a wave of sectarian hostility that would sweep away all these benefits.

If remedial legislation promised to produce more harm than good, then clearly one would have to look to the longer term for a solution. Laurier in fact pleaded for time in the many meetings he had with the delegate. The Conservatives, the prime minister noted, took six years to arrive at a remedy, why then were the Liberals required to produce one immediately? The Liberal leader admitted that he was personally dissatisfied with the Laurier-Greenway agreement, but saw it only as a first step.[25] This was according to Merry del Val the feeling of almost all the Catholic members of the Liberal caucus. The delegate accepted Laurier's contention that Ottawa had many means of exerting quiet pressure on the province without danger of arousing public hostility.[26] The government could secure administrative concessions from Manitoba, which would give the Catholics most of what they wanted. In this way, they could look forward to denominational schools in all but name, as was the case in the Maritimes. Laurier even held out the possibility of an eventual legislative restoration of Catholic schools. What he wanted, however, was to exhaust all the conciliatory means at his command before adopting energetic ones, if necessary.[27]

Having himself opted for a longer-term approach, the delegate took an active part in Laurier's conciliatory strategy and sought to improve the existing accord by extracting further concessions from Premier Greenway. In part this meant reminding politicians about the Holy See's expectations. The papal envoy clearly told Laurier that Rome would never accept a solution that depended on the whims and goodwill of public men. Catholic rights were recognized by the constitution, irrespective of how narrowly one interpreted the Judicial Committee's decision; the federal government had the power and the duty to defend them; its leaders also had committed themselves publicly to their restoration. Rome would not rest then until Manitoba adopted a law that fully satisfied the Catholic minority.

These reminders seemed to have the intended effect. Merry del Val was favourably impressed by the goodwill that existed at both the federal and provincial levels. Greenway, whom he described as the archetypal Manitoba political leader for the foreseeable future, was essentially a speculator 'senza pregiudizii, senza scrupoli, e senza principii.' While anxious to work out an administrative settlement regarding Catholic schools, he wanted at all costs to avoid public discussion and confrontation.[28] It was therefore imperative, according to Merry del Val, that the issue be taken out of politics.

Two meetings were arranged with Greenway at Laurier's house away from public view so as not to arouse Protestant suspicion and anger.[29] The delegate made it clear that he did not wish to deal directly with the Manitoba premier, to avoid any impression that the Holy See was negotiating with him. Using the federal government as intermediary, Merry del Val suggested a number of administrative changes to the school legislation. These concerned the institution of administrative districts where Catholics would have control of their own schools; the nomination of the archbishop of St Boniface to the provincial advisory board of education; the appointment of a Catholic inspector and examiners, as well as the use of school texts, subject to the archbishop's approval; teacher training and certification procedures that would not offend the convictions of members of religious orders; the use of Catholic ratepayers' taxes to support their own schools even in areas where legally they were not sufficiently numerous.[30] The delegate considered that these conditions, added to the clauses of the Laurier-Greenway accord, would confer a denominational character on minority schools. Catholics then could work with their municipalities to exploit the law to full advantage, while still retaining their demands for the complete restoration of their rights.[31]

Greenway accepted all these conditions, except for the one relating to school taxes. He refused, however, to give them legislative expression for fear of triggering extremist reaction in both Catholic and Protestant camps. When pressed by the delegate for written guarantees that could be submitted to Rome, the premier temporized, saying that he had to consult his cabinet. Finally the Manitoba government apparently agreed to the terms of an order-in-council incorporating these conditions, but declined to send the papal envoy a copy, again on the pretext that such a move would fan the flames of sectarian passion.[32] Meanwhile, as a gesture of good faith to the delegate, Laurier withheld from Manitoba interest payments of $300,000 on school lands until a satisfactory settlement of the question was reached.

Throughout these arduous negotiations, Merry del Val considered the archbishop of St Boniface a veritable thorn in his side. 'Raising the cry "all or nothing," he has absolutely refused until now to come to terms in any way with the Protestant government of Manitoba, with which unfortunately he will have to reckon for many years in a province where French Canadian Catholics are only 20,000 against almost 200,000 English-speaking Protestants.'[33] The provincial government might even have made concessions to the minority at an earlier date had it not been for the Langevin. Merry del Val contrasted the prelate's fractious and partisan manner with that of Archbishop Taché who had been quite open to an alliance with the Liberals in the wake of the Conservative government's inaction over the schools question.[34]

Considering Langevin and the Quebec hierarchy's hostility to the Liberals, the delegate felt obliged to exclude the archbishop of St Boniface from negotiations and to keep him and most French-Canadian bishops in the dark regarding the nature and objectives of his discussions with the civil authorities. On these crucial matters he confided only in the episcopate of Ontario, Bishops Lorrain and Emard, and some other 'prudent' ecclesiastics. To have acted differently, he claimed, 'would have destroyed in twenty-four hours all that was achieved, and immediately provoke old struggles without ever any hope of ending them.'[35]

These views were echoed by Greenway and Laurier. In fact, the prime minister sent a complaint directly to Rome about the archbishop's negative behaviour. Langevin could not hope to prevail, Laurier maintained, by isolating himself from the rest of the population of Manitoba. 'C'est, au contraire, en prenant part à la vie civile du pays où il vit, et en rencontrant sur un pied d'égalité ses concitoyens de croyances différentes, avec lesquelles la Providence l'a placé. Il y a raison de croire que la majorité ... lui accorderait facilement comme privilège ce qu'elle refuse de reconnaître comme un droit.'[36]

Merry del Val wondered what the archbishop of St Boniface had to offer as an alternative to the new package. Langevin seemed to want Catholic schools to remain outside of the provincial system, maintaining themselves through private donations.[37] But apart from the establishments of excellence run by religious communities in Winnipeg and St Boniface, the condition of country schools profoundly dismayed the delegate. They were poorly equipped and their teachers, despite their zeal and self-sacrifice, often incompetent. 'Thus for example in one school neither the teacher nor the children knew how to translate into English, an indispensable language in Manitoba.'[38]

The papal envoy noted that French Canadians were poor, and those of Manitoba even more so. By following the archbishop's course, parents would either eventually refuse the burden of double taxation and opt for public schools, or reject provincial aid and condemn their children to a permanent state of inferiority and to the disdain of the majority. Merry del Val was convinced that the archbishop's schools could not generate the funds necessary to provide children with a sound education in line with the requirements of the times and parents' expectations. On the other hand even Langevin admitted that in many areas of the province the Laurier-Greenway agreement could be used to good advantage to secure the substance of a Catholic education. In Winnipeg the situation was more complex, but the delegate was sure that by negotiating with municipal authorities, Catholics could obtain a settlement similar to that in New Brunswick. A real problem only existed in remote areas where the Catholic population was scattered. If, however, Langevin were less absolute, he would allow Catholic children in those regions to attend public schools and have religious instruction provided after hours, as already happened in some far-flung communities even in the most Catholic province of Quebec.[39] The delegate was puzzled by Langevin's conviction that the attempt to draw maximum advantage out of a difficult situation was tantamount to a renunciation of the minority's rights.

But despite Greenway's assurances and Laurier's seductive ways, Merry del Val left Canada in mid July empty-handed. Yet Laurier had assured Rome in June that Manitoba was about to adopt measures satisfactory to the apostolic delegate.[40] A few days after this assurance, Merry del Val sent a coded telegram to Rampolla stating that he soon expected to have an authentic copy of the Manitoba government's resolutions.[41] What went wrong? The delegate and Laurier blamed Conservative Catholics close to Langevin who embarrassed Greenway by circulating rumours regarding his negotiations with Merry del Val. As a result, the government had been forced to postpone its order-in-council. 'Nevertheless,' confirmed the delegate, 'Mr. Greenway's cabinet has not withdrawn its verbal guarantees, and declares itself always prepared to help institute schools which would be in fact if not in name under the purview and direction of Catholics.'[42]

THE EPISCOPATE: MAKING THE BEST OF A BAD SITUATION

Not surprisingly the Quebec episcopate disagreed with the delegate's position on the schools question. Bégin challenged the accuracy of Merry del Val's historical account. To the delegate's contention that the legislation of 1890 abolishing denominational schools was a bipartisan measure, the archbishop replied that the Manitoba Liberal party had proposed the bill, that this was done as a government measure, and that the Conservatives opposed it. On the other hand, Bégin continued, it was the federal Liberals who were responsible for the failure of remedial legislation. Their tactic of filibuster was the single most important element in its defeat. 'Même présentée tardivement ... elle [the bill] aurait pu être votée sans l'obstruction, qui est le fait non des libéraux seuls, mais du parti libéral seul comme parti.'[43] Only seven Catholics bolted party ranks to vote in favour of the measure on second reading; the rest preferred their partisan ties to their commitments as Catholics.

Bégin criticized Merry del Val for his knowledge and appreciation of the facts surrounding the crisis. He found astonishing the delegate's contention that just before his death Archbishop Taché was preparing to turn to the Liberals for support. The documents certainly did not bear out such a claim, he argued. While Taché may have been disgusted with the Conservatives, he knew that the Liberals had nothing to offer.

But the archbishop was not prepared completely to exonerate the Conservative party. He recognized that a number of Protestant Conservatives, with the backing of Governor General Aberdeen, delayed presentation of the remedial bill until very late in the session and that Orangemen actively participated in the filibuster. Still, all Catholic Conservative and a majority of Protestants, true to their party tradition, were prepared to see the measure through before dissolution. If the opposition Liberals had shown such determination, the bill would have become law. This being the case, Bégin did not understand the delegate's scepticism at the possibility of passing and implementing the bill. After all, the important thing was to get the measure on the books. As Bishop Gravel pointed out, even if Greenway refused to comply with the law, 'il n'est pas immortel.' Politicians came and went, laws endured.[44]

Yet, to their great dismay, the episcopate had to admit that the Laurier-Greenway accord, not remedial legislation, had won the day. Bégin believed that the governing Liberals had achieved their objective by a series of devious moves. He concluded: 'Leur responsabilité est immense devant Dieu; elle ne sera pas moins grande devant l'histoire impartiale qui les jugera. Mais peu leur importe le jugement de l'histoire; il leur suffit de garder le pouvoir aussi longtemps que possible.'[45]

Despite what the Quebec hierarchy might have thought of Merry del Val's perspective and accomplishments, Leo XIII's papal encyclical, *Affari vos*, forced them to work within the terms of the Laurier-Greenway agreement. By the same token, in declaring the accord 'defective, imperfect, and insufficient,' the encyclical compelled Laurier to try to wring further concessions from a recalcitrant provincial government, whose only acknowledgment of the delegate's mission was the appointment of two Catholics, one as school inspector and the other as a member of the advisory board of education. Consequently, further negotiations were held between Laurier and Langevin early in 1898 under the auspices of Archbishop Bruchési of Montreal. At issue was the way in which the Langevin's private schools could be brought into the public system. Talks focused particularly on textbooks and teacher certification. In the end Langevin accepted a *modus vivendi* which he termed imperfect and precarious because 'une vie languissante et incertaine vaut mieux que la mort.'[46]

This tacit agreement brought relief to the archbishop's schools in rural areas, which became eligible for public funding. But children in urban centres still remained at the mercy of boards hostile to the minority. Meanwhile new regulations issued by the government kept the feeling of harassment and frustration alive in all Catholic communities. Teachers were required to sign an oath guaranteeing that they were not dispensing religious instruction during regular school hours. In addition the government insisted on the use of expurgated public school textbooks, rather than Catholic ones, in Catholic areas. After consulting with the Propaganda,[47] Langevin accepted these restrictions, in the hope that the government eventually would accept textbooks which were 'au moins chrétiens.' The archbishop added for Rome's benefit: 'Tout cela prouve que nous ne sommes pas aussi libres que nous le voudrions; mais nous ne demeurons pas inactifs, et nous nous efforçons de profiter des avantages matériels considérables de ce régime.'[48]

In contrast, Langevin's urban schools were in desperate straits. The Winnipeg Board of Education refused to make them the slightest concession, which only exacerbated their severe financial problems. Laurier secretly provided Langevin with federal funds in 1898, which afforded them partial relief, and again the following year after the archbishop reminded him of their plight. At the same time the prime minister promised to have the provincial government rescind the oath regarding religious instruction and adopt the textbooks used in Ontario separate schools; but on both counts he was unsuccessful.[49]

For Rome's benefit, Langevin insisted that the Catholic minority had not been insensitive to Laurier's acts of goodwill. They had neither agitated politically nor organized public demonstrations.[50] Catholics sincerely sought to make the best of the current situation. But he also stressed that this public silence led people to believe that the Manitoba schools question was resolved, a position that perfectly suited the politicians. Langevin doubted that Protestants would show as much patience and restraint if their co-religionists in Quebec were subjected to such ill-treatment.

Throughout this period Bégin watched events in Manitoba with scepticism and in silence. He was determined that Rome should not regard the Quebec episcopate as a stumbling-block to conciliation.

He applauded Langevin's faithful execution of the Holy See's wishes. But he had no illusions concerning the durability of the new arrangement. He confided to Langevin:

C'est un château de cartes que le moindre souffle du fanatisme protestant suffira à renverser bientôt; c'est un marché qui ne lie en aucune manière vos adversaires ... Nos opportunistes politiques ... cherchent par dessus tout ... de se maintenir au pouvoir. Qu'il est triste d'avoir à traiter une question si ... vitale pour notre pays avec des hommes sans convictions.[51]

On the eve of Diomede Falconio's installation as apostolic delegate, Bégin deplored the fact that Laurier was again insisting in public that the Manitoba schools question was settled. He pointed out to the Propaganda that no legislative measure had been adopted either by Ottawa or Winnipeg to implement the understanding reached with Merry del Val.[52]

FALCONIO: THE CALL OF DUTY

Falconio's introduction to Canadian political life was anything but serene. He hardly had time to unpack his bags when he was embroiled in a public controversy between Laurier and Langevin over this very question. The delegate termed Laurier's public statement a painful incident, but noted that the archbishop of St Boniface's public rejoinder provided grist to the partisan press's mill. Fearing that the quarrel might degenerate into an open break with disastrous consequences for a final resolution of the question, Falconio called both men together for private talks.

The pope's representative came away from these discussions convinced of Laurier's sincerity and goodwill; he was satisfied that Laurier's desire to change Manitoba's school legislation through amicable means remained constant and firm. He was impressed with the prime minister's quick response to Langevin's complaint about the sorry state of Catholic schools in Winnipeg: the Liberal leader promised to deal with the matter immediately.

Even at this early stage in the delegate's tenure, it is clear that his perspective was broadly that of Merry del Val and Laurier: federal intervention was constitutionally questionable and politically dangerous. A definitive arrangement in favour of Catholic education would have to await happier times and in any case depended on provincial action. In the mean time it was necessary to take the issue out of politics, elevating it to a question of right 'so that [the political parties] will not exploit it as they did in the past to their own advantage to the great detriment of harmonious relations between the clergy and the faithful.'[53]

But 'elevating' the schools question out of politics was more difficult than Falconio imagined. Langevin believed that the coming to power in Winnipeg of a new Conservative government, sympathetic to Catholic demands and led by Hugh John Macdonald, signalled a fresh start. He recommended that the Canadian hierarchy present a new petition to Ottawa in order to bring the issue back into the public eye. At the same time he urged Falconio to meet with the federal opposition leader, Charles Tupper, in an attempt to persuade him to pressure Macdonald to make more concessions.[54] The delegate, however, suspected that these suggestions were dictated by partisan considerations.[55] He told Langevin that the other French-Canadian archbishops considered a petition untimely and that in any case Ottawa had already recognized the rights of Manitoba Catholics by issuing its remedial order-in-council in 1895. The initiative was now clearly with the province. In deference to the delegate, Langevin therefore wrote to Macdonald reminding him that Manitoba had not responded to Ottawa's remedial order and asking for relief on behalf of Manitoba Catholics.[56] The premier replied that, while he was sympathetic to the archbishop's cause, he had no intention of risking his political future in its defence.

Meanwhile the collapse of yet another round of negotiations between the Catholics of Winnipeg and the local public school board strained relations even more between the delegate and the archbishop of St Boniface. Once again Falconio suspected Langevin of having acted impetuously, without advice, and out of partisan motives. Nineteen hundred was an election year and, since the Winnipeg school board was dominated by Liberals, the sudden desire of Catholic spokesmen to reach an understanding with them, after three years of struggle and privation, looked to the papal envoy like another attempt to embarrass the Liberal party.[57] He urged Winnipeg Catholics to be patient and to consider the long and hard sacrifices made by their co-religionists in England and the United States in support of their schools.

Langevin saw through Falconio's veiled accusations. He pointed out to an apparently uninformed delegate that the minority's initiative had been part of an ongoing process of negotiations begun two years earlier under the Laurier-Greenway agreement.[58] Their current initiative was prompted by the dire circumstances of Winnipeg's Catholic schools which needed $9,000 to stay open, $3,000 of which were salary arrears of sisters who had not been paid in two years.[59] He assured the delegate that the talks in no way compromised the minority's demands, since Catholic spokesmen were seeking simply what their rural counterparts already enjoyed. But public trustees in Winnipeg refused to give them this and insisted that Catholic schools fully adhere to the terms of the education act. As a result, the talks collapsed. Langevin maintained that his behaviour throughout had been completely disinterested: 'On m'accusera de partisannerie, peut-être, mais je suis fort du témoignage de ma conscience, et je défie mes accusateurs de prouver ce qu'ils avancent. Je n'ai vu aucun homme politique ...et j'ai évité même d'en voir depuis près de trois ans ... précisément afin de ne pas donner prise à des accusations malveillantes.'[60]

The archbishop admitted that personally he preferred his Winnipeg schools to remain outside of the system and survive through the private donations, pending a definite resolution of the question. But for this to be a realistic option he needed money; therefore he asked the delegate to authorize a special collection in all the dioceses of Canada in support of his 'free schools.'[61] Falconio replied that the many bishops he consulted were opposed to the idea of a collection and seemed to think that the archbishop had enough money at his disposal to finance his schools.[62] Well before this letter arrived, however, Langevin put his proposal to Rome.[63] The pope himself approved the petition and asked Falconio to recommend the special collection to the Canadian hierarchy.[64] However, the delegate only approached the French-Canadian archbishops.[65]

Falconio was also active on behalf of Winnipeg Catholics. He received positive assurances from Laurier that, in future, Liberal members of the Winnipeg school board would give sympathetic consideration to the minority's demands. As a result, the delegate asked Langevin not to make any new approaches to the board without his permission. He implied that if on the previous occasion the archbishop had first consulted with him and the 'civil authorities,' not only might the archbishop have achieved success, but he certainly would have avoided criticism of his behaviour as well as the polemics of the party press.[66] Commenting on Premier Macdonald's refusal to abrogate the school law in response to the Ottawa's remedial order, the delegate lectured Langevin on the folly of putting all one's eggs in the same political basket, since the Conservatives whom the archbishop so admired had no more to offer than their Liberal predecessors. A few days later Falconio announced that H.A. Constantineau, the Oblate rector of the University of Ottawa and a personal friend of Laurier,[67] was going to Winnipeg to make new overtures to the school board in co-ordination with Langevin.

The archbishop of St Boniface was saddened by so many signs of the delegate's lack of confidence in him. 'Les avancés de politiciens intéressés semblent avoir plus de poids auprès de Votre Excellence que le témoignage de celui qui seul est le père des enfants catholiques du Manitoba et dont la conscience épiscopale doit offrir plus d'assurances de sincérité que les agissements des faiseurs politiques.' Langevin insisted that Laurier could not have been ignorant of the last approach made to the Winnipeg school board since he himself had facilitated it through the good offices of a local Liberal. The timing of the move seemed appropriate, coming as it did after the defeat of a hostile provincial government and a prominent Winnipeg Liberal trustee's assurances of its success. The failure of the talks showed that Laurier himself could not control the fanaticism of some of his followers on the board. If on the other hand, Premier Macdonald did not seem very forthcoming regarding the restoration of Catholic rights in the province, Langevin was not surprised: '... faut-il s'étonner ... qu'un premier ministre protestant refuse de risquer pour nous sa vie politique sur une question dont un premier ministre catholique s'est servie, en la compromettant à jamais, pour arriver au pouvoir?'[68] Clearly Falconio and Langevin had diametrically opposed views on the question of who bore ultimate responsibility in resolving the issue.

Despite the encouragement that Langevin drew from his Oblate confrère's arrival in the West, Constantineau's mission was a failure. The fault, according to the rector, did not belong to the Winnipeg school board, which was well disposed, even though Laurier had not followed through on his promise to exert influence on trustees. Nor was the stumbling block the archbishop. It was rather the Irish Catholics representing minority interests at the talks, who for partisan motives refused to give Laurier a settlement on a silver platter in an election year.[69]

The matter, however, was more complicated than even Constantineau suggested. Irish spokesmen had demanded written guarantees from the board that Catholic and Protestant children would not be mixed together. Trustees refused, arguing that to do so would be a violation of the law; but they did offer verbal assurances to that effect. Both Falconio and Laurier wanted Winnipeg Catholics to accept this offer of goodwill. The minority balked, demanding that Laurier first provide them with a legal opinion confirming their right under the accord to separate schools in order to counteract the views of the board's own legal advisers.[70] So, while partisan considerations may have influenced the minority's spokesmen, there were also solid legal grounds for behaving as they did.

This phase of the Manitoba schools question was related not only to local concerns, such as the fate of Catholic schools in Winnipeg, but also touched upon an issue central to western grievances against Ottawa – the Dominion lands policy, and specifically the federal government's control of school lands. Premier Macdonald told Langevin that if Ottawa were willing to put Manitoba's share of these lands at his disposal, he in turn would resolve the educational question once and for all.[71] But just as with the Catholic schools of Winnipeg, so this issue became a political football that Laurier and Macdonald's successor, Rodmond Roblin, tossed back and forth, each refusing to take the initiative of bringing about an accommodation. Meanwhile the delegate and the archbishop stood on the sidelines, cheering their favourite player and accusing each other of partisanship.

Even so, things looked promising in the early days of 1901. Falconio informed Rome that Laurier was more than ever committed to the full restoration of Catholic educational rights in Manitoba. In a letter solicited by the delegate for the Holy See, the prime minister even claimed to prefer a separate to a common school system, finding the former better suited to the needs of Canada's mixed population. He noted however that, despite Roblin's goodwill, the people of Manitoba were opposed to it. Since the federal government was in no hurry to hand the school lands over to the province, there was enough time to prepare public opinion for the change. But Laurier made it clear that he was against re-establishing the dual administrative system abolished in 1890, even though he did hold out the prospect of an early settlement of the question through concurrent legislation if Roblin were really intent on satisfying the minority's demands.[72]

Langevin, too, was optimistic. Laurier assured him that he had no intention of making political capital out of the question. He also told the archbishop that he was seeking the opinion of prominent lawyers regarding the ability of Catholic schools to retain their sectarian character once they came under the Winnipeg board's jurisdiction.[73] Just as Laurier seemed accommodating, so too did Roblin. '[Il] me parait bien disposé,' observed one of Langevin's collaborators, 'mais comme tous les politiciens il a la prudence du serpent sans avoir, je crois, la simplicité de la colombe. Toutefois je dois dire qu'il m'a laissé une bonne impression.' Even as the premier acknowledged that a good deal of distrust marked relations between the two levels of government, he stressed the importance of collaboration in order to resolve the issue.[74]

This new-found harmony was as lasting as a winter thaw. Soon the cold, harsher than ever, returned to embitter relations between Winnipeg and Ottawa. An angry Langevin accused Laurier of lacking the ability or the will to move things forward. 'Tout est facile, tout va se faire, tout est presque fait, quand on voit M. le Premier Ministre, mais pratiquement les difficultés restent insurmontables et *rien ne se fait*! Et c'est toujours la faute à nous, la minorité catholique, à nous que l'on accuse de faire de la politique!' The issues of school lands and Catholic education in Winnipeg now became inextricably mixed and further complicated the overall resolution of the question. On school lands, the archbishop felt that it was up to the federal government to set conditions for their cession.[75] Langevin demanded action, not words, from Laurier. Despite the prime minister's glowing promises, two years had gone by and still the problems regarding the teachers' oath and the use of Catholic textbooks remained unsolved. The Catholic schools of Winnipeg were now burdened with a heavier debt and the sisters still had not been paid. 'Et il a fallu se taire pour ne pas l'embarrasser, pour ne pas l'empêcher de *faire son possible* ... Nous espérons que M. Laurier fera, non pas ce qu'il appelle son possible, mais son devoir.'[76]

Relations between the delegate and the archbishop now reached breaking point, as both Laurier and Falconio dismissed these complaints. Langevin poured out his frustration to Cardinal Ledochowski. The delegate, he maintained, showed more confidence in Laurier 'qu'en nous tous ici, au Manitoba.' Yet Falconio had never taken the trouble to study the Manitoba schools question on site away from Ottawa's influence, despite Langevin's repeated invitations to spend a few months in the West. The delegate's views were so biased, maintained the archbishop, that he, Langevin, refused to have anything more to do with him on the issue.[77] Falconio responded to Langevin's accusations in kind. The previous veiled accusations were now plainly and mercilessly laid bare. He described Langevin as frivolous, impetuous, restless, and termed his complaints libellous, pure invention, odious insinuations without the slightest semblance of truth. To Ledochowski he asserted: 'It seems that Mgr Langevin loves wars of faction and race, and in the ardour of his actions he does not weigh their consequences, making himself rebellious to all sound advice no matter from whom it may come.'[78]

Falconio was even more direct with Cardinal Rampolla. He deplored 'Mgr Langevin's animosity toward the Federal Govenment, which he constantly tries to obstruct for partisan motives.'[79] These same motives impelled the archbishop never to utter a word of criticism of the Roblin administration which, according to Falconio, quickly could have resolved the vexed question of Catholic schools if it had had the slightest inclination. Instead that government had shown its hostility to the cause by trying to abrogate the Laurier-Greenway accord. This Falconio considered to be clear evidence that the schools question was not a party but a denominational issue. Still, Langevin was so anxious to please Roblin that he wanted Ottawa to cede the school lands, Laurier's trump card and Manitoba Catholics' only hope for the re-establishment of their schools, in return for the smallest concessions which Greenway himself would have made at an earlier time if the archbishop had been at all inclined to negotiate with him. Langevin even pushed frivolity to the point of revealing to the premier Laurier's intention to use the school lands as a negotiating tool. 'If Laurier were not Catholic and so strongly devoted to the Pope,' Falconio dreaded to think what the consequences might be. In any case, he told Rampolla, he was giving up all hope of altering the archbishop's dangerous character.[80]

Negotiations resumed between Winnipeg Catholics and the public school board a few days later, but in the apparent absence of a legal opinion supporting the Catholic position and of a framework which a federal-provincial accord might have provided, respective positions remained unchanged. The board asked the Catholic community to trust in their goodwill, even as they passed resolutions insisting that neither sectarian dress nor Catholic textbooks would be tolerated in their schools. These resolutions 'vous en diront plus que je ne pourrais en faire sur l'esprit de fanatisme et de bigoterie étroite qui

anime ces Messieurs ... Or quel traitement peut-on espérer de sem-
blables gens?' reported A.A. Cherrier, the chief Catholic negotiator, to
the delegate.[81] Falconio was genuinely shocked by this turn of events.
The board's resolutions, he argued, had no basis either in Manitoba's
school law or in that of any other province. Indeed, in Nova Scotia
where the legislation was broadly the same as in Manitoba, religious
communities were allowed to wear their habits.[82] The delegate urged
Laurier to have the resolutions annulled.

For his part, Cherrier maintained that the failure of negotiations
once again could be laid at the feet of federal and provincial politicians for whom the interests of the party in power were uppermost.
He said this knowing that the delegate suspected him of partisan
behaviour. He assured Falconio, however, that he had been raised in
a Liberal family and, far from seeing Laurier's rise to power with
trepidation, had welcomed it. 'Les libéraux s'en sont aperçu [sic],
aussi que n'ont-ils pas fait pour accaparer ma petite influence?'[83] He
remained firm in his defence of Catholic rights, even though these
political intrigues disgusted him and he wanted to leave 'ce théâtre
d'angoisses et de déboires sans cesse renouvelés.'[84] He also expressed
the fear that, anxious to reach an accommodation, Langevin would
succumb to the politicians' intrigues.[85]

In the summer of 1901 Roblin finally made Langevin some concrete promises. In return for the interest on the school lands totalling
$100,000, he committed himself to supporting the Catholic schools of
Winnipeg even without school board funds. He also agreed to build a
Catholic teachers' college in Winnipeg, to modify the teachers' oath
so as to allow religious exercises and instruction, and to have a new
bilingual reader printed at the expense of the province.[86] A few weeks
later Langevin reported that Roblin's attempts to bring the Winnipeg school board to heel again had been unsuccessful. He maintained that it was the fanaticism of four Protestant trustees, not
party politics, that proved to be the stumbling block.

In view of Roblin's concessions, the archbishop wanted Laurier to
transfer interest payments on school lands to the province. Failure to
do so would lead to a crisis,[87] since two Winnipeg schools were so
desperately short of funds that they would close down without
immediate relief.[88] Falconio refused to sanction such a course.[89] The
archbishop, however, insisted. Even Roblin's opponents, he argued,
recognized that the premier had done all he could to facilitate a
settlement. He had repeated his offer to support the Catholic schools

of Winnipeg without school board subsidies if necessary.[90] Undeterred, Falconio revived instead the idea of a national collection in support of Langevin's hard-pressed Winnipeg schools as an alternative to the archbishop's proposal.[91] While grateful, Langevin felt that some recognition of Roblin's goodwill was necessary and so he pressed ahead with a formal petition to Laurier for the interest payments. But this request apparently remained unfulfilled. And there the matter stood until Falconio left for his new posting in Washington.

SBARRETTI: 'NEITHER IRRITATING ACTIONS, NOR FEEBLE
ACQUIESCENCE'

Archbishop Donato Sbarretti took up his charge in Ottawa with precise instructions on the Manitoba schools question which indicated Rome's apparent concern over the lack of progress in attempts to reach an overall settlement. He was told to exert influence upon the government 'neither through irritating actions, nor feeble acquiescence' in order to obtain full legal recognition of Catholic rights. 'And the problem is especially serious,' he was told, 'since it could spread from the province of Manitoba to those other provinces of Canada, where the rights of the church are better recognized, but where they would be more difficult to defend successfully after a first and all too easy capitulation in Manitoba.'[92]

The delegate's arrival coincided with a new initiative on Langevin's part which stemmed from the realization that political parties, both federal and provincial, refused to countenance legislation formally restoring Catholic education in the province. In conjunction with J.A. Macdonnell, a Catholic lawyer from Alexandria, Ontario, Langevin believed that the solution to this impasse lay in a petition to the king reminding him of the promises made by the crown to the inhabitants of the North-West prior to their entry into Confederation.[93] Once the sovereign acknowledged the legitimacy of these promises, Ottawa would then cede to Manitoba its share of crown lands in return for a commitment that a portion of their revenues would be spent in support of Catholic education.[94] This would avoid legislation which everyone agreed would be opposed vehemently by Manitoba Protestants.

Sbarretti confidentially asked the archbishops of Canada for their reactions to Langevin's initiative. Opinion was generally favourable, although divided: O'Brien of Halifax,[95] Bégin of Quebec, and O'Connor of Toronto were in favour; Duhamel of Ottawa and Bruchési of Montreal were non-committal; Gauthier of Kingston was against. Bégin believed that the timing of the petition was right. Both the new king and his government displayed an openness on such questions as home rule for Ireland, the treatment of Boers in post-war southern Africa, and Catholic education in England. With the Merry del Val mission still smouldering in his mind, Bégin said that he was unsure whether the Canadian episcopate would act in concert on this issue. 'Déjà il a éprouvé un insuccès parce que l'Autorité Supérieure n'a pas cru devoir soutenir l'attitude qu'il avait prise. Ira-t-il se risquer encore une fois et amoindrir peut-être davantage son prestige?' In any case, he believed that the petition should have Rome's full backing so as to ensure the support of the English hierarchy 'laquelle nous a fait défaut en 1896' and of the Catholic social and political élite in both England and Canada.[96]

The other archbishops' reactions were less enthusiastic. O'Connor's was a faint endorsement. 'Assuming the statements in the enclosed Petition to be correct, I see no reason why it might not be sent to the King.' He added, though, that bishops should be left free to sign it and that he would not do so for fear of provoking an anti-Catholic backlash which would jeopardize separate schools in Ontario. 'In our times,' he explained, 'constitutional rights are made little of by majorities' which he described elsewhere in the letter as 'the mob.'[97] The archbishops of Montreal and Ottawa worried about the reception the king would give to the petition. The move was extremely serious, they maintained, and Catholics could not risk failure. Bruchési wanted to be assured of the pope's support before further committing himself, while Duhamel preferred to hear his colleagues' reactions before signing the petition.[98]

Charles Hugh Gauthier of Kingston opposed the measure. He doubted that the king would or could act on behalf of Manitoba Catholics. Besides, he considered the move 'inexpediant' [sic] since it would provoke sectarian ire in the same way as had the action of the Dominion government in 1868 [sic]. Gauthier added that Langevin had on several occasions asked his colleagues to sign 'kindered' [sic] documents, but they had refused.[99] In an earlier letter, the archbishop admitted 'to his shame' that he was not well enough informed on the Manitoba schools question, but promised to study it.[100]

In the face of these reactions, the delegate provided Rome with a tempered assessment of the situation. Although he would like to believe that King Edward 'with the sentiments of justice and equity that so distinguish him'[101] would take up the cause, he confessed that he did not hold out much hope for the petition's success. Still, he believed that the king's intercession would have very positive results, even if these were not immediately apparent. As for episcopal backing for the petition, Sbarretti thought that the response of Ontario archbishops was particularly eloquent, although he assured Rome that they would follow any lead set by the Holy See.

Meanwhile the perennial negotiations between Winnipeg Catholics and public school trustees resumed once more. Roblin apparently had actively intervened in the Winnipeg school board elections of 1902 against extremist candidates. One of these, however, managed to get re-elected. The premier wanted talks to reopen in the latter's absence and urged Langevin to comply. Although the archbishop was still leery about such a procedure, Sbarretti pressured him to accept, arguing that these negotiations were the minority's only hope for the foreseeable future.[102] A sceptical archbishop of St Boniface soon sounded a note of optimism as he observed that both the federal and provincial governments were actively working in favour of a settlement and that all the Liberal trustees seemed favourable to the Catholic position.[103] A few weeks later, though, Laurier reported that the latest round of talks had failed.[104] Once again accusations of partisanship were flung about,[105] but the continued refusal of the school board to provide Catholics with adequate guarantees proved once more to be the real stumbling-block. Soon the plight of Winnipeg Catholics was overshadowed by the question of Catholic school rights in the territories about to enter Confederation as the provinces of Saskatchewan and Alberta. As for Manitoba, that school question finally was resolved in 1916 when the newly elected Liberal administration simply abolished the privileges enjoyed by the Catholic minority under the Laurier-Greenway agreement.

CONCLUSION

Laurier's position on the Manitoba schools question may have sprung from political conviction, but clearly it was also a politically comfortable position to take. There were many advantages to following the 'sunny ways': the party avoided the disastrous dissension that wracked the Conservatives in an election year; leaders were spared the need to articulate a position clearly ('sunny ways' was a strategy rather than a bargaining position); this allowed them to appeal to various and even divergent sectarian interests in the electorate, if we assume the Manitoba schools question was an issue at the local level. In Quebec Laurier stressed Catholic rights, in Ontario the rights of the provinces. All this was politically astute, and very successful.

But the emperor had no clothes. Laurier may have promised the Catholic electorate to do better than remedial legislation, but during discussions leading up to the Laurier-Greenway agreement he appears not to have had a clearly defined bargaining position. How else can one explain the accord's failure to improve on what already existed in fact in Manitoba or to provide legislative protection for Catholic education? As such, then, the understanding neither satisfied the requirements of the Brophy judgment by the Judicial Committee of the Privy Council, nor the prime minister's own private and public commitments. And yet Laurier was quite satisfied to rest on his laurels, declaring through the governor general that the question was now settled.

Only under pressure from the apostolic delegate did he reverse himself by stating that the agreement was simply a temporary solution, a first step in the eventual restoration of Catholic schools. He even made a profession of faith in Catholic education for the benefit of the Holy See, which surely must be seen as a novel twist to his political convictions. Laurier insisted to Merry del Val that Ottawa had many means of exerting behind-the-scenes pressure on Manitoba to bring about a satisfactory accommodation. Yet, apart from Ottawa's withholding interest payments on school lands, there is no evidence that Laurier used any pressure tactics to achieve his stated purpose.

The prime minister made a liberal display of his goodwill and of his promises: promises to abolish the teachers' oath; promises to have Catholic readers accepted by the province; promises to bring the Winnipeg school board around to an agreement; promises to provide Winnipeg Catholics with a legal opinion to back their position. But these promises were seldom followed by actions. Father Constantineau himself had to admit that Liberal trustees on the Winnipeg school board had not been prepared for his mission of conciliation, despite Laurier's assurances to that effect. Yet had not the prime minister blamed Langevin for the failure of previous negotiations between the board and the minority, arguing that the archbishop, by acting alone, had not given him the opportunity to ensure the success of the minority's initiative? When his 'sunny ways' seemed ineffectual, Laurier could always use Langevin as a convenient whipping-boy for his oversights and his failures. Or he could blame a political opponent like Roblin.

It could be argued that Laurier had other concerns than the fate of four thousand schoolchildren in a remote part of Canada, but such a view would be making light of his commitments to the Catholic electorate, the apostolic delegate, and the Vatican. One could contend that the prime minister was not omnipotent, that he could not control the actions of locally elected officials, let alone a hostile premier and an uncompromising archbishop. But this raises a question of political responsibility. Who proposed the 'sunny ways' in the first place? Laurier himself told Merry del Val that if this strategy did not succeed, coercive means would have to be considered. The responsibility for restoring Catholic rights in Manitoba belonged ultimately to Ottawa. This was clearly recognized in the judgment of the Judicial Committee of the Privy Council, and blaming the province for the lack of progress in the minority's status was simply an abdication of that responsibility. But considering the political stakes involved, it is apparent that the prime minister simply lacked the will to entrench the minority's educational rights in law. Courage, clarity, commitment, and consistency generally have not been the hallmarks either of Canadian politicians or of those in other western democracies. Laurier's refusal to stake his career on the problems of a tiny minority then should surprise no one.

If Laurier responded to the political exigencies of the moment, the Holy See had pressing concerns also. Throughout Leo XIII's pontificate, the thrust of Vatican foreign policy had been to try to reach an accommodation with governments, in contrast to the splendid isolation that had marked the pontificate of Pius IX, who refused to come to terms with the emergence of the modern state. Policy and personal inclination impelled both Merry del Val and Falconio to seek an accommodation with the Canadian government. But these considerations do not sufficiently explain the position taken by apostolic delegates who identified themselves completely with Laurier in this question. It is true that they stepped into a highly polarized situation and, in this context, found it difficult to remain detached. But there is no evidence that they were influenced in the slightest by anyone other than the prime minister and his clerical supporters in the episcopate and lower clergy.

This is particularly evident in Merry del Val's case. So anxious was he to show that the Conservatives were not as lily-white as some believed that he lost all sense of balance in his analysis and glossed over the Liberals' real failings. Bégin correctly pointed out how uneven was the delegate's comparison of the two parties; he saw only perfidy in the Conservatives' championing remedial action, and only sincerity in the Liberals' obstructionism. And though he minimized the real influence exerted within the Conservative government by Catholic members, he maximized the will of their co-religionists in the Liberal party to re-establish Catholic schools in Manitoba. The Conservatives' faults were very real, but this did not hide certain facts that Bégin highlighted. The school legislation of 1890 in Manitoba was a Liberal government measure and not primarily a sectarian issue. It is true that Protestant legislators overwhelmingly supported it, but there was one notable exception which Merry del Val ignored – Rodmond Roblin. Similarly, in 1896 the parliamentary filibuster in Ottawa was a Liberal party tactic, even though individual Conservatives supported it. The opposition therefore had to bear primary responsibility for the defeat of the remedial bill.

Merry del Val's report showed a marked empathy for Laurier and his political position which did not extend, however, to his opponents. This may have had to do with the fact that the prime minister was a nominal Catholic, whereas the leader of the opposition was Protestant. In any case, the delegate showed a great deal of indulgence toward the leader of a party which, as he put it, having reached the threshhold of power after wandering in the political wilderness for so long, refused to support an 'odious measure' like remedial legislation. The delegate then justified the prime minister's failure to pursue remedial action after taking office, stressing Laurier's precarious political situation, the strength of Protestant antagonism, the tenuous status of Catholic rights and privileges. He did not provide hard evidence for his Cassandra-like pronouncements, ignored the fact that there were differing perceptions concerning these issues, and simply dismissed those who did not share his views as rabid partisans.

But the most glaring shortcoming of Merry del Val's mission was his failure to follow through on his negotiations with Laurier and Greenway. Both he and the Vatican let the fate of Manitoba Catholics rest on the goodwill and empty promises of politicians: that the province would incorporate the Delegate's demands in an order-in-council; that Winnipeg Catholics would be brought into the accord; and that the minority would not be molested any further. The future showed how hollow these promises were. But Manitoba was far away from Merry del Val's preoccupations once he returned to Rome.

Falconio, too, was generous with Laurier. Even though the prime minister made several public statements to the effect that the schools question was settled, the new delegate was quick to qualify Laurier's most recent reiteration of this position as a misunderstanding. He steadfastly maintained that the provincial government had the primary responsibility for reinstituting Catholic educational rights and that Ottawa's role could only be one of persuasion. Falconio also agreed with the prime minister that the schools question required a long-term perspective and that in the interim public opinion could be brought around slowly to a position of magnanimity toward the minority. He never bothered to ask, however, whose responsibility it was to change public opinion. Certainly Laurier did nothing to bring about this change.

Both Merry del Val and Falconio underestimated the difficulties involved in producing a lasting settlement. Their desire to raise the educational issue above politics was commendable, even if it ignored the fact that partisanship did not merely happen to be the foible of one archbishop, but was an intrinsic part of this question – so much so that it stymied all genuine efforts to bring about an agreement. In fact partisanship was embedded in the culture of local communities as well as in provincial and federal administrations. It was, of course, as easy for the delegates as for Laurier to find scapegoats when they encountered setbacks, but finding solutions was much more difficult.

The delegates' perspective was predicated on the belief that 'sunny ways' would dispel the storm clouds of intolerance and usher in a climate of mutual acceptance and understanding in which Catholic rights would be fully recognized. Merry del Val did not seem to realize that Canada was not England, where the Catholic minority finally was receiving equitable treatment in civil rights and education. In Canada, as in other colonial outposts or frontier areas, the roots of intolerance ran deeply; the mood was not one of generosity. Instead, the culture that came to predominate in the central and western parts of English-speaking Canada was narrow and unaccommodating. It did not apparently occur to the delegates that the position of Catholics could get worse, that Protestant intolerance might well sweep away the last vestiges of Catholic rights, as indeed happened in the West over the next fifteen years.

Yet had not the French-Canadian hierarchy warned that the failure to entrench Catholic educational rights in Manitoba would endanger these rights elsewhere? Instead of heeding the warnings and advice of bishops who possessed an historical consciousness, particularly in questions involving the precariousness of minority rights, the delegates preferred to listen to the Ontario episcopate, to archbishops such as Walsh and Gauthier who confessed their ignorance of an issue which should have riveted their attention. These were men who walked in the shadow of Protestant intolerance and, despite the constitutional guarantees protecting their schools, feared that the assertion of their rights would invite only repression. Their fears were those expressed by Merry del Val and Falconio, fears about schools, subsidies, and jobs – fears that nevertheless were not felt by Archbishop O'Brien of Halifax, despite the legal uncertainty of Catholic rights in the Maritimes. In any event, the French-Canadian bishops were determined not to be an obstacle to the 'sunny ways.' Once they understood that Rome wanted to pursue this course, they withdrew from movements of agitation in favour of the Manitoba minority. Bégin even refrained from expressing his views on the matter except in strictly confidential correspondence.

Langevin was therefore left to be the sole champion of the minority's cause. Was he the man for such a heavy burden? It has been said that he was partisan. If, however, he supported the Conservatives in 1896, it was not from political atavism. They promised what he, and Taché before him, had been seeking since the inception of the crisis. If, on the other hand, he opposed the Liberals, it was because they did not offer legislative safeguards for Catholic rights in the province.

He has been accused of intransigence. But when Rome decided that the accommodation had to be tried, he reluctantly complied. Should he have followed the road to conciliation sooner? It is unlikely that either Langevin or the French-Canadian hierarchy could have obtained what the full weight of Vatican diplomacy achieved, which in any case was not much. Merry del Val certainly expected a more conciliatory attitude from him. But since the delegate excluded him from his talks with Greenway and Laurier, it was difficult for the archbishop to identify himself with a process in which he was not involved. In the aftermath of the Merry del Val mission, the archbishop was left to seek out improvements to a bad situation from a hostile provincial government. If Catholic schools functioned in this period, it was only because they were situated in communities that were ethnically compact and homogeneous. Dissatisfied with this partial accommodation, however, Langevin sought concessions for urban Catholics who were mostly non-French-speaking. Despite these and other efforts to serve the many ethnic communities under his care, he was criticized by members of his English-speaking flock for, among other things, favouring his own group. At the same time he was pressured by Laurier and Falconio to accept the Winnipeg school board's professions of goodwill. Yet the fact that intransigent trustees always managed to be represented on the Winnipeg board boded ill for a compromise that patently went against the intent of the law and could only survive through the forbearance of all board members.

When Rodmond Roblin came to power, Langevin showed him some sympathy, not simply because he was Conservative but because the new premier had voted against the 1890 legislation and was well disposed toward the Catholic minority. But the sincerity and goodwill of a Roblin – or for that matter of a Laurier – were not enough to vanquish ingrained partisanship and Protestant bigotry. This Langevin well knew. His actions were not those of one who was rabidly partisan or unyielding, but one who realized that the 'sunny ways' recommended by Rome, the apostolic delegation, the Liberal party, and the Ontario episcopate led to a dead end. This was the drama which Langevin lived from day to day and its full impact would only be felt later by the minority. The Manitoba schools question really was a story of broken promises and broken dreams.

Chapter Six

Pariahs of the Nation: Immigrants within the Church

The human cargo of emigrants massed together on the docks of Liverpool could not have escaped Archbishop Falconio's attention as he waited in September 1899 to board the *Vancouver* for Quebec City. Liverpool was one of the busiest emigration depots in Europe and from there over one hundred thousand Englishmen, Irish, Scandinavians, and even Eastern Europeans left the old continent each year, lured by the prospect of economic gain and religious and political toleration in the new world. Given his elevated rank, Falconio would not have brushed shoulders with this mass of humanity on the docks, nor would he have appreciated the cramped conditions in which they travelled as steerage passengers, since he himself had a first-class ticket. Was the archbishop even aware as he crossed the Atlantic that immigration would be a major issue of his administration as apostolic delegate?

The establishment in 1899 of a permanent delegation in Canada coincided with the arrival of the first large wave of non-English and non-French speaking immigrants to this country. Since many of these newcomers were Catholic, the question arose as to how the Canadian church's structures would be modified to meet their needs. The issue was not new. It had manifested itself on a bigger scale and in starker terms in other parts of the Americas where immigrants formed much larger and more compact communities. But in Canada, where the different components of the country's charter groups already experienced such difficulty reaching an accommodation within the church, the immigrant question complicated an already complex problem of ethnic relations. In general the hierarchy in Eastern

Canada was not particularly sensitive to the needs of non-charter Catholic immigrants. If some elementary services were provided in a few dioceses, it was usually as a result of outside pressure.

The arrival around the turn of the century of a large number of Ukrainians from the Austro-Hungarian empire, or Ruthenians as they were then called, posed particular problems. Most of them were Uniate Catholics, descendants of Orthodox Christians who in 1595 recognized the primacy of the see of Peter. Rome in turn accepted their particular liturgy and discipline. This meant recognition not only of separate religious practices but a different religious sensibility. Ukrainian churches had, and continue to have, a distinctive external and internal architecture. The mass is said in Old Slavonic behind the iconostasis or screen separating the sanctuary from the nave. Statuary is as foreign to church interiors as the recitation of the rosary is to devotional exercises. At the turn of the century many of the Uniate lower clergy were married. In addition, it was not unusual in some cities of Eastern Europe to find as many as three bishops, each belonging to a different rite but all in communion with Rome, sharing the same diocese. Were these complex structures to be carried over to the new world?

Irish domination of the Catholic hierarchy in the United States, and extreme sensitivity to anything that might appear to be foreign interference, made immigrants unable to identify with the church through its practices and leadership. Schisms occurred in a number of immigrant communities, particularly from Eastern Europe, as a result of the Irish-American hierarchy's failure to respond adequately to their concerns. There was greater awareness of the immigrants' particular spiritual needs in Western Canada and a general commitment to provide requisite services, perhaps because the local church was dominated by French-speaking Oblates. But neither these bishops, nor the apostolic delegate, were equipped to confront the special problems posed by Ukrainian immigrants. It was only because of outside pressure that a resolution eventually was found to these problems, but not in time to prevent the outbreak of schism.

THE VATICAN AND IMMIGRATION

The Holy See became sensitive to the fact of emigration at the time of the first mass movement of people out of Italy in the 1880s which stirred the public conscience and sparked a lively debate among the country's educated élite. Before then Rome must have viewed mass emigration as a Northern European – and therefore largely Protestant – phenomenon. Catholics who emigrated in large numbers either did so in a very structured setting, as the Germans through their *Rafaelsverein* (an organization set up in the 1870s, to meet the immigrants' spiritual and physical needs), or they went to countries considered to be culturally compatible. But the mass exodus of Italians after 1880, many of them seeking economic opportunities in the United States, created problems of spiritual care never before confronted by the Holy See. Bishops from Brazil, Argentina, and the United States wrote to Rome about the desperate material and spiritual condition of Italian immigrants in their countries.

The testimony of the American hierarchy particularly held the Propaganda's attention. At that time the episcopate of the United States was largely the preserve of the Irish, a phenomenon which at least one historian with tongue in cheek described as 'hibernarchy.'[1] These bishops were anxious to prove to their Protestant compatriots in this burgeoning age of American might that Catholics, although a minority, were as American as the best of them. But it was difficult to keep up the appearance that the church belonged to the mainstream when hundreds of thousands of European Catholic peasants were pouring into the country every year. The shadow of foreignness cast by these immigrants was certainly not dispelled by their insistence that the church serve them in their own language. Worse still, peasants from southern Italy clung tenaciously to public displays of religious practices which confirmed widely held Protestant assumptions that Catholicism was synonymous with superstition and idolatry. The American hierarchy's desperate search for respectability was suffering a severe setback. But there was yet another issue separating the episcopate from recently arrived Catholic immigrants. Italians in particular were reluctant to make financial contributions to a church that did not reflect their cultural concerns. For their part, the bishops who generally subscribed to a managerial or self-help model of ecclesiastical development accused these immigrants of taking advantage of the church by seeking all the benefits without sharing the burdens. These complaints found their way to Rome in the American hierarchy's general indictment against Italian immigration. The bishops asked the Holy See to encourage changes in Italy that would promote more enlightened emigration to the Republic.

The concerns of the American hierarchy were not necessarily those of the Holy See. In the early 1880s Rome tried to sensitize the archbishops of Italian port cities, starting points of the immigrants' *via dolorosa*, to the deplorable spiritual conditions of those who crossed the Atlantic. The Propaganda looked to the creation of structures such as the *Rafaelsverein* to care for the immigrants' material and spiritual needs from the time they left their village to their settlement in the new world.[2] But these pious hopes resulted in little concrete action. As a result, the Propaganda sought more authoritative measures to focus attention on the serious plight of Italian immigrants. A background paper was prepared in 1887, reputedly by Giovanni Battista Scalabrini, bishop of Piacenza, to inform the Propaganda's actions.[3]

The document was a realistic assessment of the immigrant experience. It bluntly stated that the mass exodus from Italy often assumed all the features of a white slave trade. Immigrants, it argued, were preyed upon by agents of shipping companies 'which speculate on their misery and do not attend to their personal welfare. They are thrown together in overcrowded ships without distinction to age and sex in conditions detrimental to health and morality.'[4] Once in the new land, they were victimized either by their ignorance of the host country's language and customs or by go-betweens such as ethnic bosses or proselytizing Protestant ministers who, while they promised a wide range of social services, were sure to exact their due.

But the immigrants' trials did not end there. The report painted an even gloomier picture of those who already were settled in the United States.

It is humiliating to have to admit that after the Indians' disappearance from the United States and the Negroes' emancipation, it is the Italian immigrants who have become the pariahs in the great American Republic. One need only mention that they are held in such contempt for their filth and their poverty that the Irish of New York gave them the free use of the *basement* of [a church] to come together for worship.[5]

The document observed that while Italians remained outsiders, other immigrant communities were well integrated into the political and economic fabric of America. The reason was that these groups retained their native language and identity and as a result formed compact communities within the republic. The Italians, on the other hand, were fragmented because of their many dialects and particularistic cultures. Since they were unable to establish structures allowing them to act as a group, they experienced a double form of alienation. The first generation became inward-looking, clinging to the customs of the old-country village culture which aggravated their isolation. Their offspring, acculturated by American schools and deprived of institutions reflecting their Italian heritage, lost their language and their faith. 'Slowly these poor families undergo change and lose themselves in only a few years in the great American nation and ultimately nothing remains of their Italian culture but their name.'[6] This situation of cultural fragmentation was made worse by the geographic dispersal of Italian migrants ('da New York a San Francisco, dall'Ontario al Texas').

Cultural factors were believed to be primarily responsible for the Italian immigrants' marginalization. The report suggested that through such structures as 'national' parishes, parochial schools, and social welfare agencies specifically tailored to the immigrants' needs, the church was in an ideal position to bring Italians out of their cultural and geographic ghettos and foster their integration into American life. The document went on to argue that language and religion were inextricably tied: the Catholic faith could only flourish in a familiar linguistic setting. The stronger the immigrants' attachment to Italian, the surer the foundations of religion. English-speaking churches, it maintained, were not only linguistically alien but actually contributed to loss of faith in the first as well as succeeding generations.

A comprehensive set of measures was recommended to deal with this desperate situation. These included the institution of local and national immigration committees in Italy, the United States, and other parts of the Americas to tend to the immigrants' spiritual and material needs. But more important was the establishment of a seminary in the northern Italian city of Piacenza, to train priests specifically for pastoral work among Italian immigrants. Considering how dispersed these people were in the new world, it was proposed that 'flying missions' be established in order to serve them wherever they might be, whether in big cities or in bush camps. Leo XIII enthusiastically endorsed these resolutions and announced his intention of sending a representative to the United States to conduct a full inquiry into the condition of Italian immigrants. This envoy, a bishop, would be given extensive powers. But to avoid giving offence to episcopal sensibilities, the pope wanted a letter sent to the American bishops inviting them to suggest the limitations that reasonably could be placed on his representative's authority.

NORTH AMERICAN RESPONSES TO VATICAN INITIATIVES

The American hierarchy strenuously opposed the pope's move on the grounds that it would leave their church vulnerable to accusations of foreign domination. They also disagreed with the premises of the Propaganda's report. They considered filth, sloth, poverty, and religious indifference to be atavistic to southern Italians. Nevertheless, although Rome was not immune from such quasi-racist assumptions – as clearly was indicated by the preference for northern Italian priests – the Propaganda insisted that religious indifference was more the result of neglect by the American church than a cause of the immigrants' aloofness.

The American hierarchy's stance limited the concrete results of the Holy See's initiatives. Apart from the founding of a Scalabrinian seminary in Piacenza, Leo XIII had to be satisfied with the publication in late 1888 of the letter *Quam ærumnosa*, addressed to the episcopates of North and South America.[7] This document, borrowing liberally from Propaganda's report, tried to rouse the bishops to the immigrants' plight. Despite these modest achievements, the report and the papal letter are important because, among other things, they elicited a response, no matter how perfunctory, from the Canadian hierarchy to the condition of Italian immigrants in Canada.[8] These documents also serve as yardsticks by which to measure the Canadian church's later treatment of non-Italian immigrants.

Of the Canadian episcopate, only Cardinal Taschereau bothered to reply to *Quam ærumnosa*. He stated rather cryptically that the few Italians who ventured into his ecclesiastical province as part of railway construction gangs had gone long since because they found the climate too rigorous.[9] For his part, Archbishop Fabre only volunteered information on Montreal's Italians whose numbers he seriously underestimated when pressed by the Propaganda. He claimed: 'Ils ne comptent que pour quelques centaines en hiver; en été leur nombre est moins considérable. Quelques familles seulement sont établies à Montreal; les autres n'y sont pas fixes.'[10] The threat of competition from a newly established Protestant mission headed by an Italian ex-priest was what finally goaded Fabre into seeking a more stable and long-term arrangement for their spiritual care. After a few false starts the archbishop finally found an Italian priest who agreed in 1895 to serve his compatriots in Montreal.

The situation in the other archdioceses is sketchy. In Ottawa the archbishop's secretary, a French-Canadian graduate of the Urban College in Rome, began to look after the local Italians in 1892. His pastoral work, coming as it did on the heels of *Quam ærumnosa*, was probably in response to pressures from the Propaganda. The priest apparently served his immigrants devotedly until he was transferred to another position ten years later.[11] It is not known whether the Italian mission continued after his departure. In Toronto auxiliary Bishop Timothy O'Mahony asked Rome for Italian catechisms and pious readings in 1884 to counteract Protestant proselytizing efforts among the immigrant population. He observed that many destitute Italian migrant workers had recently arrived in the city because the Canadian Pacific Railway defrauded them of their wages.[12] Years later the Redemptorists of St Patrick's cared for Toronto's Italians until the establishment of their first national parish in 1908. What happened in the period between O'Mahony's letter and the time the Redemptorists took charge of these immigrants is unclear. In London two fresh graduates of the Urban College reported in 1883 that they were catering to the city's thirty-five Italian families, most of them Sicilian, left largely unattended prior to their own arrival.[13] In the West, the polyglot Oblate community occasionally ministered to Italian railway and mine workers.[14] All of this indicates a rather sporadic and haphazard approach to the spiritual care of Italians, which was a far cry from the measures advocated in the Propaganda document.

The arrival of a distinguished Italian prelate in the person of the first permanent apostolic delegate did not significantly change things. Falconio actually turned away a number of Italian priests who offered to come to Canada to serve their compatriots,[15] explaining that, apart from the Italians living in Montreal whose needs were adequately met, the others were too few and too dispersed to be served with priests from their own country. Besides, he maintained, many of them were well cared for at no extra cost by clerics who had learned their language while studying in Rome. Clearly, the geographic spread of Italian immigrants in Canada and the difficult financial circumstances of Canadian dioceses heavily influenced the church's response to the Holy See's policy on Italian immigrants.

THE PLIGHT OF UKRAINIAN IMMIGRANTS

If Italian immigrants were in a state of relative spiritual neglect in *fin de siècle* Canada, the condition of Ukrainians was much worse. Their sheer number, their pattern of compact settlement and consequently their visibility, their grinding poverty in these pioneer years – all these factors conspired to make them hold in Canada the unenviable status reserved for the Italians in the United States. However, their religious position was far more complicated and depended to a large extent on the policies established by Rome and on events south of the border.

In the early 1890s the American hierarchy complained to Rome about Ukrainian priests, many of whom were married, arriving in the United States without proper papers and showing a marked disregard, if not downright disrespect, for their ecclesiastical superiors. Nor was the welcome the bishops accorded these priests particularly warm, as Archbishop Ireland's reception of Archpriest Alexis Tovt made glaringly clear. Without being too subtle about it, Ireland questioned the validity of the Uniate priest's ordination and of the bishop who had given him holy orders.

The American bishops were not so much bothered by the failure of these clerics to follow proper ecclesiastical procedures for immigrating to the new world as by their being married. So concerned were they that married clergymen represented a fundamental threat to clerical celibacy and a cause of public scandal that they determined to stop their immigration. 'The possible loss of a few souls of the Greek rite,' argued the American archbishops in 1893, 'bears no proportion to the blessings resulting from uniformity of discipline.'[16] In the event, the few souls lost to the church numbered 220,000 by the beginning of the new century.

Bowing to these pressures, the Congregation of Oriental Affairs of the Propaganda Fide decreed that only celibate priests could emigrate from Austria-Hungary to the Americas and that, in doing so, they had to submit to the authority of local Latin bishops. The decree also prescribed proper procedures for clerical emigration.[17] The subjection of Uniate priests to Latin bishops represented a notable departure from past practices and caused a great deal of resentment among the clergy and laity of the Eastern rite. In the aftermath of this decree an agreement was drawn up between Vicar General Albert Lacombe representing the bishops of St Boniface, St Albert, and Prince Albert, and present and future Ukrainian missionaries operating in their dioceses. The bishops fully recognized the Uniate priests' freedom to operate within their own rite subject to the exclusive authority of the local bishop. They also offered to help these missionaries financially if the immigrant faithful did not provide them with sufficient support. This agreement remained a dead letter, not only because so few Uniate priests ventured to the Canadian West, but also because, the bishops of the area were not prepared to assume the financial burdens implied in the accord.

A few years later the Congregation for Oriental Affairs became concerned that Ukrainian immigrants were not receiving proper spiritual care. As a result, a decree was issued stipulating that the archbishops of those North American ecclesiastical provinces with sufficiently large numbers of Ukrainian settlers were to designate a 'suitable' celibate Uniate priest to look after their interests. 'In the absence of such, a Latin priest, well accepted by the Ruthenians, to whom would be entrusted under the authority of the local bishop the supervision and direction of the people and clergy of the Ruthenian rite [would have to be named].'[18] These pieces of legislation determined the response of the Canadian episcopate to Ukrainian immigrants.

The principles underlying these acts were perhaps noble; the reality was quite different. Since an estimated 97 per cent of the Uniate clergy were married at the time, the 1894 decree had the effect of cutting off virtually all clerical immigration to Canada at a time when Ukrainians were arriving in unprecedented numbers. A French-Canadian priest observed in 1898 that two hundred Ukrainian families had settled recently at Star (Vegreville), in the diocese of St Albert. They had been left to their own devices until two Orthodox clergymen began to court them, at which point auxiliary Bishop Legal was dispatched to keep them steady in the faith.[19] Throughout the West the dearth of Uniate priests was indeed dramatic. In the diocese of St Albert at the turn of the century only one such priest and a Polish Oblate served the Ukrainians, whereas in the archdiocese of St Boniface, two Polish Oblates looked after fourteen thousand recently arrived immigrants from Galicia.[20] Falconio feared that this situation would cause many of the twenty-thousand-odd Ukrainian Catholics to leave the church.

There was no doubt that in this context the Ukrainians were ripe for proselytism and the Russian Orthodox church was only too happy to step into the breach. Orthodoxy had a rite and a discipline which in many ways were familiar to the immigrants. It also offered definite financial advantages to the hard-pressed Ukrainian settler since the Russian government subsidized its clergy operating in North America. But the danger to the Ukrainian's faith also came from elsewhere. Falconio noted that immigrants 'in general were little given to piety, were greedy for gain and freedom and under the constant influence of Protestants who dominate them.'[21] The newcomers depended on the Protestant capitalist not only for jobs but on a whole range of social services freely dispensed by sectarian agencies. Falconio deplored the fact that Protestants opened the doors of their schools wide to these immigrants' children, even persuading some to study theology.

However, the absence of a Uniate clergy was also being exploited by Ukrainian laymen and itinerant priests within the fold. Although the situations in Canada and the United States were quite different, the American experience none the less affected events north of the border. Immigrants were influenced by Ukrainian Americans through newspapers, letters, and visits, or by Ukrainians back home whose perspective was shaped by happenings in the United States. These counselled their Canadian compatriots to be wary of or even to reject the authority of the Latin bishops, to keep the ownership and administration of church property in their own hands.[22] As a result, a movement arose within the laity which challenged the bishop's prerogative to own and manage church property, a challenge that was upheld by the Judicial Committee of the Privy Council in 1907.[23]

Proselytism and the lay movement drove the ecclesiastical authorities to be more attentive to the needs of Ukrainian immigrants. But pressure in this direction also came from the outside. A Ruthenian delegate to the Austrian *Reichsrat* asked the foreign minister what the government was doing about the religious care of his compatriots in America. The minister replied that he was fully aware of the deplorable state in which the Ukrainians found themselves and that he was actively corresponding with the Vatican on this question. The crux of the problem, he maintained, was the prohibition of married clergy in the new world. The ambitions of the few celibate clergy that could be found in Galicia and Hungary did not extend westward to the Americas, but upward to the episcopate.[24]

Meanwhile the Austro-Hungarian ambassador pressed the Holy

See for an effective solution to the problem. He cast doubts on the North American hierarchy's willingness to implement the decree concerning the designation of clergy for the care of Ukrainians in their diocese. The results of the bishops' inaction, according to the ambassador, were very serious; the apostasy of so many immigrants was not only a spiritual, but a social blight, as return migrants often became political subversives. Speaking on his government's behalf, he requested that Rome name priests accredited to the respective apostolic delegations of Canada and the United States as apostolic visitors to oversee these neglected Ukrainian immigrants.[25]

The Holy See reacted quickly. After studying the ambassador's proposal, Cardinals Satolli and Ciasca together with the two secretaries of the Propaganda gave it their approval, subject to certain conditions. They wanted the apostolic delegates concerned to be consulted. They also sought a number of expedients by which the appointment of apostolic visitors could be made without tarnishing the prestige of episcopal office in North America.[26] Finally, they insisted that the government of Austria-Hungary pay the visitors' costs of transportation and support.[27] These recommendations met with the full approval of the pope, who clearly was preoccupied by the seriousness of the problem.[28] As a result, Secretary of State Rampolla communicated the Austro-Hungarian government's concerns to the Holy See's representatives in Washington and Ottawa and sought their opinion concerning these appointments.[29]

OPPOSITION TO SPECIAL STATUS

The American hierarchy, ever anxious to avoid being tarred as un-American, reacted predictably. The apostolic delegate, Sebastiano Martinelli, questioned the special status which apparently was being conferred on the Ukrainians. Were not other immigrants exposed to the same spiritual dangers? And would not the appointment of a Visitor serve to excite national jealousies? Was not the populous Polish community as deserving of special attention? Martinelli pointed out that Ukrainian settlements were too sparse in the United States, and the immigrants themselves too poor, to support their own churches and clergy. Significantly he added: 'It is the wish ... of the American Bishops and Government that the even the Ruthenians along with those belonging to other nationalities should assimilate with the Americans to form one people. If we permit an exception for the Ruthenians in time other nationalities would make their claim to exceptional status.'[30]

But the response of the Canadian hierarchy was equally negative. Archbishop Langevin termed it 'une vraie calamité.'[31] His whole perspective was coloured by his negative impression of the itinerant Uniate clergymen he had met in previous years. Better, he thought, to bring the Ukrainians gradually to the Latin church, subjecting them to zealous priests who already had shown their devotion to ecclesiastical authority. Langevin in fact was proposing that some of his clerics, without abandoning their own rite, take on certain aspects of the Eastern liturgy 'qui suffiraient pour satisfaire ces pauvres gens ignorants et pleins de défiance vis à vis des Latins.'[32] Eventually, he hoped, one could look forward to unity of worship and concord among the different strains of the immigrant population. The archbishop added that one of the two Polish Oblates who was ministering successfully to the Ukrainian population could be given a kind of superintendence over them. At the same time the Oblate superior general in Rome might consider sending other Polish subjects to Canada and perhaps even founding a seminary in Galicia. This last proposal, he hoped, might strengthen relations between Rome and the Eastern church and help to dissipate Uniate hostility to the Latin clergy.[33]

But the nomination of an apostolic visitor he considered a sure recipe for chaos. It would mean the perpetuation in Canada of a dual structure, of two hostile clans warring in the bosom of mother church. And Langevin offered as evidence the suspicious and belligerent attitude that some Uniate priests had shown him, clearly believing that such behaviour was common to all Ukrainian clergymen. 'Le mauvais esprit montré par les prêtres Ruthènes qui sont venus ici, en ces derniers temps, et le peu de garantie de piété, de désintéressement et de fidélité au St-Siège qu'offre le clergé ruthène de Galicie, ne nous donne [sic] guères de confiance dans le succès de ces prêtres défiants et exigeants qui tourneront le peuple contre les évêques latins.'[34] Canada would have not only bad priests, but in a few years married ones as well, since the nomination of a visitor was the Trojan horse that would introduce this scandalous innovation into the country. Before long, Langevin predicted, the Ukrainians would even have their own bishop![35]

While less categorical than his metropolitan, Bishop Grandin shared Langevin's preoccupation with the Uniate clergy's lack of zeal and their hatred of everything Roman. 'C'est plutôt parce [que les Ukrainiens] ont eu des prêtres de leur langue qu'ils sont passés au schisme, que parce qu'ils en manquaient ... Ce sont des prêtres de leur nation et de leur rite résidant aux États-Unis qui les ont, paraît-il, toujours prévenus contre nous.' Grandin cited the example of Ivan Zaklynski, a Ukrainian priest, who on visiting his countrymen at Star advised them that they would be better off to become Orthodox than to submit to Latin clergy. It was clear, the prelate continued, that this priest followed his own advice since he pointedly refused to call on either his bishop or his Latin counterparts during his lengthy stay in the diocese. Grandin even doubted that Zaklynski had ever been to confession in all the time he was in the Territories.

Not that the Uniate priest could afford to be without the sacrament. In fact the bishop of St Albert had heard disturbing rumours about Zaklynski's personal conduct. But worse still were comments regarding the clergyman's fees for spiritual services, including confession, dispensed to 'ces pauvres ignorants,' which only served to confirm Protestant misconceptions about Catholicism. Grandin added that even as commendable a priest as Paul Tymkiewicz, who came to the West in 1898 highly recommended by the Propaganda, had stirred up his compatriots against episcopal ownership of their church. The bishop held Tymkiewicz indirectly responsible for the loss of the building when a number of parishioners in whose name it was registered embraced Orthodoxy. Rather than having to submit to such fractious behaviour, Grandin preferred that Ukrainians not be entirely satisfied when they requested their own priests.[36]

In contrast to Langevin, however, the bishop of St Albert still felt that only a good Uniate priest could ward off the dangers of schism and instil in the faithful a proper respect for ecclesiastical authority. To avoid all the dangers of a dual system, Grandin recommended that the proposed visitor be subject to the immediate authority of the apostolic delegate. Grandin also warned Falconio about the heavy financial burdens which his diocese would have to bear in providing for the personal and liturgical needs of Uniate priests, as well the construction of new churches. The episcopal corporation, he insisted, could not take on such heavy commitments without external support.[37]

Falconio held an amalgam of both these views. He suggested that Rome send a distinguished Uniate priest to Canada who should be designated not as a Visitor under the apostolic delegate, but as a vicar general under the authority of the respective bishops. This formula, he felt, would safeguard the prestige of the episcopate, who might take umbrage at having to relinquish part of their authority to another prelate.[38] In any case, the delegate was of the firm opinion that the Ukrainians would have to be brought prudently and gradually into the Latin church so as to preserve the long-term unity of authority and rite in Canada. He saw the nomination of the Visitor as a means to that end. Falconio clearly shared Langevin's preoccupation with the poor quality of Uniate priests, insisting that only those truly devoted to the See of Peter should be allowed to emigrate from Austria-Hungary. And only two or three of those would be necessary to cater to the needs of the more populous settlements in Canada. Ukrainians living in isolated communities would have to be content with Latin priests speaking their language. In this way the financially hard-pressed dioceses of the West would not be overburdened.[39] Falconio then assured the Propaganda that despite the vehemence of Langevin's position, the episcopate would accept whatever formula was considered best in Rome. But he insisted that the problem was truly critical and that the Holy See had to act quickly.

While awaiting action from Rome, the delegate and the episcopate took a number of initiatives to improve the Ukrainians' spiritual condition. In the spring of 1900 the diocese of St Albert dispatched Albert Lacombe on a European mission whose aim included the provision of better care to the hard-pressed Ukrainian immigrants.[40] From Rome Lacombe reported that the Holy See was opposed to the proposal that Latin priests go over to the Eastern rite. Such a move, it was felt, would be inappropriate in a country where the Latin church was so preponderant. Rome was responding here to a request made a few months earlier by a Polish priest in Lacombe's diocese who sought permission to follow both the Latin and the Eastern rites because of the financial liability of becoming a Uniate priest at the exclusive service of poor Ukrainian settlers.[41] Lacombe met with the ambassador of Austria-Hungary to the Holy See. Though very kind and devout, the diplomat declined to provide the vicar general with a letter of recommendation for his trip to Vienna and points east,[42] doubtless fearing that Lacombe's efforts to recruit Ukrainian clergymen would undermine his own lobbying for an apostolic visitor.

In the event, it was a well-recommended Lacombe who travelled in Austria-Hungary with letters from Archbishop Falconio and the apostolic nuncios in Vienna and Brussels. He met with the foreign minister, with Bishop A. Szeptycki of Stanislav (now Ivano-Frankovsk) whom he described as 'un saint évêque remarquable par sa science et son zèle,'[43] and even with Emperor Franz Joseph. Commenting on this event, Lacombe told Bishop Legal: 'Je vous en prie, ne riez pas de votre vieux sauvage!'[44] alluding to the vicar general's long service among the Cree Indians. His discussions with these men were all couched in terms of the imminent departure of two apostolic visitors to North America whose expenses, together with those of other Uniate missionaries, would be paid by His Apostolic Majesty's government.[45]

In the wake of these talks, Falconio extended an invitation to Bishop Szeptycki, apparently the man who would be choosing the apostolic visitors and himself freshly designated Greek Catholic archbishop of Lvov and metropolitan of Galicia, to visit Canada in order to assess how desperate the needs of his compatriots really were.[46] The archbishop readily accepted the invitation, subject to Rome's approval.[47] But that was precisely the stumbling-block. Cardinal Ledochowski believed that such a visit would infringe upon legislation which ordered Eastern Catholics living in North America to be subject to their Latin bishops.[48] The archbishop of Lvov therefore had to decline the invitation. But Rome was aware that the situation of Ukrainian immigrants in Canada required an immediate if partial solution. A few days after his negative response to the Szeptycki mission, Ledochowski announced that Uniate priests belonging to the Basilian order would soon be leaving for Canada. Falconio greeted the news with enthusiasm. But he took the opportunity to tell the Propaganda that the Oblate bishops of the West were not sufficiently sensitive to the limitations of their order to cater to the spiritual needs of an increasingly cosmopolitan population. The arrival of members of a different religious community, he thought, should spur the Oblates to seek the help of yet more communities. Falconio himself had tried unsuccessfully to convince his fellow Franciscans from Cincinnati to serve central and eastern European immigrants to the West.[49] He regarded the arrival of the Basilians as providential and believed that 'if well disposed, they could induce these Ruthenians in centres where the immigrant population is mixed to attend Latin churches and perhaps with time and prudence even bring them all to a unity of rite.'[50]

The delegate was correct in detecting a certain complacency among the Oblates, especially in Langevin. It was not that the archbishop was opposed, as were many of his American colleagues, to the adoption of more intensive or even special measures to care for Ukrainian immigrants. But he himself did not actively pursue this course; he was content to leave the initiative to others, such as Grandin and Falconio, while praising the scarcely adequate work done by his own priests. The sense of urgency that had driven the archbishop in the schools question was not as readily apparent in this issue. Langevin also implicitly accepted the perspective of Polish and German priests on the Ukrainian population, apparently oblivious to the prejudices and hostilities which historically marked the relations between these European peoples.

The archbishop, for example, was quite convinced that the Polish Oblate, Albert Kulawy, was slowly gaining the confidence of the Ukrainians he had served for two years. Langevin stated that in some communities Kulawy was considered one of their own.[51] The Polish priest was certainly zealous in his care of eastern European immigrants. In a letter to Langevin he provided a colourful account of his peregrinations in the Dauphin district of Manitoba which he covered in two weeks, visiting one thousand families in eleven centres.

I travel during the night often on a conveyance drawn by slow-footed oxen or 'per pedes apostolorum' which is called in French, the coach of St-Francis. One night I carried my portable chapel which is very heavy 16 miles, then I slept in a hay-stack, the cold was intense and the hay anything but warm. It was like Bethlehem, but Bethlehem in Manitoba.[52]

Kulawy noted that although he was received with diffidence by most Ukrainian settlers, their initial reaction quickly changed when he showed them a willingness to speak their language and learn their hymns. He added significantly that the zeal of Latin priests would certainly compare favourably in the eyes of these settlers with the mercenary instincts of itinerant Uniate clergymen who invariably put a price on the spiritual services they offered.[53]

Despite Kulawy's obvious enthusiasm for his work, he was not exempt from old feelings of Polish superiority. He maintained for instance that the dangers which threatened his Ukrainian flock came largely from within their community, from the preachers of socialism and even atheism. 'Unhappily,' he added, 'the Ruthenians are more exposed to be deceived and to fall away because of their ignorance. The Poles, on the contrary, reject these impious attacks with courage and success because they are better taught and more religious.' Elsewhere Kulawy stressed that many of the immigrant communities commonly considered to be Ukrainian contained Polish settlers as well. 'I say this because it is thought that we receive ... only an inferior class of Ruthenians ... the truth being, that there are also many Poles amongst these emigrants ... profoundly attached to the Bishop, to the Pope, to the Holy Roman Church.'[54] The comparison between these two peoples scarcely could have been more unfavourable to the Ukrainians.

Kulawy and his brother William, Oblate pastor of the Polish parish of the Holy Spirit in Winnipeg, sought to encourage Ukrainians to contribute to the building and the support of churches which could be used by all Catholics. Langevin noted that Albert Kulawy was achieving some success in this regard, notably in the settlement at Stuartburn, while the Ukrainians of Winnipeg were attending the Church of the Holy Spirit in growing numbers, celebrating their feast days according to the Julian calendar. Only a small minority, he claimed, insisted on worshipping in a miserable little chapel which they themselves had recently built.[55] On the whole, Langevin concluded, the cases of apostasy had been rare among Ukrainians in the wake of Kulawy's ministrations and very few died without the sacraments.[56] The Propaganda was certainly satisfied with these achievements and Ledochowski asked the apostolic delegate to say as much to the Polish Oblate.[57]

FALCONIO'S FACT-FINDING EFFORTS

Although Falconio shared Langevin's long-term goal of 'Latinizing' the Ukrainians, he was a great deal more sceptical about the acceptability and efficacy of Polish priests serving these immigrants. He was haunted by the spectre of apostasy and sought reports from the field that might counterbalance Kulawy's and Langevin's excessive optimism. These bore out what Falconio would come to term the Ukrainians' obstinacy in clinging to their rite and their intense suspicion of anything Latin.[58] Soon the delegate's worst fears were confirmed. He reported in March 1901 the distressing news that twenty leading Ukrainian families in the diocese of St Albert had gone over to Orthodoxy, while in Winnipeg Ukrainian youths were being trained for the ministry in a Protestant college. The delegate also told Rome that only a few Ukrainians actually attended the Church of the Holy Spirit in Winnipeg; most of them preferred their own little chapel where they conducted religious services in the absence of an officiating clergyman. Clearly, he maintained, Polish priests would not keep these people within the fold.[59]

But if Falconio expected a quick remedy to this situation with the imminent arrival of the Basilians, he was to be disappointed. Their departure from Galicia was postponed. Archbishop Szeptycki informed Falconio in the fall of 1901 that, to compensate for this delay, he was sending his secretary and former alumnus of the Ruthenian College in Rome, Wasyl Zholdak, 'qui sera j'en suis sûr bon mission-aire et répondra au désir de l'épiscopat du Canada.'[60] This news, which the delegate received only a few days before Zholdak actually reached Ottawa, delighted him. Falconio could now look forward to some action. 'J'espère qu'il vous sera d'un grand secours et qu'il pourra s'opposer efficacement à la propagande protestante parmi ses compatriotes,'[61] he wrote to Langevin. Falconio capitalized on this visit by asking Zholdak to provide him with detailed information on the spiritual conditions of Ukrainian immigrants. He wanted a report outlining the number and distribution of Ukrainian settlements in the West, describing Protestant and Orthodox proselytizing activity, and assessing the extent of apostasy. Falconio also asked the priest to determine the likelihood of the Ukrainians following the Latin rite.[62]

In Winnipeg Szeptycki's secretary found Langevin ever optimistic about the progress being made in ministering to the Ukrainian population. The archbishop pointed to the recent establishment by the Oblates of an immigrant school under the direction of a Polish teacher which catered to one hundred German and 'Polish-Galician' students. The potential which immigrants were coming to represent in redressing the balance between Catholics and Protestants in the West was beginning to influence the archbishop's perspective. If the flow continued, he predicted, 'nous deviendrons assez forts pour faire respecter la Constitution du pays ou pour nous suffire à nous-mêmes.'[63] Langevin stated his willingness to do even more for the Ukrainians, but in the absence of financial help from the Propaganda, pleaded poverty. He noted that his support of the Catholic schools of Winnipeg and the prodigious growth of the archdiocese limited his capacity better to serve these immigrants.[64] In time, however, he hoped for the establishment of a Catholic normal school which among other things would train teachers to instruct immigrant children in their own language. 'Nous pouvons [ainsi] sauver les 4,000 enfants Galiciens qui sont dans mon diocèse.'[65] Falconio showed much less enthusiasm for this idea, pointing out that French and English were the only generally recognized languages of the country.[66]

Langevin's optimism contrasted singularly with Zholdak's assessment of the situation in the archdiocese of St Boniface. In a peculiarly slavicized Italian, the priest described to Falconio his attempt to found a Ukrainian parish in Winnipeg according to canon law and under the dependence of the archbishop. He had to admit, however, that the problems were great. The Uniate priests who had visited Winnipeg before him had caused much mischief and the articles appearing in *Svoboda*, a Ukrainian newspaper published in New Jersey, stymied his efforts. In fact, according to Zholdak, the problem had its origins in the United States. It was from there that disaffected priests such as Zaklynski came, preaching independence from Latin episcopal authority everywhere they went. Zaklynski was now living in Winnipeg, apparently with a divorcée, and somehow considered himself exempt from the archbishop's jurisdiction. Because of priests like him, Ukrainians all over North America feared that their submission to the local bishop would put them on the slippery slope to Latinization. This fear led Ukrainians in ever growing numbers to leave the church.

To counteract this rapidly deteriorating situation, Zholdak modestly proposed that a vicariate be erected for his compatriots living in North America. The vicar apostolic would be in charge of all the priests belonging to his rite and the ownership of all church property would be vested in his name. In this way the religious disorders that afflicted Ukrainian communities would cease and a feeling of unity would develop between the adherents of the Eastern and Latin rites. Zholdak begged the apostolic delegate to make this his cause and to act as the spokesman for the Ukrainians before the Holy See. This and other reports submitted by Szeptycki's secretary shook Falconio. He soon wrote to Rome urging that in view of the critical situation, Uniate priests be sent as soon as possible to Canada and, he added significantly, 'some ecclesiastical superior of their own rite.'[67]

Meanwhile, as a result of pressures from the Austro-Hungarian government, a special commission composed of cardinals from Propaganda and Extraordinary Ecclesiastical Affairs strongly recommended in August 1901 that two visitors be assigned to the respective apostolic delegations in North America. But it took almost five months before Cardinal Ledochowski broke the news to Falconio,[68] and another five months went by before the name of the visitor was known.[69] Apparently the American hierarchy's hostility to the appointment of a special envoy from Galicia was causing delays in Rome. By the spring of 1902 the situation was considered so critical that Cardinal Rampolla, speaking in the pope's name, ordered Ledochowski to bring the issue up at a full congregation of the Propaganda.[70]

As the cardinals were deliberating, Zholdak reported that the spiritual condition of Ukrainians living in the diocese of St Albert was even worse than in St Boniface. Their faith, he believed, was in imminent danger since all of them were exposed to the seductions of Orthodoxy. The Russian imperial government was spending a great deal of money to help build churches in the region: in Vegreville there were already three large ones and two more under construction. Orthodox priests also were distributing basic necessities, including food, to the many poor Ukrainian settlers.[71] In addition to material assistance, the Russian Orthodox clergy were dispensing 'propaganda' liberally. They were playing on the settlers' fears of Latinization and depicted Uniate priests as lackeys of the Roman church, which cared so little for the Ukrainians that it refused to grant them their own bishop. In contrast, Orthodox bishops showed their pastoral devotion by visiting scattered Ukrainian settlements. Zholdak noted that the activities of the Russian Orthodox church were being abetted by the national movement among Ukrainian Catholics in the United States. He referred to a meeting then taking place in Harrisburg, Pennsylvania, with its stridently pro-Ruthenian and anti-Latin tones. The editors of *Svoboda* were writing to all literate Ukrainians in Canada, stirring up antipathy to established ecclesiastical authority. Zholdak urged Falconio to put pressure on Rome so that Archbishop Szeptycki might be permitted to come to Canada.[72]

Lacombe fully endorsed the Uniate priest's perspective. He told Falconio that a large number of the forty thousand Ukrainians living in the Territories were unfamiliar with many of the tenets of their faith. 'Malgré leur grande douceur de caractère et leur amour de la religion, [ces Galiciens] semblent malheureusement avoir plus de confiance dans leur rite que dans leur foi. C'est ce que les évêques

Grecs-Ruthènes eux-mêmes m'ont répété, lors de mon voyage dans leur pays.' Lacombe warned that a catastrophe was imminent unless prompt and energetic action were taken. He dismissed as illusory the expectation that the children of Ukrainian immigrants would take on the Latin rite. The proof of this was that the ranks of the Orthodox church were swelling day by day. The vicar general insisted that Ukrainians had to have their own clergy. He also seconded Zholdak's plea that Szeptycki be allowed to visit Canada.[73]

Relief finally came in the autumn of 1902. From Galicia, where he had spent the summer, Zholdak reported that he was returning to Canada with Basilian priests and sisters.[74] Before departing from Hamburg aboard the *Noltke* destined for New York, Zholdak asked the well-connected Lacombe to obtain railway ticket reductions for himself and his companions for the trip from New York to Winnipeg. The 'omnipotent' vicar general was also requested to ensure that they would not have to pay duty on the ornaments and chalices they were bringing with them.[75] From Cracow, Wladimir Ledochowski, a Jesuit provincial and nephew of the now deceased cardinal, expressly wrote to Falconio to assure him that the priests who were being sent were known to him personally and were all excellent clergymen.[76]

For his part, Szeptycki informed the delegate that the Propaganda had formally appointed Zholdak as apostolic visitor. He noted that, although this position was not very well defined in church canons, the episcopate of Western Canada would have nothing to fear from his former secretary, who by all accounts had earned their confidence during his earlier visit. This is why, Szeptycki added, he had recommended Zholdak for the position. The archbishop of Lvov repeated how much he would have liked to come to Canada, but 'outre des difficultés des temps (mouvement socialiste, grèves, etc.) qui réclamaient ma présence continuelle, j'ai été retenu jusqu'ici par l'opinion du feu Cardinal Ledochowski, qui était décidément contraire à ce voyage.' Now that the Propaganda had a new cardinal prefect, he noted, he would renew his request since 'je considérerais cela pour la plus grande grâce de Dieu si je pouvais être au moins pendant quelques mois missionnaire.'[77]

News of the imminent arrival in the West of Uniate priests and nuns sparked a certain rivalry between the dioceses of St Boniface and St Albert. The new titular bishop of St Albert, Emile Legal, quoted an article in the *North-West Review* which seemed to suggest that the Galician missionaries were all destined for the archdiocese. He pointed out that the need was greater in St Albert which only had one priest to care for the Ukrainians, whereas St Boniface now had six. Legal argued that his metropolitan had done nothing to help recruit these priests who had come to Canada thanks to the efforts of Lacombe and Zholdak, and that he had even been opposed to their coming. Langevin 'a même condamné, en plusieurs circonstances, les démarches du Père Lacombe,' whose travel expenses had been paid by St Albert. The bishop believed it would be a grave injustice if his diocese were deprived of the fruits of its labour. Legal was certainly correct in emphasizing his metropolitan's opposition to Uniate priests. As late as August 1902 the archbishop told the new prefect of the Propaganda, Girolamo Maria Cardinal Gotti, that it was his firm intention to have the Ukrainians of his archdiocese cared for by Latin religious. He succinctly repeated why he thought this was the best course. 'Le passage de prêtres séculiers Ruthènes au sein de nos colonies a fait plus de mal que de bien et ceux qui sont vraiment religieux parmi ces peuples, s'attachent facilement aux prêtres latins quand ce sont de saints religieux missionnaires.'[78] In any event, the *North-West Review*'s report turned out to be incorrect since Legal ended up with all the Uniate priests and nuns.

SBARRETTI: COMPETITION FROM THE ORTHODOX

With the arrival in early January 1903 of the new apostolic delegate, lobbying on behalf of the Ukrainian immigrants resumed in earnest. Zholdak reported to Sbarretti that there were sixty thousand Ukrainians in Canada, one hundred and eighty thousand in the United States, and another sixty thousand in Brazil. The state of the Ukrainian Catholic church, wracked by schism in these last two countries was deplorable. But in Canada the situation was even worse for lack of Uniate priests. He insisted that unless a Ukrainian bishop were appointed, the clergy from Galicia would never agree to serve in Canada.[79] Sbarretti, who was pleased to have such a hard-working apostolic visitor dedicated to resolving what the delegate considered a serious and urgent problem, none the less was non-committal on the idea of a Uniate bishop. 'Such a proposal is of extreme importance; and perhaps the local Bishops would not be favourably disposed to it. I understand however that it would have no little influence in keeping the Ruthenian Catholics in the true faith.'

Meanwhile, in response to a request for more information from Sbarretti, Zholdak provided population statistics on the scattered Ukrainian settlements.[81] He stressed how attached these immigrants were to their religion: in many areas settlers had built their own chapels where they gathered on Sundays to recite prayers and sing psalms. Zholdak believed that a number of these communities were sufficiently established to provide for a priest, whose livelihood he estimated would cost them $600 a year. But he believed that two dangers threatened the immigrants' faith. One came from the public school system. The teachers, often themselves Ukrainian and trained in the West's government-funded normal schools, filled immigrant children with anti-Catholic prejudices and biblical instruction was given according to Presbyterian principles.

The other danger came from visiting Orthodox bishops, the most active and notorious of whom was the impostor Bishop Serafim. The latter, who prompted Langevin to remark 'il n'a de séraphim que le nom,' went about ordaining scarcely literate peasants to the priesthood. The immigrants, however, were delighted suddenly to have in their midst so many priests chosen from among their number and independent of the 'French' hierarchy. Serafim also enjoyed *Svoboda*'s unqualified support.[82] Langevin, of course, was not so impressed. He sought to show where the devotions of the Serafimite clergy really lay by recounting to the Propaganda an incident that occurred during Serafim's visit to Winnipeg. The 'prelate' was saying mass in the local immigration office, assisted by a deacon whom he recently ordained. 'Lorsqu'il s'est agi de communier avec le calice, [le diacre] a bu si abondamment que le soidisant [sic] "Seraphim" lui a crié: "Mais laissé [sic] m'en un peu."'[83] The venue for this mass was provided by Cyril Genik, a Canadian immigration agent and translator of Ukrainian birth whom Langevin sought to have dismissed because of his support for Serafim.[84]

But since Serafim skilfully exploited the settlers' deep-seated concerns and prejudices, he could not be underestimated. In reaction to his growing popularity and under Zholdak's influence, Langevin began to pay more attention to the spiritual needs of his Ukrainian faithful. While certainly not going as far as to demand the appointment of a Ukrainian bishop, he made a formal request to Rome on behalf of the Western Canadian episcopate and with the support of the delegate that Archbishop Szeptycki be permitted to visit his compatriots in their new homeland. He also asked for two Uniate priests for his archdiocese, which was a notable departure from his previous position.

A by-product of this rivalry between Uniates and Orthodox in Winnipeg related to which denomination would be the first to build the church that would win the hearts and minds of the immigrants. Uniates at that point only had the small provisional chapel of St Nicholas where Zholdak regularly said mass. Langevin and the Uniate priest wanted a large church that would be a rallying point and the source of pride for all of Winnipeg's Ukrainian Catholics and possibly even their repentant Orthodox compatriots. In fact Zholdak had been bluntly told by some immigrants that if he succeeded in building them a church before Serafim did, they would follow him instead of his rival. Consequently, Langevin wondered whether the Austro-Hungarian government or even the emperor himself might not be persuaded to erect a Ukrainian church in Winnipeg. He even offered to go to Vienna to plead his case personally before Franz Joseph 'que nos Ruthènes appellent toujours Notre Empereur.'[85] Meanwhile, the archbishop borrowed money to purchase the land and build the rectory of the church, but he insisted that his limited financial resources prevented him from doing more.[86]

But this raised the question which earlier had been a bone of contention in the diocese of St Albert: who would be entrusted with the ownership of church property? Ukrainian Catholics in Winnipeg began a court challenge of the archbishop's prerogatives. This prompted Langevin to seek passage of a provincial law that would oblige Ukrainian churches to be incorporated as episcopal property. But Zholdak pointed out how counter-productive a move this was since it made Orthodoxy all the more attractive to the Ukrainians.[87] The issue of property rights was also hotly contested in the diocese of St Albert where the Basilian superior, Platonid Filas, asked the Delegate whether his priests could accept churches which currently were administered by lay trustees.[88] In light of these developments, Sbarretti once again pleaded with the Propaganda to allow Szeptycki to visit Canada. Such a visit would reinforce the Ukrainians' allegiance to the church and induce more Uniate priests to settle in Canada.

Archbishop Szeptycki did not come to Canada until the very end of Sbarretti's term as apostolic delegate. The Eucharistic Congress of 1910 in Montreal finally provided the prelate with the pretext that he needed.[89] But during Sbarretti's mandate the original nucleus of three Uniate priests serving in the West slowly grew as other Galician clergymen came to this country and as a handful of French Canadian and European members of religious commumities changed over to the Eastern rite.[90] These new additions, however, could not keep pace with the phenomenal growth of the Ukrainian population in this period. Not until 1907 was the Holy See finally able to designate a Uniate bishop for the Ukrainians of the United States, and even then his authority depended on that of each Latin bishop in whose diocese the Uniate communities resided. Canada's Ukrainians would have to wait another five years before receiving their bishop. But in contrast to the American experience, he was to be independent of his Latin colleagues and was to answer solely to the apostolic delegate in Canada.[91] With the arrival of Bishop Nicetas Budka serious attempts were finally made to provide adequate religious services to the Ukrainian Catholic population.

CONCLUSION

At the end of the last century the Canadian hierarchy was not prepared to cope with the arrival of thousands of Catholic immigrants speaking neither English nor French. The local church's response to this new situation was conditioned essentially by external factors; happenings in the American church, together with the reactions of the Holy See and the Austro-Hungarian government to these events, were certainly decisive.

Catholic immigration to the United States occurred almost a generation earlier than in Canada, was on a scale simply unknown here, and caused more far-reaching social and cultural tensions. At the time of these immigrants' arrival in the United States, the Irish, who dominated the ecclesiastical leadership, barely had managed to erase the stigma of their own immigration. Now they saw themselves as Catholic gatekeepers of the nation. They were anxious that their church appear thoroughly American in its leadership, its liturgy, its administrative practices. So insistent were they that immigrants quickly assimilate into the mainstream that they were largely insensitive to the newcomers' needs, particularly those of southern Europeans who appeared to be so tenaciously different from the norm. In defence of the American hierarchy, it may be said that they were fighting at the time against a conception of the United States, clearly expounded by spokesmen of different immigrant communities, as a coalition of autonomous ethnic groups each preserving its distinctive culture and language. Clearly they were worried that such notions would retard the process of assimilation. But their concern prevented them from addressing the immigrants' immediate cultural and material needs in effecting the transition to American culture.

The Holy See responded to this situation with the Propaganda's 1887 report and with a series of measures derived from it. The document was filled with a number of the same cultural misconceptions as were propagated by spokesmen of various American immigrant communities. Briefly, the report suggested that Italian culture could be perpetuated in the United States by the institution of ethnic parishes which would elevate the immigrant out of his particularistic village-bound culture to acceptable old-world standards. It was assumed that language and religion were intimately bound together and that the loss of the first ultimately would lead to perdition. Despite its false premises, the document had the merit of recommending a number of concrete measures to help in the immigrants' integration and spiritual care, thus filling a vacuum left by the episcopate's general inactivity. But this was one instance where the wishes of the Holy See were overriden by a compact and determined élite within the American church who were intent on applying the Monroe Doctrine to ecclesiastical affairs by blocking any measure that appeared to subject an immigrant group to 'foreign' interference.

In any event, it was the Propaganda document on immigration, reacting as it did to an essentially American problem, that awakened the Canadian episcopate's awareness of Italian immigrants. But in responding to Rome's concern, the bishops were content to deal with the immigrants' needs in a casual and almost haphazard way. The hierarchy was not so much motivated, as were their American colleagues, by the desire to be seen as loyal and patriotic by the wider community, as by different factors. For one thing, many of the Eastern Canadian bishops lived in rapidly urbanizing sees in which the expanding population placed heavy burdens on diocesan resources. For another, Italian immigrants, who came to Canada in much smaller numbers, were birds of passage particularly in the early period of immigration, spending the winter in the cities and then going off in the spring to jobs to the Canadian wilderness. This made it extremely difficult, though not impossible, to assess the size of the community, as diocesan statistics showed by underestimating, at times even ignoring, the Italian presence. The apostolic delegate largely accepted these constraints since he himself was more preoccupied with the financial exigencies of Canadian dioceses than by the needs of a sparse, scattered, and largely transient immigrant population, in spite of the noble principles enunciated by the Propaganda document.

External factors were also fundamental in determining the Canadian episcopate's reception of Ukrainian immigrants. But whereas the Holy See had a different perspective from the American hierarchy on the question of Italian immigration to the United States, they substantially agreed on the place of the Ukrainian immigrants within the American church. In general, Rome was wary of the presence of married clergy in the Americas and was quite willing to place Uniate immigrants under the authority of Latin bishops. It was only when the Austro-Hungarian government began making strong representations which emphasized the concrete results of these policies that Rome finally changed course.

The Propaganda's decree of 1894 provoked a great deal of anger among Ukrainians in Europe as well as the new world. They thought this measure gave the lie to the Holy See's oft-repeated assurances that Catholics of the Eastern rite were in no way inferior or subservient to those of the Latin church. Small wonder then that the few Uniate priests coming to Canada after that time showed so little respect for episcopal authority and stirred up their compatriots' feelings against the domination of 'French' bishops. But it must be stressed that these bishops were just as much heirs of a situation that was not of their own making as were the Ukrainians.

Despite these external constraints, the Western Canadian bishops were not particularly aggressive in their pastoral care of these new arrivals, nor sensitive to their needs. Indeed, the episcopate's response is reminiscent of that of their American colleagues to Italian immigrants. It is true that the bishops did not stand idly by as Ukrainians began arriving in Canada in ever growing numbers. It is also true that the initiatives which they did take were not blessed with success. The Western hierarchy, for example, tried twice to obtain priests fron Galicia, in 1898 and again in 1900. They also appealed unsuccessfully to a number of religious communities to come and serve these immigrants. Langevin even tried to induce members of his own clergy to go over to the Eastern rite.

But the Ukrainians' needs were immediate and urgent. De

Barbézieux put the Catholic population of the ecclesiastical province of St Boniface, not including the Ukrainians, at 76,877 in 1901.[92] If we assume as he did that the latter numbered thirty thousand, then almost one-third of the population of the ecclesiastical province was cared for by one Uniate and three Polish priests (one of whom only served the two hundred families of Winnipeg). In this context, thinking, as Langevin obviously did, of long-term solutions such as sending Latin priests to Galicia to be trained in the Eastern rite was clearly insufficient. It may be argued that Langevin had other more pressing matters on his mind, notably the re-establishment of Catholic schools in Manitoba. In fact the archbishop felt that such schools were basic to the continued presence of Catholics in the West. But the opposite was also true: the lack of spiritual services placed the faith of Ukrainian immigrants in immediate danger. What sense then would there be in fighting for Catholic schools if a sizeable number of people would be lost to the church?

On the whole, the Ukrainian immigrants' plight did not elicit much sympathy from the Western Canadian hierarchy, nor for that matter from the apostolic delegate. These newcomers were characterized as ignorant, superstitious, and stubborn. Falconio observed that they were 'unwilling or unable to adapt to the Latin rite.'[93] Langevin, who was already was sensitized to the problems of minority cultures, ought to have known better when he stated that Polish priests could provide adequate care for his Ukrainian flock. But perhaps it was because of his own cultural conditioning that he perceived their problem as merely one of language. In any case, the prelate did not want Uniate priests in his archdiocese, nor would he countenance the appointment of a Uniate bishop. Although Grandin showed more flexibility, he was certainly no more generous in his opinion of Ukrainian immigrants, nor any more aggressive in finding adequate solutions to their spiritual condition. It was through his vicar general, Lacombe, who was much more sympathetic to Ukrainians, that Grandin showed greater willingness to receive Uniate priests in his diocese.

In the final analysis, however, only the threat of large-scale defections from the church and the insistent diplomatic pressures of the Austro-Hungarian government prompted the episcopate to provide better care for the Ukrainians. To his credit, Diomede Falconio played an important role in this respect, but only after the Austro-Hungarian government's Roman initiative. And it is not clear whether the delegate ever abandoned the vain hope of bringing the Ukrainians to the Latin church. Certainly his early efforts, like his attempt to bring the Franciscans from Cincinnati to the West, were directed to that goal. But what is perhaps ultimately more important is that Falconio had an activist approach. He expressly sought out information from the apostolic visitor, with whom he worked closely. This may have made him more receptive to the appointment of a Uniate bishop in Canada. While neither he nor his successor ever clearly advocated such a course, they realized that the gravity of the problem required new solutions and they goaded the Canadian episcopate into trying to find a more imaginative approach to the care of these immigrants.

The Canadian episcopate was certainly more willing than their American counterparts to provide spiritual services to immigrants in their own language. But the problem of rite proved to be a major stumbling-block. If in the end, contrary to the American experience, the bishops accepted the appointment in Canada of a Uniate bishop independent of his Latin colleagues, the reason must be found in their unflinching fidelity to Rome's will. It is a pity that this fidelity did not stand them in good stead in their confrontations with the Liberal party over Manitoba schools.

Chapter Seven

The Delegate as Arbiter

When he became apostolic delegate, Diomede Falconio was concerned with both the trappings and the substance of office. Not only did he require a residence befitting the dignity of his position which he felt should in no way be inferior to his counterpart in Washington; he also asked to have the same powers as his colleague, noting that currently the Canadian delegate's faculties were no greater than those of a common bishop.[1] The prefect of the Propaganda, Cardinal Ledochowski complied with his request. The apostolic delegate was given the power to hear the grievances of priests and laymen against their bishops and to resolve them, either by mutual consent or if necessary by his own authority. 'Aside from the added prestige that will accrue to Y[our] L[ordship],' observed the cardinal prefect, 'this measure also has the advantage of allowing an on-site and closer examination of some cases in which distance itself makes it sometimes harder to obtain abundant and detailed information.'[2] Scarcely two months after his arrival Falconio already reported that 'various outstanding quarrels between Bishops, priests, and laymen are keeping me sufficiently busy.'[3]

The conventional wisdom presented by apostolic delegates was that at the heart of the crisis in the Canadian church lay a question of authority: too little episcopal authority for the early delegates, too much for the later ones. It may be argued that these various envoys were referring to two different periods in the Canadian church's history and therefore two different problems: 1877 was not 1897, Fabre and Taschereau were not Bruchési and Bégin. This point certainly has received ample recognition here, with the stress laid on the new-found unity of action and direction which characterized the Quebec hierarchy by the turn of the century.

Yet even in this later period of apparently excessive episcopal authority, the bishops reputed to be most autocratic complained about turbulent elements in the lower clergy, complaints that would have sounded very familiar to Conroy. The 1896 federal election provided painful evidence for some bishops of their inability to rally the diocesan clergy to a common cause, and restrain them from pursuing an opposite course. Archbishop Duhamel wrote: 'La politique devient de plus en plus la grande préoccupation ... malheureusement d'un certain nombre de prêtres dont les évêques ont à se plaindre.'[4] Laflèche for his part denounced the lower clergy for their 'blindness' and 'stubbornness' in failing to follow the episcopate's guidelines – a situation he thought had been caused by the liberalism taught at the Séminaire de Québec since 1876. 'Eh bien, cette ivraie a grandi depuis ce tems, et elle a produit son fruit, certes qui est bien amère [sic].'[5] The bishop was shocked to find that during Merry del Val's mission the lower clergy openly criticized their superiors without being reprimanded by the delegate.[6] Bishop Gravel lamented the fact that 'un homme du mérite et du savoir de Mgr Bégin [est] tenu en échec, mais dans un échec tel qu'on pourrait l'appeler de l'impuissance par le groupe libéral dont les têtes sont au Séminaire?'[7]

Between an unruly lower clergy and an authoritarian episcopate, where did the truth lie? Admittedly, the Canadian church lacked sophisticated governing structures which might act as a break on episcopal power. Bégin, for one, saw this as a sign not of the bishops' untrammelled authority, but rather as a result of the Canadian church's long-standing position as a missionary institution. This meant that while canon law was not applied in its strictest form in Canada, it was certainly not ignored. Despite the absence of structures, he argued, the governance of the church was an orderly and reasonable affair, not simply based on the bishop's whims.[8]

Bégin's hypothesis in part may be tested by analysing the appeals, contained in the Falconio papers, of priests and laymen against their ecclesiastical superiors. Apart from giving us a fascinating inside look at the workings and life of the church, these cases provide concrete evidence on the nature of episcopal government and on the precise role played by the apostolic delegate as arbiter of such disputes.

The Canadian church certainly was an anomaly with respect to its counterparts in the older and more established parts of the Catholic world. Canadian bishops usually ruled without the assistance of canonically instituted cathedral chapters. The chapter of the diocese of Quebec was suppressed at the time of the Conquest as part of the British effort to create a simplified structure of ecclesiastical government which then could be controlled more easily by the governor. Thereafter there were no cathedral chapters in Canada until one was established in Montreal in the early years of Bourget's episcopate. His cathedral canons held specific offices in the diocesan administration and lived a communal life together in the bishop's palace and under his watchful eye. If subsequently other Quebec prelates created their own cathedral chapters, it was only at Rome's repeated insistence that they conform more closely to canonical practices.[9]

Bourget's model was more the exception than the rule. Even in Montreal, personality conflicts between Bourget's canons and Fabre, the bishop's successor, led to the chapter's breakdown and eventual modification.[10] In some other Quebec dioceses this body had purely honorific functions. Canons did not live with their bishop, nor did they necessarily counsel him on diocesan matters. But the most blatant example of this lack of governing structure was in the archdiocese of Quebec which, at the beginning of the twentieth century, still had no chapter. This situation led one canonist to remark that there 'l'évêque, et à défaut le vicaire général, est tout.'[11] The hierarchy justified their lack of enthusiasm for this institution by pleading poverty, since the financial burden of maintaining the canons fell on their shoulders. It is certainly open to question whether the absence of a chapter really did mean that the bishop was a law unto himself. The fact remains, however, that even if some clerics shared in the burdens of episcopal office, they tended to be chosen not according to objectively determined and commonly accepted criteria, but at the discretion of the bishop.

The tendency for potential one-man diocesan rule was further reinforced by the absence of formal ecclesiastical courts.[12] Parish priests might find themselves at the mercy of their bishops who acted as judge and jury in disciplinary cases, a practice that was contrary to canon law. The right of appeal to Rome in such cases remained largely theoretical unless priests were prepared to be very patient in the face of the Curia's proverbial slowness. As one anonymous Russian commentator observed, the Curia 'usually thinks in centuries, often in generations, but only under the pressure of extraordinary circumstances in years, never in shorter spans of time.'[13] This situation was aggravated by the failure in most dioceses to hold synods which the Council of Trent prescribed should be called yearly to define, among other things, the relations between priests and their bishop. Although the first Council of Quebec (1851) formally endorsed this tridentine precept, most Canadian bishops failed to implement it.

The issue of nominations to parishes clearly underlined the possibility for episcopal caprice. There were virtually no fixed benefices in Canada at the end of the last century, which meant that parish priests could be appointed and removed from their charges at the bishop's discretion. Such a practice was contrary to tridentine canons. But worse still, bishops routinely assigned pastors to parishes without first holding a competition to determine the most qualified candidates, which was also against commonly accepted practices.

Little wonder then that Merry del Val should have remarked so pointedly on the Canadian church's failure to observe church canons. This feeling was echoed by Falconio, who reported to Rome that Canadians did not seem to consider the prescriptions of canon law to be binding on them. He described as despotic the bishops' financial administration of their dioceses and decried their casual procedures for distributing offices and charges. 'The Canadian cleric,' he observed, 'submits to this absolute form of subordination which is without limit and without control, either through deference, or because he does not wish to compromise himself with his Bishop on whom he depends almost entirely for his future.' Falconio proposed that the position of parish priests be regularized so that 'the clergy could be promoted according to law and not according to the will of he who governs.'[14] He also proposed that priests should not be transferred from one parish to another without serious cause.[15] Ledochowski fully concurred with these recommendations. He pointed out that such principles were already enshrined in decrees adopted by provincial councils in Quebec and Toronto. The cardinal prefect urged Falconio to press for the appointment of permanent pastors in the more established parishes, so that little by little local practices could be brought into line with established procedures.[16]

Falconio was convinced that, faced with such an unstructured institution as the Canadian church, the delegate had a crucial role to play in bringing conflicts and misunderstandings to an end. 'In fact,' he asserted with some pride to the cardinal prefect, 'not a few disputes that were outstanding for years have been peacefully resolved in the brief period since the founding of this Delegation.'[17] Of the forty-five cases taken from the Falconio papers during his three-year mandate, some followed the proper channels of ecclesiastical litigation, going from the bishop, to the diocesan court, to the metropolitan, and finally to the apostolic delegate; others were simply direct calls for the delegate's intercession. Questions involving marriage dispensations or annulments, membership in secret societies, larger political issues (like the nomination of an Acadian bishop or the linguistic status of the University of Ottawa) have not been considered either because they were too personal or because they have been studied elsewhere.[18] Excluded also are those cases which, although begun during Falconio's tenure, did not elicit a clear response from the delegate. It should be noted that such cases were quite numerous and carried on into Sbarretti's administration.

On first impression, Falconio's views regarding episcopal autocracy would seem to be vindicated since thirty-nine (81 per cent) of the forty-five cases were directed against the bishop (see Table 10). Of course, not all of those who had grievances bothered to appeal to the apostolic delegate. Priests especially might hesitate to complain about their bishop. As one clergyman who was removed from his office by Archbishop Bruchési observed: 'Au Canada, un appel au Délégué Apostolique équivaut à une déclaration de guerre contre un évêque et ... en définitive le "pot de fer" écrase infailliblement le "pot de terre."'[19] In general, priests who took this step must have felt that they had little to lose. Clerical appeals perhaps should be seen as the tip of the iceberg. But when we consider that there were over three thousand priests in Canada during Falconio's term of office,[20] it would be fanciful to conclude on the basis of the relatively small number of appeals made to the delegation that the church was wracked by widespread institutional disorder and discord. A proper assessment of this question will have to await studies comparing the number and nature of appeals to the delegations of various countries.

Although the civil province of Quebec accounted for roughly 70 per cent of the Canadian clergy (about 2,100 secular and religious priests) and 64 per cent of the Catholic population, only twenty-one appeals (47 per cent) originated from there. This may be a reflection that the church in Quebec was better structured than its counterparts in English Canada, with a much higher incidence of diocesan synods, cathedral chapters, and ecclesiastical courts. On the other hand, French-speakers who constituted 80 per cent of priests[21] and 75 per cent of the Catholic population in Canada were involved in thirty (67 per cent) of these cases, four of them against English-speaking bishops. For their part, English Canadians were protagonists in twelve (27 per cent) appeals to the delegate, while those of German origin accounted for two. Finally, one case originated from an émigré Syrian priest who wandered for a short time through Quebec.

These appeals dealt with issues already identified as problems in Falconio's correspondence and largely involved applications of canon law.[22] They may be categorized as shown in Table 11. Of the twenty-six cases dealing with clerical appointments, eleven (42 per cent) came from Quebec and the rest from English Canada, although in total, sixteen French Canadians were implicated as opposed to eight English Canadians, one Frenchman, and one Syrian. The diocese of Rimouski alone provided five of these cases since Bishop Blais had inherited the fruits of his predecessor's administrative negligence. In fact, it was the chaotic situation in the diocese that prompted Cardinal Taschereau to insist in 1890 that the Propaganda force Jean Langevin's resignation, arguing that his suffragan had ordained several unworthy candidates to the priesthood.[23] These priests were now proving to be the bane of Blais's existence.

One of them complained to Falconio that he was being kept against his will at St-Benoit-Joseph Labre de Longue Pointe, an institution run by the Frères de la Charité for the care of 'the insane, the infirm, the epileptics, and the sick.'[24] This was not the first time that he appealed to a higher authority. Shortly after Blais's installation as titular bishop, the priest had objected to the prefect of Propaganda that he was being locked up without apparent cause in the 'department for lunatics and maniacs' of St-Jean-de-Dieu asylum. In a subsequent appeal to Rome the obviously well-connected clergyman managed to obtain affidavits of good conduct from the ubiquitous Callixte Marquis, as well as from a number of parish priests and even judges.

Asked to supply information on this latest request, Blais told Falconio that the priest had been ordained by Langevin without having completed studies in a classical college or in the Grand Seminary. His drunken and generally immoral behaviour was a constant source of public scandal. The clergyman wandered all over Quebec and had been held in various jails and institutions. At one

TABLE 10

Parties Involved in Appeals to the Apostolic Delegate

	No.	%
Priests vs bishops/superiors	25	55.5
Parishioners vs bishops	14	25.5
Parishioners vs priests	4	9.0
Priests vs priests	1	50.0
Sisters vs priests	1	5.0

TABLE 11

Nature of the Appeals to the Apostolic Delegate

	No.	(% rounded)
Parish or clerical appointments	26	60
Parish issues/schools	13	30
Politics	4	10

point a fire mysteriously broke out and destroyed the building where he was being detained in St-Hyacinthe. Strong circumstantial evidence pointed to his having been the cause of the blaze. Considering his unstable and unedifying behaviour, Blais felt that he had no alternative but to keep him at St-Benoit-Joseph Labre. Falconio fully agreed.[25]

Langevin ordained another hapless young man who initially had been rejected for the priesthood in the archdiocese of Quebec. The new pastor sexually assaulted a number of young boys in his parish and so Langevin removed him from his charge and sent him to a remote corner of the diocese as a missionary in the local settlement. But when even these inhabitants protested against the priest's behaviour, the new bishop ordered him to retire to the Trappist monastery at Oka. Subsequently, after spending a few years in the United States, the cleric returned to Rimouski. A short time later, however, '[il] avait déjà trouvé le moyen de conduire dans un endroit isolé de la cathédrale et d'y violenter un jeune protestant, qui venait recevoir des leçons de cathéchisme chez le curé.' At this point Blais had the cleric confined at Longue Pointe and his action fully was endorsed by the delegate.[26]

A third clergyman from Rimouski who found himself in the United States called on Falconio to intervene on his behalf. He explained that after receiving holy orders from Langevin he had left the church and studied to become a Presbyterian minister. Now repentant, he wanted Blais to reinstate him as a member of the diocesan clergy. Falconio promptly offered the wayward priest a mission in Minnesota, explaining that a position could not be found for him in Rimouski, given the diocese's limited resources. A few months later, however, the anguished cleric again appealed to Falconio, saying that the bishop of Duluth would not have him and that Blais ('qui a su mettre son prédécesseur [Langevin] à la porte et le faire mourir de chagrin') hated him. Evidently moved by this letter, the delegate reminded Blais that it was the bishop's duty to find a suitable place for his diocesan clergy. But Falconio soon did an about-face when he discovered that the priest had a number of illegitimate children living in the diocese. At that point he advised the clergyman to retire to Oka since Blais had neither a position nor the funds to support him. A few days later the delegate had another shock when he learned that at the same time as the cleric was seeking Falconio's assistance, he was also corresponding with a Baptist minister in the hope of securing a position in his church. In the face of such apparent bad faith, the delegate summarily dropped the case.[27]

Clerical morality was also at issue in the case between a priest of the diocese of Chicoutimi and Bishop Labrècque, but in this instance, the delegate actively intervened to secure an accommodation. The cleric in question, deprived of his parish because of misconduct, had gone to serve various Catholic communities in Iowa. A few years later, armed with testimonials to his good conduct by the local clergy, he petitioned Falconio for reinstatement in his home diocese. Labrècque responded to this request by telling the delegate that some time earlier the priest had been publicly condemned to the lash and imprisonment for indecent assault on a young woman. It was not at all apparent to Labrècque that the cleric had amended his ways, since he now seemed to be addicted to alcohol and to other unspecified 'vile vices.' Falconio consequently advised the priest to withdraw to the Trappist monastery at Oka. The cleric tried to follow this advice, but at first the monks would not have him and it was only at the delegate's express insistence that they finally relented. Falconio also prevailed upon Labrècque to pay for the cleric's lodgings at the monastery. After a subsequent relapse into drink, the unfortunate priest finally found shelter at St-Benoit-Joseph Labre. Once again it was the delegate who got the Séminaire de Québec to see to his financial support.[28]

Problems of priestly morals were sometimes linked to the phenomenon of immigration. At a time when every year large numbers of people were arriving in Canada from Europe, it is not surprising that in their midst there should be the odd priest who saw the new world as an escape from difficult circumstances in the old. Nor is it surprising that two such cases would concern the archdiocese of Montreal, which of all Canadian cities was most likely to provide such priests with opportunity.

Compelled to leave his native France because of 'serious moral misdeeds,' a cleric sought a position in Montreal. Bruchési, who was not particularly welcoming, flatly told him that there were no appointments available. When Falconio intervened, emphasizing that the priest needed the means to support himself, the archbishop revealed that the French clergyman had arrived in Montreal with an alleged niece and that, since then, gossip about his eccentric behaviour had not stopped. While Bruchési was prepared to allow him to say mass in the archdiocese, he obviously preferred that the Frenchman return to his mother country. But despite the archbishop's opinion, Falconio counselled the priest to find himself a retreat in the Montreal area and live off the pension provided by his native diocese and the fees from his masses.[29]

The Syrian priest, for his part, complained to the delegate that he was being persecuted by his compatriots in Montreal and Quebec City, as well as by the local ecclesiastical authorities. Placed under interdict in the archdiocese of Quebec, arrested in Montreal simply for having accepted the faithful's donations for masses, he demanded that the delegate institute an inquiry into his mistreatment. Falconio sought information on the immigrant priest's status from the Catholic Patriarch of Antioch, Kyrillos VIII. He was told that the Syrian clergyman had led a scandalous life in his home country and left for the new world without his superiors' permission. Despite this news, Falconio tried to bring about a reconciliation with the ecclesiastical authorities in Montreal when the priest showed signs of wanting to amend his ways. At that point, however, the clergyman brought forward a set of exhorbitant demands, including claims for financial loss, on which he refused to compromise. The delegate's secretary then informed the headstrong Syrian that the delegation was no longer willing to involve itself in his case.[30]

Of the eleven cases where disputes over clerical appointments were related to priestly morality, six originated in Quebec and concerned breaches of chastity. Almost all of the recorded cases in English Canada, however, dealt with issues of money or drinking. The bishop of Alexandria, for example, suspended a parish priest for being a chronic public alcoholic, but had to reinstate him when parishioners petitioned for clemency. The delegate urged Bishop Alexander Macdonell to send the intemperate cleric on a long vacation to Ireland and to place him in another parish on his return. Macdonell was opposed to such a course, arguing that his diocese was too poor and positions too few. But a short time later he again was forced to discipline the backsliding priest. The latter then appealed to the delegate, claiming that he had been treated worse than an apostate. Since he had been stripped of his livelihood, he demanded that Macdonell pay for his board. Falconio, who was obviously not impressed with the priest's sentiments of repentance and due submission, scolded him, saying that he had only himself to blame for his troubles. He urged the cleric to make a formal promise to his bishop to renounce alcohol forever. The only comfort that the delegate could bring himself to offer the fallen priest was the vague hope that Macdonell eventually might find him a place.[31]

An Irish priest who worked in Halifax for a number of years complained to Falconio that the archbishop arbitrarily withdrew his faculties, forcing him to seek a position elsewhere. Originally attached to the diocese of Cork, the clergyman who now found himself in the United States felt that he had some claim on Halifax and demanded that a position be found for him there. Archbishop O'Brien denied any such obligation and added for good measure that he had no openings. His lack of sympathy for the cleric stemmed from the latter's addiction to alcohol which had caused him to mismanage parish funds and even to misappropriate subsidies from the Department of Indian Affairs meant for the support of native people. The case took another twist, however, when the Propaganda, to whom the wayward priest also appealed, decided that he indeed did belong to Halifax, a sentence that O'Brien simply refused to accept. At this point Falconio sought to bring about some kind of settlement. He pressured the archbishop to pay for the priest's placement in an institution, arguing that in any event the Propaganda would eventually force him to do so. As for the clergyman, Falconio lectured him abundantly on proper respect for episcopal authority and on the cause of his misfortunes. It is not clear how the case finally resolved itself since it ended abruptly when the priest, now living at the Trappist monastery at Oka, asked Falconio for a letter of recommendation.[32]

Parishioners in Peterborough had become so incensed with the personal and insulting remarks made from the pulpit by their priest that some refused to attend church. Falconio demanded an explanation and action from an apparently unperturbed bishop. Richard O'Connor promptly suspended the clergyman after a committee of investigation accused him of 'conduct unbecoming a priest,' apparently for the misappropriation of funds. O'Connor, who found that the cleric's great ambition was to accumulate money, told the delegate of his own readiness to place him in the local House of Providence at the expense of the diocese, on condition that he first make financial restitution. The priest at this point appealed to the delegate, recognizing his crime but alleging 'extenuating circumstances.' Anxious to avoid a trial, Falconio once again tried to work out a settlement. Ultimately the priest was confined to an institution and stripped of all jurisdiction except the right to say mass.[33]

A long-standing dispute between Bishop Dowling and a priest in the diocese of Hamilton resulted in the latter's suspension for not paying the annual parish assessment for Catholic schools. The cleric appealed to the Propaganda on the grounds that his Brantford parishioners were poor and therefore could not meet their obligations. Rome apparently declined to hear the case, but obviously sided with the bishop since he was given permission to divide the pastor's parish. When Falconio became apostolic delegate, the priest sent him details of the case 'for his information.' Dowling sought to justify his actions, arguing that the rector persistently begrudged payment of parish dues, although he always had more than enough money on hand. At this point Falconio advised the clergyman to consider his bishop's claims a priority and to settle them as quickly as possible. A few months later the pastor again turned to the delegate and complained that his health was deteriorating rapidly as a result of Dowling's constant harassment. The bishop then was prevailed upon to give the hard-pressed rector a six-month holiday. But in announcing the news, the delegate did not hide his own sentiments when he told the cleric of his hope 'that you will do all that is in your power in order to gain more and more the esteem of your bishop.'[34]

Only one case could be found in the Falconio papers involving an English-Canadian clergyman in an alleged breach of priestly chastity. The cleric, from the diocese of Chatham, complained to the delegate of being harassed by the sisters of the local Hôtel Dieu hospital, by neighbouring parish priests, and even by the bishop. After serving as curate at the cathedral and spiritual director of the Hôtel Dieu sisters, both prestigious positions, he had been forced by his detractors to take a parish in a remote corner of the diocese. Not even there did his 'traducers' give him respite, however. As a result the priest sought a post in another diocese on his own initiative, but lacking the proper papers, he was unable to find any. Meanwhile Bishop Rogers gave him an ultimatum to leave Chatham or face suspension.

The cleric denounced the entire procedure: 'Even pagan Rome,' he argued, 'had higher purer principles than to condemn the accused unheard or absent.' He depicted himself as a victim of episcopal tyranny. Bishop Rogers, he alleged, was rough and violent, a man of low birth and no breeding. This explained why, in the priest's mind, Rogers had treated him so shabbily, denying him common hospitality and forcing him to incur hotel expenses in order to defend himself. The bishop also had allowed himself to blurt out 'in his usual manner' innuendoes and 'insinuations of [the cleric's] veracity' without the slightest shred of evidence. But this was to be expected from a man who lacked the most elementary theological training. Rogers, explained the priest, had only spent a few months in a Canadian seminary and what little he knew came from the one hour of private instruction that he had been given as a young cleric by the then bishop of New Brunswick, Thomas Louis Connolly. The priest warned the delegate not to be taken in by Roger's possible protestations of infirmity and old age. The bishop, he assured Falconio, was strong and vigorous. Rogers slept eight to ten hours a day. He enjoyed his food and ate copious amounts.

At the delegate's insistence, the aggrieved cleric was finally given a position in the diocese. At the same time an unsigned document bearing the episcopal letterhead reached the delegation accusing the priest of 'immoral intimacy' with a prominent widow in the town of Chatham. The woman in question wrote to Falconio insisting that she and the priest were victims of malicious rumours. She explained that the accused cleric had visited her house on several occasions to attend to her dying husband and to provide her with spiritual succour. Subsequently, she had taken pity on the priest during his time of adversity and offered him financial and moral assistance. But she emphasized that their later meetings had always been conducted in the presence of a member of her family. Still, she complained, their enemies gave them no peace. She thus resolved to sell her business and move to New York, far away from the omnipresent gaze of the community.

After a litany of complaints against the bishop who continued to persecute him, against unnamed enemies who were fomenting unrest among his Acadian parishioners, against his own inability to find a servant 'although there were plenty of women in the parish,' the priest finally announced his own intention of seeking employment elsewhere. Falconio, through his secretary, expressed pleasure that the cleric would be going to 'some congenial place.' But the only solace the delegate could bring himself to give the priest was to remind him not to forget his papers when leaving the diocese.[35]

Apart from problems of priestly morality, nervous disorders accounted for four disputes over appointments. In Charlottetown, for instance, a parish priest complained to the delegate that he had been deprived of his parish on the basis of false accusations of immorality. Further investigation revealed, however, that the cleric suffered from symptoms of paranoia and that, contrary to his allegations, the bishop had given him only help and support.[36] In Alexandria half the members of one parish protested against their priest who was prone to fits of bad temper and who was feared as a strict disciplinarian. With the delegate's approval, Bishop Macdonell dutifully admonished the choleric clergyman. But when it came out that during one of his rages the priest allegedly struck a parishioner, Falconio insisted that in future more severe measures would have to be contemplated.[37] In Quebec Bégin justified the demotion of a priest to an 'inferior' parish when the latter's overly sensitive and impetuous personality caused serious difficulties in parish administration. Falconio not only supported Bégin, but repeated word for word the archbishop's reprimands to the priest.[38]

An interesting case in this regard involved a cleric initially of the archdiocese of Montreal who had been transferred to Sherbrooke. He had an extremely nervous personality (Bruchési even suspected that he might be epileptic), tended to be offensive with his parishioners, and was often vituperative in the pulpit, to the point that some laymen threatened to leave the church or take legal action against him. Bishop LaRocque wanted to remove him from the pressures of parish work, and since there were only parochial appointments available in Sherbrooke, suggested that Bruchési give him a chaplaincy in the archdiocese. LaRocque believed that, in any event, the problem was largely Montreal's responsibility because the archbishop apparently had known of the cleric's condition at the time of the transfer but he failed to inform Sherbrooke about it. 'Il faut bien l'avouer, à notre confusion, la franchise fait quelque fois défaut même chez les évêques,' LaRocque told the delegate.

Falconio advised the priest to retire from his parish and to live off his mass offerings, as well as a pension drawn from the ecclesiastical fund. But the clergyman would not go that easily. He stood on his rights, insisting that if he were to be stripped of his appointment, due process would have to be followed. In addition, he demanded greater financial compensation. But when the bishop went ahead and removed him from his charge, the priest complained to Falconio that he had been punished 'sans que Vous ne m'ayez condamné, ni soutenu dans l'épreuve. Si c'est ainsi qu'on rend justice dans l'église catholique, je vais voir ailleurs et je regrette de Vous dire que les tribunaux civils sauront mieux faire.' The threat, however, proved empty and Falconio remained unmoved.[39]

As often as not, disputes over clerical appointments were simple matters of administrative or jurisdictional conflict. Of the eleven such cases, three originated from Quebec and eight from dioceses in English Canada, although all but one of the priests involved were French Canadian. A pastor in the diocese of Rimouski, removed from his parish without apparent cause, went to Rome to appeal directly to the Propaganda. His challenge was successful. But he returned home to discover that he was forbidden to say mass in several parts of the diocese, although Bishop Blais insisted that he had not been suspended. The priest therefore demanded a parish and was supported by such prominent Liberals as Israel Tarte and Adélard Turgeon, as well as the ex-Liberal envoy to Rome, Jean-Baptiste Proulx. Archbishop Bégin, whose advice was sought on the matter, considered the cleric wilful and unreasonable since he had refused a perfectly good parish in Peterborough. In any event, on the delegate's insistence the priest was given a parish in Rimouski, but was removed from it a short time later, 'owing to the feebleness of his mind and the utter incapability to rule over even a small mission like the one at Matapédiac.' The author of these words, Falconio's secretary, blamed the priest's advisers for leading him on.[40] The case still had not been resolved when Falconio left for Washington, but his response certainly left no doubt as to where his sympathies lay.

Another cleric complained of being denied permission to say mass, this time in the archdiocese of St Boniface. The priest explained that he had been forced to leave the Oblate order and take up a position in the neighbouring diocese of Fargo, North Dakota, because of long-standing disagreements with Archbishop Langevin over a number of issues. From time to time he returned to St Boniface to visit his family, but on one occasion found himself under Langevin's ban. The archbishop even forbade his priest's cousin, a pastor in the archdio-cese, to receive him in his house. 'Mgr Langevin est d'ailleurs fort bien connu,' explained the aggrieved cleric, 'Il a le don de prêter l'oreille aux rapports de celui-ci, de celui-là ... Et souvent sur des rapports entendus, il agi [sic] avec une précipitation et une impru-dence que je n'ose qualifier.' The priest appealed against the arch-bishop's proscription; but the delegate advised him not to press the issue unless he were prepared to obtain affidavits challenging Langevin's unspecified allegations. The only comfort that Falconio, who certainly had no great love for Langevin, provided was to advise the priest to bear his cross with patience; otherwise, by continuing to antagonize the archbishop, he ran the risk of losing even his position in Fargo.[41]

While this cleric ultimately accepted his lot with resignation, another in the diocese of Pembroke got an American canon lawyer, P. Baart – who successfully defended a number of priests in appeals before the apostolic delegation in the United States – to take up his interests. As a result the priest obtained satisfaction from his bishop. The antagonism, which went back a number of years, arose when N.Z. Lorrain ordered the parish priest to take an inferior appoint-ment. The latter refused and appealed to Archbishop Duhamel, the metropolitan. Lorrain justified himself by arguing that since the cleric never officially belonged to the diocese, the bishop was under no obligation to honour his claims to a good parish. Eventually an arrangement was worked out: the priest agreed to take another appointment on the understanding that in doing so he would not be prejudicing earlier claims. A few years later, however, Lorrain effec-tively tried to demote him by making him curate, rather than pastor, of a parish. The priest rejected the position and turned to the delegate, demanding a parish similar to the one he initially had ac-cepted and claiming damages as well.

At this point the canon lawyer entered the fray. He proposed an accommodation to Falconio: his client would withdraw all claims on condition that he be recognized as a member of the diocesan clergy and given a yearly pension of $400. The delegate objected to the sum, arguing that pensions in Quebec were half that amount and that Pembroke was a poor diocese. The canon lawyer, evidently a skilled negotiator, managed to get Lorrain to agree to pay a reduced pension quarterly in advance and to drop a clause which would have stopped payments if the priest found employment outside the diocese.[42] Clearly the intervention of a canon lawyer expedited the resolution of the case and made both Falconio and Lorrain much more cautious in their response to the priest's claims.

The problems concerning the rights of clergymen, initially appointed to one diocese but working for many years in another, were not unique to Sherbrooke or Pembroke. They caused more than one bishop some anxiety in the wake of a Roman decree published in 1898 which formalized procedures for incardination, the process by which priests were recognized as belonging to a specific diocese. The decree deliberately sought to break with a tradition according to which incardination was governed by informal agreement. Bruchési put the bishops' concerns succinctly: if he were to be made responsible for all the priests of the archdiocese of Montreal loaned to other bishops, he would have never-ending worries. Falconio urged Bruchési and others to regularize the position of such priests and to come to mutually acceptable arrangements.[43]

The issue in Chatham was not about priests who were away, but about a chaplain who held the same position in a community of sisters for thirty-five years. The case was a by-product of the increasingly haphazard administration that marked the close of Bishop James Rogers's forty-four-year episcopate. A member of the Hôtel Dieu Sisters of Tracadie demanded an inquiry into the conduct of their chaplain who, by interfering repeatedly in the community's affairs, had caused bitter factionalism. After receiving detailed information from the mother superior, Falconio demanded the priest's resignation on the grounds that his long tenure had no justification in canon law. The delegate then appointed a nearby priest to conduct a canonical visitation of the community and strictly forbade the sisters to speak to anyone from outside, especially their ex-chaplain who happened to be pastor of the adjacent parish.

The visitor found that, because of the sisters' lack of proper training and education, the chaplain had been obliged to tend both to their temporal and spiritual well-being. He had dedicated little time to their spiritual edification, and his meddling had caused factionalism which in turn bred too much familiarity between him and a number of sisters, although the investigator was quick to point out that there had never been a hint of scandal. In the wake of the visitor's recommendations, Falconio had the ex-chaplain removed from his parish to avoid further contact with the community. This was done much against his and apparently his parishioners' will. Meanwhile the new chaplain, a French Jesuit, complained to the delegate that his predecessor had been 'un loup rapace qui les [the sisters] immola selon son bon plaisir.' The root of the problem, he argued, was 'que cet excellent peuple acadien est inscandalisable. Dans sa simplicité, il était incapable de croire qu'une action quelconque, si elle était commandée ou faite par un Prêtre put jamais être coupable, et ... les Novices ont toujours été tirées de ce milieu.' The problem also clearly lay with the old bishop who had an unbounded confidence in the former chaplain.[44]

In the diocese of London it was an ethnic conflict between French Canadians and English-speakers in the town of Windsor that prompted Bishop Fergus McEvay to remove a French-Canadian curate from his charge.[45] The two communities shared the same church under a unilingual pastor of Irish origin. But McEvay expressly had asked for a curate from the archdiocese of Montreal to serve the needs of the French-speaking members of the parish whose numbers were swelling with the influx of Quebec immigrants to Essex County. The curate soon alerted McEvay to the fact that large numbers of French-Canadian workers, as many as one-third the adult parishioners, refused to go to church on Sunday because they felt alienated from its cultural environment. With the Montreal priest's support, the call soon went up for an ethnically homogeneous parish. But since French Canadians had contributed to the building of the original church, they demanded some form of compensation. The matter went from the bishop to the metropolitan and finally to the apostolic delegate for adjudication. Falconio sought an expedient. He confirmed the removal of the curate, but also required the transfer of the Irish pastor. The delegate proposed the appointment of a bilingual incumbent who also would oversee the founding of a new French-Canadian parish. Although the question of compensation was not addressed, the French Canadians found the arrangement satisfactory.[46]

Ethnic conflict was also involved in appeals to the delegate on parish issues. Of the five cases in this category originating in dioceses located in English Canada, three dealt with ethnic tensions. Some parishioners of Grand' Digue appealed to the delegate against the decision of the bishop of St John to annex them to a neighbouring parish. Falconio was particularly impressed by their threat to go to the local Protestant church if matters were not arranged to their satisfaction. He urged the aged bishop, John Sweeney, to reconsider his decision. The diocesan authorities, however, blamed the conflict on 'meddlesome priests' who were agitating the Acadian question. They pointed out that although the annexation was justified because of distance, the faithful rejected the rector of the new parish because he was a French Canadian from Quebec. Falconio advised the Acadians to submit to the bishop's decision or direct their appeal to Archbishop O'Brien, the metropolitan.

But the Acadian rector of the parish from which the inhabitants were to be detached was insistent, raising the spectre of mass defections from the church unless the bishop relented. He depicted his compatriots as victims of Irish and Quebec clergymen who did not understand Acadian national aspirations.

Ces Messieurs [French-Canadian clergy] se montrent, ouvertement, leurs ennemis, autant que les Irlandais ... Leur joug, ajouté à celui des fils de l'Irlande, est devenu à peu près intolérable à notre peuple. La foi diminue tous les jours ... ce triste état de choses ne peut que s'aggraver, à moins que les Acadiens n'obtiennent des évêques et des prêtres de leur nationalité.

The delegate, who earlier had recommended the appointment of an Acadian bishop to Rome, was not insensitive to this plea. He reminded the new bishop of St John, Timothy Casey, that only serious motives could justify annexations and that these should not be implemented without prior consultation with the pastor and the parishioners concerned. Casey, however, insisted on pursuing his objective, arguing that the faithful's objections were unfounded.[47]

In Hamilton Bishop Dowling proved to be a little more responsive to ethnic factors. Members of St Clement's parish, diocese of Hamilton, wanted their dues to be directed to St Mary's in neighbouring London diocese. Both were German-language parishes. The claimants argued that they lived closer to St Mary's, which they had helped to build on the understanding that they could continue to worship there. Bishop Dowling apparently had taken account of the distance separating these families from St Clement's by allowing them to attend another church in his diocese. But the pastor of that parish was not German-speaking. An appeal therefore was made to the delegate through the rector of St Mary's. Falconio's private view was that the petitioners should be annexed to the diocese of London.

Dowling promptly set up a committee of inquiry which challenged the parishoners' key contention regarding their proximity of St Mary's. The appellants then were told that, although they were free to attend whatever church they pleased, their dues had to go to St Clement's. A vindicated bishop boasted to Falconio that 'in dealing with the German element in this diocese, my invariable rule is to consult my German Council, a course which has been highly approved by Propaganda and for which I received the congratulations of His Eminence Cardinal Ledochowski.' Anxious as well to show his sensitivity to the petitioners' concerns, Dowling appointed a German to the parish adjacent to St Clement's, although, as he pointed out, Germans were only a minority there. Falconio expressed full satisfaction with the bishop's actions and explanations.[48]

While Germans were restive in the western part of the province, French Canadians agitated in eastern Ontario against their Scottish bishop. The issue was education. French Canadians in the diocese of Alexandria wanted Macdonell to do something about the lack of French instruction in the local separate schools. They asked that one course be added to the English-language curriculum to allow their children to learn the rudiments of French, as well as some prayers and the catechism in their native tongue. Macdonell dismissed their request as purely sentimental, arising out of agitation imported from Quebec and inspired by French nationalism. Ontario, he proclaimed, was an English-speaking province and knowledge of French did not serve any useful purpose. Those who clung to it did so from sentiment, not social ambition. By appealing to the bishop, Macdonell contended, these diocesans were trying to take the law into their own hands. Instead of going through the proper channels of legitimate constitutional redress, they expected special treatment.

The delegate ignored the more strident aspects of Macdonell's letter in his reply to the French Canadians of Alexandria. He assured them that, although their bishop was not opposed to the teaching of French, it was not his responsibility to provide such courses but that of the civil authorities. In the absence of unanimity within the community as to language of instruction, however, Falconio believed that little could be done unless French Canadians were willing to create their own French-language separate schools. But despite the assurance with which the delegate intervened in this issue, it was clear that he had a rather imperfect knowledge of the Ontario school law. In rather stilted English he expressed the improbable opinion that 'it was against the law to have the French course in the public schools.' The French Canadians of Alexandria quickly understood that there was little to be hoped for in pursuing their complaint and the matter ended there.[49]

In the neighbouring archdiocese of Ottawa the issue was also education. But the focus, rather than being on ethnic antagonism, involved local support for Catholic schools, pitting Archbishop Duhamel against the French-Canadian parishioners of St-Joseph d'Orléans. The question is important because it makes clear the delegate's fundamental position on denominational, as opposed to public, education. The inhabitants of Orléans sent their children to a public school where religious instruction nevertheless was provided and Catholic symbols prominently displayed. But Archbishop Duhamel insisted that they become supporters of the separate school system. The parishioners pleaded that the size and limited resources of their community simply would not allow for the support of two schools, each having qualified and competent teachers. Duhamel would not be moved. He deprived the parishioners of the sacraments until they were ready to acknowledge the error of their ways.

They appealed to the apostolic delegate, who sided completely with their archbishop. Falconio reminded the inhabitants that Duhamel spared no effort to reach a satisfactory arrangement with them, inconveniencing himself three times to talk to them. The delegate admitted that the arguments put forward by the parishioners were not without merit. He emphasized, however, that their primary obligation was to support Catholic schools; in time the rest, like their concerns for quality education, would follow. The tolerance shown by the local public school for religious symbols and instruction was, he affirmed, against the law and should be seen only as an ephemeral measure. 'Il n'est pas sage pour les catholiques de préférer l'incertain au certain,' Falconio sententiously stated. How Archbishop Langevin would have been delighted with these words, had they been intended for Manitoba politicians, instead of poor Franco-Ontarian farmers! The delegate urged the inhabitants to submit to their archbishop's will so that they could do their Easter duty.[50]

Most appeals based on parish issues were related to more concrete considerations than ethnicity and sectarian education. Nine of the thirteen cases studied fell into this category, eight of them came from Quebec and only one, involving another group of Germans in the diocese of Hamilton, was from Ontario. In such questions the laity were moved either by considerations of personal convenience or financial benefit.[51] The inhabitants of St-Damase mission, for instance, challenged Archbishop Bégin's choice for the site of their new church and threatened apostasy if the matter were not rectified. Bégin, whose actions eventually were vindicated by the delegate, argued that because of the parishioners' ill-will, a consensus had been impossible to achieve. He therefore made the choice on his own initiative and dismissed as hollow the threat of apostasy.[52] The archbishop explained that very often material and personal factors determined the parishioners' choice of church site. They were aware, for instance, that property values increased when houses were located near a church. Since 'on ne peut pas mettre une église à toutes les portes de maison,' the good of the community had to prevail even if this caused dissatisfaction among some parishioners.[53]

In the archdiocese of Montreal, politics, not real estate, was apparently what divided Bruchési and the parishioners of St-Ignace Loyola, Berthier County. The parish, made up of farmers, fishermen, and sailors, had, according to the archbishop, experienced the usual intense factionalism over the routine parish administration. But things got out of hand when fighting actually broke out in the church over the election of its wardens. Blood was spilled and the rector was attacked. Bruchési was determined to make an example of these obstreperous parishioners and so imposed an interdict on them. As bells tolled, the sacrament was removed from the church and the altar stripped to the singing of the 'Miserere.' A concerned Falconio who read about this punishment in the local newspapers requested information and urged prudence and a speedy settlement. The interdict was soon lifted when the parishioners begged Bruchési's forgiveness and then proceeded to elect their wardens by acclamation! The archbishop later informed the delegate that the rivalry had been sparked by party politics.[54]

Specific appeals against the clergy's meddling in politics were relatively few. One came from Quebec and three from the Maritimes. In the archdiocese of Montreal the much-maligned Jean-Baptiste Proulx accused a neighbouring pastor of slander for an article published in a Laurentian newspaper on the Manitoba schools question. Proulx went through the usual channels of appeal; the paper generated by this case was quite voluminous. Basically, Proulx was trying to have himself cleared of allegations that he had conducted his Rome mission of 1896–7 without the authorization of his ecclesiastical superiors. Falconio eventually was able to bring about an amicable settlement by having Proulx's accuser publish a retraction in the newspaper.[55]

In Charlottetown a priest got into trouble for his newspaper articles which used intemperate language to describe the provincial government. The Conservatives were depicted as 'traitors' and a 'gang of outlaws,' while their newspapers were termed the 'reptile press.' The priest was also accused of being offensive to his colleagues in the clergy, as well as to his superiors. As a result Bishop J.C. McDonald forbade him to publish any material not previously submitted to the diocesan authorities. An appeal was made to Archbishop O'Brien, who considered the injunction too general and ordered McDonald to make it more restrictive. The bishop refused and turned to Falconio for support. The delegate, however, advised McDonald to follow proper canonical procedures in issuing his prohibition. The bishop accepted the advice and withdrew his appeal against O'Brien's sentence.[56]

Meanwhile in the neighbouring diocese of Antigonish the parishioners of Heatherton, who had been deprived of the sacraments for four years because of their reaction to the bishop's pastoral letter on the federal elections of 1896, appealed to the delegate to put an end to their torment. In his defence, Bishop John Cameron argued that these people had given scandal by walking out of the church when the pastoral was read. For a public offence he demanded public reparation, but the majority who, he alleged, were not of good faith, refused to bend. Falconio soon drew up a statement of redress acceptable to Cameron, which the guilty parties were required to make either singly or as a group. A spokesmen for the appellants soon reported that all had complied and finally had been admitted to the sacraments.[57]

In the same diocese some parishioners accused their pastor of interfering in the elections of 1900. This complaint was supported by none other than Laurier himself. Apparently at vespers the priest quoted the opinion of an unspecified bishop who termed the prime minister an infidel. Falconio, who reflected the Vatican's nervousness over the question of clerical interference in politics, demanded

TABLE 12
Nature of the Decisions Rendered by the Delegate

In favour of	No.	%
Bishop	28	76
Appellant	2	5
Compromise	7	19
Total	37	

a public retraction if the accusations were true. Although the belea-guered priest denied the charges, the delegate stated that he was in possession of affidavits from 'honourable men' which challenged his disclaimer. Cameron took the trouble to refute the accusations in detail. After receiving the bishop's explanation, Falconio concluded that the allegations had been false or exaggerated. To Conservative M.P. F.D. Monk the delegate asserted: 'with very few exceptions the clergy, in the exercise of their civil rights, conducted themselves pru-dently and ... even the actions of those in the few cases mentioned, were generally misunderstood, owing, I suppose, to party spirit.'[58]

Overall, it is not difficult to determine in whose favour the apostolic delegate intervened in appeals by priests and laymen against episcopal authority. Of the thirty-seven such cases, bishops most often emerged triumphant (see Table 12). Even in the remain-ing cases where they were not directly involved as parties, their judg-ments, whether privately expressed or implicit, or their behind-the-scenes actions, were frequently upheld by the delegate. In the two cases where the appellants were victorious one concerned the priest from the diocese of Pembroke, who likely won because of a canon lawyer's intervention; and the verdict, although satisfactory, was only a partial victory for the cleric. The second case was a more clear-cut triumph of parishioners over their bishop. Some families had un-successfully petitioned their bishop, Elphège Gravel of Nicolet, to attend a church in the neighbouring diocese of Sherbrooke, which happened to be closer to them. They appealed to the apostolic dele-gate who reversed the bishop's decision and even chastised Gravel for not being more attentive to the spiritual needs of these parishioners. 'Il y a des âmes qui souffrent beaucoup de l'état actuel des choses,' Falconio reminded him.[59]

In two other instances the delegate's action indirectly went against the bishop. The outcome of the appeal of the Hôtel Dieu sisters of Tracadie was an implicit criticism of Bishop Rogers. But in the second case, that of the libel suit involving two priests from the diocese of Montreal, Falconio's intervention was more of a help than a hindrance to Archbishop Bruchési whose relations with Proulx had been strained for a number of years. It is true that through the delegate's action, the appellant secured a partial retraction of the newspaper allegations against him, something that neither the archbishop, nor his diocesan court, was able to do. But it is also true that the archdiocesan authorities did not want to confront Proulx's main contention that Archbishop Fabre had sanctioned his Liberal-inspired mission to Rome. Falconio's intervention was more a face-saving device than an indirect criticism of Bruchési's behaviour.

Only seven disputes, five of them relating to clerical appointments, were resolved by amicable means. In five of these, the delegate fundamentally did not alter the position initially taken by the bishop, looking instead for some expedient to make the decision more palatable to the appellant. In the other two, the delegate made sure that his actions did not appear to be an infringement of episcopal prerogatives. The case involving the pamphleteering priest in the diocese of Charlottetown, for example, upheld the bishop's right to discipline him, although requiring that proper canonical procedures be observed. And, while in the Halifax case Falconio insisted that Archbishop O'Brien maintain the Irish priest whom the Propaganda considered one of his subjects, at the same time, he lectured the intemperate cleric on the archbishop's magnanimity in the face of his own persistent failings.

In the final analysis, the delegate did what he was told to do by the Holy See – to act as a support to episcopal authority. While his actions were in harmony with his instructions from Rome, they clearly were in contradiction with his own observations concerning the exaggerated power wielded by the episcopate in Canada. Ultimately, perhaps Bégin was correct: although the Canadian church did not adhere to the outward forms of canonical practices, in fact episcopal power was no more arbitrary in Canada than anywhere else in the Catholic world.

CONCLUSION

Apostolic delegates Merry del Val and Falconio were correct in insisting that ecclesiastical government in Canada become more formalized in both structure and method. It is clear that procedures for parish appointments had to be regularized and these positions made more permanent. In addition, the status of priests belonging to one diocese but lent to another for long periods of time had to be clarified. It is also evident, however, that no clergyman who challenged his bishop's decision on a parish nomination emerged totally victorious. Nor were missionary priests who demanded positions in their dioceses of origin ever fully vindicated. Perhaps some mistakes of diocesan administration might have been avoided if bishops had routinely consulted with advisers – mistakes such as the ordination of unworthy priests, clerical charges held for inordinately long periods of time, or unduly harsh episcopal strictures against priests or parishioners. Even though some of these excesses did occur in dioceses having cathedral chapters or other consultative bodies, the delegates' argument regarding due process was ultimately a compelling one.

But Merry del Val and Falconio went too far when they identified the failure to adhere to canonical forms and structures as the cause of episcopal autocracy, which in turn they made central to the crisis in the Canadian church. For one thing, in their perspective the crisis was confined almost exclusively to the province of Quebec which paradoxically had the most advanced forms of ecclesiastical government in Canada with chapters, tribunals, and synods. The English-Canadian church lacked such structures but was considered to have the most thoughtful and moderating elements in Canadian Catholicism. And even if we were to add to the cases investigated here an indeterminate number which never made it to the delegate for fear of reprisals, we are still far from the image of an aberrant institution characterized by unbridled episcopal authority. There were surely instances of abuse of power in both the English- and French-Canadian churches, but these were not so widespread as to undermine the whole ecclesiastical edifice.

Then where did this perception come from? Falconio and especially Merry del Val's mandates were dominated by the political question, which in Quebec was also a nationalist one. Previously, issues related to this question had caused dissension within the hierarchy and so the focus of attention was generally on the bishops. At the turn of the century, however, the Quebec bishops were united, except for one or possibly two exceptions. But the church was still divided because a growing number of the lower clergy were challenging their superiors on these issues. It is open to debate whether, as some bishops alleged, the politicization of Quebec's lower clergy was more widespread in this period; it was certainly more tangible. Even more problematic is Laflèche's contention that this politicization originated in the pernicious teachings of the Séminaire de Québec. The fact remains, however, that in the face of an episcopate determined to prevent backsliding on such issues as the Manitoba schools question, the clergy, sympathetic for whatever reason to the Liberal party, felt restive and expressed their frustrations to the apostolic delegates. In this way episcopal autocracy became a *leitmotiv* in the delegates' reports and dispatches to Rome, although in fact Falconio's own actions as arbiter tended to disprove this accusation.

Politics certainly permeated all aspects of society in *fin de siècle* Canada and the church could not avoid its pervasive influence. Even some of the cases analysed here hint at its importance within the church. The example of two of the priests from Rimouski who appealed to the delegate with letters of support from prominent provincial or federal politicians, judges, and clerics well known for their Liberal sympathies is an indication that clerics were not unaware of the use that could be made of political connections for promoting their ecclesiastical career and interests. On the other hand the case of the parishioners who had the misfortune to incur Bruchési's interdict reveals how disruptive political factionalism could be at the local level, even insinuating itself in parish administration; while that of laymen in the diocese of Antigonish who complained with affidavits about their pastor's unwarranted interference in politics illustrates how easily the position of a parish priest and even a bishop could be challenged on the basis of *ex parte* evidence.

Apart from the importance of politics in the life of the church, what other observations may be gleaned from these cases? One is that values such as comfort, material gain, and personal advancement were certainly not extraneous to the spiritual life of Catholics. Parishioners whose choice of place of worship was determined by such factors as real estate values, convenience, or the fear of having to pay new levies; diocesans who threatened their bishop with apostasy if they did not obtain satisfaction on a variety of parish questions; laymen who preferred to support public to Catholic schools because of the material advantages involved as well as the tolerance shown for religious instruction in such schools; all these are indicators that religious sentiment often encompassed very practical and material considerations.

Questions of language and nationality were also vital in the popular mind to the practice of religion. Acadians, dissatisfied with being served by just any French-speaking priests, demanded their own clergy. Franco-Ontarians, alienated by Irish pastors or by English-language Catholic schools, required religious institutions catering to their cultural needs. Germans preferred worshipping in churches staffed by clergymen speaking their language. These demands would become ever more pressing in the course of time as immigration brought a more culturally diverse population to Canada.

Finally, examples of priestly deviance, although certainly more numerous than the cases brought to the apostolic delegate's attention, still were marginal when considered in the context of the total number of Canadian priests. These cases, together with those involving clergymen with pronounced nervous conditions, illustrate the high status enjoyed by the priestly office in Catholic cultures, and show the few options open to those who could not live up to its high standards. This was an era when leaving the priesthood or even the church was tantamount to cutting oneself off from one's community of origin. We get an implicit sense of all the tension and ambivalence generated by such a course of action in the case of the Catholic/Baptist clergyman's desperate search for security and identity.

In general, deviant clerics lived a life of intense isolation and rejection. Bishops might send them to missionary outposts in their dioceses out of the respectable citizenry's sight. They might try to have them transferred to neighbouring dioceses suffering from shortages of priests or to some far-flung corner of the continent. If these clerics proved to be truly incorrigible, the insane asylum or the home for wayward priests was a final solution. The fear of scandal was uppermost in the minds of ecclesiastical superiors, and in this era of intense conformity their preferred methods for dealing with deviant clerics were removal or confinement. But the underlying cause of these priests' behaviour remained unresolved.

Conclusion

Canada was born of ethnic tension. In the nineteenth century this conflict took on sectarian characteristics since religion generally was regarded as an essential component of ethnic identity. Although at first the point of dissension concerned the rights and privileges to be enjoyed by the religious minority, eventually the issue became the very cultural character of the country. Essentially the question was framed in the context of Catholic-Protestant relations since other religious denominations were almost non-existent (although it is interesting to note that Etienne-Paschal Taché's education bill of 1855 made provision for the creation of separate schools in Canada West for Blacks and Jews; this clause was then struck from the final draft of the legislation). Since schools were seen by Victorian Canadians who subscribed to a progressive assumption of their age as fundamental tools for shaping society both socially and culturally, it is not surprising that education should be at the centre of the conflict.

Every colony and region entering into Confederation experienced such tensions and resolved them in different ways. In Quebec a settlement most generous to the Protestant minority was achieved mainly because many prominent members of the Canadian socio-economic élite were drawn from its ranks. As a result Quebec Protestants enjoyed a large degree of institutional autonomy, together with a number of specific political guarantees, both formal and informal. In Ontario a separate school system came into existence in the Union period largely because of the unified action of French-Canadian legislators who triumphed over their politically divided colleagues from Canada West. Ontario Catholics as a body were neither demographically strong nor socially prominent enough to influence this course of events on their own. The establishment of a separate school system generally was regarded with disfavour by Ontario Protestants, whose reactions ranging from the tolerant antipathy of Egerton Ryerson (who expected that the system would wither away) to fierce opposition on the part of voluntarist groups. The system was then entrenched in article 93 of the British North America Act as part of a package of measures primarily intended to protect the Protestant minority in Quebec. In Nova Scotia, although the Catholic minority was subjected to sectarian harassment in the late 1850s and to a common school system in 1865, a *modus vivendi* soon emerged that allowed for the existence of *de facto* Catholic schools. At the time of Confederation such schools existed in the other Maritime colonies as well as in the North-West.

Confederation created an expectation among Catholic spokesmen – one that the political élite did not discourage – that their co-religionists in the provinces and territories of Canada could look forward to the same magnanimous treatment accorded the Protestants of Quebec. Article 93 of the BNA Act was seen as symbolic of this equality. It mattered little to these spokesmen that the clause only extended constitutional protection to Catholic schools whose existence had received prior legal recognition. Equity demanded that the Protestant and Catholic minorities of the country be treated equally. If necessary, the clout exercised by a politically compact body of French-Canadian politicians could again be invoked to achieve this goal. This belief in equality was articulated by religious leaders and newspapers at the time of the New Brunswick schools question and repeated by a variety of spokesmen over the next fifty years.[1]

Arthur Silver is quite correct in arguing that Quebec's French-speaking political leaders were primarily concerned in 1867 with achieving the widest possible autonomy for their province within Confederation; that they largely ignored the existence of French-speaking communities in other parts of Canada; and that they had no particular interest in trying to export their model of a bilingual society to the rest of the country.[2] By the same token, they could not have ignored, nor would their religious leaders have allowed them to do so, the existence of Catholic minorities elsewhere in Canada. It is significant that on the eve of Confederation Hector-Louis Langevin, writing to his brother, a priest, stated: 'Nous accordons aux Protestants du Bas Canada la protection qu'ils doivent avoir et en considération de cela nous étendrons notre protection aux 700,000 ou 800,000 catholiques du Haut Canada & des Provinces Maritimes.'[3] It is difficult to imagine that the clergy would have countenanced supporting the new political arrangement if they so much as suspected that it would imperil existing institutions and leave Catholic minorities at the mercy of hostile majorities.

And yet their expectation of equity turned to bitter disillusion in the next half-century. Conceived in conflict, Canada would be marked by conflict in its formative years. Crises soon erupted in New Brunswick and the North-West. The schools controversy in New Brunswick eventually resulted in an accommodation similar to the one worked out in Nova Scotia, in part because of French-Canadian and Irish Catholic political pressures, but also because of the outbreak of violence. The crisis underlined how precarious Catholic institutions and the supposed rights on which they rested really were. While in the North-West such institutions were safe, at least for the time being, their architects were subjected to unfair treatment. Louis Riel and Ambroise Lépine were repeatedly denied the amnesty promised by various public officials. Instead, the majority harassed and persecuted them, while the minority considered them champions of the Catholic cause and therefore victims of Protestant arbitrariness.

Some ten years later the Jesuit Estates controversy would rekindle latent sectarian hostility and trigger a chain of crises in the Canadian West and Ontario. As a result, in Manitoba and the Territories the sons of Ontario farmers gave themselves the common school system denied them in their province of origin. In Ontario a separate school system which had met with tolerance, but not genuine acceptance, was assailed by the opposition and the system's weakest component, the bilingual schools, eventually would be abolished with regulation 17. By the outbreak of the First World War, Canada, except for Quebec, had an English Protestant face and Catholic minorities were expected to fit into this cultural mould. The dream of a Canada where the two dominant denominations, together with their minorities, would live side by side in harmony was shattered.

The Catholic church in Canada lived within this climate of ethnic confrontation, and ecclesiastical leaders, whether consciously or unconsciously, in some way were actors in this conflict. The church, particularly in Quebec, was marked by a high degree of ideological unity inspired by Pius IX's reaction to the revolutions of 1848 and especially by his encyclical *Quanta cura* and its *Syllabus of Errors*. Even so, the institution was afflicted by serious tensions based on personality and vested interest. These tensions in turn influenced the response of the Quebec hierarchy to the crises that shook Confederation. Despite their ideological compactness, bishops might find themselves on opposite sides in these confrontations. Some, while not themselves French-Canadian nationalists, might defend positions that would advance the cause of nationalism (of which religion was an integral part). Others, without being anti-nationalists, would inhibit its development.

Bishop Bourget for one had a strong sense of historical continuity. He often saw his actions as extensions of a tradition that stretched back in time from his predecessor, Jean-Jacques Lartigue, to the first archbishop of Quebec, Joseph-Octave Plessis, to the founder of the Canadian church, François de Laval. He revered these prelates because they stood as champions of the rights of the church against the encroachments of the state, whether these took the form of royal Gallicanism or British supremacy. In his mind, the rights of the church went hand in hand with the rights of Catholics. For this reason the bishop was a prime advocate of an amnesty for Riel in the early days. He was also the most active churchman in the agitation in favour of the educational rights of New Brunswick Catholics.

Yet, for a variety of reasons, Bourget's actions did not rally his colleagues in the episcopate. Taschereau feared among other things the consequences of the church's becoming too involved in political questions. (Bourget's stands had already alienated the Conservative party.) The archbishop preferred quiet diplomacy, although there is little evidence that he was particularly active as a behind-the-scenes lobbyist. And while Bourget's public and private interventions made a contribution, at least on the intellectual level, to French-Canadian nationalism, no such transcendent vision inspired his metropolitan. So Taschereau left no legacy in this regard, either in intellectual or in concrete terms; he seldom went beyond judgments about the inopportuneness of Bourget's actions.

The same is true of Taschereau's English-speaking colleagues. Archbishop Lynch may have considered himself leader of the Canadian church, he may have championed many causes, notably Irish ones, but the fate of Riel and New Brunswick Catholics apparently left him indifferent. Archbishop Connolly, on the other hand, like Taschereau, was a proponent of quiet diplomacy; but as a strong supporter of the Conservative party he was unlikely to embarrass the government over New Brunswick schools. In fact it was only when the party was safely in opposition that the archbishop of Halifax finally called together his suffragans to publish a letter on the issue. Except for Bishop Sweeney who was from New Brunswick, inaction best characterized the response of the English-speaking hierarchy to these issues.

Bourget failed to rally his brother bishops and was ultimately defeated in Rome because of high-level lobbying on the part of the ruling Liberal party and clerics at the Séminaire de Québec who were hostile to him. These also managed to discredit the bulk of the Quebec clergy by smearing them with accusations of political partisanship and electoral interference. Bourget saw the writing on the wall and resigned and his mantle fell to Laflèche. But the bishop of Trois-Rivières was not made of the same stuff as his master: he lacked Bourget's charisma, his energy, his vision. Laflèche was also more prone to interpret events in conspiratorial terms, a tendency common to unconditional followers of Pius IX, but which in his case became almost obsessive. In the bishop's defence, it may be argued that he was sorely tried. Viewed with suspicion and ostracized by Rome, punished for his alleged obstinacy, Laflèche certainly did not have an easy time defending his causes either in Quebec or at the Vatican. But neither was he particularly effective as an organizer or an advocate of these causes.

Nevertheless, the bishop was the living link between Bourget and another great ecclesiastic, Nazaire Bégin. The archbishop of Quebec not only had a deep personal commitment to Catholic minority rights, but also a strong sense of the church's historical role in their defence. Like Bourget, he was a prelate with energy, charisma, and vision; but unlike the bishop of Montreal, he was a man of wide culture and learning. Bégin gave the lie to Conroy's assertion that the Quebec clergy's interference in politics was caused by their profound lack of education. During the 1896 elections the archbishop believed that it was opportune for the episcopate to speak out publicly on behalf of Manitoba Catholics, much as Bourget had done for the New Brunswick minority in 1872. Both churchmen contended that voters and legislators were morally bound to uphold Catholic rights and that it ultimately fell to the church to judge their good intentions. Bégin went so far in his vindication of the clergy's right to speak out on the moral aspects of public issues that he justified the controversial sermon Laflèche delivered just prior to the elections of 1896. 'Son unique but,' he maintained, 'était de forcer les libéraux à répudier cette erreur [the absolute independence of the Catholic MPS' political conscience] ou à renoncer à l'appui des catholiques sincères.'[4] For his efforts, Bégin maintained, Laflèche had received only outrageous insults from the party press.

Yet this is the same man who some twenty years earlier bemoaned Laflèche's ignorance, his narrow-mindedness, and bad faith, and who yearned for his downfall. In the intervening period was it Laflèche or Bégin who had changed? Or to put it another way, were the episcopates of Bourget and Laflèche simply an eccentricity in the history of the Quebec church, as some political and religious historians conveniently maintain, or worse still, an ideological reign of terror, a temporary madness from which the church soon recovered? Was Bégin – ever Taschereau's man of confidence, hand-picked to succeed the cardinal in the see of Quebec – part of the much-vaunted Taschereau tradition, if indeed such a tradition ever existed? It is interesting to note that in the aftermath of the Manitoba crisis Bégin was at pains to explain why his position regarding the Liberal party seemed so different from the one taken by his predecessor in 1882. Taschereau, he insisted, would not have written in 1896 what he wrote in 1882 when he distinguished between doctrinal liberalism and the Liberal party; nor had he expressed then the ideas that Liberals later attributed to him. The archbishop, he argued, had not denied the party's dangerous tendencies; he simply sought to prevent the condemnation of a political party on the basis of the opinion of an individual bishop, of a group of priests or laymen. By an irony of fate, Merry del Val turned these words against their author: the delegate accused an extremist rump of French-Canadian bishops of appropriating the authority of the Canadian church in their attempt to condemn the Liberal party for its position on Manitoba schools.

In the final analysis, Bégin was defeated by two forces in the closing years of the last century. One was the campaign spearheaded by Benjamin Pâquet and Taschereau in the 1870s and 1880s which succeeded in convincing Rome that their clerical opponents were ignorant, intemperate, and politically motivated. Bégin, as we have seen, actively collaborated in this campaign. The other was the timorousness and general passivity of the English-speaking hierarchy over questions of Catholic rights.

This was especially true of the Ontario episcopate. Betraying the mentality of a besieged minority, these bishops did not see themselves as belonging to a wider Canadian Catholic community which represented 42 per cent of the total population. They did not find strength in the fact that they lived next to a populous province where 92 per cent of the population was Catholic. The Quebec church's French-speaking character apparently prevented them from identifying themselves with the majority component of Canadian Catholicism. They chose instead to see themselves as alone, as isolated, a small minority representing 18 per cent of the population against a huge and menacing Protestant majority. And while Archbishop O'Brien of Halifax, whose schools did not enjoy constitutional guarantees, proved to be a bolder champion of minority rights in Manitoba, the bishops of Ontario believed that any public act on their part might jeopardize the Catholic educational system in their province, which had such guarantees.

But apart from these fears, the Ontario bishops showed an alarming lack of concern for the fate of their Manitoba co- religionists. On separate occasions archbishops Walsh and Gauthier each admitted that they were not up to date on current aspects of the Manitoba schools question. The Ontario hierarchy neither provided moral support to Archbishop Langevin in his hour of need, nor endorsed any of his initiatives to break the stalemate that beset the schools question. And they proposed no alternate strategies. Like Lynch before them, they remained passive and impassive to the fate of Catholic minorities elsewhere in the country. Was their behaviour determined by the fact that these minorities were French-speaking? At the time of the New Brunswick schools question there were at least as many English- as French-speaking Catholics in that province, but Lynch did not seek to help them. Was it the fear of antagonizing a not unfriendly provincial government in Ontario that motivated him? But, as we have seen, of all the Catholic minorities of Canada the one in Ontario was surely the most constitutionally secure. It is difficult to understand why the bishops were so hesitant. Perhaps their background best explains their position.

A majority of the Ontario hierarchy in the latter part of the nineteenth century were immigrants, mostly Irish, whose cultural frames of reference were the British Isles or the United States. As a result, they would not have shared with Bégin or Bourget a consciousness of the historic struggle for the achievement of Catholic rights in Canada. Their experience was limited to conducting business with a

generally indifferent provincial government through quiet diplomacy. They seemed to ignore the fundamental fact that this approach
had been made possible by the political agitation of French-Canadian
churchmen and legislators in the Union period, which eventually
resulted in guarantees for the separate school system in the BNA Act.
The episcopate appeared instead to believe that it was their approach
that had given birth to separate schools in Ontario and that as a result
it was universally valid.

But the Ontario bishops were not alone in betraying an insular
perspective. It is obvious that the highly fragmented components of
the Canadian church were not keeping pace with political developments initiated by Confederation. Bishop Bourget implicitly understood that these arrangements required greater co-ordination among
the local churches and so advocated ecclesiastical structures reflecting the new political reality. But his call was heeded neither at home
nor in Rome. To the contrary, further fragmentation occurred. The
elevation of Taschereau to the cardinalate might have provided the
opportunity to bring together the scattered fragments of Canadian
Catholicism, but it seems clear that Taschereau did not have the
temperament to act as the leader of the Canadian church by fostering
collaboration and cohesion.[5]

Thus the outbreak of the Manitoba schools question found the
Canadian church unprepared and unused to common action. The
Quebec church, on the other hand, was already able to act in concert
thanks to the persistent efforts of Bourget. In the face of the English-
speaking hierarchy's general passivity, the Quebec bishops were
compelled to act alone. In this context, Merry del Val's proposal that
the Canadian church only undertake common initiatives at the
instigation of the Ontario hierarchy surely would have condemned
the institution to immobility. Falconio understood the dynamics of
the hierarchy much better and for this reason recommended the
institution of a national synod – a proposal which a majority of
English-speaking bishops did not endorse.

The Quebec hierarchy's support for Catholic schools in Manitoba
remained unwavering throughout the crisis. At first all bishops, with
one or two exceptions, felt that such schools could best be re-
established through remedial legislation. When as a result of Rome's
position this course of action was no longer viable, the episcopate
continued to provide moral and financial assistance to Archbishop
Langevin, despite their own feelings about the futility of concessions

obtained through the Laurier-Greenway agreement. Their support raises a question about the personality of Archbishop Langevin. Historians have tended to depict the prelate as ignorant, imprudent, and intransigent. He was undoubtedly a man of many faults. The archbishop was impulsive and high-strung, with a certain eagerness to please. He obviously lacked the education, the interests, and the polish of a Bégin. His response to the spiritual needs of Ukrainian immigrants revealed a relative narrow-mindedness.

Yet it is difficult to escape the impression that he was made a scapegoat by politicians, ecclesiastics, and historians. As the visible head of the Manitoba Catholic minority, Langevin was and remains an easy target on which to pin the blame for problems arising out of the Laurier-Greenway accord. But surely his role was not to make any easier the life of politicians whose fundamental axiom was to avoid controversy at all costs. In upholding the rights of his faithful, Langevin was carrying out his duty. Yet Cherrier's correspondence with Falconio reveals a much less intransigent, much less determined personality than has emerged from contemporary and historical representations of the archbishop. Indeed, if at one point Cherrier feared that Langevin might accept unacceptable compromises, it seems clear that the prelate could not have been the wild-eyed extremist described by his opponents then as now. Nor would a prudent and otherwise sensible prelate like Bégin have supported him so consistently. Despite his drawbacks, Langevin, like Bégin, had a visceral sense of the historic struggle for Catholic rights in Canada and the church's role in that struggle. He too made an intellectual contribution to a dualistic vision of Canada, even though in practice he was unsuccessful in realizing his objectives.

Rome was not opposed in principle to ethnic aspirations in this period. Its treatment of Ukrainians and Acadians indicates a certain sensitivity to such concerns. It is true that the Holy See responded to the Ruthenian question as a result of diplomatic pressures and threats of schism. But respond it did. If the Acadians' call for a bishop of their own was not immediately heeded, it was because the vacancies in New Brunswick's two sees had just been filled and Rome would not countenance the creation of a third diocese in light of the province's relatively small Catholic population. By the same token, the Holy See surely would not have impeded the affirmation of Catholic rights in Canada, even if its definition of such rights was narrower and more legalistic than that of Bourget or Bégin. What

Rome wanted above all was that ethnic or religious questions not divide the local church and that as much as possible they not trouble relations with civil authorities.

But the problem was precisely that. Although Bishop Bourget's positions on the *programme catholique* and the New Brunswick schools question were found to be doctrinally sound by Roman canonists, these issues bitterly divided the Quebec hierarchy and gave rise to violent public quarrels. As a result the Holy See ordered the bishops to remain silent on such questions. Roman officials must have been swayed by the arguments of Taschereau and some of his suffragans that Bourget was needlessly provoking a government which on numerous occasions had shown sympathy for the Catholic cause. These top administrators had met leading Canadian Catholic politicians who went to Rome at the time of Confederation to confirm their party's good intentions towards the church. Taschereau insisted as well that Bourget also was antagonizing the Protestant majority by his actions. Since Quebeckers only represented one-third of the Canadian population, the archbishop maintained that they were sure to lose any confrontation with the majority. The archbishop seemed to forget that Quebeckers were not the only Catholics in Confederation. Still, he was correct in pointing out the relative under-representation of his co-religionists in the Canadian Parliament.

These same conflicts within the church recurred when the Liberals came to power in Ottawa. By 1876 the Quebec church again was making a public spectacle of its divisions, and partisan newspapers appropriated various clergymen to their own cause. Benjamin Pâquet, among others, repeated arguments articulated by Taschereau a few years earlier and laced them with alarmist cries of sectarian violence and civil war. Such dire predictions later would be dismissed as utterly groundless by Bégin himself. But nevertheless they were effective. Pâquet's warnings were confirmed by the self-important archbishop of Toronto, who had his own axe to grind against the Quebec hierarchy. Lynch also gave his blessing to the Roman mission of his suffragan, John Walsh, who together with the former Liberal senator, Sir Edward Kenny, sought to vindicate the ruling party's position on various ethnic and religious questions.

Hearing such discordant voices on the nature of Canadian political parties and fearing that an otherwise friendly government would be alienated by the actions of certain bishops, Rome once again imposed silence on its unruly Quebec church and dispatched Bishop Conroy on a mission of reconciliation. The choice of a prelate from the British empire was significant. The Holy See was looking for someone who understood the complexities of the British parliamentary system and could situate the crisis in the proper context of relations between Rome and Great Britain. Aware that Canada was a colony of Britain, the Holy See was not interested in pursuing a course that would antagonize British interests.

Rome faced more urgent problems of church-state relations in this period, what with Italian unification, the German and Swiss *Kulturkampfen*, the abrogation of the Austrian *Concordat*, and the threat of French and Belgian anti-clericalism. Compared with these problems, the issues raised by some Canadian churchmen must have seemed trifling, especially since politicians themselves were so anxious to show their goodwill. Officials at the Holy See must have believed that Bourget and his allies were getting carried away when they described in the highly ideological language of the times the dangers awaiting the Canadian church.

But the language that Bourget and his followers used should not blind us to the point they were trying to make. While not doctrinally dangerous, the Liberal party was certainly opportunistic, alternately playing to the clerical gallery and, when the political moment was right, attacking it. It is true that opportunism is not the prerogative of any one party in Canadian political history, or for that matter in any other country. What Bourget and his followers denounced, however, was the ease with which French-Canadian Liberals assailed the church, something that distinguished them from their Conservative colleagues, who never openly engaged in such tactics. With their sense of the contemporary state of Canadian ethnic relations, Bourget and his allies felt that this tendency boded ill for Catholic rights. The Manitoba schools question would prove them correct, for while the Conservatives finally introduced remedial legislation, Laurier – who publicly professed his filial devotion to the church – opposed the measure.

But all that was still in the future. The Conroy mission confirmed the Holy See's suspicions about the political eccentricities of the Quebec clergy. By temperament a scholar and a diplomat, the Irish prelate had no sympathy with nationalism, either in Ireland or in Canada. Like his mentor Paul Cardinal Cullen, archbishop of Dublin, Conroy was predisposed to negotiating with the civil authorities. Nationalism to him was just another obstacle, on the same level as

private interests or personality quirks, impeding his mission. Conroy
was no one's dupe, neither Mackenzie's nor Lynch's nor Taschereau's. Yet his was ultimately an idealistic vision of things. One
wonders whether his model of the nineteenth-century cleric really
existed, since he so readily dismissed the entire clergy of North
America as ignorant and base. This idealized vision allowed him to
judge the Quebec clergy as severely as Lord Durham had the French
Canadians some thirty years earlier and for the same reasons. His
analysis of the situation was ill-conceived, as the perpetuation of the
crisis in the Quebec church showed. Conroy did not imagine that
relations between Catholic and Protestant, English and French,
would get worse in the next few years, nor that the Quebec church,
far from being a cause of dissension, was merely an actor in a wider
conflict over the cultural character of Canada.

Rome continued to impose silence on the Quebec episcopate in
questions regarded as purely political. Not even as trusted a collaborator as Smeulders could deter officials at the Holy See from pursuing
such a course. But this prelate, coming as he did from a minority
culture, had an instinctive understanding of the Quebec clergy's
concerns. Through contacts with such clerics as Laflèche and Taché,
he came to realize that the future of Catholicism in Canada depended
on a strong Catholic Quebec. Only in this way could the type of
compromises inimical to Catholic interests which occurred in the
1870s be prevented. His mandate, however, was not wide enough for
him to act as an effective spokesman on behalf of the Quebec clergy.
His other handicap was that he became a prisoner of the conspiratorial language of Laflèche, which did nothing to alter Rome's perception of Canadian problems.

With its carrot and stick approach, the Holy See kept the Quebec
clergy well in line until the next crisis erupted. But the ineffective-
ness of Rome's policy of distributing honours and promotions as a
means of correcting what were perceived to be dangerous tendencies
in the Quebec church was soon revealed. Structural changes such as
the creation of three ecclesiastical provinces and the establishment of
a virtually autonomous university in Montreal; personality changes
resulting from the replacement of every Quebec bishop with a new
incumbent by the end of the century; Taschereau's own elevation to
the College of Cardinals – all these events amounted to little, since
the crisis when it hit was just as intense as it had been twenty years
earlier.

Instead of rethinking its approaches and strategies, the Vatican persisted in its tried and true ways. In fact fresh evidence from the United States tended to confirm a number of preconceptions held by Roman officialdom. For one thing, the Franco-American clergy and faithful were proving to be just as unruly and indifferent to ecclesiastical authority as their Canadian cousins. For another, their insistence on the intimate link between language and religion was being disputed by such high dignitaries as the apostolic delegate in Washington. Citing the example of the Franco-Americans of Hartford, Connecticut, Archbishop Satolli asserted:

It is ridiculous ... to affirm that if they do not maintain their native language exclusively in the home and at church they risk losing their faith, as if the latter were tied to one or other language for every nation. Indeed the inevitable course of events for every immigrant nationality shows that change and uniformity of language and customs [occur] within one generation at the very latest. Already the Germans have little by little understood this, and they are convinced that their supposed Cahenslyism was a utopia.[6]

The 'narrow' views of the French-Canadian clergy, whether native or expatriate, were also confirmed by such prelates as archbishops Corrigan and Ireland as well as Cardinal Vaughan of Westminster. Rome lent a great deal of weight to their testimony, undoubtedly believing that these men were expressing not only personal opinions but also the views of their governments. Only Cardinal Ledochowski, another member of a minority culture, did not accept this vision of things. Did the Vatican not expect the French Canadians of Quebec to follow in the footsteps of their American cousins and submit to the 'inevitable' empire of the English language?

One thing is certain. Even more than twenty years earlier, the crisis leading up to the Merry del Val mission was set by the Vatican bureaucracy in the broader Anglo-Saxon context. In the United States the defeat of Cahenslyism coincided with the triumph of manifest destiny. North of the border, Canada, with the possible exception of Quebec, was clearly becoming an English country, both linguistically and culturally. The dominion of English-speaking peoples was not only a North American but a world reality as Britain achieved the pinnacle of power. The sun of the British empire obscured for Rome the fact that French Canadians comprised the overwhelming majority of Canadian Catholics. In this context the

Vatican's choice of the very English Merry del Val was no accident.

Just like Conroy before him, the apostolic delegate had his own version of manifest destiny: the fervent belief that the English-speaking peoples of the world would return to the Roman fold. This conversion would be effected by emulating, not fighting them, indeed by surpassing them in their own strengths and so winning their admiration. Merry del Val here betrayed the mentality typical of minority groups, with their delusions of grandeur founded on what are perceived to be the majority culture's qualities. Given the international context, such views were taken very seriously at the Vatican.

It is not surprising that Merry del Val should favour the Ontario episcopate as instruments for his plan of conversion. The irony was that without the influx of French Canadians from Quebec and the natural increase of Franco-Ontarians these bishops could not have succeeded in maintaining the Catholic population at current levels. But this was ignored by Merry del Val, as were the past political excesses of a Lynch and a Cleary. Instead the Ontario bishops were presented as paragons of intellect and rational discourse, those essential ingredients for the successful conversion of English-speaking Protestants.

The Vatican's Anglo-Saxon perspective was also evident in the appointment of Falconio as first permanent apostolic delegate. While the prelate spoke broken English, his French was almost non-existent. His experience of North America was considerable, his knowledge of Quebec minimal. Even so, Falconio was much more attuned than his predecessor to ethnic issues, as his attitude toward Ukrainians and Acadians showed. But there were limits to his willingness to accommodate such concerns, especially if they disrupted the unity of the church or good relations with government.

The Manitoba schools question was one such issue. The defeat of remedial legislation immeasurably complicated things. In light of the constitutional limbo into which the question fell at that point, it was virtually impossible for the apostolic delegate to bring about an equitable settlement. It remains true, however, that Falconio, Merry del Val, and Rampolla showed as much unbounded confidence in the Catholic Laurier as did the French Canadians in their native son. Hindsight would reveal that this confidence was unwarranted. No more than in the 1870s were the Liberals willing to risk defeat for the sake of a small minority.

Rome's policies with regard to the relatively small and distant Canadian Catholic community is certainly understandable. The results of those policies, however, are no less perceptible. In the aftermath of the defeat of the 1837 rebellions, the church emerged as a major player in Quebec. The times favoured a conservative response to the question of *la survivance* and the church had the human and institutional resources to take up the challenge, not only on behalf of the French Canadians of Quebec, but increasingly on behalf of those who left the province.

The politics of the Union and Confederation periods gave rise to another major player in the cultural life of the colony – the political parties. When Persico so astutely observed that 'tutto è politica,' he was astonished to see how in Canada political parties managed to infiltrate and attempt to control every aspect of life, including, he might have added, the church. But prelates such as Bourget demonstrated a will to keep the church free of the influence of political parties, especially in the assertion of Catholic rights. As long as this will remained strong, the process by which the minority gave in to the majority on a number of religious and linguistic questions in this formative period in Canada's history was at least hampered. It was no doubt this resistance to the process of cultural homogenization that Charles Lindsey found so exasperating. But that will was defeated in the 1870s, in large measure because of the Holy See's policies. Rome in Canada did not, as Lindsey feared, side with the assertive spokesmen of Catholic rights. It might be more correct to say that Rome was on the side of the big battalions!

This defeat in turn prepared the way for the one in 1896. As a result, although Catholics constituted the single largest Christian denomination in Canada, they saw themselves as a minority, weak and marginal. The perception of the Ontario hierarchy had become the dominant one. It is significant that this defeat also signalled the decline of French-Canadian political power and ushered in the one-sided 'compromises' that followed.

Notes

Introduction

1 Charles Lindsey, *Rome in Canada* (Toronto 1877), 4
2 L.O. David, *Le clergé canadien, sa mission, son œuvre* (Montréal 1896); *Histoire du Canada* (Montréal 1909); Charles Langelier, *Souvenirs politiques*, 2 vols. (Québec 1902, and 1912)
3 Crunican, *Priests and Politicians*
4 Rumilly, *Histoire de la province de Québec*

CHAPTER ONE: Toward a National Church?

1 Archivio della Sacra Congregazione di Propaganda Fide, Roma, (APFR), nuova serie (NS) vol. 195, rubrica 154, Diomede Falconio al Cardinal Prefetto M. Ledochowski, 6 giu. 1900. In this letter Falconio described the Canadian winter as hard beyond words ('durissimo oltre ogni dire').
2 James A. Schmeiser, 'The Development of Canadian Ecclesiastical Provinces, Councils, Rituals and Catechisms,' *Studia canonica* 5 (1971): 135–65
3 Grisé, *Les conciles provinciaux de Québec et l'Église canadienne*
4 Terry Murphy, 'The Emergence of Maritime Catholicism, 1781–1830,' *Acadiensis* 13, no. 2 (Spring 1984): 29–49. See also Terry Murphy and C.J. Byrne, eds., *Religion and Identity: The Experience of Irish and Scottish Catholics in Atlantic Canada* (St John's 1987). On the early history of Irish Catholics in Halifax, see T.M. Punch, 'The Irish Catholics, Halifax's First Minority Group,' *Nova Scotia Historical Quarterly* 10, no. 1 (March 1980) 23–40.

5 In mission territories, raising an area to the status of a vicarate is a preliminary step to its becoming a diocese. The vicariate is administered by a vicar apostolic who has the status and powers of a bishop. He does not, however, belong to an ecclesiastical province but is under the direct and immediate supervision of the Holy See. And whereas diocesan bishops within an ecclesiastical province deliberate on questions of discipline, dogma, and morals in provincial councils, these issues are determined in a vicariate between the vicar apostolic and the Holy See. The formula of the vicariate was used throughout Canadian history from the establishment of episcopal authority in Quebec in 1659 to the ecclesiastical organization of remote northern regions.

6 Because of London's hostility to the creation of more than one bishopric in Canada, the Holy See gave MacEachern the unusual title of auxiliary suffragan bishop. Although he had, like Burke, a defined territory to administer, as an auxiliary bishop he depended for his authority on Bishop Plessis of Quebec. See Edgar Godin, 'Établissement de l'Église catholique au Nouveau Brunswick,' Société canadienne d'histoire de l'Église catholique (SCHEC) *Sessions d'études* (1981): 37–56.

7 Léon Thériault, 'L'Acadianisation de l'Église catholique en Acadie, 1763–1953' in Jean Daigle, ed., *Les Acadiens des Maritimes: Études Thématiques* (Moncton 1980): 293–369; Martin Spigelman, 'Race et religion: les Acadiens et la hiérarchie catholique irlandaise du Nouveau Brunswick,' *Revue d'Histoire de l'Amérique française* 29, no. 1 (juin 1975): 69–85; Johnston, *A History of the Catholic Church in Eastern Nova Scotia*, II: 402–5. In later years tensions did not completely subside between the Irish and the Scots. In the diocese of Charlottetown, for example, complaints against the Scots monopoly of the local church were heard from Irish clergymen at the turn of the century. See Archivio Segreto Vaticano (ASV), Delegazione Apostolica del Canadà (DAC), box 6, Irish priests to Donato Sbarretti, 11 Nov 1907.

8 The Acadians also had their own institutions of higher learning. See, for example, Georgette Desjardins, 'Le rôle des religieuses Hospitalières de Saint-Joseph dans l'éducation au Madawaska depuis 1873,' SCHEC *Sessions d'étude* (1981): 57–66; Alexandre Savoie, 'Les communautés religieuses et l'enseignement au Nouveau-Brunswick depuis 1867,' ibid., 67–78.

9 I.R. Robertson, 'The Bible Question in Prince Edward Island from 1856 to 1860,' *Acadiensis* 5 (1975–6): 3–25, and 'Party Politics and

Religious Controversialism in Prince Edward Island from 1860 to 1863,' *Acadiensis* 7 (1977–8): 29–59; Johnston, *History of the Catholic Church*, 279–82; M. Hatfield, 'H.H. Pitts and Race and Religion in New Brunswick Politics,' *Acadiensis* 4 (1975): 46–65; J.I. Little, 'New Brunswick Reaction to the Manitoba Schools' Question,' *Acadiensis* 1 (1972): 43–58

10 Murphy, 'Emergence,' 40–5; this interpretation is questioned in Hatfield, 'Pitts and Race and Religion.'

11 F. Wilson, 'The Most Reverend Thomas L. Connolly, Archbishop of Halifax,' Canadian Catholic Historical Association (CCHA) *Annual Report* 11 (1943–4): 55–108; David Fleming, 'Archbishop Thomas L. Connolly: Godfather of Confederation,' CCHA *Study Sessions* 37 (1970): 67–84; Trombley, *Thomas Louis Connolly*

12 Johnston, *History of the Catholic Church*, 489

13 Ibid., 491

14 G.F.G. Stanley, 'The Caraquet Riots of 1875,' *Acadiensis* 2 (Autumn 1972): 21–38; P.M. Toner, 'The New Brunswick Schools Question,' CCHA *Report* 37 (1970): 85–95

15 ASV, DAC 157, Cameron to D. Falconio, 15 Jan. 1901

16 Macdonell was given the same title as Angus MacEachern, auxiliary suffragan to the bishop of Quebec.

17 In the diocese of Kingston, Macdonell's successors were Rémi Gaulin (1840–57), a French Canadian; Patrick Phelan, administrator of the diocese (1852–7), titular bishop (1857), an Irishman trained at the Séminaire de Saint-Sulpice in Montreal and a member of the Seminary; Edward John Horan (1857–74), born in Quebec of English-speaking parents, trained at the Séminaire de Québec where he became a professor of natural history. The bishops of Toronto were Michael Power (1842–7), born in Halifax of Irish parents, studied at Quebec and Montreal, pastor of various French-Canadian parishes in the Montreal region; Armand de Charbonnel (1850–60), a Frenchman and Sulpician, member of the Séminaire de Saint-Sulpice in Montreal. The first bishop of London was Pierre Adolphe Pinsonneault (1855–66), a French Canadian and Sulpician. In Hamilton Francis Farrell (1855–74), an Irishman trained at the Grand Séminaire de Montréal, became the first bishop.

18 Quoted in Stortz, 'John Joseph Lynch, Archbishop of Toronto,' 40

19 For studies on conflicts between the Irish hierarchy and other ethnic groups within the church of the United States, see Tomasi, *Piety and Power*; Colman Barry, *The Catholic Church and German Americans* (Milwaukee 1953); Savard, *Jules-Paul Tardivel*; Robert Rumilly, *His-*

toire des Franco-Américains (Montréal 1958); Anthony Kuzniewski, *Faith and Fatherland: The Polish Church War in Wisconsin* (Notre Dame 1980).

20 Stortz, 'Lynch'

21 M. Nicolson, 'Irish Tridentine Catholicism in Victorian Toronto: Vessel for Ethno-Religious Persistence,' CCHA *Study Sessions* 50 (1983) 433–4

22 Stortz, 'Lynch,' ch. 2

23 Archives of the Irish College in Rome (AICR), Lynch to Msgr. T. Kirby, rector of the Irish College, 26 May 1880

24 APFR, Scritture riferite nei Congressi, America settentrionale (SC) vol. 16, Lynch to Bishop George Conroy, 10 May 1877, ff.78–81; APFR, Scritture originali riferite nelle Congregazioni generali (SOCG) 1015, Lynch au Cardinal Giovanni Simeoni, 17 mai 1882; AICR, Lynch to Kirby, 6 July 1886

25 APFR, SOCG 1015, Lynch a Simeoni, 19 genn. 1881: 'I francesi della [*sic*] Canada non lascieranno una sola impressione permanente in questo paese.'

26 See Choquette, *L'Église catholique dans l'Ontario français du dix-neuvième siècle*, esp. ch. 9; Cartwright, 'Ecclesiastical Territorial Organization,' 176–99.

27 This figure was reached by subtracting the number of French living on the Ontario side of the diocese of Ottawa, 26,116 (taken from Choquette, *Église*, 143) from the total number of French living in Ontario, 75,383, as indicated by the 1871 census.

28 Scots, 10,000; Amerindian, 2,000; Germans, 12,000. The number of Scottish Catholics is based on an estimate by Donald Akenson, *The Irish in Ontario: A Study in Rural History* (Montreal 1984), that they constituted 3 per cent of the Scots living in Ontario. The figure for Amerindian Catholics is based on census statistics for the counties of Manitoulin, Algoma West, East, and Central, and Parry Sound. the figure for German Catholics is an estimate based on samples drawn from a project on class, mobility, and households in nineteenth-century Ontario, conducted by Gordon Darroch and Michael Orenstein. The samples estimated the number of German Catholics to the overall population of the province, the percentage of German Catholics to the total German population, and the proportion of German Catholics to the Catholic population. The sample varies in size from 86 to 1,866 and produced estimates of German Catholics ranging from 11,426 to 12,611. The figure 12,000 was therefore considered a fair guess. I wish to thank Gordon Darroch for providing me with these

figures. For further information on German Catholics, see J.A Lenhard, 'German Catholics in Ontario,' CCHA *Report* (1936–7): 41–5; J.A. Wahl, 'Father Louis Funcken's Contribution to German Catholicism in Waterloo County, Ontario,' CCHA *Study Sessions* (1983): 513–31. Wahl quotes a letter written in the 1850s by a Jesuit, John Holzer, which gives a German Catholic population of 12,000 in the Waterloo area. Holzer undoubtedly was exaggerating to emphasize the pastoral needs of the German community.

29 I arrived at these figures in a rather complicated manner. To obtain the Catholic population of the ecclesiastical province of Toronto, I took the total number of Ontario Catholics according to the 1871 census, 274,162, and subtracted the Catholics living on the Ontario side of the diocese of Ottawa, 52,427. The latter figure is based on Choquette's statistics (p. 143) amended to include Catholics in the northern portion of Lanark County who belonged to the diocese of Ottawa. Thus I arrived at 221,735 Catholics in the ecclesiastical province of Toronto. To obtain the number of Irish Catholics in the province of Ontario, I once again took the total Catholic population and subtracted from it the French, German, Scottish, and Amerindian Catholics and arrived at 174,779. This figure is lower than the estimate by Akenson (188,912), which does not take into account the presence of German Catholics in Ontario, and that (182,000) by Houston and Smyth, *The Sash Canada Wore*. I then subtracted from this number the Irish living in the Ontario portion of the diocese of Ottawa, 26,529. The latter figure was reached by adding the Irish Catholic population in the counties constituting the diocese of Ottawa as provided by Cartwright ('Ecclesiastical,' 180). The Irish Catholics of the ecclesiastical province of Toronto therefore numbered 148,250, or 67 per cent of the total Catholics.

30 The numbers are taken from de Barbézieux, *L'Église catholique au Canada*.

31 Within the two Irish ecclesiastical provinces, the French numbered 89,738 in 1901. I estimate the Scottish Catholics at 12,000. The 1901 census reveals that outside the ecclesiastical province of Ottawa, the Germans numbered 16,000, the Italians, 5,000; the Poles and Ukrainians, 3,000; the Indians and half-breeds, 5,000. These figures are approximations. A conservative estimate of the non-Irish Catholic population consequently would be 130,738. The total Catholic population in the ecclesiastical provinces of Toronto and Kingston was 279,793 in 1901. Thus the Irish constituted 53 per cent of the Catholic population in this region.

32 See Stortz, 'Lynch,' ch. 5; Walker, *Catholic Education and Politics in Ontario*, ch. 4.

33 Martin Galvin, 'The Jubilee Riots in Toronto, 1875,' CCHA *Report* (1959): 93–107. The *British American Presbyterian* and the *Christian Guardian* believed that religious processions should be made illegal.

34 G. Kealey, 'The Orange Order: Religious Riot and the Working Class' in G.S. Kealey and P. Warrian, eds., *Essays in Working Class History* (Toronto 1976), 31.

35 See Walker, *Catholic Education,* chs. 5 and 6.

36 Ibid., 82–5. The theory of the power of the Catholic vote is based on the assumption that since Protestants were divided evenly between Liberals and Conservatives, Catholics could swing elections in a number of constituencies and thus make a government. It does not seem to have occurred to proponents of this theory that Catholics too might be tempted to split their votes between the two parties and that in any case they never did vote as a bloc.

37 ASV, DAC 157, D. O'Connor to Falconio, 20 Nov. 1900

38 Ibid.

39 Ibid., F. McEvay to Falconio, 19 Nov. 1900

40 Ibid., V. Marijon à Falconio, 14 nov. 1900

41 Lemieux, *L'établissement de la première province ecclésiastique*; Champagne, *Les débuts de la mission dans le Nord-Ouest canadien*; Gilles Chaussé, 'Deux évêques missionnaires: Mgr J.N. Provencher et Mgr J.J. Lartigue,' SCHEC *Sessions d'étude* (1970): 51–60

42 In 1970 a special issue of the SCHEC *Sessions d'étude* was dedicated to the early history of the Catholic church in the west. The issue included among others the following articles: D. Roy, ''Mgr Provencher et son clergé séculier,' SCHEC *Sessions d'étude* (1970): 1–16; Gaston Carrière, 'The Oblates and the Northwest, 1845–1861,' CCHA *Study Sessions* (1970): 35–65; Lucien Lemieux, 'Mgr Provencher et la pastorale missionnaire des évêques de Québec,' SCHEC *Sessions d'étude* (1970): 31–49; Léon Pouliot, 'Mgr Bourget et la mission de la Rivière Rouge,' ibid., 17–30; Nive Voisine, 'L'abbé Louis-François Laflèche, missionnaire dans l'Ouest,' ibid., 61–9.

43 Morice, *Histoire de l'Église catholique dans l'Ouest canadien,* livre 5, ch. 6

44 APFR, SC 20 Faraud à Simeoni, 24 juin 1878, ff.253–4

45 See Robert Painchaud, 'Les exigences linguistiques dans le recrutement d'un clergé pour l'Ouest canadien, 1818–1920,' SCHEC *Sessions d'étude* (1975): 43–64.

46 See Champagne, *Débuts de la mission dans le Nord-Ouest,* ch. 4, for

Bishop Grandin's attempts to depart from the moral rigours of Tridentine Catholicism in dealing with aboriginal peoples whose religious practices were not predicated on a sedentary existence. See also Abel, 'Prophets, Priests and Preachers,' 211– 24.

47 See Morice, *Histoire*, livre 10, ch. 7, for a description of Bishop Paul Durieu's pastoral techniques among British Columbia's Amerindians.

48 J.-P. Wallot, 'Religion and French Canadian Mores in the Early Nineteenth Century,' *Canadian Historical Review* (March 1971): 51–94; Lemieux, *L'établissement*

49 In 1820 Rome gave Bishop Jean-Jacques Lartigue the same unusual title as Angus MacEachern in Prince Edward Island, auxiliary suffragan of the bishop of Quebec. He became titular bishop of Montreal in 1836. See Lemieux, *L'établisement*, 120–5.

50 J. Monet, 'French Canadian Nationalism and the Challenge of Ultramontanism,' CHA *Historical Papers* (1966): 41–55; R. Perin, 'Nationalism and the Church in French Canada, 1840-1880,' *Bulletin of Canadian Studies* 1, no. 1 (May 1977): 27–38

51 R. Perin, 'Clercs et politiques au Québec, 1865–1876,' *Revue de l'Université d'Ottawa* (avr.- juin 1980): 168–90; 'St-Bourget, évêque et martyr,' *Journal of Canadian Studies* 15 (Winter 1980–1): 43–55

52 Archives du Séminaire de Saint-Sulpice, Montréal (ASSM) 'Notes biographiques et historiques par M. Rousseau et al.,' n.d.

53 This reference appeared in his pastoral letter on St-Jean Baptiste Day, dated 31 May 1868 and cited in N. Fahmy-Eid, 'Ultramontanisme, idéologie et classes sociales,' *Revue d'Histoire de l'Amérique Française* 29, no. 1 (juin 1975): 49–68.

54 See Choquette, *L'Église*, passim.

55 A.I. Silver, 'An Introduction' in J.P. Tardivel, *For My Country*, trans. Sheila Fischman (Toronto 1975), xix

CHAPTER TWO: Rome: Another Canadian Metropolis

1 APFR, Lettere e Decreti della Sacra Congregazione e Biglietti di Monsignore Segretario (LDB) 1884, Simeoni a Smeulders, 12 lug. 1884, f.361. E d'uopo che Ella vada al buono della questione ... Molto più poi insisto su questa maniera di procedere perche gli Emi[nentissimi] Card[inali] che nelle Congreg[azioni] gen[erali] debbono sempre occuparsi di varie e molte volte complicate questioni, non hanno tempo di leggere lunghissime esposizioni.'

2 Fernand Dumont, 'Du début du siècle à la crise de 1929: un espace

idéologique' in F. Dumont et al., *Idéologies au Canada français, 1900–1929* (Québec 1974), 1–13

3 APFR, LDB 1883, Simeoni a Smeulders, 15 dic. 1883 f.658. 'Le invio copia di una circolare di questa S[acra] Cong[regazione] riguardante il Museo. Se Ella all'occorenza potesse trovare degli oggetti interessanti per il Museo stesso, La interesso a procurare di farne raccolta.'

4 To get an idea of the variety of issues dealt with by Propaganda, see Monique Benoit, 'Inventaire des principales séries de documents intéressant le Canada, sous le pontificat de Léon XIII (1878–1903), dans les archives de la Sacrée Congrégation "de Propaganda Fide" à Rome' (Ottawa: Archives publiques du Canada–Université Saint-Paul 1985).

5 APFR, SC 18 Manning to Conroy, 17 Oct. 1877, ff.472–3

6 The notoriously conservative Abbé Bellenger of Deschambault wrote to George Conroy: 'Ils [certains prêtres] ont voulu seulement marquer la ruse de cet homme qui pour épier l'occasion favorable de passer ses idées sur les hommes et les choses du Canada à quelques Cardinaux se présente à leur porte, les mains remplies d'intentions de messe. Du reste le fait des intrigues et des artifices de l'abbé Pâquet est bien connu à Rome ... [D'après] ... non seulement des employés subalternes des congrégations, mais aussi ... des hauts personnages ... il serait difficile de régler les difficultés du Canada, tant que l'abbé Pâquet serait à Rome.' Ibid., Bellenger à Conroy, 20 déc. 1877, ff.915–8. Taschereau responded to these accusations: 'Mgr Pâquet, sur la demande même de plusieurs chefs d'ordres et de Cardinaux, leur a passé des intentions de messes, afin d'aider de pauvres prêtres et religieux de Rome à subsister. L'auteur, obéissant à son caractère soupçonneux et dépourvu de toute charité, voit en cela *une clef d'or pour se ménager de puissantes influences.* En frappant Mgr Pâquet, il frappe les Cardinaux eux-mêmes, car si c'est un péché d'acheter un Cardinal, c'est un plus grand péché qu'un Cardinal se vende.' Ibid., Taschereau à Conroy, 5 déc. 1877, ff.692–3

7 See Fogarty, *The Vatican and the Americanist Crisis*, ch. 4.

8 APFR, Acta (1876), Rapporto Roncetti. Roncetti was rewarded handsomely for his services. He was soon consecrated an archbishop by Cardinal Franchi and immediately designated as apostolic internuncio to Brazil. At the same time, he was named apostolic delegate to Argentina, Uruguay, Paraguay, and Chile. In 1879 he was promoted to apostolic nuncio in Bavaria. He died two years later in October 1881 at the age of forty-seven.

9 APFR, LDB 1876, Franchi a Persico, 1 magg. 1876. 'Crederei che l'uno

potrebbe esser quello di inviare nel Canada un Rappresentante della
Santa Sede il quale risiedesse in Quebec, e potesse dar indirizzo ai
Vescovi tanto per le questioni attuali, quanto per quelle che potessero
insorgere in appresso ... circa l'opportunità e convenienza dell'espedi-
ente che si penserebbe adottare non che circa la maniera con cui la
S.V. crederebbe opportuno doversi mettere in pratica; e le difficoltà
che potesse incontrare.' See Gabriel-Marie Dumas, 'Le cardinal Ignace
Persico, capucin, curé de Sillery, et sa mission secrète au Canada,'
SCHEC, *Sessions d'étude* 32 (1965): 11–19. The supposed secret mission
was nothing more than Franchi's instructions.

10 APFR, LDB 1876, Franchi a Persico, 18 lug. 1876
11 Archives of the Archdiocese of Toronto (AAT), Taschereau à Lynch, 1
   sept. 1876
12 See Giovanni Miccoli, *Fra mito della Cristianità secolarizzazione*
   (Casale Monferrato 1985).
13 APFR, LDB 1876, Franchi a Cauchon, 25 magg. 1876. '... e molto più per
   la sollecita premura con cui si adopera nel tutelare gl'interessi della
   Chiesa.'
14 Ibid., Franchi a Persico, 5 lug. 1876. Alexis Tremblay alleged clerical
   interference in his defeat in the Charlevoix by-election of 1876 which
   saw Hector Langevin emerge victorious.
15 See Pierre Savard, 'Le journal de l'abbé Benjamin Pâquet, étudiant à
   Rome, 1863–1866' in *Aspects du catholicisme canadien-français*, 47–
   71.
16 APFR, SC 14, N. Bolduc à Roncetti, 1 juil. 1876
17 APFR, SC 18, Pâquet à Conroy, 25 nov. 1877. '... Il en est un (péché)
   toutefois dont je n'aurai jamais la contrition, c'est d'avoir contribué
   pour une large part à la nomination et à la mission de V.E. comme
   Délégué Apostolique.'
18 AAT, Cauchon to the Lieutenant-Governor of Ontario, 10 Aug. 1876.
   Cauchon, after failing to convince Lynch to intervene in Rome on the
   party's behalf, asked the lieutenant-governor to pressure Lynch to do
   so. 'Pray see his Grace and urge upon him the need for immediate
   action. Let us not leave a stone unturned.'
19 Archives de l'Archevêché de Montréal (ACAM), 901.147, Godefroi
   Lamarche à Bourget, Fabre et Laflèche, 1 fév. 1877
20 For a historiographical discussion of the Holy See and apostolic delegates in Canada, see Matteo Sanfilippo, 'La Santa Sede, il Canada e la
   Delegazione Apostolica ad Ottawa,' *Annali Accademici Canadesi* 2
   (autunno 1986): 112–19.
22 APFR, Acta 247 f.289. '[Il Delegato] Procurerebbe pure di scandagliare

o di preparare i mezzi di rendere stabili o meglio non infrequenti le visite di un Rappresentante del Sommo Pontefice nell'unione Canadese.'

22 Ibid.

23 APFR, LDB 1877, Istruzioni per Mgr Conroy, Deleg. Apost., 6 magg. 1877, ff.170–1. For the historical context within the Quebec church which prompted these instructions, see Nive Voisine, 'Rome et le Canada: la mission de Mgr Conroy,' *Revue d'Histoire de l'Amérique Française* 33, no. 4 (mars 1980): 499–519. Voisine does not take into account the divergence of views within the Propaganda itself and argues as if Rome had a monolithic position on the political question.

24 APFR, SC 15, Conroy a un canonico, 23 apr. 1877, f.212. 'Spero che si farà intendere ai pellegrini canadesi che la Propaganda ripone piena fiducia nel Delegato. Altrimenti questi torneranno pronti a resistere.'

25 Archivio della Sacra Congregazione per gli Affari Ecclesiastici Straordinari (AAES), folder 34, pos. 82–3, Estratto di lettera al D[elegato] A[postolico] del C[anada] da un sacerdote respettabilissimo dimorante a Montreal, 13 dic. 1877. This information was excerpted from H.A. Verreau à Conroy, 21 déc. 1877. Verreau, principal of the Jacques Cartier Normal School in Montreal, was a confidant of Conroy. According to Verreau, Agnozzi asked James Lonergan, a priest from the diocese of Montreal then studying in Rome, to lead the opposition movement.

26 Ibid., Conroy a Eminenza Reverendissima [Franchi], 14 dic. 1877. The fact that this and other confidential letters written by Conroy to Franchi are in this archive tends to confirm the hypothesis that there was dissension within the Propaganda itself and that the prefect needed to keep these letters in a place which would not be accessible to certain members of the Propaganda.

27 Ibid., Conroy a Franchi, 28 dic. 1877

28 Ibid., Conroy a Franchi, 4 genn. 1877

29 APFR, LDB, Simeoni a Laflèche, 6 apr. 1877; Simeoni a J. Langevin, 7 apr. 1877; Simeoni a Laflèche, 28 giu. 1877

30 APFR, SOCG 1010, R. Laflamme, C.A.P. Pelletier, F. Langelier, F.X. Marchand, H. Starnes, P. Bachand, et A. Chauveau à Simeoni, accompanied by a covering letter by L. Letellier de Saint-Just, 21 août 1878, ff.78–82

31 Ibid., Letellier de Saint-Just à Léon XIII, n.d., ff.85–93

32 APFR, Acta 247, f.290. The Propaganda considered Conroy's report on the political question in Canada to be '*importantissima*.' They added:

'Egli pose un freno alle bollenti questioni fra i due partiti politici, Liberale e Conservatore, che dividevano i Vescovi, il Clero e il popolo nella provincia di Quebec.' (He put a break on the fiery controversies between the two political parties, Liberal and Conservative, which divided the bishops, the clergy and the people of the province of Quebec.)

33 APFR, SC 21, Persico a Simeoni, 10 genn. 1881, ff.486–7

34 APFR, SC 22, Laflèche à Simeoni, 7 sept. 1882

35 These were led by canons of the cathedral chapter whom Bourget had handpicked. 'La plupart des chanoines lui [Fabre] firent une opposition sourde ou manifeste, et ne pouvant consentir à vivre sous le même toît et à s'asseoir à la même table que leur Evêque, ils donnèrent successivement leur démission. Deux seulement conservent leur titre, encore faut-il dire que l'un d'eux âgé et infirme n'habite plus à l'évêché.' See APFR, SC 23, Note sur la réorganisation du chapitre de Montréal, juil. 1883. This was an anonymous opinion solicited by Cardinal Simeoni. The bishops supporting Laflèche were Duhamel of Ottawa and to a lesser extent Moreau of St-Hyacinthe. After being rebuked by Rome and Conroy, Langevin of Rimouski sank into despondency and inactivity.

36 In 1881 Rome received Thomas Hamel, rector of Laval University, and Antoine Racine, bishop of Sherbrooke, as well as Ignace Bourget, A. Dumesnil, a priest from St-Hyacinthe who claimed to represent the majority of the clergy of Montreal, A. Villeneuve, a priest and notorious pamphleteer from that city, and politician F.X.A. Trudel. In the new year they were joined by Laflèche and Dominique Racine, bishop of Chicoutimi.

37 These positions emerge for example on the university controversy. Leo XIII instituted in 1881 a special commission of three cardinals from the Propaganda to look into this quarrel which divided Montreal from Quebec City. Cardinal Franzelin, a Jesuit, was quite sympathetic to Montreal, but not to the point of forcing a reconsideration of the whole university question. Cardinal Mertel for his part simply believed that it would be unseemly for the Propaganda to be forever revising its decisions. The third cardinal was Giovanni Simeoni. See APFR, SOCG 1020, ff.289–9.

38 APFR, SC 27, Bégin à Zitelli, 7 avr. 1881, ff.760–1. Zitelli was a long-time personal friend of Pâquet who regarded him as his *minutante*. See Savard, 'Le journal,' n. 38. They were possibly students together in Rome.

39 Dominique Racine used Brichet as a conduit for information destined for the Propaganda. See APFR, SC 28, D. Racine à Simeoni, 14 fév. 1883, ff.1151–2.

40 Ibid., Bégin à Marquis, 25 janv. 1880[1883]. Bégin affirmed that Persico was defending 'les intérêts de la Sainte Église,' which in Bégin's mind were those of the archdiocese of Quebec.

41 Ibid., D. Racine à Howard, 7 mai 1883, ff.775–6

42 APFR, SC 26, Relazione sulla divisione della diocesi di Trois Rivières, febb. 1878. 'è un uomo che non merita la stima della S. Sede ... Occupato sempre di cose secolari, intrigante, e poco [sollecito] della salute dei suoi parrochiani ... egli ha messo disordine dappertutto.'

43 APFR, SC 27, Bégin à Zitelli 7 avr. 1881, ff.760–1. The fact that Bégin could express his thoughts so unashamedly to the most important *minutante* at the Propaganda tends to indicate some complicity between Roman officials and the archdiocese of Quebec.

44 APFR SC 28, Marquis à Zitelli, 14 fév. 1883, ff.1141–2. This passage refers to a limp which Laflèche developed when he was a missionary in the North-West.

45 Ibid., Bégin à Marquis, 25 janv. 1880 [1883] ff.1143–6. The italics are Bégin's.

46 Ibid., extract from a letter by J.B.Z. Bolduc on 30 Apr. 1883 and cited by Marquis in notes presented to the Propaganda ff.770–3. Note the misogynism expressed in this and subsequent quotations, which was quite typical of men of the church in the nineteenth century. The italics are in the original.

47 Ibid., extract from a letter by A. Racine, 30 avr. 1883, ff.770–3

48 Ibid., extract from a letter by A. Racine, 9 mai 1883, ff.783–8

49 APFR, SOCG 1020, extract from a letter by Bégin, 11 août 1883, ff.340–3

50 The change of policy occurred sometime between June and August of 1883. See APFR, SC 28, ff.798–9.

51 APFR, SOCG 1020, Marquis au Cardinal Domenico Jacobini, 25 août 1883, ff.340–3. Marquis was quoting a letter from Pâquet who was urging the appointment of a delegate. APFR, SC 23, Laflèche à Simeoni, 29 août 1883, ff.434–5. Laflèche was particularly adamant about Zitelli and Brichet.

52 APFR, LDB 1883, Istruzioni per l'abb. Smeulders, commissario apostolico, ff.587–9

53 APFR, LDB, Simeoni a Smeulders e Taschereau, 27 ago. 1884, f.445. For a historical account of the complexities of the university question, see André Lavallée, *Québec contre Montréal: la querelle universitaire,*

1876–1891 (Montréal 1974), who provides a mechanistic interpretation of the question based on economic determinism. See also Germain Lavallée, 'Mgr Antoine Racine et la question universitaire canadienne 1875–1892,' *Revue d'Histoire de l'Amérique Française* 12: no. 1 (juin 1958): 80–107; no. 2 (sept 1958): 247–61; no. 3 (déc. 1958): 372–86; no. 4 (mars 1959): 485–516.

54 APFR, SC 24, L.G. Monnin à Simeoni, 8 janv. 1885, ff.63–6

55 APFR, SC 26, L. Desilets à Simeoni, 15 mai 1885 ff.1000–1. Desilets complained that although Laflèche's opponents had easy access to the pope, he had to wait two years for an audience with the pontiff. Senator F.X.A. Trudel for his part wrote a despairing letter to Rome: 'J'avoue que je n'ai jamais pu comprendre pour quel crime nous avons été traités d'une façon si implacable à Rome. Car enfin, seconder leur vieil évêque [Bourget], un saint, de l'aveu de tous, dans ses efforts pour doter son immense diocèse, un diocèse grand comme l'Italie, d'une université catholique *nécessaire*, ne devrait pas être un péché à jamais irrémissible.' He ended his complaint with these words: 'Voilà l'espèce de justice que je trouve à Rome, après avoir 20 années durant, soutenu dans la presse et devant les tribunaux, des luttes incessantes pour faire triompher le principe de l'indépendance de l'Église! pour *prouver* que l'on peut avoir justice devant l'autorité ecclésiastique et qu'il ne faut pas citer les prêtres ou les Évêques devant les tribunaux civils.' See APFR, SC 30, Trudel à Simeoni, 15 déc. 1887, ff.562–5.

56 Miller, *Equal Rights: The Jesuits' Estates Act Controversy*, provides the background for this change of climate within the church. The Jesuit Estates' Act strained relations between English and French Canadians to the breaking point. It fuelled anti-Catholic hostilities in English Canada, hostilities that would have an immediate and negative impact on French and Catholic minorities outside Quebec. It made French Canadians feel that there was little room for them not only in Ontario and the West, but also in the overall cultural make-up of the new Dominion. Before this threat from the outside, many churchmen felt that it was high time to put the quarrels of the past behind them.

57 APFR, SC 31, Labelle à Jacobini, 16 juin 1890, ff.877–8

58 Ibid., Labelle à Simeoni, 9 mai 1890, ff.845–50

59 AAES 64, pos. 142, Taché à J.A. Ouimet, 1 mai 1894

60 Ibid., Taché à Ouimet, 3 avr. 1894

61 APFR, NS 240, Bégin à Ledochowski, 20 avr. 1894, ff.11–15. (From this point on the rubrica number will only be indicated if it is not 154.)

Archbishop Duhamel was of the same opinion. The newspaper articles and speeches of fanatical Protestants, he asserted, did not find a response among the Protestant masses. The agitation around the Jesuit Estates bill had shown that remedial legislation would provoke neither a sectarian nor an ethnic war. The politicians, he felt, who spoke in Cassandra-like terms of schism and war ignored recent developments in Canadian history. See ASV, DAC, Duhamel à Merry del Val, 12 avr. 1897.

62 'Les fanatiques' warned the hierarchy, 'ne sont encore au pays que le petit nombre; mais ce n'est pas en capitulant devant eux et en les habituant à des concessions désastreuses pour la cause de l'Eglise qu'on tempèrera leur audace.' AAES 91, Déclaration de l'Episcopat canadien touchant la question scolaire 23 mars 1897. This document was signed by archbishops Duhamel and Bégin, by bishops Laflèche, Moreau, Lorrain, Gravel, Blais, Labrècque, Emard, LaRocque, Maxime Decelles, auxiliary bishop of St-Hyacinthe, and Florent Bourgeault, administrator of the archdiocese of Montreal following Fabre's death.

63 ASV, Spogli dei Cardinali: Oreglia di San Stefano, Laflèche à Oreglia, 25 déc. 1895

64 The bishop of Nicolet doubted that the forthcoming federal elections would bring together a majority of members of Parliament in favour of remedial legislation. See APFR, NS 240, Gravel à Ledochowski, 3 avr. 1895, ff.64–7. The bishop of St- Hyacinthe for his part believed that the Liberals would soon be in power, but added: 'L'impression générale dans le pays est que les libéraux seront impuissants à régler cette mesure, et qu'à leur tour, il leur faudra descendre du pouvoir. Le ministère fédéral d'aujourd'hui reviendra ensuite au timon des af- faires, et conduira la question des écoles à bonne fin. Tel est l'espoir fondé des Evêques et de tous les amis de l'ordre et du droit.' See ibid., Moreau à Ledochowski, 3 avr. 1895, ff.72–5.

65 Ibid., Gravel à Ledochowski avec un précis historique de la question scolaire au Manitoba, 8 déc. 1894, ff.28–39

66 Ibid., Ledochowski a Vaughan, 3 genn. 1895, ff.41–2. 'Produre[bbe] un senso di disgusto e di alienazione che potrebbe anche sfruttarsi dagli agitatori politici che non mancano in Canada.'

67 Ibid., Moreau à Ledochowski, 3 avr. 1895, ff.72–5; Gravel à Ledochow- ski 3 avr. 1895, ff.64–7; J.M. Emard à Ledochowski, 4 avr. 1895, ff.61–3

68 Ibid., Bégin à Ledochowski, 1 mai 1896, ff.118–20

69 Ibid., Ledochowski ad Fabre 8 Juliis 1896, ff.129–30; Ledochowski ad Langevin, 7 Juliis 1896, ff.180–1

70 AAES 79, pos. 161, Walsh to Laurier, 31 Jan. 1896 (copy)

71 ASV, Delegazione Apostolica degli Stati Uniti (DASU), section VI, f.23, Power to Mgr F.J. Rooker, Secretary of the delegation, 8 Feb. 1896

72 The governor general's wife asked Archbishop Walsh of Toronto to write to Satolli urging him to restrain an immoderate Quebec clergy. Walsh does not seem to have obliged. See Crunican, *Priests and Politicians*, 180–1, a splendid and well-balanced study of the clergy's involvement in the Manitoba controversy.

73 ASV, DASU II, f.4a, Satolli to Fabre, 10 May 1896

74 ASV, DASU VI, f.23, Satolli aux archevêques du Canada, 30 avr. 1896

75 Ibid., Walsh ad Satolli 14 Maiius 1896: 'non necessariam, certe inopportunam et imo periculosam.'

76 Ibid., Cleary to Satolli, May 1896

77 Ibid., Duhamel à Satolli, 15 mai 1896; Fabre à Satolli, 11 mai 1896

78 Ibid., Bégin à Satolli, 14 mai 1896

79 ASV, Segreteria di Stato (SS), rub. 280, Satolli a Rampolla, 30 giu. 1896. 'E poichè i Vescovi generalmente si erano adoperati (obbligandovi anche i sacerdoti) a favore dell'opposto partito [Tories]; non saranno da temere alcun danno per gl'interessi della Chiesa in quella vasta regione? Nel partito liberale sono molti ed eccellenti Cattolici; e se il clero si fosse mantenuto superiore ai partiti, oggi riconoscerebbe i vantaggi di tale dignitoso contegno.' 'Tutti risposero che se il S[anto] P[adre] lo manda essi lo riceveranno docilmente e volontieri, salvo di non essere gravati per mantenerlo (Timmerunt ubi non erat timor), ma non veggono la necessità.'

80 AAES 82, pos. 161, Requête des députés et sénateurs libéraux du parlement fédéral à Léon XIII nov. 1896; Requête des députés et conseillers législatifs de la province de Québec à Léon XIII 4 déc. 1896. (Henceforth the position number will only be indicated if it is different from 161.)

81 ASV, DAC 26, folder 'Proulx vs. Landry,' déclaration 29 août 1896. Proulx accused the bishops of Rimouski, Trois-Rivières, Chicoutimi, St Boniface, and Antigonish. This document, however, is rather mysterious since only a few weeks later Proulx wrote to Fabre denying that the object of his Roman mission was to accuse the bishops and to ask for an apostolic delegation. He assured his archbishop that 'la politique n'est rien pour moi, rien, rien, rien' (see Proulx à Fabre, 23 nov. 1896). This did not prevent him from accepting a gratuity of $250 from Laurier for services rendered during his two-month stay in Rome (see Laurier à Proulx, 23 nov. 1896). Dominique Gonthier, for his part, was paid $20 a month for acting as the

Quebec bishops' agent in Rome (see Charland, *Le Père Gonthier*, 121). Proulx's document is also mysterious because Fabre did not appear critical of his colleagues' behaviour during the elections of 1896. In fact his only comment to Ledochowski after the federal election was to praise the joint pastoral for its noble, worthy, and impartial tone. Would he have freely put his name to a document incriminating his brother bishops?

82 ASV, SS rub. 280, Aristide Rinaldini a Rampolla, 19 ott. 1896
83 AAES 86, Norfolk to Rampolla, 21 Jan. 1897
84 AAES 86, Vaughan a Rampolla, 18 genn. 1897
85 AAES 89, *The Tablet*, 6 Feb. 1897
86 See Lovell Clark, ed., *The Manitoba School Question: Majority Rule or Minority Rights* (Toronto 1968), 116–17.
87 ASV, DAC 76, *Ragioni che consigliano l'invio di un Delegato al Canada*. This memorandum was printed in London.
88 APFR, NS 240, Bégin à Ledochowski, 14 nov. 1896, ff.489–90
89 Ibid., Projet d'encyclique, ff.491–6
90 Ibid., Ledochowski ad Langevin, 12 Dec. 1896, f.535
91 Ibid., Cavagnis a Agostino Ciasca, 13 genn. 1897, f.563
92 Proulx confessed in rather florid terms to Fabre, 'Il s'est recontré ici des personnes très respectables du reste, qui se sont donné bien du trouble pour me fermer plus d'une porte, en vain toutefois; il m'était pénible de voir que des catholiques fussent sous l'impression que, par les petits détours d'une politique risquée, on pourrait empêcher d'arriver au Père commun, la voix, ne fut-ce du plus humble de ses enfants ... et [je] passe à travers cette toile d'embarras comme l'oiseau passe à travers une toile d'araignée.' ASV, DAC 26, folder 'Proulx vs Landry,' 23 nov. 1896
93 *La Gerarchia Cattolica, la Famiglia e la Cappella Pontificia* (Roma 1897). See Luigi Bruti-Liberati and Nicoletta Serio, 'Inventaire des documents d'intérêt canadien dans les archives du Vatican 1878–1903' (Rome 1987) for an idea of the type of issues dealt with by the Congregration for Extraordinary Ecclesiastical Affairs. This inventory may be consulted at St Paul's University, Ottawa, or at the National Library or National Archives of Canada.
94 APFR, NS 240, Bégin à Ledochowski, 3 janv. 1897, ff.582–8
95 Ibid., Ledochowski a Cavagnis, 4 febb. 1897, f.828. 'Il partito liberale è premuroso che tal parola non giunga prima delle imminenti elezioni nella Provincia di Quebec, affine di riuscire vittorioso anche in questo.'
96 Ibid., Esposto sulla questione politica nel Manitoba e sulla questione

relativa dei Vescovi Canadesi, ff.565–75. 'Ma l'opera dei Vescovi è fraintesa e combattuta da alcuni come ingerenza indebita.'

97 Ibid., Cavagnis a Ciasca, 19 febb. 1897, ff.837–8

98 APFR, NS 241, Sacra Congregazione degli Affari Ecclesiastici Staordinari: Canada, febb. 1897, ff.161–221

99 APFR, NS 240, Cavagnis a Ciasca, 19 febb. 1897

100 Ibid., Ledochowski ad Bégin, 20 Februarius 1897, f.834

101 See Hennesey, *American Catholics* ch. 15.

102 AAES 89, Cavagnis a Rampolla, 23 febb. 1897

103 APFR, NS 120, Rampolla a Ledochowski, 9 mar. 1897, f.489

104 APFR, NS 241, Larocque à Ledochowski, 5 mars 1897, ff.3–15

105 Ibid., Gravel à Ledochowski, 5 mars 1897, ff.16–18. AAES 90, Laflèche à Rampolla, 8 mars 1897; Labrècque à Rampolla, 9 mars 1897

106 APFR, NS 241, Duhamel à Ledochowski, 8 mars 1897, ff.21–5

107 APFR, NS 114, Bégin à Ledochowski, 24 mai 1897, f.277. For details of Gonthier's mission, see Charland, *Le père Gonthier*.

108 APFR, NS 241, C.B. Rousseau à Ciasca, 16 sept. 1897, ff.748–9

109 AAES 98, Laurier à Rampolla, 1 juin 1897

110 APFR, NS 120, Cavagnis a Ciasca, 22 giu. 1897; Ledochowski a Merry del Val, 26 giu. 1897, f.503

111 AAES 102, ponenza, 11 dic. 1897. APFR, NS 241, Cavagnis a Ciasca, 25 ott. 1897, ff.775–7

112 Ibid., Bégin à Ledochowski, 19 janv. 1898, f.952

113 APFR, NS 295, Langevin à Ledochowski, 18 sept. 1899, f.185–6; Larocque à Ledochowski, 25 sept 1899, f.191–2; Bégin à Ledochowski, 12 oct. 1899, f.195–6

114 Ibid., Laurier à Rampolla, 30 oct. 1897; Russell à Rampolla, 24 nov. 1897; Marchand à Rampolla, 19 nov. 1897

115 AAES 109, pos. 173, ponenza sulla Delegazione Apostolica Permanente in Canada, 11 lug. 1897. This position paper indicates that these decisions were made on 11 Dec. 1897.

116 AAES 111, pos. 181, Russell to Vaughan 18 Apr. 1899

117 ASV DAC 178, file 'Correspondance avec Rampolla,' Rampolla a Falconio, 5 magg. 1899

CHAPTER THREE: The Delegation

1 APFR, NS 295, Falconio a Ledochowski, 3 nov. 1899 f.208. 'Ottawa, oltre all'essere la Capitale e sede del governo, è la città più centrale, avendo da un lato le provincie dove domina l'elemento francese e dall'altro l'inglese.'

2 Ibid., 'Desiderei anche sapere se debba rivolgermi alla generosità dei Vescovi e dei fedeli per i fondi necessarii per l'acquisto del locale. Per ora abito all'Università.'

3 ASV, DAC 178, Rampolla a Falconio, 25 nov. 1899

4 APFR NS 295, Ledochowski a Falconio, 4 dic. 1899. Rampolla later confirmed that Ledochowski's was also the express wish of the Holy See ASV, DAC 178, Rampolla a Falconio, 4 genn. 1900.

5 ASV, DAC, Letter Book Falconio (LBF), Falconio à Bruchési et Bégin, 13 déc. 1899, p. 26

6 Ibid., Falconio à Bruchési et Bégin, 17 déc. 1899, p. 28

7 APFR, NS 295, Falconio a Ledochowski, 21 dic. 1899, f.220. 'Mal soffrendo che il rappresentante di Sua Santità non abbia una propria abitazione come nei vicini Stati Uniti.'

8 ASV, DAC 6, folder 'Montréal: divers,' Bruchési à Falconio, 14 déc. 1899; DAC 5, folder 'Simon Fraser,' Bégin à Falconio, 17 déc. 1899

9 APFR, NS 295, Ledochowski a Falconio, 13 genn. 1900

10 ASV, DAC LBF, Falconio a Ledochowski, 31 genn. 1901, p. 136. 'L'abitazione è stata acquistata, e fra giorni sarà mobiliata, con offerte assolutamente spontanee dei Vescovi e con una somma largita dai benemeriti Padri Sulpiziani di Montreal, senza alcuna sollecitazione da parte mia.' Contributions were as follows: the Sulpicians, $6,000; the archdiocese of Quebec, which also covered for the diocese of Chicoutimi, $2,500; $1,000 each from the archdioceses of Montreal, Kingston, and Ottawa, and from the dioceses of London, St-Hyacinthe, Hamilton, Toronto, and Rimouski.

11 APFR, NS 295, Duhamel à Gotti, 9 oct. 1903, ff.270–1

12 See Dumas, 'Le cardinal Ignace Persico,' 11–13.

13 APFR, NS 241, Alexis Pelletier à Ledochowski, 14 août 1897

14 Details of these resolutions may be obtained from Grisé, *Les conciles provinciaux de Québec.*

15 APFR, SC 14, Persico a Franchi, 20 apr. 1876

16 Ibid., Persico a Franchi, 28 lug. 1876

17 APFR, SC 15, Lynch à Franchi, 25 mai 1877. The portrait was by the nineteenth-century Italian painter Vincenzo Pasqualoni and is still housed at the Seminary.

18 Ibid., Conroy a Franchi, 25 magg. 1877, ff.292–5. 'Tutto ciò che V.E. ha inteso sullo stato delle cose del Canada è al di sotto del vero, tanto per il bene quanto per il male. Il bene è maggiore di quel che si crede e il male è anche maggiore. Sarebbe difficile di concepire l'idea di un popolo migliore, e più crudelmente tormentato da discordie intestine.'

19 Ibid., Conroy a Franchi, 5 ott. 1877, ff.447–8
20 AAES 34, pos. 83, Conroy a Franchi, 11 genn. 1878. 'Ho sofferto molto per qualche settimana dal freddo atroce di questo clima. Ieri il termometro segnava 30 gradi sotto zero!'
21 APFR, SC 26, Rapporto sulla divisione della diocesi di Trois-Rivières, ff.135–146
22 See Paul Johnson, *A History of Christianity* (Harmondsworth 1976). 'The monks were often formed, or formed themselves, into black-robed squads for the execution of the Church's business, first to smash up pagan temples, later to rampage through the streets and basilicas in time of doctrinal controversy ... They were taken in bands to Church councils to bully hostile delegates and try to influence the outcome' (p. 94).
23 APFR Acta 247, Relazione di Monsig[nor] Conroy sulla Questione Politica nel Canadà, f.320. 'Ora una tale mancanza di movimento intelletuale Cattolico è da ripetersi in gran parte dal mediocre ingegno dei Prelati Quebecesi. La razza dominante inglese, come ben sa stimare le doti dello spirito dovunque esistono, così difficilmente s'inchina innanzi alla mediocrità anche seduta sul trono episcopale. Quindi accade che la Chiesa Cattolica non fa quel progresso che si potrebbe giustamente aspettare in un paese dove ella si trova in una posizione così singolarmente favorevole come il Canadà.'
24 Ibid., 'A me sembra che sarebbe ormai il tempo di far capire a questi sacerdoti che non appartiene ad essi di occuparsi di queste cose, ma che loro pretto dovere sì è d'obbedire ai loro superiori ecclesiastici.'
25 APFR, SOCG 1010, Mémoire S. Tassé à Simeoni, 5 mai 1878, ff.100–3
26 APFR, SC 15, Conroy a Franchi, 28 sett 1877
27 APFR, SC 20, Conroy a Franchi 6 dic. 1877, ff.40–2
28 APFR, SC 26, Rapporto sulla divisione della diocesi di Trois-Rivières, ff.135–46
29 AICR, Thomas Power, Bishop of St John's, to Kirby, 11 July 1878
30 *La Minerve*, 5 déc. 1883
31 APFR, SC 23, Smeulders a Simeoni, 26 sett. 1883, ff.491–2. Smeulders's secretaries were a Dutch deacon, Amédée de Bie, and a French priest, Pierre Daïdé. Daïdé had lived in Quebec for a while and also had been secretary to a president of Ecuador.
32 Ibid., Smeulders à D. Jacobini, 23 oct. 1883
33 APFR, SOCG 1020, Joseph Desflèches à D. Jacobini, 7 août 1884, f.209. Archbishop Desflèches was, like Smeulders, a consultant at the Propaganda.

34 APFR, SC 26, Relatio de divioni diocesis Trifluvianae, 27 Augustus 1884

35 They were Benjamin Pâquet and his brother Louis-Honoré, both of whom were, in Smeulders's estimation, more clever and wilier than the devil in administrative matters. See APFR, SOCG 1020, Smeulders ad Simeoni, 22 Jiuliis 1884, ff.376–7. Marquis was another who through guile managed to influence the Propaganda's views. Smeulders begged Simeoni to warn Zitelli (optimo nostro amico ... quem sincere amo et in magna æstimationem habeo) to break with Marquis. See APFR, SC 23, Smeulders ad Simeoni, 12 Februarius 1884, f.765. Finally, there was Thomas Etienne Hamel, rector of Laval University, a hard, impulsive, and intractable man. See APFR, Acta 253, Relatio Commisarii Apostolici in Canada de Controversia Lavallensem inter et Scholam Medicinæ et Chirurgiæ Marianopolitanam, n.d.

36 Ibid., Smeulders ad Simeoni, 26 Aprilis 1884, f.401. 'Archiepiscopus cum suis vulpibus quae demoliuntur vineam Domini.'

37 In Smeulders's opinion, Antoine and Dominique Racine, respectively of Sherbrooke and Chicoutimi, were in this last category. They had 'as their supreme law to agree in all things with the Archbishop.' See APFR, SC 26, Relatio Commissarii Apostolici de divisione Diocesis Trifluvianae, 27 Augustus 1884, ff.742–55. 'Quibus suprema lex est, in omnibus assentiri Archiepiscopo.' Of Zéphirin Moreau, bishop of St-Hyacinthe, Smeulders conceded that he was an extremely pious and temperate prelate, but he could not say as much about his intelligence. See APFR, Acta 253, Smeulders ad Simeoni, 26 Aprilis 1884, f.401. Edouard Fabre of Montreal was weak, hesitating, and timid. See APFR SC 26, Relatio de divisioni diocesis ... Under the guise of obedience to his archbishop, Fabre allowed many wily subterfuges to slip by. See ibid., Relatio de controversia ...

38 According to Marquis, the university would fall into the hands of heretics if Laflèche were allowed to have his way. See APFR, SC 28, Marquis à Zitelli, 14 fév. 1883, ff.1141–2. Of the Jesuits, Smeulders observed: 'Itaque Patres Societas omnino irreprehensibiles sunt, et quidquid sub hoc aspectu a Jesuitophobis Lavallensibus in contrarium insinuari potest sunt malitiosæ nugæ et calumniæ ... Societas est securum et forte propugnaculum conservandi orthodoxiam in doctrina.' See APFR, Acta 253, Smeulders ad Simeoni, 26 Aprilis 1884, f.401. (Therefore the Jesuits are altogether blameless, and whatever can be insinuated to the contrary from the 'Jesuitophobes' at Laval is malicious nonsense and slanderous ... The Society is a strong and sure defence for the preservation of the true faith.)

39 An indication of the state of mind of the university administration is
provided in the following passage which speculates about the closing
down of the university: 'Ce sera pour nous un immense débarras, un
soulagement que nous seuls sommes en état d'apprécier à sa juste
valeur, parce que nous seuls avons eu à subir les dépenses, les
sacrifices les plus pénibles de toute sorte, les inquiétudes, les persécu-
tions, les avanies, et les bêtises de la pire espèce depuis 20 ans.' See
APFR, SC 28, Bégin à Marquis, 25 janv. 1880 [1883], ff.1143–6.
Smeulders replied: 'Certe expensæ illæ non possunt considerari ut
titulus cui respondere debeat compensatio. Deinde quædam expensæ
proponuntur ut *sacrificia* pro Universitate facta, quiæ ab aliis potiori
iure habentur ut *lucrosæ speculationes*. Et adhuc prætendunt sibi
deberi compensationem! Hoc revera est nimis rabbinicum.' See APFR,
Acta 253, Smeulders ad Simeoni 29 Martius 1884, f.399. (Certainly
these expenses cannot be considered as a *title* for compensation. But
they [Laval administrators] presented these expenses as a *sacrifice*
made for the university, which gave them the right to *profitable
speculation*. And from this they pretend that compensation is owed to
them. In truth these things are too rabbinical.) Note the anti-Semitic
sentiments.

40 Ibid., Smeulders ad Simeoni, 26 Jiunius 1884, f.412. 'Nam Archiepiscopus liber a noxio influxu, in continuo contactu cum sapientissimis
Cardinalibus et Praelatis romanis, brevi suam cogitandi rationem
modificaret, et utile servitium S. Sedi praestare posset.'

41 Ibid., Smeulders ad Simeoni, 29 Martius 1884 f.399. 'Erunt semper
duo galli inter unam collectionem gallinarum.'

42 APFR, SC 26, Relatio de divisione ...

43 When Taschereau commented on the questionable morality of some of
the professors at the Catholic École de Médecine, Smeulders observed
that similar accusations could be levelled at Laval professors. He then
added: 'Sed sermo sit de iure iustitia et æquitate et non descendamus
ad cuppam lavatoriam.' See APFR, Acta 253, Relatio de controversia
Lavallensem ..., ff.413–24. (But let the discussion be about law,
justice, and equity and let us not descend to the level of lurid lavato-
ries.) Similarly, when called upon to adjudicate a quarrel between an
'ultramontane' layman and the rector of Laval University, he dismissed the layman's allegations and described the whole event using
Horace's happy phrase: 'Parturiunt montes, nascetur ridiculus mus.'
(The mountains gave birth and a ridiculous mouse was born.) APFR, SC
23, Smeulders ad Simeoni, 24 September 1884, ff.1169–76

44 Ibid., Smeulders ad Simeoni, 10 December 1884, ff. 1288–9. 'Scio enim

me monacum esse, non astutum diplomaticum, et aliunde in actioni-
bus meis nihil intendi aliud, nisi quod conferat ad majorem Dei
gloriam, Ecclesiae utilitatem, et Apostolica Sedis decorem, quem prae
oculis usque habui atque tueri pro viribus conatus sum.'

45 Ibid., Taschereau à Simeoni, 29 déc. 1884, f.1312
46 APFR, SC 26, Taschereau à Simeoni, 4 déc. 1884, ff.918–19
47 Ibid., D. Racine à Léon XIII, 5 avr. 1885, ff.978–9
48 Ibid., Gravel à Simeoni, 18 fév. 1885, ff.946–7. It is interesting that
Gravel should have considered Smeulders to be a stranger even
though he was French-speaking, whereas a Roman (read Italian) or
British prelate seemed to him less foreign.
49 *Enciclopedia Cattolica*, VIII
50 AAES 91, Merry del Val a Rampolla, 19 mar. 1897. He observed: 'il
fatto è grave e complica sempre più una situazione già difficile.' (This
is a serious development which complicates even more an already
difficult situation.)
51 Ibid., Merry del Val a Rampolla, 20 mar. 1897
52 Ibid., Merry del Val a Rampolla, 30 mar. 1897. 'Tutti deplorano lo
stato penoso al quale sono ridotti moltissimi cattolici al Canada in
conseguenza delle lotte politiche, e delle imprudenze commesse da
molti nel clero.' Although Corrigan was seen as a leader of the
conservative faction in the American church and therefore hostile to
Archbishop Ireland's party, he was not particularly sympathetic to the
cultural aspirations of immigrant groups. At the time of the 1896
federal elections an open letter was circulating in the United States
signed by C.F. St-Laurent, a pseudonym for a priest from the diocese
of Montreal. The document outraged an Irish American hierarchy
which, as we have seen, had been fighting the 'ethnicization' of the
church for many years. It certainly did nothing to endear the Irish
bishops to their French-Canadian diocesans, some of whom had been
in the vanguard of the ethnic cause for over twenty years. The letter
stated: 'Depuis trop longtemps, à certains endroits, on nous traite en
parias de la famille catholique; ... comme si une foule des établisse-
ments religieux n'étaient pas en bonne partie le fruit de nos travaux
et de nos sueurs ... Les Canadiens ne sont pas d'une race abâtardie;
leurs prêtres ne sont pas des mercenaires qui n'ont droit qu'à la plus
maigre pitance et au mépris des autres nations ... Le Souverain
Pontife ne demande pas qu'on nous mène au ciel à coup d'anglais; il
veut que l'on s'adresse au peuple dans sa langue ... Il sait que le
prêtre est fait pour le peuple, et non le peuple pour le prêtre. Son

action en faveur des Italiens résidant aux États-Unis, montre avec
quelle surabondance qu'il ne veut pas l'unification forcée.' It is not
hard to image then that the American hierarchy easily would accredit
rumours of a turbulent and politically active clergy in Quebec.

53 *La Presse*, 29 mars 1897
54 AAES 91, Merry del Val a Rampolla, 19 mar. 1897
55 AAES 100, Rapporto di Mgr Delegato, sett. 1897, ff.3–60, f.26
56 AAES 92, Marois aux évêques de la province ecclésiastique de Québec,
3 avr. 1897; Merry del Val a Rampolla, 12 apr. 1897. 'Protestai energi-
camente contro la slealtà della sua condotta, e contro l'audacia dimos-
trata intramettendosi in una corrispondenza particolare tra i Vescovi
e il Rappresentante della Santa Sede.' Bishop Moreau for his part
objected to the delegate's interpretation of the incident. 'A moins de
croire que Sa Sainteté ne veuille interdire aux évêques la liberté de se
communiquer mutuellement leurs vues sur la situation; à moins de
croire que le Déléguée ait reçu instruction d'isoler les évêques les uns
des autres afin d'obtenir de chacun isolement, ce que l'on craindrait
ne pouvoir obtenir d'eux réunis,' he could not justify the delegate's behaviour. He also condemned Merry del Val's harsh language 'qu'un
évêque n'oserait employer vis-à-vis le dernier de ses prêtres, et cela, le
plus souvent sur la foi de rumeurs dont Son Excellence a dû reconnaître elle-même la fausseté.' See APFR, NS 241, Moreau à Bégin, 22
mai 1897, ff. 350–2.
57 AAES 94, Merry del Val a Rampolla, 21 magg. 1897
58 AAES 100, Rapporto di Mgr Delegato, f.3. 'La triste situazione religiosa
esistente oggi nel Canada, e più specialmente nelle provincie di lingua
francese.'
59 Ibid., f.46. 'Se la questione delle scuole del Manitoba è gravissima, lo è
assai più uno stato di cose che questa questione ha fatto nascere in
varie provincie del Canada, e che mette in pericolo imminente la fede
di migliaia di persone, fa odiare i sagramenti della Chiesa, disprez-
zare l'autorità dei Vescovi e del Clero, distrugge ogni disciplina
ecclesiastica, allontana sempre più gli acattolici, rovina la pace delle
famiglie, e causa la perdita di tante e tante anime.'
60 Ibid., f.17
61 Ibid., f.57. 'Non vi è infatti nessuno che possa oggi dirigere
l'Episcopato canadese che la malattia ha colpito l'egregio Card.
Taschereau.'
62 AES 94, Merry del Val a Rampolla, 7 magg. 1897. In the same letter,
the delegate claimed to be on good terms with the archbishop. But

subsequent correspondence and his final report make clear that
Merry del Val felt piqued at what he termed Bégin's avoidance. He
related how the archbishop, in the only meeting with which he
favoured the delegate (nell'unico abboccamento che mi favorì [Rap-
porto, f.25]), refused to discuss substantial issues. However, noted the
delegate, Bégin was in the same period writing long reports to Rome
on the Manitoba schools question. Merry del Val complained of the
cold reception he received from the Quebec bishops. It is clear that
these had a less than respectful regard for the pope's young representative. Because of his age, he was referred to as 'il ragazzino' (the
little boy), while more malicious tongues, commenting on his fastidi-
ousness and his overly refined and elegant manner, called him 'la
ragazzina' (the little girl). See Charland, *Le père Gonthier*, 47.

63 AAES 94, Merry del Val a Rampolla, 26 apr. 1897
64 AAES 92, Merry del Val a Rampolla, 3 apr. 1897. This letter contains
the following ambivalent sentence. 'Your Most Reverend Lordship will
notice from the story of this worthy Prelate that this is not the first
time that the vehemence of his otherwise admirable zeal has pushed
him beyond the limits of prudence in political contests.' (L'E.V.R.
rilieverà dalla storia di quel degno Prelato che non è la prima volta
che la veemenza del suo zelo, ammirabile peraltro, lo ha spinto ad ol-
trepassare i limiti della prudenza nelle agitazioni politiche.)
65 AAES 91, Merry del Val a Rampolla, 30 mar. 1897. 'E discutibile la
prudenza di questo passo frettoloso dell'egregio Prelato ...'
66 AAES 98, Merry del Val a Rampolla, n.d. received on 24 July 1897
67 AAES, Rapporto di Mgr Delegato, f.20
68 AAES 92, Merry del Val A Rampolla, 3 apr. 1897. 'E una delle poche
persone di vedute veramente elevate, che ho [*sic*] incontrato finor fra
gli ecclesiastici del Canada.'
69 AAES, Rapporto di Mgr Delegato, f.4. '... dei quali gli uni cercano di
unirsi maggiormente coll'elemento inglese, mentre che gli altri
vogliono mantenersi nell'atteggiamento riservato e quasi esclusivo di
altri tempi.'
70 Ibid., f.54. 'Il Canada dovrebbe e potrebbe essere il baluardo e
l'appoggio principale della Chiesa in tutto il continente dell'America
settentrionale; ma procedendo le cose come vanno oggi, perderà defini-
tivamente la sua posizione tradizionale e nulla farà nell'avvenire.'
71 AAES 95, Merry del Val a Rampolla, 21 magg. 1897. 'Essi si sono
guadagnati la stima degli uomini pubblici e degli stessi protestanti in
modo tale da esercitare un influenza grandissima nel paese. Dopo una
lotta lunga, perseverante hanno saputo conseguire le loro scuole sepa-

rate, dei sussidi considerevoli per i principali Istituti cattolici, e delle facilitazioni d'ogni sorta per le opere cattoliche. Ma cio non hanno ottenuto colla violenza, denunziando persone, proibendo giornali e sacramenti, od offendendo i partiti politici da una parte ed il fanatismo protestante dall'altra. Senza menomare o nascondere i principii cattolici, nell'applicazione di questi fanno piuttosto appelo al buon senso ed ai sentimenti di giustizia dei loro concittadini per migliorare passo a passo la lora posizione.'

72 AAES 98, Merry del Val a Rampolla, n.d. 'Non posso sperare di sfuggire alle denunzie di quelli che dapprima erano contrarii all'invio di un Delegato, e che in seguito avrebbero voluto diriggerne l'azione.'

73 APFR, NS 120, Observations sur un rapport présenté par s[on] Ex[cellence] Mgr Del Val à la S[acrée] C[ongrégation] des Affaires Ecclésiastiques Extraordinaires en sept. 1897, à l'occasion de sa Délégation au Canada 3 juil. 1902, ff.558–93, f.592

74 Ibid., f.560

75 APFR, NS 241, Moreau à Ledochowski, 9 août 1897, ff.726-30

76 APFR, NS 120, Observations sur un rapport, f.561

77 Ibid., f.564

78 Ibid., f.559

79 Ibid., f.587

80 Ibid., f.589

81 Ibid., f.591

82 ASV, DAC LBF, Notice biographique sur son Ex Mgr Diomede Falconio et ses Secrétaires; *Catholic Register* (Toronto) 15 Feb. 1917

83 François Marie Étienne de Clavette was a French Franciscan who had been ordained in Montreal in 1898; Edward Fisher was an English Franciscan ordained in France and expelled from that country by the Ferry government. In 1901 Fisher returned to England because of illness. He was replaced by an American Franciscan, Francis Schaefer.

84 To get an idea of the varied nature of the problems Falconio was called upon to deal with, see Matteo Sanfilippo, 'Inventaire des documents d'intérêt canadien dans *l'Archivio Segreto Vaticano* sous le pontificat de Léon XIII (1878–1903): Délégation Apostolique du Canada, Délégation Apostolique des États-Unis, *Epistolæ ad Principes* et *Epistolæ Latinæ*, et autres séries mineures' (Rome 1987). Copies of this inventory are available for consultation at the St Paul University, Ottawa, at the National Library and National Archives of Canada.

85 APFR NS 195, Falconio a Ledochowski, 6 giu. 1900, ff.134–8. 'I cattolici

in generale sono, veramente pratici. Se qualcuno manca a Messa nei dì festivi o al Precetto Pasquale è marcato a dito.'

86 APFR NS 215, Rapporto sulla Chiesa Cattolica in Canada, 3 dic. 1901, ff.710–45

87 Ibid., Rapporto sulla Propaganda Protestante nel Canada, 20 mar. 1901, ff.619–41

88 Ibid., Rapporto sulla Chiesa, 3 dic. 1901

89 ASV, DAC 115, Ledochowski a Falconio, 13 genn. 1902. 'Cio che sopratutto conviene aver di mira è l'accordo tra Prelati di nazionalità rivali tra loro.'

90 Ibid., Falconio aux Archevêques du Canada, 15 mai 1902

91 Ibid., Bruchési à Falconio, 5 juin 1902

92 Ibid. Although coadjutor bishops were consulted, vicars apostolic were not.

93 Ibid., Falconio a Gotti, 29 ott. 1902

94 ASV, SS 280, folder 3, Ireland à Rampolla, 18 sept. 1901

95 APFR NS 265, Rampolla a Gotti, 18 sett. 1902, f.16; note by Mgr G. Della Chiesa, 20 sett. 1902, f.18; Rampolla a Gotti, 18 nov. 1902

96 *The Catholic Record*, 17 Jan. 1903

97 Champagne, *Débuts de la mission dans le Nord-Ouest*, stresses the dismal state of theological education in mid nineteenth-century France, characterized by poorly qualified teachers, superficial textbooks, and the briefest course of studies. This situation lasted until the last quarter of the century. See esp. pp. 17–22.

98 Hennesey, *American Catholics*, 178

99 Ibid., ch. 14

CHAPTER FOUR: Tutto è politica

1 APFR, SC 18, Fabre à Conroy, 1 déc. 1877, ff.710–11

2 Ibid., Fabre à Conroy, 5 déc. 1877, ff.704–5

3 See Noel Bélanger, 'Une introduction au problème de l'influence indue, illustrée par la contestation de l'élection de 1876 dans le comté de Charlevoix' (Licence en histoire, Laval University 1960). This thesis is very much a product of the Quiet Revolution. It is a true reflection of the guilt felt by progressive clergymen at the time who believed that the Catholic church had abused of its power and intimidated the laity for over a century. But Bélanger, too, based his evidence on sworn affidavits to indict certain clergymen of undue interference in the Charlevoix by-election of 1876. Yet even this evidence

suggests that the accused priests did not use the sacraments to cow the electorate, as was later widely assumed. On the other hand, these affidavits do point to an attitude of condescension which seemed to mark the relationship between Liberal politicians and the habitants. Over and over again these politicians depicted the Quebec farmer as a vulnerable creature easily intimidated by 'his betters' and therefore in need of protection. The actions of the habitants, however, prove that they were quite able to look after themselves. After all, did they not walk out en masse from church when their pastors presumed to suggest how they should vote? If the habitants were so easily intimidated, why did the Conservative win the by-election by the slimmest of margins? It would seem instead that the Liberals were using the clergy as convenient scapegoats and the habitants as foils in their attempts to unseat the Conservative candidate.

4 A.T. Galt, *Civil Liberty in Lower Canada* (Montreal 1876); *Church and State* (Montreal 1876)
5 AAT, Lynch à Bourget, fév. 1876
6 Ibid., Lynch to H.R. Casgrain, 18 Feb. 1876
7 Walker, *Catholic Education*, ch. 2. Stortz makes clear that Lynch publicly intervened in politics a number of times, often silencing or censuring priests who supported opposing political views. See Stortz, 'Lynch,' passim.
8 AAT, Taschereau à Lynch, 1 mars 1876
9 APFR, SC 19 Bourget à Taschereau, 8 mars 1876, f.10 (copy)
10 APFR, SC 14, Persico a Franchi, 20 apr. 1876. 'E questo non per tutelare principî religiosi, ma semplicemente per fini politici o personali.'
11 Ibid., 'la vita sociale del Canadà è eminentemente politica. Lo stesso commercio colle arti ed industrie trovasi intimamente dipendente dalla politica.'
12 For details of the Conroy mission, see R. Perin, 'Troppo Ardenti Sacerdoti: The Conroy Mission Revisited,' *Canadian Historical Review* 61, no. 3 (Sept. 1980): 283–304; N. Voisine, 'Rome et le Canada: La Mission de Mgr. Conroy,' *Revue d'Histoire de l'Amérique Française* 33, no. 4 (mars 1980): 499–519.
13 APFR, SC 15, Conroy a Franchi, 25 magg. 1877. 'Ho accettato il suo invito, e spero di poter ricevere da lui tali informazioni che saranno di non lieve utilità per la spedizione degli affari della Delegazione.'
14 Ibid., Conroy a Franchi, 9 giu. 1877, ff.314–5
15 Ibid., Conroy a Franchi, 30 nov. 1877, ff.484–5. 'Egli mi riceve colla

più squisita cortesia, e mi trattava con tutti i riguardi che si con-
cedono ad un ambasciatore di alcune delle grandi potenze ... Mise
ancora a mia disposizione la sua carrozza nobile e fece di tutto per
colmare di onore l'indegno Rappresentante del Santo Padre.'

16 Ibid.

17 APFR, SC 17 (Italian translation), Dufferin a Conroy, 27 mar. 1878

18 APFR, SOCG 1010, Requête des prêtres du diocèse de Montréal à
Simeoni, 25 mai 1878, ff.97–8; Mémoire Stanislas Tassé à Simeoni, 12
juil. 1878, f.100–3. The author of this second memorandum argued
that more clerics would have signed it had they not been intimidated
by their bishops who opposed it. An earlier meeting of the pastors of
the diocese of Montreal had passed resolutions expressing similar
sentiments to those in the Requête. See APFR, SC 18, Procès verbal de
l'Assemblée des curés du diocèse de Montréal, 27 août 1877. See also
Archives du Séminaire de St-Sulpice, Montréal, Projet de mémoire à
la Sacrée Congrégation de la Propagande au nom de la majeure partie
du clergé du Bas Canada, 19 mars 1878. This last document, which is
in draft form, does not appear to have been sent. It is there that
Quebec is represented as the 'boulevard du catholicisme dans la
confédération.'

19 APFR, Acta 247, Relazione di Mgr Conroy sulla Questione Politica nel
Canadà, n.d., f.305. 'Chi riesce ad assidersi, come Ministro , al ban-
chetto della nazione, diviene ricco. Chi non appartiene al partito
trionfante, rimane povero. Quindi, nel Canadà più forse che altrove, si
vede comunemente un uomo pubblico passare da un partito all'altro
per motivo d'interesse personale.'

20 This was one of the key ideas of a memorandum which Conroy himself
elicited from an Ottawa priest, James I. Chisholm. The priest argued
that because of the heterogeneous nature of Canadian political
parties, none meddled in religion. The church therefore enjoyed a
great many advantages and it would be imprudent to challenge this
situation, as was being done in Quebec. Chisholm admitted that he
could not read French newspapers and that he did not have a first-
hand experience of what was happening in Quebec. He could not
therefore say whether priests denied penitents absolution simply for
voting Liberal or for supporting Liberal Catholics. In any case, he
thought, nominal Catholics could be supported as long as they were
not hostile to religion. He feared however that the Quebec clergy
identified the Liberal party with European liberalism to the overall
detriment of the Canadian church. See APFR, SC 16, Chisholm to
Conroy, n.d. ff.29–36.

21 This idea was also expressed in a complacent memorandum written by Archbishop Lynch, in which the Irish and French Canadians were compared to the latter's disadvantage. According to Lynch, the Irish clergy knew the difference between a liberal in politics and a liberal in religion, whereas the French 'are local and cannot see beyond their own horizon.' He ended by observing that the appointment of an Irishman as apostolic delegate was considered a special favour by the English-speaking prelates of Canada, who were twelve in number, whereas the French, who were only seven, would have preferred a Frenchman or Italian. 'All the other provinces are not to be sacrificed to the interests of Quebec, rich in every resource, but alas in great confusion.' See ibid., Lynch to Conroy, 10 May 1877, ff.78–81. None of these overtly Irish views found their way into Conroy's report.

22 He said as much to Prime Minister Mackenzie, showing him 'some very bad speeches' made by the leaders of the Liberal party in Quebec. Mackenzie replied that he had strictly forbidden Liberals from making such speeches and that he had punished their authors by not giving them the places in government they had wanted. Conroy added: 'I think that it will do him some good to know that Catholics will not let themselves be insulted with impunity' (Credo io che gli farà bene il sapere che i Cattolici non si lascieranno insultare con impunità). APFR, SC 15, Conroy a Franchi, 30 nov. 1877, ff.484–5

23 APFR, Acta 247, Relazione Conroy, f.304. 'I suoi compagni hanno vomitato in quella e in altre occasioni bestemmie le più luride contro la Chiesa, il Papato, il Clero.'

24 Charles de Montalembert (1810–70) was a French liberal Catholic who coined the slogan 'A Free Church in a Free State.' He tried to effect a synthesis between traditional Catholic thought and modern Liberal democracy. His position was viewed with suspicion and hostility in Rome, the more so when he rejected the idea of papal infallibility.

25 APFR, Relazione Conroy, f.306. 'Ora, il partito, come associazione, non assume la responsabilità degli errori professati da alcuni dei suoi membri, quando questi errori sono stati sbandati dal programma generale del partito.'

26 Ibid., f.303

27 Horace, *Epistles*, I.ii.16. Conroy did not seem to have his Horace handy since he inverted the word order of the quotation. It should be: 'Iliacos intra muros peccatur, et extra.' Many thanks to my colleague Paul Swarney whose thorough knowledge of Horace allowed me to identify Conroy's quotation.

28 Ibid., f.305. 'E valga il vero, avanti al 1841 quando non esisteva il
Parlamento, i Cattolici Francesi erano trattati da schiavi dagl'Inglesi
padroni. Ma dal giorno in cui il sistema parlamentare cominciava a
funzionare, cioè dal 1841 fino al presente, la storia del Canadà è la
storia del progresso continuo della Religione.'

29 Ibid., f.312. 'Dall'alto del pulpito, nel confessionale, nei giornali religiosi, nelle Lettere Pastorali il Clero Cattolico per molti anni non cessa
di denunciare come empio il partito Liberale, senza distinguere i
buoni dai cattivi, e senza badare all'eterogeneità degli elementi dei
quali quel partito si compone.'

30 Ibid., f.314

31 APFR, SC 17, Mémoire des six curés de Jacques Cartier à Conroy, 19
sept. 1877, ff.182–203. The memorandum was signed by F. Bourgeault, G. Chevrefils, N. Piché, F. Perrault, F.X. Laberge, and P.
Dupuis. St Alphonsus Liguori was an eighteenth-century Neapolitan
theologian, founder of the Redemptorist order, who turned away from
the rigorous Jansenist morality of his day and proposed instead a
more subtle and less rigid set of moral standards. Sinners, he taught,
should be brought back to the fold through patience, charity, and
moderation, rather than severity and fear. In judging their behaviour,
a confessor above all had to look at their conscience, not only at
external factors which in themselves might constitute occasions of sin.
In the nineteenth century Liguori was considered to be in the vanguard of Catholic ethics. Bishop Bourget was very active in encouraging the spread of his teachings in Canada.

32 APFR, SC 16, Curés de Jacques Cartier à Fabre, 15 déc. 1876, ff.132–8

33 APFR, SC 17, Direction donnée par six curés de Jacques Cartier, 24 déc.
1876, ff.173–6. Commenting on the passage in the collective pastoral
of 1877 which asserted that the bishops had not wanted to condemn a
political party, the pastor of Ste-Geneviève, one of the incriminated
clerics, told his parishioners: 'M.F. c'est ce que je vous ai toujours
enseigné. Vous le savez, je vous ai toujours dit que du moment qu'un
candidat ne serait que libéral en politique, vous aviez une parfaite
liberté de voter pour lui.' Ibid., Commentaire de la lettre pastorale
collective du 11 oct. 1877 par le curé de Ste-Geneviève [F. Perreault] à
ses paroissiens, ff.177–9.

34 APFR, SC 16, six curés, 15 déc. 1876

35 APFR, SC 17, Fabre aux six curés de Jacques Cartier, 9 déc. 1876,
ff.88–9

36 APFR, SC 19, J.L. Mougeau à certains paroissiens de Ste-Elisabeth

(comté Joliette), 28 déc. 1876. Mougeau was Fabre's secretary and was writing in the bishop's name.

37 Laflèche did not follow his lay nationalist disciples into Mercier's parti national which, the bishop felt, was a thinly disguised attempt to put the Liberal party in power in Quebec City. In his eyes, Mercier was exploiting Riel's hanging for purely partisan purposes. Acting on information provided by his close colleague Bishop Taché, Laflèche argued that the Métis leader was not the nationalist martyr he had been in 1869, but simply a misguided, unorthodox, and highly unstable figure. It would be foolish therefore to overturn old political alliances on the basis of such ephemeral and uncertain forces. Laflèche felt that this judgment of his was fully vindicated when the parti national, reeling from accusations of corruption, collapsed only six years after its formation.

38 APFR, Acta 253, Smeulders ad Simeoni, 8 Maiius 1884, f.403

39 APFR, SC 26, Relatio Commissarii Apotolici de divisione Diocesis Trifluvianae, 27 Augustus 1884, ff.742–55

40 APFR, SC 23, Taché à Laflèche, 15 janv. 1883, ff.436–7 (copy). Smeulders got this information directly from Taché who acted as the Commissioner's privileged adviser during the archbishop's three month stay in Montreal. Smeulders regarded Taché as the saintliest and most disinterested prelate in Canadian Catholicism.

41 APFR, Acta 253, Smeulders ad Simeoni, 26 Aprilis 1884, f.401

42 Ibid., Smeulders ad Simeoni, 10 December 1883. 'Directe vel indirecte, et forsitan inconscios periculi, favere gliscenti occulto Liberalismo aut maconismo, vel saltem eorum propagationi eos non sufficienter resistere.'

43 Ibid., Smeulders a D. Jacobini 16 apr. 1884, f.400. 'E vero che l'Arcivescovo ed i Signori di Laval attribuiscono quell'antipatia a mancanza d'istruzione e per che non sono all'altezza dell'odierno progresso della civiltà; ma, communque sia, mi pare che tutti non sono asini, massimamente spettata la qualità delle persone delle quali si tratta, fra le quali trovo uomini che sono riguardati come le Sommità della Giurisprudenza, e della magistratura, avvocati renomatissimi, e che hanno fatto con honore i loro corsi a Roma ecc. ecc. Sarei piuttosto a dire "Vox populi, vox dei." '

44 APFR, NS 240, Bégin à Ledochowski, 24 juil. 1896, ff.197–202

45 Bishop Sweeney of St John, who had led the fight for Catholic schools in New Brunswick, apparently took no public stand on the Manitoba schools question. His colleague, Bishop Rogers of Chatham, refused to

identify himself publicly with a cause 'tainted' by French-Canadian nationalism. He only committed himself to remedial action at the very last moment in the electoral campaign of 1896. See Jack Little, 'New Brunswick Reaction to the Manitoba Schools' Question,' *Acadiensis* 1 (Spring 1972): 43–58. Bishop Cameron of Antigonish seems to have been the only prelate among the Maritime bishops who strongly and publicly advocated the restoration of Catholic rights in Manitoba.

46 APFR, NS 240, Fabre à Ledochowski, 10 mai 1896, ff.122–4

47 Ibid., Emard à Ledochowski, 11 mai 1896, ff.149–52

48 See especially Crunican, *Priests and Politicians*, ch. 9.

49 AAES 80, Attestation que Mgr Bégin veut faire signer aux députés lors des élections de 1896

50 Ibid., Marois à J.E. Rouleau, 3 juin 1896. Marois makes it clear in this letter that it was Bégin who asked him to reply to Rouleau's query as to whether it was a mortal sin not to follow the direction laid out in the pastoral letter. It is inconceivable that Marois would have given this reply without the archbishop's approval.

51 Ibid., Marois à Rouleau, 7 juin 1896

52 The dubious candidate here was Henri Joly de Lotbinière; ibid., 11 juin, 1896.

53 Ibid., Bégin à Joly, 9 juin 1896

54 APFR, NS 240, Bégin à Ledochowski, 24 juil. 1896, ff.197–202

55 Ibid., Moreau à Ledochowski, 6 août 1896, ff.210–14

56 Ibid., Emard à Ledochowski, 21 juil. 1896, ff.206–9

57 Ibid., Notes présentées dans l'assemblée du 6 mai 1896 par Mgr Emard, ff. 131–48

58 ASV, Spogli Oreglia, Laflèche à Oreglia, 23 déc. 1896. Laflèche was also shocked by Proulx's decision to act as Laurier's agent in Rome: 'Je ne puis m'expliquer cette attitude chez un prêtre de sa valeur!' As for Emard, he considered the bishop pretentious, 'lui le plus jeune des évêques,' and accused him of diluting the meaning of the pastoral letter. 'Sans être *libéral*, me disait un de nos collègues, Mgr Emard est un *opportuniste* dans la force de ce mot; ce qui ne vaut guère mieux dans mon humble opinion.' The colleague in question was undoubtedly Moreau.

59 Ibid., Laflèche à Oreglia, 23 déc. 1896

60 APFR, NS 240, Bégin à Ledochowski, 3 janv. 1897, ff.582–8

61 Ibid., Bégin à Ledochowski, 14 janv. 1897, ff.823–5

62 AAES 90, Laflèche à Rampolla, 8 mars 1897

63 AAES 92, Merry del Val a Rampolla, 7 apr. 1897. 'Non appena avuta notizia del mio arrivo in Ottawa, mi mandò il suo aiutante di campo

per invitarmi immediatamente a pranzo ... Portò poi la sua gentilezza al punto di offrirmi con calda insistenza l'alloggio nel suo palazzo; e ieri venne a prendermi in carrozza per darmi occasione di parlare con tutta libertà della mia missione. Per il pubblico, massime per quello protestante inglese, questa dimostrazione del Governatore ha non poca importanza, mantenendo alto il prestigio della S[anta] Sede.'

64 AAES 94, Merry del Val a Rampolla, 21 magg. 1897. 'Pochi anni fa quando entrò in Diocesi questo degmo. Arcivescovo lo ricevettero coi sassi, ed oggi ancora basterebbe un atto meno che prudente per sollevare il grido di abbasso il Papa.'

65 Ibid., Merry del Val a Rampolla, 26 apr. 1897

66 AAES 100, Rapporto di Mgr Delegato, ff.14–16

67 Ibid., f.59. 'Il Cardinale Taschereau colla sua prudenza e energia sostenuta dalla Santa Sede giunse a domare gli animi, ed imporre a separare la religione dagli interessi dalla politica, è ciò malgrado la violenta opposizione del Vescovo di Trois Révières [sic] e di altri. Oggi egli è sparito dalla scena e si lavora a distruggere la sua opera.'

68 Ibid., ff.18, 58

69 AAES 94, Merry del Val a Rampolla, 21 magg. 1897

70 Ibid.

71 AAES, Rapporto di Mgr Delegato, ff.45–55

72 APFR, NS 120, Observations sur un rapport présenté par s[on] Ex[cellence] Mgr Del Val à la S[acrée] C[ongrégation] des Affaires Ecclésiastiques Extraordinaires en sept. 1897, à l'occasion de sa Délégation au Canada, 3 juil. 1902, f.588

73 Ibid., f.577

74 Ibid., f.579

75 APFR, NS 241, Langevin à Ledochowski, 12 mai 1897, ff.151–3

76 APFR, Observations sur un rapport, f.584

77 Ibid.

78 Ibid., f.591

79 Ibid., f.572

80 Ibid., f.574

81 Ibid., f.576

82 Ibid.

83 APFR, NS 241, Bégin à Ledochowski, 2 août 1897

84 APFR, NS 295, Bégin A Ledochowski, 12 oct. 1899, ff.195–6

85 APFR, NS 195, Falconio a Ledochowski, 6 giu. 1900, ff.134–8

86 Ibid., in which he stated that there was no difference among the political parties on the religious question

87 APFR, NS 215, Rapporto sulla propaganda protestante nel Canada, 20

mar. 1901, ff.619–41. Falconio described Canada as one of the freest countries in the world. Freedom of worship was, he maintained, a fully accepted fact.

88 APFR, NS 195, Falconio a Ledochowski, 8 nov. 1900, f.156. 'La vittoria del partito liberale con alla testa un cattolico e la gran maggioranza di deputati cattolici, ci fa sperare migliori disposizioni verso la nostra santa religione.'

89 APFR, NS 215, Rapporto sulla propaganda protestante

90 Ibid., f.728

91 AAES 114, pos. 193, Falconio a Rampolla, 8 magg. 1901

92 P. Sylvain, 'Libéralisme et ultramontanisme au Canada français: affrontement idéologique et doctrinal (1840–1865)' in W.L. Morton, ed., *The Shield of Achilles* (Toronto 1968); Voisine et Hamelin, *Les ultramontains canadiens-français*; Eid, *Le clergé et le pouvoir politique au Québec*; Voisine, *Louis-François Laflèche*

93 Paul Crunican, 'Bishop Laflèche and the Mandement of 1896,' CHA *Historical Papers* (1969): 52–61

94 Walker, *Catholic Education*, ch. 6

95 Ibid., ch. 1

96 R. Perin, 'St-Bourget: Évêque et Martyr,' *Journal of Canadian Studies* 15, no. 4 (Winter 1980–1): 43–55

CHAPTER FIVE: A House of Cards

1 APFR, NS 242, Falconio a Ledochowski, 29 apr. 1901, ff.279–80. 'Eminenza, ubbidiente ai desiderii del Sommo Pontefice, lasciai la mia diocesi per recarmi in queste regioni dove, per circa sei mesi si è ricoperti di ghiacci e di neve e dove questioni acerbe, per anni ed anni han disturbato la pace. A tutto mi son sottomesso.'

2 Lupul, *The Roman Catholic Church*; Robert Choquette, 'Adélard Langevin et les questions scolaires du Manitoba et du Nord-Ouest, 1895–1915,' *Revue de l'Université d'Ottawa* 46, no. 3 (juil.– sept. 1976): 324–44; Ramsay Cook, 'Church, Schools and Politics in Manitoba, 1903–1912,' *Canadian Historical Review* 30, no. 1 (March 1958): 1–23; Gilbert Comeault, 'La question des écoles du Manitoba, un nouvel éclairage,' *Revue d'Histoire d'Amérique Française* 33, no. 1 (juin 1979): 3–23; and 'Les rapports de Mgr L.-P.-A. Langevin avec les groupes minoritaires et leurs répercussions sur le statut de la langue française au Manitoba,' SCHEC, *Sessions d'études* (1975): 65–85

3 Except for those cited above. See also W.L.Morton, 'Manitoba Schools and Canadian Nationality, 1890–1923,' CHA *Report* (1951): 51–9; Cornelius Jaenen, 'The Manitoba Schools Question: An Ethnic Interpretation' in Martin Kovacs, ed., *Ethnic Canadians: Culture and Education* (Regina 1978), 217–31.

4 See Lupul, *The Roman Catholic Church*, esp. chs. 4–6.

5 APFR, NS 240, Langevin à Ledochowski, 8 oct. 1896, ff.250–6. ('I raised my eyes to the mountains from whence come my support.') Langevin was forty-one at the time.

6 Ibid., Bégin à Ledochowski, 4 nov. 1986, ff.411–6

7 AAES 80, O'Brien to Langevin, 10 Nov. 1896

8 Ibid., Walsh to Langevin, 11 Nov. 1896

9 Comeault, 'Question des écoles du Manitoba,' 10–11

10 Lovell Clark, *The Manitoba School Question: Majority Rule or Minority Rights?* (Toronto 1968), 117

11 W.L. Morton, *Manitoba: A History* (Toronto 1957), 248

12 APFR, NS 240, Langevin à Ledochowski, 18 nov. 1896, ff.533–4

13 Ibid., Moreau à Ledochowski, 5 fév. 1897, ff.850–2

14 *Dictionary of National Biography* 22, Supplement (Oxford 1917), 1199–1204. The baron was awarded an honorary degree from Laval University in 1896.

15 AAES, Rapporto di Mgr Delegato, f.4

16 Ibid., f.7. 'Voglio credere che non pochi del partito aspettavano sinceramente dal tribunale una sentenza favorevole.'

17 Ibid., f.10. The delegate noted that the Conservatives spent more time than the Liberals obstructing the remedial bill. Their leader, Charles Tupper, encouraged a number of Protestant members to support the measure with assurances that it never would become law. He even allowed candidates opposed to the legislation to carry the party banner during the elections.

18 Ibid., f.12. 'Il partito Liberale ... si sentiva prossimo al potere da tanto tempo ambito ... Alla vigilia di una elezione per esso di tanta importanza non volle inimicarsi una sezione grande degli Elettori prestando la sua cooperazione ad una misura odiosa, e dall'altra parte non voleva cedere ai Conservatori il vantaggio.'

19 Ibid., f.29

20 AAES 92, Merry del Val a Rampolla, 7 apr. 1897. 'Egli si trova in circostanze difficilissime, e non mi ha voluto nascondere che la S[anta] Sede ha in mano in questi momenti la sua posizione politica.'

D'altra parte a mio giudizio è molto discutibile la prudenza di un azione precipitata nell'attuale stadio acuto della questione. Un passo men ponderato nel modo di agire potrebbe portare sconvolgimenti politici e religiosi di somma gravità.'

21 Ibid., Merry del Val a Rampolla, 12 apr. 1897
22 AAES, Rapporto di Mgr Delegato, f.32
23 Ibid., f.34. 'Con una maggioranza questa volta enorme di protestanti decisi più che mai a negare ai cattolici la minima concessione.'
24 AAES 94, Merry del Val a Rampolla, 21 magg. 1897. 'Ora domando: ... sarebbe poco meno che un delitto sacrificare 50,000 fanciulli cattolici nell'Ontario ed altrettanti nelle provincie marittime, e sollevare l'antipatia dei protestanti contro i cattolici in tutte le sfere della società, negli impieghi ed uffici pubblici, e nelle stesse famiglie solo per volere difendere in astratto e senza neanche riuscire nella pratica ciò che assolutamente parlando sarebbe il diritto di 4,000 fanciulli del Manitoba per i quali in via amministrativa e con altri mezzi si puo per adesso provvedere?'
25 AAES, Rapporto di Mgr Delegato, f.14
26 Ibid., f.36
27 AAES 94, Merry del Val a Rampolla, 26 apr. 1897
28 AAES, Rapporto di Mgr Delegato, f.37
29 AAES 94, Merry del Val a Rampolla, 7 magg. 1897
30 AAES 98, Laurier à Rampolla, 1 juin 1897
31 AAES 94, Merry del Val a Rampolla, 21 magg. 1897
32 AAES, Rapporto di Mgr Delegato, f.39
33 AAES 94, Merry del Val a Rampolla, 26 apr. 1897. 'Alzando il grido di "tutto o niente" si è assolutatmente rifiutato finora a intendersi in qualsiasi maniera con il Governo protestante del Manitoba, col quale purtroppo avrà da contare per molto tempo in una provincia dove i cattolici Canadesi francesi non sono che 20,000 di fronte a quasi 200,000 protestanti di lingua inglese.'
34 The delegate cited as evidence a letter in AAES 64, Taché à Ouimet, 1 mai 1894 (cited in ch. 2, note 59), at the bottom of which he wrote: 'Important *secret* correspondence between Mgr Taché and the *Conservative* minister Ouimet ... which shows that Mgr Taché had no illusions as to the sincerity of the Conservative party and that he intended to turn to the Liberal party.' (Importante corrispondenza *segreta* di Mgr Taché con il Ministro *Conservatore* Ouimet ... che rivela che Mgr Taché non si faceva illusione sulla sincerità del Partito Conservatore e che egli intendesse rivolgersi al Partito liberale.)

35 AAES 94, Merry del Val a Rampolla, 21 magg. 1897. 'Sarebbe distruggere in 24 ore tutto cio che si è fatto, e ravvivare immediatamente le
antiche lotte senza più speranza di uscirne.'

36 AAES 98, Laurier à Rampolla, 1 juin 1897

37 AAES, Rapporto di Mgr Delegato, f.41. According to the delegate,
fifteen former Catholic schools had accepted the terms of the Laurier-
Greenway accord. The rest, those in Winnipeg and the countryside,
were schools established by the archbishop and under his control.

38 Ibid., f.44. 'Così p[er] es[empio] in una scuola nè la maestra nè i
fanciulli sapevano tradurre l'inglese, lingua indispensabile nel
Manitoba.'

39 Ibid., f.43. The delegate gave examples of communities in the dioceses
of Sherbrooke and Ottawa where this was done.

40 AAES 98, Laurier à Rampolla, 1 juin 1897

41 AAES 95, Merry del Val a Rampolla, 3 giu. 1897

42 AAES 98, Merry del Val a Rampolla, n.d. received in Rome on 24 July
1897. 'Nondimeno il Gabinetto del Sig. Greenway non ritira le assicu-
razioni date a voce, e si dichiara sempre disposto a facilitare
l'impianto di scuole di fatto, se non di nome, che sarebbero sotto la
vigilanza e la direzione di cattolici.'

43 APFR, NS 120, Observations sur un rapport, 3 juil. 1902

44 AAES 92, Gravel à Merry del Val, 3 avr. 1897

45 APFR, NS 241, Bégin à Ledochowski, 2 août 1897, ff.663–70

46 APFR, NS 242, Langevin à Léon XIII, 1 sept. 1898, ff.51–4

47 Ibid., Langevin à Ledochowski, 9 sept. 1898, ff.71–2; ASV, DAC 69,
Ledochowski ad Langevin, 14 Januarius 1899; APFR, NS 242, Langevin
à Ledochowski, 1 mars 1899, ff.80–1; Rampolla a Ledochowski, 3
magg. 1899, f.86

48 Ibid., Langevin à Ledochowski, 1 mars 1899, ff.80–1

49 Ibid., Langevin à Ledochowski, 18 sept. 1899, f.101

50 APFR, NS 295, Langevin à Ledochowski, 18 nov. 1899, ff.185–6. He
pointed out that the bishops of his ecclesiastical province deliberately
refrained from publishing a petition to the governor general on behalf
of Manitoba's urban Catholics so as not to embarrass the government.
He himself decided against launching a public appeal for funds in
support of his schools for fear that his action might be interpreted as a
political gesture against the provincial Liberals who were seeking re-
election.

51 APFR, NS 242, Bégin à Langevin, 6 déc. 1898, ff.64–5

52 APFR, NS 295, Bégin à Ledochowski, 12 oct. 1899, ff.195–6

53 Ibid., Falconio a Ledochowski, 3 nov. 1899, ff.208–9. 'Affinchè questi non abbiano a sfruttarla, come per lo passato, a proprio beneficio, con grave jattura della concordia fra il clero ed il popolo cattolico.'

54 ASV, DAC 69, Langevin à Falconio, 13 fév. 1900

55 ASV, DAC LBF, Falconio à Langevin, 26 fév. 1900, p. 43

56 ASV, DAC 69, Langevin to Macdonald, 2 June 1900

57 ASV, DAC LBF, Falconio à Langevin, 4 avr. 1900, pp. 51–2

58 ASV, DAC 69, Langevin à Falconio, 14 avr. 1900

59 Ibid., Langevin à Falconio, 12 juil., 21 avr. 1900. The delegate was poorly informed on the financial situation of the Catholic schools of Winnipeg. Prior to receiving these detailed figures from Langevin, Falconio thought that a $2,000 donation which Laurier had made to these schools would cover costs. See ibid., Falconio à Langevin, 16 juin 1900.

60 Ibid., Langevin à Falconio, 4 juin 1900

61 Ibid., Langevin à Falconio, 7 avr. 1900

62 Ibid., Falconio à Langevin, 16 juin 1900

63 APFR, NS 242, Augustin Dontenwill à Ledochowski, n.d., received in Rome 17 May 1900, ff.177–81

64 ASV, DAC 178, Luigi Veccia a Falconio, 19 giu. 1900

65 ASV, DAC 69, Falconio à Langevin, 5 sept. 1900

66 Ibid., Falconio à Langevin, 11 juin 1900

67 Choquette, *Language and Religion: A History of English-French Conflict in Ontario*, 19, refers to Constantineau as Laurier's confessor.

68 ASV, DAC 69, Langevin à Falconio, 21 juin 1900

69 Ibid., Constantineau to Laurier, 10 July 1900

70 Ibid., Langevin à Falconio, 11 juil. 1900; Constantineau to Falconio, 20 Sept. 1900

71 ASV, DAC 69, Langevin à Falconio, 4 juin 1900

72 Ibid., Laurier à Falconio, 6 fév. 1901; AAES 113, Falconio a Rampolla, 8 febb. 1901

73 ASV, DAC 69, Langevin à Falconio, 13 fév. 1901

74 Ibid., A.A. Cherrier à Langevin, 26 fév. 1901

75 Ibid., Langevin à Laurier, 20 mars 1901; Langevin à Falconio, same date. Langevin criticized Laurier's choice of spokesman in the talks that were to be held between the two levels of government on the question of school lands. The man designated by Laurier was Edward Farrer, a *Globe* editorialist, who was very critical of Roblin's railway policy. Langevin proposed instead the chairman of the Winnipeg board of education who was a Liberal and acceptable to Roblin.

76 APFR, NS 242, Langevin à Ledochowski, 2 avr. 1901, ff.204–7

77 Ibid., Langevin à Ledochowski, 13 avr. 1901
78 Ibid., Falconio a Ledochowski, 29 apr 1901, ff.283–98. 'Ma sembra che Mgr Langevin ami le battaglie di parte e di razza, e nella veemenza del suo operare, non calcola le conseguenze e si rende ribelle ad ogni sano consiglio, non importa da chi possa emanare.'
79 AAES 114, Falconio a Rampolla, 8 magg. 1901. 'L'animosità di Mons Langevin verso questo Governo Federale, al quale cerca sempre creare imbarazzi per ragione di partito.'
80 Ibid. These arguments paralleled those used by Laurier in an earlier letter to Langevin. See ASV, DAC 69, Laurier à Langevin, 1 avr. 1901.
81 Ibid., Cherrier à Falconio, 14 août 1901
82 ASV, DAC LBF, Falconio à Langevin, 7 sept. 1901
83 ASV, DAC 69, Cherrier à Falconio, 15 juin 1901
84 Ibid., Cherrier à Falconio, 7 juin 1901
85 Ibid., Cherrier à Falconio, 14 août 1901
86 Ibid., Langevin à Falconio, 12 août 1901; document entitled 'Mémoire de l'Honorable Roblin, Premier Ministre du Manitoba. Ce que ce Monsieur est prêt à faire,' written in Langevin's hand.
87 Ibid., Langevin à Falconio, 28 sept. 1901
88 Ibid., Langevin à Falconio, 17 nov. 1901
89 ASV, DAC LBF, Falconio à Langevin, 3 oct. 1901, p. 252; Falconio à Langevin, 8 nov 1901, p 264
90 ASV, DAC 69, Langevin à Falconio, 17 nov. 1901
91 Ibid., Langevin à Falconio, 2 déc. 1901
92 APFR, NS 265, Minuta per Mgr Sbarretti, ff.31–7. 'Senza mosse irritanti, ma senza deboli acquiescenze. E la questione è tanto più grave, in quanto che dalla provincia del Manitoba potrà in breve passare a quelle altre provincie del Canadà, dove ora i diritti della Chiesa sono meglio riconosciuti, e dove sarebbe difficile difenderli con buon successo, dopo una prima troppo arrendevole capitolazione nel Manitoba.'
93 ASV, DAC 70, Macdonnell to Sbarretti, 27 Jan. 1903; Langevin to Macdonnell, 16 Jan. 1903 (copy)
94 Ibid., Macdonnell to Sbarretti, 1 Feb. 1903
95 Ibid., O'Brien to Sbarretti, 31 Mar. 1903. The archbishop said he would 'cheerfully' give his backing to such a petition.
96 Ibid., Bégin à Sbarretti, 30 mars 1903
97 Ibid., O'Connor to Sbarretti, 26 Mar. 1903
98 Ibid., Bruchési à Sbarretti, 11 mars 1903; Duhamel à Sbarretti, 25 mars 1903
99 Ibid., Gauthier to Sbarretti, 7 May 1903 (copy)

100 Ibid., Gauthier to Sbarretti, 1 Apr. 1903
101 Ibid., Sbarretti a Gotti, 5 lug. 1903
102 AAES 117, Rapporto di Mgr Sbarretti sulle scuole cattoliche in Manitoba, 11 apr. 1903
103 Ibid., Langevin à Sbarretti, 3 mai 1903
104 Ibid., Laurier to Sbarretti, 25 June 1903
105 Ibid., J.K. Barrett to Sbarretti, 26 June 1903. Barrett was the plaintiff in the court case which resulted in the Judicial Committee of the Privy Council's judgment of 1892. He was a Liberal with pronounced anti-French sentiments. He believed that the responsibility for the minority's ills belonged to Langevin and the French-Canadian Conservative politicians representing Manitoba. 'It takes French Canadians – especially the ecclesiastical portion a long time to learn wisdom and prudence. I am heartily sorry for his Grace. He is generous hearted and noble and devoutly desirous to do right, but he is unfortunately surrounded by as bad a lot of advisers as it is possible to have.' See ASV, DAC 69, Barrett to Edward Fisher, secretary to the delegate, 14 Dec. 1900. Barrett doubted that a settlement could be reached in Winnipeg as long as the archbishop was in charge of negotiations for the Catholic side. See ASV, DAC 70, Barrett to Sbarretti, 11 Mar. 1903.

CHAPTER SIX: Pariahs of the Nation

1 See Hennesey, *American Catholics*, ch. 15, and Tomasi, *Piety and Power*, ch. 4.
2 See Maria Laura Vannicelli, 'L'Opera della Congregazione di Propaganda Fide per gli Emigrati Italiani negli Stati Uniti (1883–1887),' in Pietro Borzomati, ed., *L'Emigrazione Calabrese dall'Unità ad Oggi* (Roma 1982) 135–51.
3 For Scalabrini and his dedication to the cause of the Italian immigrant, see the exhaustive biography by Mario Fancesconi, *Giovanni Battista Scalabrini, vescovo di Piacenza e degli emigrati* (Roma 1985).
4 APFR, Acta 257, Rapporto sull'emigrazione italiana con sommario, ff.683–93. 'Le quali speculando sulla loro miseria, non si dan troppo cura delle loro persone. Sono imbarcati alla rinfusa, pigiati senza distinzione d'età e di sesso in numero soverchio sui piroscafi, in condizione esiziale per l'igiene e la moralità' (f.683).
5 Ibid., f.685. 'E umiliante riconoscere come, dopo la scomparsa degl'indiani dagli Stati Uniti e l'emancipazione dei negri, sono gli emigrati italiani quelli che in gran numero rappresentano *i paria* nella grande

Reppublica Americana. Basti l'accennare che sono così disprezzati per il loro sudiciume e la loro pitoccheria, che a New York gli Irlandesi concedettero loro l'uso gratuito del *Sotterraneo* della Chiesa della Trasfigurazione, per riunirsi alle pratiche del culto.'

6 Ibid., f.686. 'Lentamente quelle famiglie povere van trasformandosi, per perdersi in pochi anni nella grande nazione americana, d'italiano non conservando che il nome.'

7 A full text of the letter may be read in G. Tassello and L. Favero, eds., *Chiesa e mobilità umana: documenti della Santa Sede dal 1883 al 1983* (Roma 1985).

8 For a good general discussion of the role of the church in the care of Italian immigrants in Canada, see Matteo Sanfilippo, 'Fonti Vaticane per la storia dell'emigrazione italiana in Canada, 1899–1915,' *Movimento operaio e socialista* 10 (nuova serie), no. 3 (sett.–dic. 1987): 327–36.

9 APFR, SC 31, Taschereau à Jacobini, 5 janv. 1889, ff.11–12

10 Ibid., Fabre à Simeoni, 28 mai 1889, ff.307–8

11 ASV, DAC 50, Deguire à Falconio, 10 oct. 1902; LBF, Falconio à Deguire, 24 oct. 1902

12 APFR, SC 23, O'Mahony a Simeoni, 14 febb. 1884, ff.769–70. (The letter, written in Italian, is full of mistakes which will not be indicated in the following text.) 'In questi ultimi giorni, parrechi Italiani sono arrivati in questa città ... Questi sono stati impiegati nei lavori della strada ferrata "Canadian Pacific" ed essedo fraudati del loro stipendio dagli uffiziali della Compania si trovano qui nella più grande miseria. Alcuni si sono ricoverati ne ospedale, attacati dal ghiaccio e dallo scorbuto – altri campano qui e là in città al meglio.'

13 APFR, SC 22, T. Cornyn a Simeoni, 14 ago. 1882, ff.937–8; James Walsh a Simeoni, 18 apr. 1883, ff.271–3

14 See, among others, APFR, NS 146, J. Bigaouette a Ciasca, 30 jann. 1898, ff.384–90; ASV, DAC 50, Falconio to H. Thayer, 4 Nov. 1900.

15 Falconio's letter book indicates that he turned away at least eight Italian priests. Of these, the papers of two clerics were in order. Three others wanted to emigrate for rather dubious reasons: to avoid military service; to live more comfortably, etc. The other three had been students of Falconio.

16 Hennesey, *American Catholics*, 193

17 Propaganda Fide was divided into two sections, one for the Latin and the other for the Eastern rites. For the Propaganda's decree, see ASV, DAC 178, printed document signed by Cardinal Ledochowski dated 12 Apr. 1894.

18 The decree was dated 4 May 1897. AAES 195, Proposta dell'I[mperiale] e R[eggio] Governo Austro-Ungarico per provvedere alla cura spirituale dei Ruteni cattolici di Galizia e Ungheria emigrati nel Canada e negli Stati Uniti di America agosto 1901. 'In mancanza di questi, un sacerdote latino, bene accettato ai Ruteni, a cui fosse affidata, sotto la dipendenza dell'Ordinario del luogo, la sorveglianza e la direzione del popolo e del clero di rito ruteno.'

19 APFR, Bigaouette à Ciasca, 30 janv. 1898

20 APFR, NS 215, Propaganda Protestante nel Canada, 20 mar. 1901, ff.619–41

21 Ibid. 'Generalmente poco dediti alla pietà, avidi di guadagno e di libertà e sotto l'influenza costante de' protestanti che dominano.'

22 APFR, NS 195, F. Olszewski, a Ledochowski 13 mar. 1900, ff.116–17 (Italian translation of Polish original)

23 See Paul Yuzyk, *The Ukrainian Greek Orthodox Church of Canada* (Ottawa 1981), 36–9.

24 ASV, SS 247, Emidio Taliani, Nunzio Apostolico a Vienna, a Rampolla, 29 magg. 1900

25 AAES 195, Count Revertera a Rampolla, 6 magg. 1900

26 The visitors, who had to be educated, zealous, and celibate, would cease being subjects of their Ukrainian bishops. They would have to request their powers from the North American episcopate and only if the latter refused, could they ask the apostolic delegate to grant them. They were expected to inculcate in their flock a sense of submission and obedience to the Latin hierarchy. They were to report their findings and make their recommendations to the apostolic delegate.

27 AAES 195, Proposta dell'I. e R. Governo, ago. 1901

28 ASV, DAC 178, Lacombe à Falconio, 9 sept. 1900

29 Ibid., Rampolla a Falconio, 2 lug. 1900

30 AAES 195, Proposta dell'I. e R. Governo. 'Desiderio ... dei Vescovi e del Governo americano sarebbe che anche i Ruteni, come quelli appartenenti ad altre nazionalità, abbiano ad assimilarsi agli americani e formare un solo popolo. Ammessa invece questa eccezione pei Ruteni potrebbe col tempo essere essa invocata anche dalle altre nazionalità.'

31 ASV, DAC 178, Langevin à Falconio, 5 oct. 1900

32 Ibid., Langevin à Falconio, 31 juil. 1900. Langevin suggested that Byzantine hymns, vestments, church architecture, ceremonies, devotions, and benedictions be retained, but that the mass and the sacraments be performed according to the Latin rite.

33 Ibid.

34 Ibid., Langevin à Falconio, 18 juil. 1900
35 Ibid., Langevin à Falconio, 5 oct. 1900
36 ASV, DAC 50, Grandin à Falconio, 31 mars 1901
37 ASV, DAC 178, Grandin à Falconio, 25 juil. 1900; DAC 50, Grandin à Falconio, 18 oct. 1900
38 ASV, DAC LBF, Falconio a Rampolla, 5 ago. 1900
39 Ibid., 4 ago. 1900
40 ASV, DAC 50, Legal à Falconio, 15 fév. 1900. Legal listed the objectives of this mission: to obtain teaching brothers for Catholic boys; to favour the immigration of good Catholic families from Europe; to provide for the spiritual care of the Métis. Not a word was mentioned of the Ukrainians in this letter.
41 APFR, Olszewski, a Ledochowski 13 mar. 1900
42 ASV, DAC 178, Lacombe à Falconio, 15 juin 1900
43 Ibid., Lacombe à Falconio, 27 sept. 1900
44 Ibid., Lacombe à Falconio, 9 sept. 1900; Lacombe à Legal, 14 sept. 1900 (extract)
45 Ibid., Lacombe à Falconio, 27 sept. 1900
46 ASV, DAC LBF, Falconio à Szeptycki, 9 janv. 1901. This invitation was supported by the bishops of the ecclesiastical province of St Boniface who petitioned Rome to that effect.
47 ASV, DAC LBF, Falconio a Ledochowski, 12 mar. 1901
48 ASV, DAC 178, Ledochowski a Falconio, 1 mar. 1901
49 ASV, DAC LBF, Falconio à Langevin, 20 mai 1900; Falconio à Grandin, 11 juil. 1901; DAC 50, Grandin à Falconio, 15 mai 1901
50 Ibid., Falconio a Ledochowski, 23 mar. 1901. 'Se ben disposti, potrebbero indurre questi Ruteni a frequentare le chiese latine nei centri misti e forse col tempo e con prudenza indurli tutti anche all'unità di rito.'
51 ASV, DAC 178, Langevin à Falconio, 31 juil. 1900
52 Ibid., Kulawy to Langevin, 8 Dec. 1900
53 Ibid., Kulawy à Langevin, 31 juil. 1900 (copy)
54 Ibid., Kulawy to Langevin, 8 Dec. 1900
55 Ibid., Langevin à Falconio, 23 nov. 1900
56 ASV, DAC 157, Langevin à Falconio, rapport sur la propagande protestante, 5 fév. 1901
57 Ibid., Ledochowski a Falconio, 1 mar. 1901
58 ASV, DAC LBF, Falconio a Ledochowski, 12 mar. 1901. Falconio believed that Kulawy's efforts had done some good ('qualche bene'), but noted that the vast majority of Ukrainians strongly were opposed to the

Latin rite. The delegate sought information on the Ukrainians'
spiritual condition from a priest serving central and eastern European
immigrants in East Assa, Manitoba, from his faithful informant in
Winnipeg, J.K. Barrett, and from a Redemptorist priest in the
Brandon area. See ASV, DAC 69, P.J. de Bresson à Falconio, déc. 1900;
DAC 178, Barrett to Falconio, 14 Nov. 1900; G.M. Godts to Falconio, 26
Mar. 1901. The latter provided a rather ethnocentric point of view.
'The people of this rite [Ruthenian] are more opposed to latin Catholics than to Protestants, they do not even know what the Rosary is, a
devotion I thought His Holiness spread all over the world.' Still, he
informed the delegate that Achille Delaere, a Redemptorist who would
later become a Uniate priest, had visited almost five hundred Ukrainian families in the Brandon area and was doing much good.

59 Ibid., Falconio a Ledochowski, 23 mar. 1901
60 ASV, DAC 178, Szeptycki à Falconio, 11 sept. 1901
61 ASV, DAC LBF, Falconio à Langevin, 12 oct. 1901
62 Ibid., Falconio a Zholdak, 13 nov. 1901
63 APFR, NS 242, Langevin à Ledochowski, 1 oct. 1901, ff.315–22
64 ASV, DAC 178, Langevin à Falconio, 20 oct. 1901
65 ASV, DAC 69, Langevin à Falconio, 4 janv. 1902
66 ASV, DAC LBF, Falconio à Langevin, 18 janv. 1902
67 Ibid., Falconio a Ledochowski 1 marzo 1902.
68 APFR, NS 215, Ledochowski a Falconio, 13 genn. 1902
69 ASV, DAC LBF, Falconio à Langevin, 6 mai 1902. The visitor was to be
   Ambrose Polanski but he never came to Canada.
70 ASV, SS 280, Rampolla a Ledochowski, 24 mar. 1902
71 ASV, DAC 178, Zholdak a Falconio, 16 magg. 1902
72 Ibid., Zholdak a Falconio, 16 magg. 1902
73 Ibid., Lacombe à Falconio, 3 mai 1902
74 Ibid., Zholdak a Falconio, 19 ago. 1902
75 Ibid., Zholdak à Lacombe, 14 sept. 1902
76 Ibid., W. Ledochowski a Falconio, 28 sett. 1902
77 Ibid., Szeptycki à Falconio, 7 oct. 1902
78 APFR, NS 242, Langevin à Gotti, 11 août 1902
79 ASV, DAC 184, Zholdak a Sbarretti, 26 febb. 1903
80 Ibid., Sbarretti a Gotti, 23 mar. 1903. 'Tale proposta è d'un eccezion-
   ale importanza; e forse i Vescovi di qui non la vedrebbero di buon
   occhio. Comprendo però che avrebbe non poca influenza per manten-
   ere alla vera fede i cattolici Ruteni.'
81 Ibid., Zholdak a Sbarretti, 24 mar. 1903 (copy). Zholdak reported that

Ukrainians were most numerous in the archdiocese of St Boniface where there were 15,000 of them grouped together in 3,293 families. In the diocese of St Albert there were 1,300 families; whereas 655 families could be found in the diocese of Prince Albert. He then broke down these statistics according to local community.

	Catholic families	Orthodox
ARCHDIOCESE OF ST-BONIFACE:		
Winnipeg	200	some
Stuartburn	650	200
Broken Head	100	some
Gonor	33	40
Gimli	550	
Glenella	20	
Cooks Creek	60	
Valley River, Sifton		
Fish River, Ethelbert	800	
Hun's Valley	50	
Shoal Lake	200	
Venlaw	100	
Yorkton	600 many of them Orthodox	
Brandon	20	

Zholdak claimed that on the whole the Orthodox in the archdiocese of St Boniface were not converts from Catholicism, but immigrants from Bukovyna in the Austrian empire, where the dominant religion was Orthodoxy.

DIOCESE OF ST ALBERT		
Beaver Creek	900 many of them Orthodox	
Rabbit's Hill	200	15
Lethbridge	80	
Edmonton	12	

DIOCESE OF PRINCE ALBERT	
Fish Creek	600
Crooked Lake	40
Domrémy	15

These statistics would tend to indicate that Zholdak's estimate of 60,000 Ukrainians was an exaggeration.

82 Ibid., Zholdak a Sbarretti, 21 magg. 1903
83 Ibid., Langevin à Sbarretti, 14 avr. 1903 (copy)
84 Ibid., Langevin à Sbarretti, 18 juil. 1903 (copy). Langevin asked Sbarretti to pressure Laurier to this effect.
85 Ibid., Langevin à Sbarretti, 18 juil. 1903 (copy)
86 Ibid., Langevin à Sbarretti, 1 mars 1903 (copy)
87 Ibid., Zholdak a Sbarretti, 6 apr. 1903
88 Ibid., Filas ad Sbarretti 10 Maiius 1903
89 See Bohdan Kazymyra, 'Metropolitan Andrew Sheptyckyj and the Ukrainians in Canada,' CCHA *Report* (1957): 75–86.
90 See Joseph Jean, 'S.E. Mgr Adélard Langevin, Archevêque de St-Boniface, et les Ukrainiens,' SCHEC *Rapport* (1944–5): 101–10. This article provides useful information and is a valuable first-hand account by a French Canadian who became a Uniate priest serving the Ukrainians in the West. The author is patently hagiographic in his treatment of Langevin.
91 It is interesting to compare the documents creating the Uniate episcopate in the United States and Canada. See Tassello and Favero, eds., *Chiesa e mobilità umana*. For the United States, the document is entitled *Ea semper* (59–66); for Canada, *Officium Supremi* (86–7) and Propaganda's decree of 1913 *Fidelibus Ruthenis* (90–7).
92 ASV, DAC 179, Fr. Alexis, 'Le Catholicisme et la race Française au Canada d'après les recensements de 1881, de 1891 et de 1901,' n.d.
93 APFR, NS 215, La Chiesa Cattolica nel Canada 3 dic 1901. 'non sapendosi o non volendosi adattare al rito latino.'

CHAPTER SEVEN: The Delegate as Arbiter

1 ASV, DAC LBF, Falconio a Ledochowski, 3 nov. 1899
2 APFR, NS 215, Ledochowski a Falconio, 22 dic. 1899, ff.210–1. 'Con cio oltre al maggiore prestigio che ne viene alla S[ignoria] V[ostra], si avrà pure il vantaggio di poter esaminare sul luogo e da vicino alcuni casi sui quali la stessa lontananza toglie talora la facilità di avere copiosi ed esatti ragguagli.'
3 APFR, NS 295, Falconio a Ledochowski, 21 dic. 1899, f.220. 'Varie quistioni pendenti fra Vescovi, preti e secolari mi tengono bastantemente occupato.'
4 ASV, Spogli dei Cardinale: Oreglia, 14 déc. 1898
5 Ibid., Laflèche à Oreglia, 23 déc. 1897
6 APFR, NS 241, Laflèche à Ledochowski, 1 juin 1897

7 APFR, NS 125, Gravel à un révérend et cher père [Gonthier?], 16 nov.
1897. Gravel complained about the bishops' general subservience to
their diocesan seminaries. 'Non seulement les séminaires continuer-
ont à se gouverner à leur guise, mais ils ne lasseront pas de se croire
chargés de faire l'opinion publique dans le pays sur toutes les questions, même à l'encontre de la direction des évêques.'

8 APFR, NS 120, Observations sur un rapport, 3 juil. 1902, ff.590–1

9 Chapters were established in the dioceses of Trois-Rivières, St-Hyacinthe, Ottawa, and Rimouski. As for the Holy See's efforts to encourage their creation, see Grisé, *Les conciles provinciaux de Québec* 177,
249, 285. There were no cathedral chapters in English Canada.

10 One anonymous observer, hostile to the chapter established by Bourget, commented that the canons' communal life had engendered an
intense factionalism even during Bourget's time. The chapter 'était
plutôt l'instigateur de toutes les mesures extrêmes dont les tristes
conséquences se font aujourd'hui si fâcheusement sentir.' He added:
'L'on conçoit sans peine le désir de Mgr Fabre de se débarrasser d'un
chapitre qui ne lui a donné que des ennuis et des déplaisirs.' See APFR,
SC 23, Note sur la réorganisation du Chapitre de Montréal, juil. 1883.

11 DAC 115, Joseph Gingras à Sbarretti, 25 juin 1903

12 Despite a formal injunction to this effect by the sixth council of
Quebec, the dioceses of Trois-Rivières, Chicoutimi, Sherbrooke,
Ottawa, and Pembroke did not have such courts. In English Canada,
only Hamilton and St John had them.

13 Cited in Joseph Bernhart, *The Vatican as a World Power* (New York
1939), 442

14 APFR, NS 215, La chiesa cattolica, f.725. 'Il prete canadese si sottopone
a questa dipendenza assoluta, senza limite e senza controllo, sia per
pietà, sia perchè non desidera compromettersi col suo Vescovo dal
quale dipende quasi assolutamente il suo futuro.' 'E che il clero sia
promosso a secondo del diritto e non già secondo la volonta di chi
impera.'

15 APFR, NS 198, Falconio a Ledochowski, 21 ott. 1901, f.853

16 Ibid., Ledochowski a Falconio, 28 nov. 1901

17 APFR, NS 195, Falconio a Ledochowski, 6 giu. 1900, ff.134–8. 'Infatti
non pochi litigi, pendenti da anni, si sono pacificamente assodati nel
breve tempo da che si è fondata questa delegazione.'

18 For the University of Ottawa question, see Choquette, *Language and
Religion*, ch. 1.

19 Archives générales de l'Ordre des Servites de Marie, Rome, A. Curotte

à Alexis Lépicier, 5 sept. 1912. Lépicier had been a professor of
Curotte's at the Urban College in Rome. Curotte attributed Bruchési's
action in his regard to the fact that 'la déception de son cardinalat
manqué l'a aigri.' This letter shows that Bruchési was already
showing signs of mental instability which would later incapacitate
him.

20 *Le Canada ecclésiastique: almanach annuaire du clergé canadien*
(Montréal 1900)

21 Included in this figure are a number of French and Belgian clergymen, many of whom had come to Canada with their religious communities, as well as priests bearing such names as Fraser, Lonergan,
Kavanagh, who were functionally French-speaking.

22 Two cases concerning property and debt and both involving appeals
against bishops have not been considered here because they were
neither particularly interesting nor germaine. One involved a dispute
between Agnes Murphy against the Sisters of St Joseph in the archdiocese of Toronto (see DAC 88); the other concerned Pierre Théberge,
a priest in the apostolic prefecture of the Gulf of St Lawrence, and the
bishop of Chicoutimi (see DAC 5). In both cases, the bishop was either
vindicated or a mutually acceptable arrangement was reached.

23 APFR, SC 32, Taschereau à Simeoni, 21 août 1890, f.215. Taschereau's
allegations were supported by the superior of the diocesan seminary
of Rimouski, P. Sylvain. See his 'Liste des prêtres ordonnés par mon-
seigneur Langevin et dont la conduite a été regrettable, avec bref
réquisitoire contre chacun des prêtres,' ff.221–30.

24 See *Le Canada ecclésiastique* (1906), 247–8

25 Unless otherwise indicated, all further references are to the Archivio
Segreto so that the abbreviation ASV, will no longer appear. DAC LBF,
pp. 138, 143–4. The case occurs in February 1901. The exact number
and location of these letters may be determined by consulting M.
Sanfilippo, *Inventaire des documents d'intérêt canadien*.

26 DAC, LBF, pp. 138, 143–4

27 DAC 5, Rimouski: C.E. Trudel, July–Dec. 1900; LBF, pp. 75–6, 118–19,
121–2

28 DAC 5, Chicoutimi: L.O. Tremblay, Sept. 1899–July 1902; there are
over twenty letters in LBF dealing with this case and it would be
tedious to list them all. See Sanfilippo, *Inventaire*.

29 DAC 26, Montréal: C.E. Perrin, Dec. 1899–July 1900; LBF, pp. 28, 31

30 DAC 179; DAC 26, Montréal: P. Giraud, Feb.–Nov. 1902; LBF, pp. 345–6,
347, 351, 362, 364

31 DAC 88, Alexandria: T.Fitzpatrick, Sept. 1900–Apr. 1901; LBF, pp. 88, 92, 93, 95–6, 171–2

32 DAC 13, Halifax: P.A. Desmond March 1900 to April 1902; there are over twenty letters in LBF on this case.

33 DAC 88, Peterborough: J.Sweeney, Sept. 1901–Feb. 1903; LBF, pp. 285, 304

34 DAC 88, Hamilton: Peter Lennon v. Bishop Dowling, Oct. 1899–May 1900; LBF, pp. 27–8. The case was first submitted to arbitration before Archbishop Walsh of Toronto in 1894. Difficulties between Lennon and his bishop continued even after the priest's retirement from parish work.

35 DAC 13, Chatham: Thomas Henry Ellison, Oct. 1899–Sept. 1900. LBF, pp. 14–15, 20–1

36 DAC 13, Charlottetown: P.J. Hogan, June–Oct. 1902; LBF, pp. 333, 349, 360

37 DAC 88, Alexandria: J. Twomey, June and July 1902

38 DAC 50, Québec: Philias Lessard, Oct. 1901; LBF, pp. 253–4, 255–6

39 DAC 26, Sherbrooke: D.P. Picotte, Aug.–Oct. 1901; LBF, pp. 238–9, 240, 247, 258

40 DAC 5, Rimouski: Simon Fraser, Mar. 1896–Nov. 1902; this case generated over thirty letters in LBF.

41 DAC 50, St Boniface: Théophile Campeau, Dec. 1900–Sept. 1902; LBF, pp. 132, 325, 354

42 DAC 50, Pembroke: A. Nolin, Dec. 1901– Mar. 1902; LBF, pp. 272, 274, 275, 285, 292, 297, 304–5, 307, 308, 311, 314, 316–17

43 DAC 26, Montréal: R. Prud'homme; LBF, p 152. A similar case may be found in DAC 157, C.A.M Paradis v. R.A. O'Connor, bishop of Peterborough, May–June 1901; LBF, pp. 119, 202–3, 207, 211, 222, 288. On Paradis, see Choquette, *L'Église catholique dans l'Ontario français*, 246–8.

44 DAC 13, Chatham: J.A. Babineau, May 1902–May 1903; LBF, pp. 334–6

45 This conflict is described in Choquette, *Language and Religion*, 117–34.

46 DAC 88, London: paroisse de St Alphonse, Apr.–Dec. 1900

47 DAC 13, St John: annexion de McDougall Settlement à la paroisse de Notre Dame, Nov. 1900–Apr. 1901

48 DAC 88, Hamilton: parishioners of Hesson against Bishop Dowling, Nov.–Dec. 1901

49 DAC 88, Alexandria: Canadiens français contre Mgr Macdonell, June 1902

50 DAC 50 Ottawa: paroissiens de St-Joseph d'Orléans contre Mgr Duhamel, Feb.–Apr. 1901

51 See DAC 88, Hamilton: parishioners of Formosa against Bishop Dowling, June–Aug. 1901; DAC 5, Nicolet: paroissiens de St-Paul de Chester contre Mgr Gravel, Dec. 1899–Mar. 1900; paroissiens de St-Zéphirin de Courval, Feb. 1901–Jan. 1902; DAC 26, Sherbrooke: paroissiens de St-Gabriel de Stratford contre Mgr LaRocque, Apr.–May 1900; Ste-Anne de Danville contre l'Évêque de Sherbrooke, Oct.–Jan. 1902

52 DAC 50, Québec: paroissiens de St-Damase contre Mgr Bégin, July–Aug. 1902

53 Ibid., paroissiens de Pintendre contre Mgr Bégin, Dec. 1899–Aug. 1902

54 DAC 26, Montréal: interdiction de la paroisse de St-Ignace Loyola, Jan. 1900

55 Ibid., J.B. Proulx contre J.M. Landry, curé de Rawdon, Apr. 1901–June 1902

56 DAC 13, Charlottetown: J.C. McDonald versus A.E. Burke, Aug.–Sept. 1901

57 DAC 13, Antigonish: the parishioners of Heatherton against Bishop Cameron, May–July 1900

58 Ibid., parishioners of Lourdes against William McDonald, their pastor, Nov. 1900–Oct. 1901. Similar complaints were made against Martin Macpherson, pastor of Little Bras d'Or, M. Laffin, pastor of Tracadie, and M. Cody, pastor of Havre à Boucher. But none of these cases were investigated.

59 DAC LBF, Falconio à Gravel, 12 mars 1900, p. 46

Conclusion

1 See Choquette, *Language and Religion*, 230–6, for the arguments used by the Unity League of Ontario to find a just settlement to the crisis created by regulation 17.

2 Silver, *The French-Canadian Idea of Confederation*

3 Cited in Andrée Désilets, *Hector-Louis Langevin: un père de la confédération canadienne (1826–1906)* (Québec 1969), 161

4 APFR, NS 120, Observations sur un rapport, f.580. Laflèche had condemned Laurier's opinion that as a politician he had to place himself above religion in order to judge the questions of the day.

5 An index of Taschereau's innate conservatism may be seen in the fact

that he was the only Canadian prelate to oppose the creation of a Canadian college in Rome. Until the foundation of this institution in 1886, Canadian clerics lived in a variety of national colleges, including the Irish, the Scots, the French, the English, the North American, and had little opportunity of interacting with one another. Taschereau believed in his typical manner that existing structures were quite sufficient.

6 ASV, SS 280, Satolli a Rampolla, 14 lug. 1895. 'Ridocolo poi che ... siasi detto che se non mantengono in casa e chiesa esclusivamente la lingua nativa, sono in rischio di perdere la fede, come se questa fosse legata ad una od altra lingua per ogni nazione. Se non che, il corso inevitabile delle cose adduce per ogni immigrata nazionalità al più tardi una generazione, il cambiamento ed uniformità di linguaggio e costumi. Ormai i tedeschi via via ciò ben' intendono, e son convinti che il loro presunto Kansleismo era un utopia.'

Bibliography

MANUSCRIPT SOURCES

Rome

a) Archivio della Sacra Congregazione di Propaganda Fide (APFR), Piazza di Spagna 48

This is the major repository of Canadian material at the Vatican up to the curial reforms of 1908 and is run very efficiently. Researchers need only a letter of introduction to have access to material that is open, theoretically at least, to 1922. The following major sources were consulted for this study.

– Acta S. Congregationis de Propaganda Fide, vols. 244 (1876)–274 (1903). These are the major decisions taken by the Congregation as a whole, together with background papers and supporting documents. The material is organized chronologically, by geographical area and by diocese.
– Scritture originali riferite nelle Congregazioni generali(SOCG), vols. 1008 (1878)–1044 (1892). Here we find the original documents upon which the Propaganda's decisions were based. This series follows the same organization as for Acta.
– Scritture riferite nei Congressi, America settentrionale, Canadà (SC), vols. 15 (1876)–32 (1891–2). Letters, briefs, newspaper clippings, statistics, and questionnaires make up this series, undoubtedly the richest source at Propaganda Fide for Canadian history. SC represents the daily correspondence received by the cardinal prefect or Secretary of the Congregation from 'the field.'

– Lettere e Decreti della Sacra Congregazione e Biglietti di Monsignore Segretario (LDB). This is a letter book of the correspondence written by the cardinal prefect or the Secretary of the Congregation and is organized by year in chronological order. The correspondence deals with the issues raised in SC or in Acta.
– Nuova Serie (NS), vols. 1 (1893)–265 (1903). In 1892 the organization of the archives was changed. Material was classified both according to standardized headings and geographical locations. This series contains all the material formerly found in SOCG, SC as well as in LDB.

b) Archivio Segreto Vaticano (ASV)
The main archival collection of the Holy See is housed in the Vatican Palaces. Access to the archives is normally given to researchers having a letter of introduction. These are then provided with a pass that gets them past the Swiss Guards and archival officials. Service to researchers here is much less efficient than at Propaganda Fide. Restrictions of all kinds limit daily access to material.

– Delegazione Apostolica del Canadà (DAC), 1899–1903. This collection contains a wealth of material that make up the papers of the apostolic delegates to Canada. In general, material is organized by apostolic delegate and according to diocese, although this is not always the case. It is an extremely rich source of documentation. An inventory (cited below) of the first apostolic delegate's papers is available at the National Archives and National Library of Canada. DAC also includes the Letter Book of Monsignor Falconio (LBF) which contains copies of the delegate's daily correspondence.
– Delegazione Apostolica degli Stati Uniti (DASU). Organized by section, this series has some material which is pertinent to Canadian history. The latter has been catalogued in the inventory mentioned below. A comprehensive inventory of the series is available for consultation at the Vatican Archives.
– Spogli dei Cardinali. These are the papers of individual cardinals. One is sometimes lucky enough to find Canadian material in them, as was the case with the papers of Cardinal Oreglia di San Stefano.
– Segreteria di Stato (SS). This material, which deals with politico-religious and diplomatic questions, is organized by subject headings (rubriche) and by year. An inventory of Canadian documents for the period under study here is cited below.

c) Archivio della Sacra Congregazione degli Affari Ecclesiastici Staordinari (AAES), Sala Borgia
This archive is distinct from ASV, is housed in separate facilities within the Vatican Palaces, and possesses its distinct personnel. Documents relate to questions of church-state relations regarded as 'delicate' and follow a geographical classification. Canadian material is found under the title 'Inghilterra. Irlanda. Malta' and is divided into folders. The latter may contain or be part of sections (posizioni) which concern specific issues. This Congregation functioned as did Propaganda with decisions taken in general congregation or by the Secretary of State with the assistance of permanent staff. An inventory of Canadian material is also cited below.

d) Archives of the Irish College in Rome (AICR)
Rectors of this college sometimes acted as agents of the English-Canadian hierarchy in Rome. The voluminous correspondence of Monsignor Kirby contains Canadian material.

PRINTED SOURCES

De Barbézieux, Alexis (T.R.P. Alexis), *L'Église catholique au Canada*. Québec: Editions de l'Action sociale catholique 1914
MacMillan, J.C. *The History of the Catholic Church in Prince Edward Island*. 2 vols. Quebec: L'Evenement Printing Company 1905, 1913
O'Sullivan, D. *Essays on the Church in Canada*. Toronto: Catholic Truth Society 1890
Savaète, Arthur. *Voix Canadiennes: Vers l'abîme tome XII: Mgr A. Langevin*. Paris, n.d.
Spetz, T. *The Catholic Church in Waterloo County*. Toronto: The Catholic Register and Extension 1916

SECONDARY MATERIAL

Reference Works
Benoit, Monique. 'Inventaire des principales séries de documents intéressant le Canada, sous le pontificat de Léon XIII (1878–1903) dans les archives de la Sacrée Congrégation "de Propaganda Fide" à Rome.' National Archives of Canada 1985
Dictionary of Canadian Biography, vols. 8–11. Toronto: University of Toronto Press 1972–85
Enciclopedia Cattolica, 12 vols. Città del Vaticano: Ente per l'Enciclope-

dia Cattolica e per il Libro Cattolico 1948–53

Fournet, A. 'Le Canada (Catholicisme)' in A. Vacant and E. Mangenot, eds., *Dictionnaire de Théologie Catholique*, vol. 2. Paris: Letouzey et Ané 1905: 1453–96

La Gerarchia Cattolica, la Famiglia e la Cappella Pontificia, 28 vols. Roma: Tipografia Poliglotta 1876–1903

Le Canada ecclésiastique: almanach annuaire du clergé canadien. Montréal: Librairie Beauchemin 1883–1903

Sanfilippo, Matteo. 'Inventaire des documents d'intérêt canadien dans l'Archivio Segreto Vaticano sous le pontificat de Léon XIII (1878–1903): Délégation Apostolique du Canada, Délégation Apostolique des Etats-Unis, Epistolae ad Principes et Epistolae Latinae, et autres séries mineures.' National Archives of Canada 1987

Serio, Nicoletta and Luigi Bruti-Liberati. 'Inventaire des documents d'intérêt canadien dans les Archives du Vatican (1878–1903).' National Archives of Canada 1987

Books

Champagne, Claude. *Les débuts de la mission dans le Nord-Ouest canadien. Mission et Église chez Mgr Vital Grandin, o.m.i.(1829–1902).* Ottawa: Presses de l'Université d'Ottawa 1983

Charland, Thomas. *Le père Gonthier et les écoles du Manitoba: sa mission secrète en 1897–98.* Montréal: Fides 1979

Choquette, Robert. *L'Église catholique dans l'Ontario français du dix-neuvième siècle.* Ottawa: Presses de l'Université d'Ottawa 1984

– *Language and Religion: A History of English-French Conflict in Ontario.* Ottawa: University of Ottawa Press 1975

Confessore, Ornella. *L'americanismo cattolico in Italia.* Roma: Edizioni Studium 1984

Crunican, Paul. *Priests and Politicians: Manitoba Schools and the Election of 1896.* Toronto: University of Toronto Press 1974

Eid, Nadia F. *Le clergé et le pouvoir politique au Québec: une analyse de l'idéologie ultramontaine du XIXe siècle.* Montréal: HMH 1978

Flynn, Louis. *Built on a Rock: The Story of the Roman Catholic Church in Kingston.* Kingston: Roman Catholic Archdiocese of Kingston 1976

Fogarty, G.P. *The Vatican and the Americanist Crisis: Denis J. O'Connell, American Agent in Rome, 1885–1903.* Rome 1974

Gaffield, Chad. *Language, Schooling, and Cultural Conflict: The Origins of the French-Language Controversy in Ontario.* Kingston and Montreal: McGill-Queen's University Press 1987

Grisé, Jacques. *Les conciles provinciaux de Québec et l'Église canadienne.* Montréal: Fides 1979

Groulx, Lionel. *L'enseignement français au Canada*, vol. 2: *Les écoles des minorités.* Montréal: Librairie d'Action canadienne française 1933

Hamelin, Jean, and Nicole Gagnon. *Le XXe siècle*, vol. 1: *1898 1940.* Vol. of *Histoire du catholicisme québécois*, ed. Nive Voisine. Montréal: Boréal Express 1984

Hennesey, James. *American Catholics: A History of the Roman Catholic Community in the United States.* Oxford: Oxford University Press 1981

Houston, C.J. and W.J. Smyth. *The Sash Canada Wore: A Historical Geography of the Orange Order in Canada.* Toronto: University of Toronto Press 1980

Johnston, A.A. *A History of the Catholic Church in Eastern Nova Scotia*, 2 vols. Antigonish: St Francis Xavier University Press 1966, 1971

Lemieux, Lucien. *L'établissement de la première province ecclésiastique au Canada, 1783–1844.* Montréal: Fides 1967

Lupul, Manoly. *The Roman Catholic Church and the North-West School Question: A Study in Church-State Relations in Western Canada 1875–1905.* Toronto: University of Toronto Press 1974

Miller, J.R. *Equal Rights: The Jesuits' Estates Act Controversy.* Montreal: McGill-Queen's University Press 1979

Moir, John S. *Church and State in Canada West.* Toronto: University of Toronto Press 1959

Morice, Adrien G. *Histoire de l'Eglise catholique dans l'Ouest canadien*, 3 vols. St Boniface–Montréal 1915

Murphy, T. and C.J. Byrne. *Religion and Identity: The Experience of Irish and Scottish Catholics in Atlantic Canada.* St John's: Jesperson Press 1987

Painchaud, Robert. *Un rêve français dans le peuplement de la prairie.* St Boniface: Editions des Plaines 1987

Rumilly, Robert. *Histoire de la province de Québec*, vols. 1–9. Montréal: Fides 1971–76

Savard, Pierre. *Jules-Paul Tardivel, la France et les États–Unis 1851–1905.* Québec: Presses de l'Université Laval 1967

– *Aspects du catholicisme canadien-français au XIXe siècle.* Montréal: Fides 1980

Savoie, Alexandre. *Un siècle de revendications scolaires au Nouveau Brunswick 1871–1971*, 2 vols. Montréal 1978

Silver, Arthur. *The French-Canadian Idea of Confederation 1864–1900.* Toronto: University of Toronto Press 1982

Sissons, C.B. *Church and State in Canadian Education.* Toronto: Ryerson Press, 1959

Tomasi, Silvano. *Piety and Power: The Role of Italian Parishes in the New York Metropolitan Area.* New York: Center for Migration Studies 1975

Trombley, K. Fay. *Thomas Louis Connolly (1815–1876): The Man and His Place in Secular and Ecclesiastical History.* Louvain: Katholieke Universiteit Leuven 1983

Voisine, Nive. *Louis-François Laflèche. Deuxième évêque de Trois-Rivières,* vol. 1. St-Hyacinthe: Editions Edisem 1980

Voisine, Nive and Jean Hamelin. *Les ultramontains canadiens-français.* Montréal: Boréal Express 1985

Walker, Franklin. *Catholic Education and Politics in Ontario.* Toronto: T. Nelson 1964

Articles

Abel, Kerry. 'Prophets, Priests and Preachers: Dene Shamans and Christian Missions in the Nineteenth Century.' CHA *Historical Papers* (1986): 211–24

Cartwright, D.G. 'Ecclesiastical Territorial Organization and Institutional Conflict in Eastern and Northern Ontario, 1840–1910.' CHA *Historical Papers* (1978): 176–99

Champagne, Antoine. 'La communauté des Chanoines réguliers de l'Immaculée Conception au Manitoba.' SCHEC *Sessions d'étude* (1970): 229–45

Choquette, Robert. 'Adélard Langevin et l'érection de l'archidiocèse de Winnipeg.' *RHAF* 28 (sept. 1974): 187–202

Crunican, Paul. 'Father Lacombe's Strange Mission: The Langevin-Lacombe Correspondence on the Manitoba School Question, 1895–96.' CCHA *Report* (1959): 57–71

Fohlen, Claude. 'Catholicisme américain et catholicisme européen: la convergence de l'"Américanisme."' *Revue d'Histoire Moderne et Contemporaine* 34 (1987): 215–30

Gill, S.D. '"The Sword in the Bishop's Hand": Father William Peter MacDonald, a Scottish Defender of the Catholic Faith in Upper Canada.' CCHA *Study Sessions* (1983): 437–52

Godin, Edgar. 'Etablissement de l'Église catholique au Nouveau Brunswick.' SCHEC *Sessions d'étude* (1981): 37–56

Huel, Raymond. 'The Irish-French Conflict in Catholic Episcopal Nominations: The Western Sees and the Struggle for Domination Within the

Church.' CCHA *Study Sessions* (1975): 51–70

Kinsky, Richard. 'Reaction of the Globe to the Vatican Council: Dec. 1869 to July 1870.' CCHA *Report* (1959): 81–92

La Pierre, Laurier. 'Joseph Israel Tarte et les évêques de Saint-Boniface.' SCHEC *Sessions d'étude* (1970): 173–95

Little, J.I. 'French Canada and the Western School Questions.' *Acadiensis* 5 (1976): 149–54

McGowan, Mark. '"Religious Duties and Patriotic Endeavours": The Catholic Church Extension Society, French Canada and the Prairie West, 1908–1916.' CCHA *Historical Studies* (1984): 102–19

McLaughlin, Kenneth. ' "Riding the Protestant Horse": The Manitoba School Question and Canadian Politics, 1890–1896.' CCHA *Historical Studies* (1986): 39–52

Miller, J.R. 'Anti-Catholic Thought in Victorian Canada.' *CHR* 66 (Dec 1985): 474–94

Moir, J.S. 'Canadian Protestant Reaction to the *Ne Temere* Decree.' CCHA *Study Sessions* (1981): 78–90

– 'The Problem of a Double Minority: Some Reflections on the Development of the English-Speaking Catholic Church in the Nineteenth Century.' *Histoire sociale / Social History* 7 (Apr. 1971): 53–67

Nash-Chambers, Debra. 'In the Palm of God's Hand? The Irish Catholic Experience in Mid-Nineteenth Century Guelph.' CCHA *Study Sessions* (1984): 67–87

Nicolson, M.W. 'Ecclesiastical Metropolitanism and the Evolution of the Catholic Archdiocese of Toronto.' *Histoire sociale / Social History* 15 (May 1982): 129–56

Proulx, Adolphe. 'Histoire du diocèse de Sault-Sainte-Marie.' SCHEC *Sessions d'étude* (1960): 71–82.

Roy, Jean. 'Le clergé nicolétain, 1885–1904: aspects sociographiques.' *Revue d'Histoire de l'Amérique Française* 35 (déc. 1981): 383–95

Voisine, Nive. 'La correspondance Langevin-Laflèche.' SCHEC *Sessions d'étude* (1967): 79–86

Theses

Bélanger, Noël. 'Une introduction au problème de l'influence indue, illustrée par la contestation de l'élection dans le comté de Charlevoix.' Thèse de licence es lettres (histoire), Université Laval 1960

Comeault, G.L. 'The Politics of the Manitoba School Question and Its Impact on L.-P.-A. Langevin's Relations with Manitoba's Catholic Minority Groups 1895–1915.' MA (history), University of Manitoba 1977

Dupasquier, Maurice. 'Dom Paul Benoit et le Nouveau Monde, 1850–1915.'
Thèse de doctorat (histoire), Université Laval 1970
La Pierre, Laurier. 'Politics, Race and Religion in French Canada: Joseph
Israel Tarte.' PH D (history), University of Toronto 1962
Nicolson, Murray. 'The Catholic Church and the Irish in Victorian
Toronto.' PH D (history), University of Guelph 1981
Perin, Roberto. 'Bourget and the Dream of a Free Church in Quebec,
1862–1878.' PH D (history), University of Ottawa 1975
Robertson, H.L. 'The Ultramontane Group in French Canada,
1867–1885.' MA (history), Queen's University 1952
Robertson, I.R. 'Religion, Politics and Education in Prince Edward Island,
1856–1877.' MA (history), McGill University 1968
Stortz, T.G.L. 'John Joseph Lynch, Archbishop of Toronto: A Biographical
Study of Religious, Social and Political Commitment.' PH D (history),
Guelph University 1980

Index